READING HLA HART'S *THE CONCEPT OF LAW*

More than 50 years after it was first published, *The Concept of Law* remains the most important work of legal philosophy in the English-speaking world. In this volume, written for both students and specialists, 13 leading scholars look afresh at Hart's great book.

Unique in format, the volume proceeds sequentially through all the main ideas in *The Concept of Law*: each contributor addresses a single chapter of Hart's book, critically discussing its arguments in light of subsequent developments in the field. Four concluding essays assess the continued relevance for jurisprudence of the 'persistent questions' identified by Hart at the beginning of *The Concept of Law*. The collection also includes Hart's 'Answers to Eight Questions', written in 1988 and never before published in English.

Contributors include Timothy Endicott, Richard HS Tur, Pavlos Eleftheriadis, John Gardner, Grant Lamond, Nicos Stavropoulos, Leslie Green, John Tasioulas, Jeremy Waldron, John Finnis, Frederick Schauer, Pierluigi Chiassoni and Nicola Lacey.

Reading HLA Hart's
The Concept of Law

Edited by
Luís Duarte d'Almeida
James Edwards
and
Andrea Dolcetti

OXFORD AND PORTLAND, OREGON
2013

Published in the United Kingdom by Hart Publishing Ltd
16C Worcester Place, Oxford, OX1 2JW
Telephone: +44 (0)1865 517530
Fax: +44 (0)1865 510710
E-mail: mail@hartpub.co.uk
Website: http://www.hartpub.co.uk

Published in North America (US and Canada) by
Hart Publishing
c/o International Specialized Book Services
920 NE 58th Avenue, Suite 300
Portland, OR 97213-3786
USA
Tel: +1 503 287 3093 or toll-free: (1) 800 944 6190
Fax: +1 503 280 8832
E-mail: orders@isbs.com
Website: http://www.isbs.com

© The editors and contributors severally 2013

The editors and contributors have asserted their right under the Copyright, Designs and Patents Act 1988 to be identified as the authors of this work.

All rights reserved. No part of this publication may be reproduced, stored in a retrieval system, or transmitted, in any form or by any means, without the prior permission of Hart Publishing, or as expressly permitted by law or under the terms agreed with the appropriate reprographic rights organisation. Enquiries concerning reproduction which may not be covered by the above should be addressed to Hart Publishing Ltd at the address above.

British Library Cataloguing in Publication Data
Data Available

ISBN: 978-1-84946-324-9

Typeset by Hope Services, Abingdon

Contents

Contributors		vii
1	Hart's Readers *Luís Duarte d'Almeida, James Edwards and Andrea Dolcetti*	1

I. READING *THE CONCEPT OF LAW*

2	The Generality of Law *Timothy Endicott*	15
3	Variety or Uniformity? *Richard HS Tur*	37
4	Hart on Sovereignty *Pavlos Eleftheriadis*	59
5	Why Law Might Emerge: Hart's Problematic Fable *John Gardner*	81
6	The Rule of Recognition and the Foundations of a Legal System *Grant Lamond*	97
7	Words and Obligations *Nicos Stavropoulos*	123
8	Hart on Justice and Morality *John Tasioulas*	155
9	The Morality in Law *Leslie Green*	177
10	International Law: 'A Relatively Small and Unimportant' Part of Jurisprudence? *Jeremy Waldron*	209

II. HART'S 'PERSISTENT QUESTIONS'

11	How Persistent are Hart's 'Persistent Questions'? *John Finnis*	227

12 Hart's Anti-Essentialism 237
Frederick Schauer

13 The Model of Ordinary Analysis 247
Pierluigi Chiassoni

14 Do the 'Persistent Questions' Persist?: Revisiting Chapter I in
The Concept of Law 269
Nicola Lacey

III. AN INTERVIEW WITH HLA HART

15 Introductory Note 277
Juan Ramón de Páramo

16 Answers to Eight Questions 279
HLA Hart

Index of Names 299

Index of Subjects 303

Contributors

Pierluigi Chiassoni is Professor of Jurisprudence at the University of Genoa.
Andrea Dolcetti is Non-Stipendiary Lecturer in Law at St Hilda's College, University of Oxford.
Luís Duarte d'Almeida is Chancellor's Fellow in Law at the University of Edinburgh.
James Edwards is Fellow and Lecturer in Law at Christ's College, Cambridge.
Pavlos Eleftheriadis is a University Lecturer in Law and Fellow of Mansfield College, University of Oxford.
Timothy Endicott is Dean of the Faculty of Law, Professor of Legal Philosophy, and Fellow of Balliol College, University of Oxford.
John Finnis is Professor of Law and Legal Philosophy Emeritus at the University of Oxford, and Biolchini Professor of Law at the University of Notre Dame.
John Gardner is Professor of Jurisprudence and Fellow of University College, University of Oxford.
Leslie Green is Professor of the Philosophy of Law and Fellow of Balliol College, University of Oxford.
Nicola Lacey is Professor of Criminal Law and Legal Theory and Fellow of All Souls College, University of Oxford.
Grant Lamond is University Lecturer in Legal Philosophy and Felix Frankfurter Fellow of Balliol College, University of Oxford.
Juan Ramón de Páramo Argüelles is Professor of Philosophy of Law, and Dean of the Faculty of Law and Social Sciences at the University of Castilla-La Mancha.
Frederick Schauer is David and Mary Harrison Distinguished Professor of Law at the University of Virginia.
Nicos Stavropoulos is University Lecturer in Legal Theory at the University of Oxford.
John Tasioulas is Quain Professor of Jurisprudence at the Faculty of Laws, University College London.
Richard HS Tur is Emeritus Fellow of Oriel College, University of Oxford.
Jeremy Waldron is University Professor at New York University School of Law, and Chichele Professor of Social and Political Theory at the University of Oxford.

1

Hart's Readers

LUÍS DUARTE D'ALMEIDA, JAMES EDWARDS AND
ANDREA DOLCETTI

I. TO THE STUDENT

'IN LAW AS elsewhere, we can know and yet not understand.' Thus began HLA Hart's 1953 inaugural lecture as Professor of Jurisprudence at Oxford.[1] To promote, not principally our knowledge, but our understanding of law: this was how Hart saw his task. *The Concept of Law* opens on a similar note. Hart's 'aim in this book', he announces, is 'to further the understanding of law, coercion, and morality as different but related social phenomena'.[2]

The point is not that there is some radical divide between knowing and understanding. To further one's understanding, of law or anything else, is to further one's knowledge. The point is that there may be things we simultaneously know and yet not fully understand. To further one's understanding of something is to further one's knowledge in depth, as it were, rather than in breadth. Hart expands on this in chapter I of *The Concept of Law*, but he had put matters more straightforwardly in a 1957 essay:

> [I]t is characteristic not only of the use of legal concepts, but also of many concepts in other disciplines and in ordinary life, that we may have adequate mastery of them for the purpose of their day-to-day use; and yet they may still require elucidation; for we are puzzled when we try to understand our own conceptual apparatus. We may know how to use these concepts, but we cannot say how or describe how we do this in ways which are intelligible to others and indeed to ourselves. We know, and yet do not fully understand, even quite familiar features of legal thinking – much in the way perhaps that a man may know his own way about a familiar

---

[1] HLA Hart, 'Definition and Theory in Jurisprudence', in his *Essays in Jurisprudence and Philosophy* (Oxford, Clarendon Press, 1983 [1953]) 21.
[2] Hart, *The Concept of Law*, 3rd edn (Oxford, Oxford University Press, 2012 [1961]) vi.

town by rote without being able to draw a map of it or explain to others how he finds his way about the town.[3]

In a sense, then, Hart does not in his work set out to tell his readers new things about law. He sets out to tell them new things *about things they already know* about law.[4] It follows that if one is to count oneself among Hart's intended readers there is a certain body of knowledge about law that one must already have. This does not mean that *The Concept of Law* is a book addressed to experts, a book for trained lawyers only. For the body of knowledge about law with which Hart is concerned is a body of general rather than specialised knowledge. It is general, in fact, in at least two ways. First, it is a body of knowledge about law that Hart takes 'virtually everyone' ('any educated man', at any rate) to have.[5] Second, it is a body of knowledge about law *in general*, not about the distinctive details of any particular legal system at any particular moment. It is knowledge about the 'structure' and 'salient features', as he often puts it,[6] of legal systems everywhere.

What propositions form part of this body of 'common knowledge'?[7] Here is a list. (1) The laws of any country 'form some sort of system'.[8] (2) Legal systems are in all countries 'broadly similar in structure'.[9] Among the points of similarity, the 'most prominent' is that (3) law's existence 'means that certain kinds of human conduct are no longer optional but in *some* sense obligatory'.[10] Another is that (4) '[t]he legal system of a modern state is characterized by a certain kind of *supremacy* within its territory and *independence* of other systems'.[11] And (5) legal systems in all countries also similarly comprise 'rules of many different types',[12] namely

> (i) rules forbidding or enjoining certain types of behaviour under penalty; (ii) rules requiring people to compensate those whom they injure in certain ways; (iii) rules specifying what must be done to make wills, contracts or other arrangements which confer rights and create obligations; (iv) courts to determine what the rules are and when they have been broken; (v) a legislature to make new rules and abolish old ones.[13]

---

[3] Hart, 'Analytical Jurisprudence in Mid-Twentieth Century: A Reply to Professor Bodenheimer' (1957) 105 *University of Pennsylvania Law Review* 964f, 971; cf also his 'Theory and Definition in Jurisprudence' (1955) 29 *Proceedings of the Aristotelian Society. Supplementary Volumes* 244f.

[4] See 'Theory and Definition in Jurisprudence' (n 3) 241; and 'Analytical Jurisprudence in Mid-Twentieth Century' (n 3) 965.

[5] *The Concept of Law* (n 2) 2f.

[6] ibid 3, 5, 51, 75, 79, 100, 240.

[7] ibid 3, 240.

[8] ibid 3.

[9] ibid.

[10] ibid 6, 82.

[11] ibid 24.

[12] ibid 9.

[13] ibid 3.

'Familiar' as these facts may be,[14] 'even skilled lawyers', Hart says, 'cannot explain and do not fully understand' much about them.[15] This may strike you as a somewhat immodest claim. How can Hart know what his readers, skilled lawyers or otherwise, do and do not understand? And supposing he were right, why should anyone bother to 'understand' those facts any better? If even professional jurists may happily go about their lives equipped with whatever little 'understanding' of law Hart is willing to grant them – what reason could one have for developing more?

To think along these lines is to miss the point of Hart's endeavour. He is not telling his readers that they *need* to improve their current understanding of law. Perhaps that common body of knowledge does contain all one needs to know about law in general. After all, what one *needs* to know about law is dependent on one's own goals. We can be sure, however, that the common body of knowledge is relatively superficial. How do we know that? Because for more than two millennia, as Hart remarks, many 'serious thinkers'[16] have been trying precisely to increase their understanding (as well as ours) of law in general – and all have felt recurrently compelled to tackle the same issues. This is solid evidence, thinks Hart, not only that there are questions to which law seems 'naturally'[17] to give rise, but that such questions are far from easy to put to rest. The 'deep perplexity' which has kept these questions alive is certainly not a product of 'ignorance or forgetfulness or inability to recognize the phenomena to which the word "law" commonly refers'.[18] It is a product of the fact that reflection on the body of knowledge we share about law soon gives rise to many puzzles. And this is why Hart thinks there will be things about law his readers do not fully understand.

To see Hart's point, consider the three 'persistent questions' he identifies at the outset of *The Concept of Law*:

> How does law differ from and how is it related to orders backed by threats? How does legal obligation differ from, and how is it related to, moral obligation? What are rules and to what extent is law an affair of rules?[19]

Take this last query – a good example of what Hart means about knowing something and yet not fully understanding it. We *know*, it seems safe to say, that 'a legal system consists, in general at any rate, of *rules*'. At first blush this 'could hardly be doubted or found difficult to understand'.[20] Yet once the 'seemingly unproblematic notion' of a rule 'is queried' – once the apparently

---

[14] ibid 5.
[15] ibid 14; cf also the 'Introduction' to his *Essays in Jurisprudence and Philosophy* (n 1) 5f.
[16] *The Concept of Law* (n 2) 1.
[17] ibid 9.
[18] ibid 5; cf also 'Analytical Jurisprudence in Mid-Twentieth Century' (n 3) 961 fn 17.
[19] ibid 13.
[20] ibid 8.

simple question 'What *are* rules?' is asked – 'dissatisfaction, confusion, and uncertainty' are sure to emerge.[21] And soon other difficult questions will be prompted by further reflection. 'What does it mean to say that a rule *exists*? Do courts really apply rules or do they pretend to do so?'[22] 'How do rules differ from mere habits or regularities of behaviour? Are there radically different types of rules? How may rules be related? What is it for rules to form a system?'[23]

These are philosophical questions about law in general: questions we face when we try to deepen our understanding of it.[24] Why should anyone mull over them? Again, Hart's claim is not that anyone should. Not everyone will consider philosophical questions unsettling or feel the urge to spend time thinking about them. Perhaps it is true that, as Richard Hare is once said to have put it, 'philosophers, like poets and gardeners, are born not made'. On the other hand, it may be that you do regard questions like these as sufficiently puzzling to arrest your attention. You will then find yourself in the company of those many 'serious thinkers' that Hart mentions. You will be joining a long-lasting discussion about law in general. *The Concept of Law* was written for readers like you.

What does Hart suppose he can bring to the 'unending' philosophical debate about law, as he calls it?[25] The adjective is not derogatory. Most important controversies in philosophy are 'unending' by their very nature, and Hart is certainly not seeking to solve, once and for all, any of jurisprudence's perennially 'persistent questions'. He also believes that many before him have made important progress in furthering our understanding of law in general. But such authors, he thinks, seem often to have assumed that the success of a theory of law is measured by its ability to explain law's many aspects in terms of a few 'basic' notions, or even a single such notion. Hart disagrees. There is no doubt, of course, that simpler theories, all else being equal, are to be preferred. His point, though, is that the explanatory power of many jurisprudential theories has often been compromised by an urge to reduce the complex structure of law to as few elements as possible.[26] For there is just no reason to presume that there is *any* 'basic' element common to all instances of what we properly call 'law'.

---

[21] ibid.
[22] ibid.
[23] HLA Hart, 'Comment' in R Gavison (ed), *Issues in Contemporary Legal Philosophy. The Influence of H.L.A. Hart* (Oxford, Clarendon Press, 1987) 38. See also Hart's 1967 'Problems of the Philosophy of Law', in his *Essays in Jurisprudence and Philosophy* (n 1) for a much richer catalogue of jurisprudential issues.
[24] The passage quoted above to n 3 continues: 'This surely is the predicament that makes the philosophical elucidation of concepts necessary and philosophy has always found its chief stimulus in this predicament'; cf 'Analytical Jurisprudence in Mid-Twentieth Century' (n 3) 964.
[25] *The Concept of Law* (n 2) 2.
[26] ibid 7, 32, 38, 41, 43, 49, 284ff.

There is little sense, in fact, thinks Hart, in trying to articulate a definition of 'law', at least if by 'a definition' one means a list of 'common qualities' necessary and sufficient for anything to count as an instance of 'law'.[27] The aspects of law that underlie each of jurisprudence's 'persistent questions' are just 'too different from each other and too fundamental',[28] he says, to be reducible to any common definitional feature.[29] This is not to claim that they are unrelated; only that they seem to be 'linked together in quite different ways from that postulated by the simple form of definition.'[30]

So Hart proposes to follow a different course. His strategy is to focus, not on the meaning of the term 'law', but on 'the distinctive structure of a municipal legal system' in 'a modern state'.[31] Why? First, because he subscribes to the 'analytical principle' that 'in the analysis of concepts' (or at any rate 'in the case of a concept so complex as a legal system'[32]) we 'need first to establish what may be called the paradigm or standard case of the use of an expression'.[33] It is then by their relations to that 'central case' – often relations 'of analogy of either form or content' – that we are to understand the 'diverse range of cases of which the word "law" is "properly" used'.[34] Second, Hart takes 'legal systems of modern states'[35] – that is, 'municipal systems which exhibit the full complement of *juge, gendarme et législateur*'[36] – to constitute the paradigmatic instance of law, the 'settled situation in which there is law'.[37]

Even here it is in terms of a 'central *set* of elements'[38] – not of any single, common feature – that the notion of a legal system, thinks Hart, is to be

---

[27] ibid 13, 213, 279.
[28] ibid 16.
[29] These are themes addressed in great detail in Frederick Schauer's and Pierluigi Chiassoni's contributions to this volume. Timothy Endicott and Leslie Green also touch upon methodological issues in their chapters; both take the opportunity to reply to Brian Leiter's 'The Demarcation Problem in Jurisprudence: A New Case for Scepticism' (2012) 32 *Oxford Journal of Legal Studies* 4.
[30] ibid 16. This was a point on which Hart insisted throughout much of his early work: see also eg 'Definition and Theory in Jurisprudence' (n 1) 22; 'Analytical Jurisprudence in Mid-Twentieth Century' (n 3) 969f; 'Dias and Hughes on Jurisprudence' (1958) 4 *Journal of the Society of Public Teachers of Law* 144f; or 'Problems of the Philosophy of Law' (n 23) 91. In 'The Ascription of Responsibility and Rights' (1949) 49 *Proceedings of the Aristotelian Society* 173 we also find the similar-sounding contention that 'usually the request for a definition of a legal concept . . . cannot be answered by the provision of a verbal rule for the translation of a legal expression into other terms or one specifying a set of necessary and sufficient conditions', though here Hart's arguments are of a very different character.
[31] *The Concept of Law* (n 2) 17, 79.
[32] 'Theory and Definition in Jurisprudence' (n 3) 253.
[33] 'Analytical Jurisprudence in Mid-Twentieth Century' (n 3) 968.
[34] *The Concept of Law* (n 2) 81, 279f; and 'Introduction' (n 15) 4.
[35] *The Concept of Law* (n 2) 3.
[36] ibid 156.
[37] ibid 23. Arguably this approach is not without costs: see Jeremy Waldron's contribution to this volume.
[38] ibid 16 (emphasis added).

'elucidated'. One should neither neglect nor seek to play down the fact that the existence of a legal system is a highly 'complex social phenomenon'.[39] The 'complexity of the notion' becomes apparent if one begins simply to catalogue 'the main elements which are present in the standard case of an advanced modern society'.[40] A 'formidable list' of features will quickly take shape:

(1) Courts.
(2) Rules conferring jurisdiction on Courts and providing for the appointment and conditions of tenure of judicial office.
(3) Rules of procedure for Courts.
(4) Rules of evidence for Courts.
(5) Substantive civil laws.
(6) Substantive criminal law.
(7) A Legislature.
(8) Constitutional rules providing criteria valid for the system for the identification of the rules of the system (sources of law).
(9) Sanctions.
(10) Possibility of argument.
(11) Universality of scope.[41]

Hart's determination to resist jurisprudence's traditional 'itch for uniformity'[42] and '"reductionist" drive'[43] is a methodological watermark of his work. It also enables him to make regular use of past theorists' main insights, incorporating them into his own theory. Time and again in *The Concept of Law* we find that Hart manages to steer a seemingly sensible middle path between competing exaggerated views on some given issue.[44] Indeed, it was not with regard to their insights about law that many past thinkers were most often mistaken. (Hart was 'heavily and obviously indebted to other writers', as he says in his Preface;[45] nor is he being too modest.) What these writers were primarily wrong about, Hart thinks, was the relative importance of their insights, whose illuminating power and centrality to legal theory they – or their followers – were somewhat prone to overstating.

John Austin's imperative theory is a case in point. In his 1832 *The Province of Jurisprudence Determined* Austin had claimed to have found *the* 'key to the

---

[39] ibid 61.
[40] 'Theory and Definition in Jurisprudence' (n 3) 252.
[41] ibid; as Timothy Endicott notes in his contribution to this volume, the *executive* functions of the state are conspicuously absent from Hart's account.
[42] *The Concept of Law* (n 2) 32.
[43] 'Analytical Jurisprudence in Mid-Twentieth Century' (n 3) 959.
[44] Which is not to say that he does not sometimes ignore or misrepresent the theses of some of his predecessors – an issue raised by John Finnis, Nicola Lacey and Pavlos Eleftheriadis in their contributions to this book.
[45] *The Concept of Law* (n 2) vii.

sciences of jurisprudence and morals': it was, he said, the notion of a *command*, of which 'laws or rules, properly so called' are, he held, 'a *species*'.[46] Now there is only one way, Hart suggests, of testing a claim like this: by checking whether this 'key' does open all the requisite theoretical doors. Can all legal rules be seen as commands or orders issued by a sovereign? Hart thinks not, and his paramount objection (among many) is that the very notion of a sovereign commander, even a legally unlimited one, is conceptually dependent on a constitutional 'rule conferring powers'[47] – something that looks nothing like a command or an order backed by threats.

To say this, however, is not to discredit Austin's theory, which contains, as Hart observes, 'strong points'[48] and 'certain truths about certain important aspects of law'.[49] For 'there is of course no doubt', says Hart – thinking of the 'vertical or "top to bottom"' image of law-making'[50] he associates with Austin – 'that a legal system often presents this aspect among others'.[51] There is indeed 'at least a strong analogy between the criminal law and its sanctions' and 'general orders backed by threats', and 'some analogy' as well 'between such general orders and the law of torts'.[52] But what about rules that 'do not impose duties or obligations', and whose 'social function' is instead to 'provide individuals with *facilities*' – with private powers – 'for realising their wishes'?[53] More importantly even, what about 'the whole official side to law'? What about the use '*in* legislation and adjudication'[54] of rules 'conferring and defining the manner of exercise'[55] of the corresponding public powers?

These are salient features of law, which become 'obscured' or 'distorted', Hart tirelessly protests,[56] if we look at 'all law from the point of view of the persons on whom its duties are imposed'.[57] Should we then make 'official activities, especially the judicial attitude or relationship to law'[58] our 'key' to jurisprudence (as Hans Kelsen, at least as Hart reads him, may be said to have done) and treat the notion of a power as explanatorily prior to that of a duty? This would be, says Hart, to make the 'opposite error'.[59] We would now be

---

[46] See J Austin, *The Province of Jurisprudence Determined*, WE Rumble (ed) (Cambridge, Cambridge University Press, 1995 [1832]) 21.
[47] *The Concept of Law* (n 2) 77.
[48] ibid 60.
[49] ibid 100.
[50] ibid 42.
[51] ibid 7.
[52] ibid 27.
[53] ibid.
[54] ibid 113 (emphasis added).
[55] ibid 31, 36, 41.
[56] ibid 7, 28, 31, 38, 40f, 49, 61, 70, 79, 80, 112, 155, 217, 285.
[57] ibid 41.
[58] ibid 113.
[59] ibid.

obscuring the *non*-official side to law, its 'social function' of guiding 'ordinary citizens in the activities of non-official life'.[60]

Hart's suggestion? The natural one: that we treat neither duty-imposing nor power-conferring rules as *the* 'key' to the science of jurisprudence, and prioritise neither the official nor the non-official sides to law – but acknowledge instead that a legal system is a 'complex union'[61] of rules of *both* kinds, and that the way in which legal officials relate to the rules that concern them *qua* officials is quite different from the way in which citizens relate to the legal rules that concern *them*.[62] This is, by Hart's own admission, the core thesis of *The Concept of Law*.[63] It is also an equanimous 'mean between juristic extremes'[64] – as are so many other claims in the book.

'Professor Hart's favorite jibe at his opponents', Lon Fuller once remarked,[65] 'was that they were not clear, that they perceived things dimly, etc.' Indeed in *The Concept of Law*, as we have just seen, Hart's stock rejoinder to rival views is that they 'obscure' important features of law. (Not surprisingly, he avails himself of kindred light-related metaphors in support of his own proposal; law can 'most illuminatingly' be characterised, he says,[66] as a union of different types of rule – which union should be assigned a central place 'in the elucidation of the concept of law'.[67]) One may have one's doubts about the strength or even the point of this Hartian rejoinder. It is not as if previous thinkers had simply failed to grasp the importance of power-conferring as well as duty-imposing rules.[68] True, some had claimed that the former could be logically 'reduced' to the latter: that both types of rule could be seen, as Hart puts it, as 'versions' of 'the same form'.[69] But Hart does not really seek to dispute the logical viability of this 'reduction', which he accuses instead – he finds this 'the natural protest'[70] – of 'concealing' or 'distorting the different social functions which different types of legal rule perform'.[71] Yet *how*, exactly, does the reductionist

---

[60] ibid 39.
[61] ibid 114.
[62] ibid 115.
[63] ibid 155, 283.
[64] ibid 213.
[65] In correspondence; see N Lacey, 'Out of the "Witches' Cauldron"? Reinterpreting the Context and Reassessing the Significance of the Hart-Fuller Debate', in P Cane (ed), *The Hart-Fuller Debate in the Twenty-First Century* (Oxford, Hart, 2010) 20.
[66] *The Concept of Law* (n 2) 94.
[67] ibid 110. It is this proposal that John Gardner describes, in his contribution to this volume (at 96) as 'an authentic "Eureka!" moment in the history of ideas'.
[68] Kelsen, for one, had discussed legal powers, eg in his *General Theory of Law and State*, A Wedberg (trans) (Cambridge, Mass, Harvard University Press, 1945) 90f and indeed at the core of the theory of 'legal dynamics' (cf ibid 110ff) is the notion of a norm-creating power. See also Hart's endnotes in *The Concept of Law* (n 2) at 284–85 and 286.
[69] ibid 24.
[70] ibid 40.
[71] ibid 38.

theorist 'distort' the point about social functions? Arguably there is nothing preventing the reductionist from consistently supplementing his logical point with a full-throated defence of the idea that law performs different 'social functions' by imposing duties and conferring powers.[72]

This is a fair criticism to press against Hart. It assumes, quite naturally, that Hart's charge that reductionist theories 'obscure' the salient features and functions is *addressed to the proponents* of such reductionist theories. But perhaps a different interpretation can be offered. Perhaps his insistent reminders that law is not *simply* a matter of orders backed by threats – or indeed not simply a matter of duties – are meant, not really as watertight rebuttals of views actually held by past theorists, but as salutary warnings to those of Hart's *readers* who might perhaps be tempted by the thought that the 'command model' does capture the workings of law.

Who might these readers be? The answer, of course, is 'students'. *The Concept of Law* was after all 'primarily designed' and written with 'undergraduate readers in mind',[73] which clearly influenced its structure and tone.[74] Why might students need to be reminded that the existence of a legal system is not simply a matter of orders or even mandatory rules? Because, first, this 'top-to-bottom' picture of law is, 'in its simplicity', immediately 'attractive'[75] (which also makes it, pedagogically, an excellent starting-point). Second, the imperative theory, Hart found, cast a 'shadow' over the (then) 'standard terminology of legal and political thought'.[76] Given that theory's 'hold over the minds of many thinkers',[77] its 'great influence on jurists',[78] it was educationally important to undermine it from an early stage.

Indeed Hart spends his first three chapters discussing, not really *Austin's* theory, but the very sort of 'simple model' of a legal system that a student who felt the initial appeal of the imperative image of law might begin by trying to articulate. Hart's discussion of this simple model, up to the conclusion that a 'fresh start' is in order,[79] seeks patiently and exemplarily to get his readers – his students – to submit to critical scrutiny ideas that they might at first regard as plausible or even obviously true. This exercise not only 'fosters clarity of thought and expression', but 'develops analytical and critical skills which may be freely transferred to other disciplines'.[80] Teaching students 'to think clearly

---

[72] Richard HS Tur raises this objection in his contribution to this volume.
[73] See *The Concept of Law* (n 2) v, 238.
[74] See ibid vii, on the 'pedagogical aim' that presided over Hart's arrangement of the book's argument.
[75] ibid 7, 42.
[76] ibid 112.
[77] ibid 100.
[78] ibid 19.
[79] ibid 78.
[80] HLA Hart, 'Answers to Eight Questions', ch 16, this volume, at 281.

and precisely even when, as is the case with the fundamental notions involved in the structure of a legal system . . . the subjects themselves may be vague': here lies, as Hart thought, the 'educational value'[81] of jurisprudence, and the 'main justification' for its inclusion in law curricula 'as a compulsory subject'.[82]

II. READING HART

For all his invectives against 'obscurity', Hart was not as clear a writer as one might have wished. Not that his prose is not accessible; indeed on reading *The Concept of Law* for the first time one has a sense that a series of level-headed theses are being laid down in simple, straightforward terms. Whether or not Hart is concerned *with* ordinary language to any significant extent – the topic is debated[83] – he certainly *speaks* it.[84] But Hart's ideas seem to grow *less* clear with every re-reading, and it is often difficult to give rigorous formulations of the claims he wishes to defend. Hart was aware of his expository flaws; in a 1988 interview given near the end of his career (the original version of which is published for the first time in the present collection), he describes himself as a 'somewhat careless writer' whose views were sometimes expressed 'inaccurately, ambiguously or too vaguely'.[85]

This dual aspect of Hart's book's discourse – a cool and readable first exposition of sensible ideas, but one that can quickly morph into something that cries out for refinement and development – has perhaps been an important factor in the book's extraordinary success. While *The Concept of Law* rapidly became, and remains, one of the most discussed books in the scholarly community, it is also successfully used to teach undergraduates in classrooms all over the world.

The present collection was put together with these two facets of Hart's book very much in mind. Though not exclusively designed *for* undergraduates, all chapters in this book (including this one) were written for an audience inclusive of students. But they critically engage with Hart's claims and theses at all steps. The overall project began two years ago, when the three editors were convening the Oxford Jurisprudence Discussion Group. In May 2011, to celebrate the 50th anniversary of the publication of *The Concept of Law*, we organised at the

---

[81] ibid vi.

[82] Hart, 'Philosophy of Law and Jurisprudence in Britain (1945–1952)' (1953) 2 *The American Journal of Comparative Law* 363; see also 'Analytical Jurisprudence in Mid-Twentieth Century' (n 3) 972f.

[83] cf Leslie Green's recent 'Introduction' to the 3rd edition of *The Concept of Law* (n 2) at xlvii–xlviii, as well as his chapter in the present volume; but contrast, also in this volume, Pierluigi Chiassoni's characterisation of what he calls Hart's 'model of ordinary analysis'.

[84] See 'Philosophy of Law and Jurisprudence in Britain (1945–1952)' (n 78) 364.

[85] See 'Answers to Eight Questions' (n 80) at 282. See also the 'Introduction' to his *Essays in Jurisprudence and Philosophy* (n 1) 7.

Oxford Law Faculty a weekly series of four events on Hart's book. Each of our speakers was invited to deliver and discuss a paper on one of Hart's chapters. Most contributors were legal and political philosophers from Oxford; the project became, in a sense, an Oxonian homage to the founder of the 'Oxford school' of jurisprudence. This collection was from the beginning a part of that project; our goal has been to put together, again with students in mind, a 'companion' of sorts to *The Concept of Law*.

The 2011 series of talks was a great success.[86] It began with a paper on chapter II of *The Concept of Law*, and rounded off with a group of four papers on those 'persistent questions' that Hart raises in chapter I. The present collection retains this structure. Part I contains essays on chapters II to X of *The Concept of Law*; each contributor focuses on a single of Hart's chapters, evaluating its claims in light of subsequent developments in the field. Part II (which we had decided might have a slightly more international shade) is dedicated to Hart's opening chapter. Here the contributors address, in more or less explicit terms, the question of how persistent Hart's 'persistent questions' have proved to be. Also included – in Part III – is the already mentioned interview in which Hart looks back at his book and its impact.

We are indebted to our contributors; to the Oxford Law Faculty, to Hart Publishing and to the Oxford University Press, for supporting our 2011 events; to Vinit Haksar, Tony Honoré and William Twining, for their generous participation in those events; to Timothy Endicott, John Gardner and Nicola Lacey, for advice and stimulus; and to Suzannah Moxey, for research assistance. We also thank Juan Ramón de Páramo, the editorial board of *Doxa. Cuadernos de Filosofía del Derecho*, Joanna Ryan and the Warden and Scholars of New College, Oxford, for permission to publish HLA Hart's 'Answers to Eight Questions'; and Jennifer Thorp, Archivist at New College, Oxford, who helped us locate the original typescript of Hart's interview.

Special thanks are due to Richard Hart, long-standing supporter of the Oxford Jurisprudence Discussion Group, who encouraged and guided our project from the beginning.

---

[86] Timothy Endicott, Dean of the Faculty, had expressed the wish that our series, reaching beyond the specialist circle of jurisprudential scholars, might captivate a broader audience and 'fill the Gulbenkian Lecture Theatre with undergraduates'. It did.

Part I

Reading *The Concept of Law*

2

The Generality of Law

TIMOTHY ENDICOTT*

IN THE 50 years since it was written, HLA Hart's *The Concept of Law*[1] has shaped legal philosophy. It has not done so by creating a school, but by doing something more fruitful, something that I am sure Hart found troubling. Yet he must also have found it rewarding. The book inspired people to explain why they disagree with it, and it still does today.

The book is durable in another way: its arguments are not dated. The tone is dated. It is the sound of 1950s England. If you want a guide to the era and to the milieu in which Hart was writing, you can find it in Jenifer Hart's autobiography, *Ask Me No More*.[2] There, you will find a kindred tone of voice and the same longing for candour and clarity, which Jenifer Hart and HLA Hart shared as members of an English intelligentsia in the 1950s, when the English did not really think of themselves as having an intelligentsia. It was a different era, and in the sound of that era, the book is dated.

But in the truths it states about the nature of law, it is not dated. And the errors in the book are, in Hart's phrase, 'pointers to the truth' now.[3] If you read the book you will find an elucidation of the nature of law, offered to you by a person who is striving for clarity. I guarantee that you will find something to disagree with. It may give you pointers to the truth.

In the eight pages of chapter II of *The Concept of Law*, Hart merely identifies a theory that he is going to address. Chapter II does not even clear the ground for the construction of his own theory (he clears the ground in chapters III and IV, by demolishing the theory identified in chapter II). Yet there is a great deal in this short, preliminary chapter. It is an accidental essay on the generality of law. I call it accidental because there is no indication that Hart set out to give an account of generality.

The simple imperative theory is, according to Hart, the theory that laws are coercive orders. He uses Austin's version of the theory in setting up his target,

---

* I am grateful for comments from John Finnis and from the editors of this volume.
[1] HLA Hart, *The Concept of Law*, 3rd edn (Oxford, Oxford University Press, 2012 [1961]).
[2] J Hart, *Ask Me No More* (London, Peter Halban Publishers, 1998).
[3] *The Concept of Law* (n 1) 17.

because Austin presented the theory more clearly and simply than Bentham did. Before identifying the errors in the theory, Hart sets out to make it a theory worth disagreeing with. A theory is worth disagreeing with not simply in virtue of being wrong, but only if we can learn something worthwhile from its mistakes. Hart suggests that we have more promise of learning something if we first show how it can best be defended. If the laws of a country are coercive orders, it might seem that they are like the commands of a gunman. But the simple imperative theory can actually distinguish law from the commands of a gunman, in various ways. In chapter II, Hart explains how that can be done, setting up a form of the imperative theory that would be worth disagreeing with. He aims to 'secure that the doctrine we shall consider and criticise is stated in its strongest form'.[4] In chapters III and IV he uses two related errors that he found in the imperative theory (in a nutshell, its account of the normativity of rules is inept, and so is its theory of a normative system) as pointers to the truth about the nature of law. Those errors will be more useful for that purpose, if the theory is presented as strongly as possible. Chapter II is an essay on ways in which the imperative theory could distinguish between laws and the commands of a gunman; Austin could have agreed with it.

The essay takes the form of a list. It is original, a little bit absent-minded, and incomplete. Hart starts numbering the features that distinguish laws from the commands of the gunman, then stops numbering them, and he never makes it very clear how many there are. And he never points out what unifies them.

The generality of law is what unites them. They all reflect the necessity, in any accurate account of laws, and in any accurate account of the existence and authority of legal institutions and of legal systems, of propositions that generalise across classes of instances. I will outline the major ways in which law is necessarily general (section I). I will start from Hart's account, but I will include aspects of generality in law that his accidental essay does not mention.

The most important respect in which Hart's account can be completed is by explaining the roles and the importance of particular norms in a legal system. Hart says that particular orders are either exceptional, or are 'ancillary accompaniments' of general forms of direction.[5] Here is the most striking incompleteness in his account of generality. I will argue in section II that particularity, too, is a necessary feature of a legal system. Particular orders are not exceptional, and it is misleading to call them 'ancillary'. This is to take nothing away from Hart's insight that law necessarily includes general rules. The generality of law is best understood in light of the necessary particularity of law, and the combination of generality and particularity is itself a necessary feature of a legal system.

[4] ibid 18.
[5] ibid 21.

In section III, I will discuss what 'necessary' means in these claims. It is a popular idea that legal theorists should not try to identify necessary features of law; I think that the popular idea is a mistake. In section IV, I will conclude by arguing that Hart's purposes call for value judgments about law. In his method of using insights into the use of language to draw conclusions as to what is necessarily the case about law, Hart shows a studied ambivalence toward the value of law. We can get further with Hart's own task – the elucidation task – if we are, instead, whole-hearted in understanding and saying what is good and bad about law. In setting the agenda for the book at the end of chapter I, Hart says that the errors of the simple imperative theory are 'a pointer to the truth'.[6] Hart's ambivalence is an error that is a pointer to a truth: that the elucidation of the concept of law depends on an elucidation of the value of law.

I. GENERALITY

A. The Generality of Laws

i. Applicability to Persons and to Conduct

The first two modes of generality lie in the scope of a law such as a criminal prohibition on murder, or an income tax. Such laws are general (1) as to the type of conduct required or prohibited or regulated, and (2) as to the persons to whom they apply. By defining a class of actions, law makers very often implicitly provide that the law that they are making is to apply generally to persons who engage in those actions. We might say that generality as to persons is just one aspect of generality in the conduct regulated by general rules; yet it is a form of generality that deserves attention because of the importance – for attaining the rule of law – of regulating not a particular person's conduct, but the conduct of persons generally in the community.

There is a class of persons who are subject to the criminal law or to the income tax, and there is a class of actions that count as murder or as earning income, and the obligations to pay the tax, and not to commit murder, apply generally to ordered pairs of persons and actions within the relevant classes. Sometimes, lawmakers come out and express the general application of a rule both to a class of persons, and to a class of actions. The Canadian prohibition on murder takes the form of a general statement that:

> Every one who commits first degree murder or second degree murder is guilty of an indictable offence and shall be sentenced to imprisonment for life.[7]

---

[6] ibid 17.
[7] Criminal Code (RSC, 1985, c C-46) 235(1).

Of course, there are legally valid orders that are particular as to the conduct required, or as to the person to whom the order applies – an order that a defendant must pay damages in a specified amount, or a sentence of imprisonment against a particular person for an offence, or an anti-social behaviour order addressed to a particular person, prohibiting a class of conduct. And general rules may be particular in some respect: a rule making a street one-way does not apply to streets in general, but to *this* street in particular. But it is general as to the class of conduct (driving on the street) and as to persons to whom the prohibition applies.[8]

ii. Time

The second mode of generality in law mentioned in chapter II is the enduring or '"standing" or persistent' character of a law.[9] Persistence is generality in applicability to a class of occasions across time. A tax law, unlike a demand from a gunman to his victim, persists in time. Laws typically apply generally across time. The time during which a law is to be in effect may be prescribed by a lawmaker (and then the rule will apply generally during that time, rather than at one particular moment). But often the lawmaker will say nothing, and then a law remains valid generally from the time of its making until it is repealed.[10]

iii. Place

Laws such as income tax laws, or prohibitions on homicide, are general as to the place at which the income is earned or the homicide is prohibited. Their extent may be regulated by complex rules as to what counts as earning the income within the relevant jurisdiction, and rules regulating borderline cases and overlaps with jurisdictions of other authorities.[11] Rules may apply in particular places, but general application in a territory is at the core of legal ordering. The reason is the relation between law and political communities.

---

[8] Are there particular *rules*? The idea of a rule involves not only normativity, but also regularity (unlike the idea of a *ruling*, which is typically particular); everything properly called 'a rule' is general in some respect. A rule may be particular in various respects, but every rule is more or less general in one or more modes. So in order to establish that generality is a necessary feature of law, it would be enough to establish that rules are a necessary feature of law. The present chapter argues not simply that law necessarily includes rules, but that law necessarily includes rules that are highly general, in a variety of respects, and that this is not only a necessary truth but an important truth.

[9] *The Concept of Law* (n 1) 23.

[10] For the best discussion of 'the general principle' that a law remains valid until it expires according to its terms, or until a deadline implied in its making, or until it is repealed, see J Finnis, 'Revolutions and Continuity of Law' in AWB Simpson (ed), *Oxford Essays in Jurisprudence. Second Series* (Oxford, Oxford University Press, 1973) 61–65.

[11] See Part XIV of the Canadian Criminal Code. Limits on the general territorial application of a law may be expressed in various ways, such as in terms of a limit on the jurisdiction of a court.

The relation between a people and a territory in a political community implies a need for laws that apply generally to the territory. Not every law need apply generally to the territory, of course; but every legal system that regulates the life of the community must include laws that apply generally to the territory. No prohibition on homicide would achieve its purpose if it were not general to the territory for which the law is made; restrictions on arbitrary detention are unfit for purpose if they do not apply throughout the territory in which executive officials exercise authority; citizenship laws that do not apply to a whole territory would not create a shared citizenship; police powers that do not effectively extend throughout a territory create enclaves for lawlessness. These forms of territorial generality – and many others – are essential to the rule of law.

Just as laws remain valid until repealed unless a lawmaker decides otherwise, they extend throughout the jurisdiction unless a lawmaker decides otherwise. As Hart says,

> In a modern state it is normally understood that, in the absence of special indications widening or narrowing the class, its general laws extend to all persons within its territorial boundaries.[12]

Such laws are general not only as to the class of conduct and as to the class of persons, and as to the time during which they apply, but also as to the territory within which the conduct is required or permitted or prohibited.

B. The General Authority of Legal Institutions

The generality of laws reflects generality in the authority of the law makers who make them. Every legal system gives authority to law makers not only to make particular orders, but to regulate the life of the community generally. And the generality of legal authority is also entailed by what Hart says, at the end of his list, about the supremacy of law. Law is made by institutions that are supreme within the system, and are independent from other institutions or persons.

Supremacy is general power. Nothing could count as a legal system, in which there was no general authority to regulate the life of the community. The supremacy of law entails at least four modes of generality: in the scope of the authority of legal institutions as to persons and as to subject matter, in the persistence in time of legal institutions, and in their authority across a territory. There is no *supreme* authority without *general* power to make law. I do not think that the authorities in a legal system need to claim unlimited authority.[13]

---

[12] *The Concept of Law* (n 1) 21.
[13] See Timothy Endicott, 'Interpretation, Jurisdiction, and the Authority of Law' (2007) 6 *American Philosophical Association Newsletter* 14–19.

But it is absolutely necessary that their authority to regulate the life of a community should extend generally across an extremely wide class of conduct.

Legal systems also necessarily have tribunals of general jurisdiction.[14] Setting up a tribunal with jurisdiction to decide a particular matter, such as an *ad hoc* war crimes tribunal, is an extraordinary measure. It can be appropriate if there is some urgent necessity for a tribunal capable of deciding the matter, and no regular tribunal has the combination of jurisdiction and effectiveness to decide the matter. But courts of regular, persistent, general jurisdiction over classes (and, in fact, over very broad classes) of legal dispute in a territory are necessary features of a legal system.

We should also point out another mode of generality in a legal system, which is not accounted for in chapter II. It reflects an incompleteness in Hart's account of the concept of law (although you may think that it is only a failure to mention something too obvious to mention). Along with rules of recognition, change, and adjudication, he should have pointed out the central role, in any conceivable legal system, of executive rules – rules authorising action (juridical and non-juridical) on behalf of the public. *The Concept of Law* does not mention the essential role in law of the executive functions of the state. This lacuna is understandable, since the legislative and adjudicative functions are paradigmatically legal functions, and we tend to think of legislatures and courts as the branches of government responsible for the law. But the *primary* functions of any state are executive, and the law must authorise and support and control those functions. A legal system necessarily confers general executive authority on agencies of the state. In fact, every actual legal system confers a complex variety of general competencies on a complex (and partly but not entirely hierarchical) array of agencies. And every legal system necessarily imposes general limits on executive action, and necessarily imposes general obligations on executive actors. Moreover, the primary responsibility for sustaining a legal system – for the rule of law – lies with the executive, and not with the legislature or the courts.[15]

Finally, just as rules of change and adjudication and executive rules are necessarily general, we can say the same of rules of recognition. Rules of recognition are necessarily general rules, for reasons that follow from the generality of rules of adjudication and of change and executive rules.

---

[14] Not necessarily 'general jurisdiction' in the sense in which the English High Court is a court of general jurisdiction; see *R (Cart) v Upper Tribunal* [2011] UKSC 28, and the discussion at first instance by Laws LJ, [2010] 2 WLR 1012.

[15] See T Endicott, *Administrative Law*, 2nd edn (Oxford, Oxford University Press, 2011) ch 1.

C. The Generality of the System

This is implied by the points made above about the authority of legal institutions within a system: the legal *system*, itself, has general authority over persons, over the subject matter of legal ordering, and over the community's territory, and the system itself persists in time.

D. A General Habit of Obedience

Finally, we should note that law is generally effective. In any legal system there is, in a phrase that Hart borrows from John Austin, a 'general habit of obedience'. All habits have at least two modes of generality: if you have a habit, you have a disposition that applies generally to instances or occasions within a class of conduct, and the habit, being a disposition, has some degree of general persistence across time. When Hart and Austin speak of a general habit, they mean a habit that is also general in a further respect: it is held generally by the members of a community. Although there may well be members of the community who do not have the habit, they are exceptions. Hart says that the general habit of obedience is a vague characteristic of law, but crucial.[16] And Hart adds something to this that I have not counted as a separate characteristic, which is that in a legal system there is 'a continuing belief in the consequences of disobedience'.[17]

In every legal system, the executive authorities of the state, in particular, have a general habit of obedience to the law (there may be exceptions, and even widespread exceptions; and exceptions to this generalisation typically depart from the rule of law).

E. Conclusion on Generality

Hart lists most of these modes of generality in chapter II,[18] but he does not present all of them as instances of generality.[19] Hart only uses 'generality' as a term for the first two modes of generality mentioned above, as to the persons

---

[16] *The Concept of Law* (n 1) 24; 'crucial' is a word we must come back to.
[17] ibid 23.
[18] To be specific, he listed generality of application of laws to persons and to conduct, the standing character of laws, the existence of a general belief in the execution of sanctions, a habit of general obedience, and the supremacy of law (which implies generality of authority).
[19] For example, Hart contrasts the persistence of law with 'the feature of generality', as two different features that differentiate law from the gunman situation: *The Concept of Law* (n 1) 22.

and conduct regulated by a law.[20] I have argued that all of the features he points out (which distinguish laws from the commands of a gunman, even under the simple imperative theory) are modes of generality in law. So are the additions I have made to the list.

As an account of generality in law, chapter II is incomplete. That is excusable, because in the rest of Hart's book, we can find much of what is needed to complete it. If he had been writing his essay on generality more deliberately, he could have pointed out that the secondary rules of recognition, change and adjudication in a legal system are all necessarily general rules. To his list of the essential framework rules of recognition, change, and adjudication, he should have added executive rules; they must be general, too.

Every legal system necessarily displays generality in (at least) the following modes:

MODES OF GENERALITY IN LAW		
Legal systems necessarily include **rules regulating the life of the community** that are general as to: **1.** Persons to whom they apply. **2.** Conduct which they regulate. **3.** The time at which they are in effect. **4.** The place in which they apply.	**Legal institutions** necessarily have general authority. Rules of change and adjudication and executive rules are general as to: **5.** The persons subject to the institution's jurisdiction. **6.** The subject matter of their jurisdiction. **7.** The time at which they have jurisdiction (persistence in existence of legal institutions is implicated in this mode of generality). **8.** The place at which they have jurisdiction.	**9. Legal systems** themselves necessarily persist generally in time, and are in effect in a territory in general, and the scope of their authority is general as to persons and conduct. Rules of recognition are necessarily general rules. **10.** The existence of a legal system necessarily involves a **disposition to obedience** (by officials and by non-officials) that is general as to the class of laws that are obeyed, the class of persons who obey, and the time and place at which the disposition subsists.

II. PARTICULARITY

Hart more or less stumbled into the account of the generality of law in chapter II, while preparing Austin's theory for demolition. It is hardly surprising that

---
[20] ibid 21.

the account is incomplete. A more complete account would explain the role of particularity in law, to put the role of generality in its true perspective.

The importance of particular legal rulings is not adequately reflected in Hart's rather by-the-by suggestion that particular norms are exceptional or ancillary. Here is what he says:

> Even in a complex large society, like that of a modern state, there are occasions when an official, face to face with an individual, orders him to do something. A policeman orders a particular motorist to stop or a particular beggar to move on. But these simple situations are not, and could not be, the standard way in which law functions, if only because no society could support the number of officials necessary to secure that every member of the society was officially and separately informed of every act which he was required to do. Instead such particularized forms of control are either exceptional or are ancillary accompaniments or reinforcements of general forms of directions which do not name, and are not addressed to, particular individuals, and do not indicate a particular act to be done.[21]

It is true that some forms of particular *legislation* are exceptional, such as an act of attainder, or an enactment designed to deprive a particular claimant of the effect of a court order,[22] or the old practice of legislative divorce. Some such acts are violations of the requirements of the rule of law, precisely because of their particularity. This does not mean that particular legislation is generally bad; but we can at least say that particular enactments are proper uses of legislative power only when there is some reason for particularity. An Act of Parliament for the creation of a railway company or other public body can be an example, and of course there are many others. But the most obvious and important example of particular legislation is the approval of a budget (as in the annual Finance Act in the United Kingdom), which includes a legislative authorisation of particular expenditure. That process in a legislature is justifiable because of the value, in the interests of responsible government, of fiscal accountability to a legislative assembly. In fact, it is so important a legislative function that you may conclude that generality is *not* the norm in legislation, after all. It is at least enough to show that particular legislation is not necessarily contrary to the rule of law. But certain sorts of particular legislation are exceptional, and the exceptionality of instruments such as acts of attainder or divorce shows something important about particularity in law: *the application of the community's legal standards to a particular case* is not (and it should not be) a standard function of the legislature. This is one aspect of the separation of powers and, like the connected ideal of the rule of law, the separation of powers is achieved by every legal system to some

---

[21] ibid 20–21.
[22] As the UK War Damage Act 1965 deprived the plaintiff of damages that had been awarded against the government in *Burmah Oil v Lord Advocate* [1965] AC 75, for destruction of property carried out by British forces to prevent the property from falling into enemy hands.

extent (even if there are defects in the separation of powers in every legal system).

But in the application of the community's standards by judicial tribunals, of course, particularity is the norm. Every court order is particular in one or more of several modes: as to persons affected, as to conduct required, and expressly or implicitly as to time and place. And particularity is essential to the executive function of government. That particularity is in turn essential to government by law, and Hart downplays it when he points out that particular orders could not take the place of general rules.

If judicial and executive orders are not exceptional, are they 'ancillary accompaniments or reinforcements of general forms of directions', as Hart suggests? It is true that they may involve the application of a general rule. Hart mentions a tax inspector's demand that you pay what you already owe, by the application of the general law. And he says that disobedience of a general rule 'may be officially identified and recorded and the threatened punishment imposed by a court'.[23] The suggestion is that the general rule is what matters, and the particular order of a court merely establishes what the general rule already requires.

This terse account of the role of orders obscures their importance. They are, in fact, necessary elements in a legal system. Let us focus on judicial orders, for relative simplicity. We need to start by understanding the importance in law of two particularising functions; in the exercise of *both* functions, a legal institution creates a new, particular norm. I will borrow the terms that Stephen Smith uses for them, in his study[24] of legal orders, and speak of:

(1) **replicative orders**, giving effect to existing duties under general rules as applied to particular cases; and
(2) **creative orders**, making a legal determination of a matter that is not determined by a general rule.

Judges carry out both functions.

A. The Legal System's Need for Particular Orders

If you have committed a serious assault, the general rule makes what you have done a crime, and it is a crime before the court so decides. You committed a crime when you committed the assault; but you are not convicted until a court makes a particular decision to convict you. It is unlawful for you to be pun-

---

[23] *The Concept of Law* (n 1) 21.
[24] S Smith, 'Why Courts Make Orders (And What This Tells us About Damages)' (2011) 64 *Current Legal Problems* 51.

ished by the state, without a particular decision of the court that you have committed assault.

Suppose that the police have caught you red-handed, and you freely admit the crime, and you do not want a trial. Why can't the state simply put you in prison? There are at least two reasons, which correspond to the two particularising functions listed above. First, the state needs to establish that the rule applies to your case. And it needs a rule-governed process for doing so, not only to be fair to you (or no judicial decision would be needed when you freely admit the crime), but also for the sake of responsible government, which requires a process by which the community (and not just the prosecution and the defendant) can be satisfied that the defendant has committed an offence.

This aspect of criminal process distinguishes it from, for example, the tort process, under which the victim of the tort need not bring the matter to a court, and the state cannot ordinarily do so unless it is the victim, and you can reach a settlement with the victim precisely to avoid a judicial process. It might seem that this aspect of process in private law shows that law simply may or may not require particular decisions. But even in the tort process, a particular decision of the court is essential, if any state action is to be undertaken on the basis that a tort was committed.

In fact, law is *necessarily* particular, not merely in the trivial sense that general rules apply to particulars, but because general rules are not enough: the system must have techniques for the rule-governed application of the law to particulars by the institutions of the system, chiefly to impose the rule of law on its own operation.

Orders typically create new rights or obligations or liabilities – even in the case of an order for payment of a fixed penalty, such as a parking ticket. Before the ticket is issued, you are liable to be fined. After it is issued, you *have been* fined, and you now have a new obligation to pay the fine (and you become liable to whatever penalties there may be for non-payment of the fine). The prohibition on parking had effect before the ticket was issued (just as a prohibition on homicide has effect before a court convicts you of homicide). But the issuance of the parking ticket has consequences such as authorisation of particular enforcement measures, which the general rule does not have. The parking ticket *is* ancillary to the prohibition on parking, in a sense, and yet Hart obscured the importance of particular orders when he dismissed them as ancillary.

The law must regulate its own application. There are various ways in which orders for the payment of a tax might be made – by courts like the English High Court, or by a specialised tribunal or commission independent of the government, or by the tax collectors themselves. Here is the essential point: if the tax collectors themselves have power to take coercive action for the collection of the tax *without* an order, the community fails (to that extent) to achieve the rule of law. The failure might be as serious as if there were no general rule, so that the tax collectors could take what they like. This is true even when there is no issue of any kind as to the nature of the primary obligation or liability under the general law, when courts issue replicative orders.

B. Particular Norms in Sanctions and Remedies

'Creative' orders involve a second, very important mode of particularity. Once a criminal conviction is entered, it may take a particular decision of the court to specify the punishment (often within a range set by legislation). This second role – determining sentence within a range – is not ancillary; at least, not in the sense that it identifies and records the effect of a general rule. Very typically, at least for most serious offences, the court's sentencing decision is a creative decision, authorised by a general rule. General legislation can constrain the discretion of judges and regulate the ways in which they exercise discretion, and legislatures have often set out to constrain and to regulate sentencing. The results involve forms of arbitrariness, insofar as fixed penalties prevent the sentencing decision from reflecting the facts that make a particular offence more or less serious than other offences of the same category. And the aspects of human situations and human conduct that make an offence more or less serious are so radically various that no legislative scheme of sanctions could provide in advance for a sentence tailored to the facts of every offence. If you try to imagine a system of criminal sentencing that assigned no discretion to the judge, you would find yourself imagining a scheme that involves radical forms of arbitrariness that are inimical to the idea of a punishment fitted to the offence. No authority could engage in *punishment*, without at least holding itself out as fitting the action to the offence. So the creativity involved in sentencing is essential to punishment.

Because this point extends more broadly to any general authority to impose sanctions and to award remedies, the making of particular orders is a necessary part of a legal system. The point applies to remedies in private law, just as it applies to sanctions in criminal law. An award of general damages very commonly creates a specific norm, for example by specifying a sum to be paid in compensation. The award is authorised by the general law, and it even seems to take the form of an *application* of a general rule of law, which may be formulated by saying that the claimant is to receive:

> that sum of money which will put the party who has been injured, or who has suffered, in the same position as he would have been in if he had not sustained the wrong for which he is now getting his compensation.[25]

[25] Lord Blackburn in *Livingstone v The Rawyards Coal Company* (1879–80) LR 5 App Cas 25 (House of Lords), cited in *Rees v Darlington Memorial Hospital NHS Trust* (House of Lords) [2003] UKHL 52, [2004] 1 AC 309.

The definite description ('that sum . . .') seems to present the amount to be awarded as if it were already determined by the general law, but of course its content is *not* determined. The reason is not simply that the rule is a general one, so that the sum depends on the facts, and is different in different cases. In many particular cases, there is in fact no rational criterion for concluding that some precise sum of money will put a party who has wrongfully suffered, for example, a chronic backache, in the same position as if the wrong had not been sustained.[26] And yet, the system needs a resolution. Ordinarily, the court's role in providing resolution requires an order for the payment of a precise sum of money, so that the defendant will know what sum to pay, and the claimant can know whether his or her legal right under the order has been fulfilled, and so that the officials of the system can know whether the defendant is in compliance with the order of the court. The determination itself is not the result of applying the general law, and yet a legal system needs the determination to be made. The award would be arbitrary, if it were determined by general rules.

Precise, preauthorised sanctions and remedies are, of course, possible. But no legal system could achieve the purpose of regulation of the life of the community entirely through such techniques. So the rule of law, in its opposition to arbitrary rule, demands a facility for particular creative orders. This is an important mode of particularity in law.

C. Determining the Undetermined

The exercise of an express discretion to impose a sentence within a range involves an authorisation and a responsibility to determine what the law has not determined. It creates a new, particular, legal norm. Determining the undetermined is characteristic of the judicial role not only in criminal sanctions and civil remedies, but also in the exercise of express discretions (as to costs, for example). It is also characteristic of the exercise of all the implicit discretions that result from vagueness in general laws. And because vagueness is a necessary, common, and important feature of general laws,[27] this form of creativity is commonly required of courts, and their role in exercising it is important, and legal systems necessarily involve this creativity.

---

[26] The precedents of the system may constrain the creative role of the court substantially, so that, for example, it may be well established in one jurisdiction that some particular sum would be an excessive award for a backache, and well established in another jurisdiction that the same sum would be inadequate. General rules of damages would have to turn into highly arbitrary tariffs, in order to remove the discretion substantially. And tariffs could never abolish the discretion of the court, because of the variety of possible injuries and of other possible losses.

[27] See T Endicott, 'Law is Necessarily Vague' (2001) 7 *Legal Theory* 379, and 'The Value of Vagueness', in A Marmor and S Soames (eds), *Philosophical Foundations of Language in the Law* (Oxford, Oxford University Press, 2011).

Courts applying the law very commonly create *new* obligations or liabilities, by specifying what is left unspecified in the law. In his terse account of the role of particularity in law, Hart neglects the fact that particular orders very commonly create *new* legal obligations and create *new* legal rights. A legal system could not operate without a facility for carrying this out.

D. Conclusion on Particularity

Hart points out that particular orders 'are not, and could not be, the standard way in which law functions'.[28] But we might just as well say that general rules are not, and could not be, 'the standard way in which law functions'. For law could not possibly function merely as a system of general rules.

Try to imagine a legal system in which there are only general rules, with no legal techniques for their application to particular cases. It would be in mere deadlock if officials of the state were unable to treat the rules as having some consequence, whenever anyone considered that the general rules have a different consequence. It would not be in deadlock if, without legal provision for any particular decision, executive officials could collect the taxes coercively, or impose punishment for crimes, when they conclude that the victim is liable to the tax or to the punishment under the general law. To imagine this scenario is to imagine the radical abandonment of the rule of law. The making of particular orders is necessary for law.

So the connection between particularity and generality in a legal system is much more complex than Hart says in chapter II of *The Concept of Law*. But the necessity and the importance of particular orders are compatible with Hart's insight that the generality of law is a necessary feature of law. And we should keep in mind one final, crucial feature of the rule of law (a respect in which, you might say, particular orders are, in a sense, 'ancillary' to general rules): in a legal system, there can be no particular orders with legal effect, except insofar as the legal official who creates a new legal obligation or liability, does so in the exercise of a general legal authorisation.

III. NECESSITY

In Hart's elucidation of one aspect of the nature of law (the necessity of generality in various modes), and in the argument that I have offered concerning the necessity of particular orders, what does 'necessity' mean? *The Concept of Law* did not expressly answer this question, but I do not think that it is difficult. Generality is a necessary feature of law if a legal system (or a legal institution, or a legal rule

---

[28] *The Concept of Law* (n 1) 21.

...) *must* have it, in order to be a legal system (or institution or rule ...). And generality is a necessary feature of law, if you and I *must* refer to it, to give a good account of the nature of law. Here is what Hart says at the beginning of chapter VIII, in summing up what is needed for elucidating the concept of law:

> We have found it necessary, in order to elucidate features distinctive of law as a means of social control, to introduce elements which cannot be constructed out of the ideas of an order, a threat, obedience, habits, and generality.[29]

We might say that if we *cannot* explain what is distinctive about law without mentioning generality, then generality is a *necessary* feature of law.

We can get a sense of what Hart means by 'necessary', from some pertinent words in chapter II. Hart writes about how people talk. He says that there is a variety of social situations in which people *characteristically* use imperative forms of speech; there are *recurrent* main types of social situation in which we address others in the imperative; those usages are marked by certain *familiar* classifications; 'pass the salt please' is *usually* a mere request; *normally* it is addressed by the speaker to one who is able to render him a service; it is quite *natural* to say that the gunman gave an order to his henchman to 'shut the door'; we do not *naturally* speak of commands in the case of government; the *standard* form of a criminal statute is general; 'we might *properly* say that the gunman ordered the clerk to hand over the money and the clerk obeyed'.[30]

We can class these low-key and sensible words into two categories. Hart uses words in the first category – words such as 'customarily', 'usually', 'normally' – to point out facts: about the way in which these words are used, and about what we do (commonly, usually, normally). Likewise, he talks about what we *would say*, and about what is done in a legal system. That is the first category: these words denote factual regularities.

The second category is the cluster of words such as 'characteristic' and 'appropriate' and 'properly'. Jeremy Bentham, too, used the word 'properly' in his own, very different methodology. Bentham claimed to identify the proper way to use words such as, for example, the word 'duty'. It is proper to use that word, according to Bentham, of a person who is liable to the infliction of some pain if he or she does not comply with the will of another.[31] When Bentham said that this use of the word is *proper*, he did not mean that it is customary or usual or normal. In fact, he thought that the customary, usual, normal way of using words such as 'duty' was misconceived.[32]

---

[29] ibid 154.
[30] ibid ch II *passim*.
[31] J Bentham, *A Fragment on Government*, JH Burns and HLA Hart (eds) (Cambridge, Cambridge University Press, 1977 [1776]) 113.
[32] See T Endicott, 'Law and Language', in J Coleman and SJ Shapiro (eds), *The Oxford Handbook of Jurisprudence* (Oxford, Oxford University Press, 2004) 939–45.

Hart uses the word 'properly' in a more diffident sort of way. Unlike Bentham, he just mixes it in (and he just mixes in the related word 'appropriately'), with the first category of words – 'usually', 'normally', what we 'would say'. Hart talks in the same breath *both* about what people say, and about what it is proper to say. From considering the ways in which people use words, he says that we can gain wisdom not merely about a word, but about *law*. There is in the Preface of *The Concept of Law* a famous reference to JL Austin, who said that we can use a 'sharpened awareness of words' to gain a sharpened 'perception of the phenomena'.[33] The idea is put more clearly by Hart himself in an endnote in *The Concept of Law*. Hart says that

> to ask in what standard sorts of situation would the use of sentences in the grammatical imperative mood be normally classed as orders, pleas, requests, commands, directions etc is a method of discovering not merely facts about language, but the similarities and differences recognised in language between various social situations and relationships. The appreciation of these is of great importance for the study of law, morals and society.[34]

Hart uses *both* categories (insights as to how we in fact use words, and insights as to how it is proper to use them) for the same purpose. The purpose is to point out characteristic features of law, in order to elucidate the concept.

The result of his elucidation in chapter II is a set of claims as to what is necessarily the case: a general habit of obedience to law, for example, is 'a further necessary feature which we must add to the gunman situation, if it is to approximate to the settled situation in which there is law'.[35] In making claims of necessity, Hart is not actually doing something distinct from saying what is characteristic, recurrent, familiar, normal, natural, standard, customary, usual, normal, appropriate, proper. He uses all those terms, along with 'necessary', in pointing out those features of law that we *must* attend to, if we are to elucidate the concept of law. And those are the same features that a rule or an institution or a system *must* display, according to Hart, if it is to count as legal.

If that is the right way to understand Hart's claims of necessity, does it simply show that Hart makes too much of his observations about how people use words? Granted that people use words in the ways he pointed out, are the associated features of law *necessary* features? Deep historical roots still nourish a tendency among some philosophers to be suspicious of such claims. For

---

[33] *The Concept of Law* (n 1) vii; Austin's full sentence is: 'When we examine what we should say when, what words we would use in what situations, we are looking again not merely at words (or "meanings", whatever they may be) but also at the realities we use the words to talk about: we are using our sharpened awareness of words to sharpen our awareness of, though not as the final arbiter of, the phenomena': JL Austin, 'A Plea for Excuses', in his *Philosophical Papers*, JO Urmson and GJ Warnock (eds), 3rd edn (Oxford, Oxford University Press, 1979) 182.
[34] *The Concept of Law* (n 1) 280.
[35] ibid 23.

millennia it has seemed to some that there is no *necessary* or *essential* content to a human concept.

You might say that the instances of *some* concepts obviously have necessary features. Having three sides is a necessary feature of triangles. If a figure does not have three sides, then for that reason it does not – it *cannot* – count as a triangle. So a figure *needs* three sides to count as a triangle, and there isn't anything wrong with saying that having three sides is a necessary feature of a triangle. But that is geometry. Perhaps we should say that there is nothing that is necessary or essential to the concepts of anything so controversial, unstable, and limned by multiple contingencies, as social theory?

Brian Leiter has recently given a vigorous statement of this view. He says that people should abandon the 'demarcation problem' in jurisprudence – the problem of how to distinguish law and morality. He says that Hart and others have tried to solve that problem by identifying necessary or essential features or attributes or properties of law that distinguish it from morality. Leiter rejects the attempt. Yet he identifies one necessary feature of law:

> The concept of law is the concept of an *artefact*, that is, something that necessarily owes its existence to human activities intended to create that artefact.[36]

Let's ask whether Leiter has a case that this is the *only* necessary truth about law. His point is that artefacts have no essential attributes, because they depend on human ends and purposes, and 'human ends and purposes shift'. Law being an artefact, it seems that what counts as law depends on something that is contingent.[37]

All sorts of truths about an artefact – say, a chair – arise from the relevant human purposes – that it was designed to be sat upon, and therefore it has extension in space and is solid and durable, and more or less fits the human form, and is bigger than a pinhead and smaller than Saskatchewan, and so on. But Leiter says:

> Chairs can be made of stone or wood or metal. Their apparent function – providing support for those who sit – can be discharged by boxes, tortoises, car seats, and steps. Moreover, some chairs have as their actual function ornamental decoration,

---

[36] B Leiter, 'The Demarcation Problem in Jurisprudence: A New Case for Scepticism' (2011) 31 *Oxford Journal of Legal Studies* 666.

[37] ibid 667. Leiter combines that argument with an 'inductive argument' from alleged past failures of philosophers to identify necessary features of law. He mentions the incompatible claims of four legal philosophers including Hart (ibid 668). But he offers no base for the proposed induction, because he gives the reader no reason to think that any particular one of the conflicting claims is untrue. They cannot all be true, so he *does* offer a sound basis for concluding that not all legal philosophers can be right. In order to conclude that there are no necessary truths that answer problems of jurisprudence, we would have to add the premise that a necessary truth must be *uncontroversially* true. We should reject that further premise; the human capacity to dispute the indisputable makes controversy an inadequate criterion for concluding that a proposition is not necessarily true.

not sitting; some serve primarily as shelves for stacking papers or books. Some chairs have arm rests, some do not; some have back rests, some do not. Because human ends and purposes shift, the concept of a 'chair' has no essential attributes.[38]

People can sit on things that are not chairs, people can do other things with chairs than sit on them, and chairs vary in form and substance. So perhaps, since 'human ends and purposes shift', chairs have no necessary features that distinguish them from other things?

It is true that human purposes may shift in all directions, from designing a piece of furniture for seating, towards stacking papers, towards home decoration, towards building a life-saving fire, and objects that people call 'chairs' can be put to all these purposes. And human purposes range more widely into parody, so that someone might make a vaudeville chair designed to collapse as soon as someone sits on it, or a modern art chair 50 feet tall or made out of egg shells. And of course, a person may remove the seat of a chair to fix it, and then you cannot even sit on it. So it seems that we cannot say that chairs are necessarily used, or necessarily *can* be used, or were even necessarily *made*, to be sat upon.

What are we to do? We shouldn't give up altogether on distinguishing law from morality (or, presumably, on distinguishing chairs from other things), according to Leiter:

> I have conceded that judges have a defeasible obligation to apply the law and that judges, like other persons, ought to do what is morally right. This statement already supposes that the two sources of norms, law and morality, are different. But of course they are *obviously* different in many cases, and many contexts! It is a mistake to assume that a distinction, to be useful for *many* purposes, has to be made in terms of *essential* properties that will demarcate *all* cases for all purposes, the way the molecular constitution of water definitely settles the status of all clear potable liquids. . . . For most purposes, we operate quite well with the method of paradigm cases, and analogies to those cases.[39]

That is a good method. Let's say that the paradigm case of a chair is a piece of furniture designed and crafted for people to sit on;[40] a chair may not be a paradigm chair, so it is *not* a necessary truth that a chair has all the features of a paradigm chair. And then, Leiter's method of analogy helps us to explain the various tricky things that may be called 'chairs' even though they do not have the traits of the paradigm. Therefore, the method of analogy helps us to

---

[38] ibid 666f.
[39] ibid 676.
[40] In fact, the concept is more complex than this suggests, and there would of course be more to be said, such as that the paradigm case of a chair is distinguishable from a stool by having a back rest (which, given certain no doubt shifting facts about human physiology, makes it apt for a particular kind of sitting or, you might say, particularly apt for sitting), and it would be possible to explain why people don't call a seat in a car or an airplane a 'chair', and to say whether a throne is too fancy to be called a 'chair'.

deal with the implications of the shifting nature of human purposes for the meaning and reference of an artefact term:

- A chair that has had its seat removed for repair may still be a chair, because of the similarities it bears to paradigm cases, and because the disanalogy to paradigm cases is accountable in light of the repair.
- And even a chair that has simply lost its seat and is not being repaired is intelligible *as* a chair in a similar way – as a defective chair.
- Borderline cases are intelligible *as* borderline both by their analogies to and their differences from paradigms.
- The vaudeville chair and the modern art chairs are intelligible as what they are, in light of the analogies *and disanalogies* to paradigms (the combination of similarities and dissimilarities makes the vaudeville chair a trick chair, and lends irony to the modern art chairs; neither would work for their human purposes without the analogies to paradigm chairs).

Leiter's method of analogy is a sound and promising method for making concepts intelligible, in spite of (or rather, in light of) the shifting nature of human purposes.

Ironically, this method of analogy is Hart's method.[41] It underlies his talk of 'necessity'. And the method actually *undermines* Leiter's view that there are no necessary truths about artefact concepts.

Nothing is a paradigm of a concept unless it has features in virtue of which we might find it useful in explaining the application of the concept. An object is an instance of the concept if it is a paradigm. And an object is an instance of the concept if analogies to paradigms justify the extension of the term to the object. We add nothing to this, if we say that an object *must* count as an instance of the concept if it is a paradigm, and that it *must* be appropriately analogous to a paradigm, if it is to count as an instance (there are many analogies between any particular table and a paradigm chair, but they do not justify calling the table a 'chair'). An object is not a chair (and we may just as well say that an object *cannot* be a chair), if the analogies to paradigms do not make sense of extending the term to apply to the object.

And this is the point of contact between the method of analogy, and necessary truths: the analogies to paradigm chairs must justify calling an object a 'chair', or it is not a chair. There is that word 'must'. It should not be off-putting to anyone who adopts the method of analogy. And accepting the method means rejecting Leiter's claim that there are no necessary truths about chairs – or about law.

---

[41] See, eg, *The Concept of Law* (n 1) 81: 'the diverse range of cases of which the word 'law' is used are not linked by . . . simple uniformity, but by less direct relations – often of analogy of either form or content to a central case'.

IV. VALUE

Paradigms of artefacts are to be identified, and analogies are to be drawn, in light of the values that are implicated in the purposes and ends of artefacts such as law or such as chairs. The paradigm of a legal system is good for the purposes for which it is worth crafting or sustaining a legal system. Legal systems are not necessarily good. Like chairs, they can be badly made, and they can be put to bad purposes. And a community needs more than just a legal system. But here is a connection between law and morality: in order to accomplish the morally good purposes for which a legal system might be adopted and established and sustained, it is necessary (for example) to make general rules. A legal system needs to offer the modes of generality that the community needs for its governance. Here is Hart again, making his first point about the generality of law:

> A policeman orders a particular motorist to stop or a particular beggar to move on. But these simple situations are not, and could not be, the standard way in which law functions, if only because no society could support the number of officials necessary to secure that every member of the society was officially and separately informed of every act which he was required to do.[42]

Hart explains the necessity of generality by referring to the impossibility of the alternative: particular orders 'could not be' the standard way in which law functions. But Hart's point – that a society could not 'support the number of officials' – is a dodge. The salient, undeniable, prior truth, patently underlying the point about the number of officials, is that trying to regulate a community without generality would ruin a legal system.

You might say that this consideration of value is not a matter of necessity, because it is *possible* to have a legal system that does not achieve the value that a good legal system would achieve. The imperfections are likely to be significant even in a good legal system. Yet the consideration of value still involves a necessity: if we want to accomplish the goods that can be accomplished through a legal system, we *need* general rules. Latent in the obvious points about a legal system made in sections I and II above is a set of allusions to the *value* of generality and to the value of particularity in the ordering of the community.

There is an evident rationale for Hart's reticence in tying necessary truths about law to assertions of value: he had a healthy wariness of portraying law as necessarily a good thing, when it is not necessarily a good thing. But the reticence is a mistake, because of the connection between the nature of law and the goods that it can achieve. Although not every legal rule is a good thing (and not every legal system is a good thing), no legal system can be a

---

[42] ibid 21.

good thing without generality and particularity in the modes set out in sections I and II. This is a necessary connection between law and value that Hart need not have denied. Indeed, it is a form of necessary connection that is supported by Hart's assertions that societies with only 'primary rules of obligation' may suffer from *defects* of uncertainty, static rules, and the inefficiency of 'diffuse social pressure' in dispute resolution and enforcement. Hart says that law provides a 'remedy' for these 'defects'.[43] Again, a legal system, with its characteristic aspects of certainty and dynamism, and its techniques for effective dispute resolution and enforcement, may be put to evil purposes; and still there is a necessary connection between law and morality, if those features of law are needed for moral purposes.[44]

There is value for a community in having rules that are general, in the ways that Hart pointed out and in other ways. The reason it can be valuable to have law lies partly in the value of generality in the ordering of the community. The paradigm case of a legal system has modes of generality and particularity because it needs them in order to serve the community in the way that (being a paradigm of a legal system) it does. Generality as to time and place are connected to the ideal of the rule of law; so are all the aspects of generality. Generality finds a place in all the best lists of the requirements of the rule of law.[45]

This connection between the nature of law and the good of a community should be obvious. A community is a generality. The application of law generally to *more than one particular person* is essential to its role as the *community's* system for the good regulation of the community's life. And a legal system could not be a legal system if only one particular person obeyed it (general obedience is 'crucial', as Hart says), because it would not be accomplishing the goods that a legal system is capable of accomplishing. So the generality of law is necessarily associated with the good of a community. It would be deeply pointless, in regulating the direction of traffic on a street, to have a one-way rule that applied to some person in particular and not to drivers in general. The rationale for prohibiting murder, in justice and for the public good, is a

---

[43] ibid 92–94.

[44] For a full explanation of Hart's ambivalence about the value of law, it is not enough to point out his sensible insight that a law or a legal system may not be a good thing; the reticence also involves his ambivalence about the objectivity of morality and, by implication, of value. This ambivalence is expressed both in the Postscript to *The Concept of Law* (ibid 253), and in the 'Introduction' to Hart's *Essays in Jurisprudence and Philosophy* (Oxford, Oxford University Press, 1983) 11.

[45] See LL Fuller, *The Morality of Law*, revised edn (New Haven, Yale University Press, 1969) ch II; J Finnis, *Natural Law and Natural Rights*, 2nd edn (Oxford, Oxford University Press, 2011) 270f; Joseph Raz, *The Authority of Law*, 2nd edn (Oxford, Oxford University Press, 2009) 214–18. For a helpful discussion of the relation between generality and clarity in the rule of law, see P Yowell, 'Legislation, Common Law and the Virtue of Clarity' in R Ekins (ed), *Modern Challenges to the Rule of Law* (Wellington, LexisNexis, 2011).

rationale that applies generally, so that a prohibition on murder ought to apply generally. Public authorities could not pursue good purposes without general authority over persons and over forms of conduct, or without general authority over a territory. When Hart says that 'In a modern state it is normally understood that . . . its general laws extend to all persons within its territorial boundaries',[46] he might have added that such a normal understanding makes sense because of the value to the community of that form of generality. Generality is necessary in, for example, taxation for good public purposes – for efficiency, and for preventing abuse by tax collectors. Endurance in time of rules, institutions, and the system itself is necessary to the very idea of law, because a community has a life that extends in time. Rules, institutions, and the system itself could not accomplish the goods that law is capable of accomplishing, if they vanished in an instant.

Every one of the modes of generality set out in section I can be related to value in this way, and the particularity of law involves the considerations of value that I set out in section II.

The generality of law, incidentally, provides one aspect of the solution to the 'demarcation problem' that Leiter rejects as an ill-formed problem. Law is general within classes (of person, of territory, of activity . . .) that correspond to a particular community, to its particular system, and to a time during which the system is in effect. Authorities, and their jurisdictions, are intrinsic to the concept of law. The generality of law cannot be understood without reference to jurisdiction. But jurisdiction is not essential to the concept of morality (though morality may require acceptance of an authority's jurisdiction). The generality of morality and the generality of law are necessarily different. And the modes of particularity that are essential to law are not essential to morality. There is much more to be said about the demarcation between the two, but this is enough to show that the 'demarcation problem' makes sense, and can be solved.

Law has a nature or essence, which is characterised by its necessary features. They are the features that must obtain if, for example, a particular norm is a law, or a particular institution is a legal institution, or a particular community has a legal system. They include the features that we must refer to if we are to elucidate the concept. Jurisprudence has a great deal more to do, besides pointing out necessary truths. But doing so is part of the project of making social life intelligible. Identifying those truths depends on identifying the value of law. Necessary truths about law (such as that it involves generality and particularity in the modes set out in sections I and II) are truths because of the value of certain aspects of paradigm cases of law, such as the generality and particularity that they involve.

---

[46] *The Concept of Law* (n 1) 21.

3
Variety or Uniformity?

RICHARD HS TUR

> Where order in variety we see,
> And where, though all things differ, all agree.[1]

I. INTELLECTUAL CONTEXT

ALL THEORIES OF law are influenced by some general philosophical assumptions, and Hart's *The Concept of Law* is no exception. The dominant school of philosophy in the mid-twentieth century, not least at Oxford, was what came to be known as 'linguistic philosophy'. Hart's *Concept* exhibits its influence through and through. Before we discuss his views on the 'variety of laws' – the topic of chapter III in Hart's book – it will prove useful to look, albeit briefly, at some traits of that school of philosophy.

Three leading linguistic philosophers whose work influenced Hart's were GE Moore (1873–1959), Ludwig Wittgenstein (1889–1951), and JL Austin (1911–1960).[2] In *Principia Ethica*, Moore advanced the sweeping generalisation that in *all* 'philosophical studies'

> the difficulties and disagreements, of which its history is full, are mainly due to a very simple cause: namely to the attempt to answer questions, without first discovering precisely *what* question it is which you desire to answer.[3]

If only philosophers were to '*try* to discover what question they were asking, before they set about to answer it', he says, 'many of the most glaring difficulties and disagreements in philosophy would disappear'.[4] The suggestion is that (to put it broadly) philosophical problems are pseudo-problems stemming from the misuse of language: that most philosophy can be reduced to linguistic therapy. Not only does the importance of language feature in Moore's philosophy, so too

---

[1] A Pope, *Windsor Forest* (1711) 1.11.
[2] See RS Summers, 'Professor HLA Hart's Concept of Law' (1963) 4 *Duke Law Journal* 631 n 7.
[3] GE Moore, *Principia Ethica* (Cambridge, Cambridge University Press, 1903) vii.
[4] ibid.

does the validity of the plain man's view. The status accorded to 'common sense' is high. This ties in with the view that philosophical problems are created by philosophers – that it is their misuse of language which creates problems. Plain men are not philosophers. They do not confuse themselves. They do not have philosophical problems. Thus will common usage – the language of the plain man based upon common sense – provide all the answers.

Wittgenstein espoused two inconsistent theories as to the nature of language and its relation to philosophising at different stages of his life. For the 'later' Wittgenstein, however, philosophy also involves the clarification of the confusion and perplexity spread by philosophers using language in the wrong context. Philosophers of the traditional type produce nonsense, which is incompatible with familiar and deep-seated common-sense beliefs. Real philosophers seek to eliminate such confusion, to overcome our bewitchment by language. As he put it, the aim of philosophy is 'to shew the fly how to get out of the fly-bottle'.[5] The point being, of course, that it was the philosophers who put it there in the first place.

JL Austin, with whom Hart collaborated at Oxford, took linguistic philosophy seriously as an end in itself rather than merely as a therapeutic or prophylactic activity.[6] He became deeply involved in the detail of common linguistic usage and was reluctant to theorise or generalise; to generalise, he thought, was necessarily to distort. His belief in the adequacy of ordinary language was astounding: he held the startling view that

> our common stock of words embodies all the distinctions men have found worth drawing, and the connexions they have found worth making, in the lifetimes of many generations: these surely are likely to be more numerous, more sound, since they have stood up to the long test of the survival of the fittest, and more subtle, at least in all ordinary and reasonably practical matters, than any that you or I are likely to think up in our arm-chairs of an afternoon – the most favoured alternative method.[7]

A lesser figure of the school presses the similar point that

> language does not develop in a random or inexplicable fashion . . . [I]t is at the very least unlikely that it should contain either much more, or much less, than [its] purposes require . . . It is at the same time very *un*likely that any invented, artificial, or *ad hoc* terminology will be an improvement on that which has already satisfied the most stringent of tests – that is, survival in (probably) centuries of constant actual use.[8]

---

[5] See L Wittgenstein, *Philosophical Investigations*, GEM Anscombe (trans) (Oxford, Blackwell, 2001 [1953]) §309.

[6] 'Much of course of the amusement and of the instruction comes in drawing the coverts of the microglot, in hounding down the minutiae': JL Austin, 'A Plea for Excuses', in his *Philosophical Papers*, 3rd edn (Oxford, Oxford University Press, 1979 [1957]) 175.

[7] ibid 182.

[8] GJ Warnock, *English Philosophy Since 1900* (London, Oxford University Press, 1958) 150.

All this seems to me seriously wrong-headed and no more persuasive than the extravagant notion that the common law is right reason itself. Of course an artificial, technical language can do certain jobs better than ordinary usage. And of course there is more to philosophy than a mere scrutiny of ordinary usage. Indeed 'the very purpose of philosophy is to delve *below* the apparent clarity of common speech'.[9] Moreover, it seems to me that ordinary usage and common sense (whatever the time, place or culture) is often trivial, platitudinous, and full of error. It perpetuates mistake, mysticism, and myth. It eliminates the need to be aware of the contribution of technical languages such as those of computer science, mathematics, or law, among many others. It seems to me to be non-critical and complacent; it accepts as justified what common sense accepts. Bertrand Russell seems to me to have gotten it about right when he said that common sense is the metaphysics of savages.[10] A view rather more congenial to mine is exceptionally and characteristically well put by Lon Fuller:

> In general the practice of ordinary-language philosophy consists in digging out and clarifying the distinctions embedded in everyday usage. In whatever field these distinctions are found, there seems to be a kind of presumption that they will prove valid and useful and that once they have been fully articulated there is no need to go further. . . . Some useful insights have been derived through this method; there is indeed a lot of tacit and subtle wisdom concealed in the interstices of everyday speech. But the tendency of the practitioners of this method has been to regard as an end in itself, what ought to be viewed as a useful adjunct to philosophical thought.[11]

Against this method's negative and demeaning vision of philosophy, I juxtapose a wider and older view of it as the critical assessment of belief, together with such conceptual analysis and revision as is necessary to that end – even where the reconstruction of concepts goes well beyond common usage. Nor do I believe that to generalise is necessarily to distort, or that general theory is to be distrusted. Rather, I believe that thinking is a unifying process, and to make sense of or to understand something is sometimes to see it as part of something more general.

My philosophical preference for uniformity contrasts sharply with Hart's emphasis on variety, which is the focus of his chapter III. Rooted as we are in these very different philosophical traditions, it is unsurprising that I favour uniformity and he advocates variety.

---

[9] AN Whitehead, *Adventures of Ideas* (Cambridge, Cambridge University Press, 1933) 223.
[10] See B Magee, *Confessions of a Philosopher. A Personal Journey Through Western Philosophy, from Plato to Popper* (New York, Random House, 1998) 43; the popular phrase appears to be Magee's own – summarising a passage in Russell's *The Problems of Philosophy* – rather than a direct quotation.
[11] LL Fuller, *The Morality of Law*, revised edn (New Haven, Yale University Press, 1969) 195f.

II. THE VARIETY OF LAWS: INITIAL SIGHTING

The thesis which I seek to advance is that Hart's emphasis on the variety of laws is overstated, dependent to a degree on linguistic philosophy, and sociological rather than conceptual. As against Hart's 'variety' thesis – set forth in chapter III of *The Concept of Law* – I argue for a 'uniformity' thesis; the claim that law in all its forms can be conceptually reduced to one logical form.

By way of introduction, let us briefly glance at chapter I. Hart suggests that any 'educated man' can identify 'salient features' of a legal system. These are:

> (i) rules forbidding or enjoining certain behaviour under penalty; (ii) rules requiring people to compensate those they injure in certain ways; (iii) rules specifying what must be done to make wills, contracts, or other arrangements which confer rights and create obligations; (iv) courts to determine what the rules are and when they have been broken, and to fix the punishment or compensation to be paid; (v) a legislature to make new rules and abolish old ones.[12]

This is a very important passage. The educated man says that law is made up of rules: these rules are of 'various sorts'[13] – or so it seems to the educated man. Hart's own programme in his *Concept*, a programme which actually commences in chapter V, is to show that law can best be elucidated by thinking of it as a union or 'fusion'[14] of primary and secondary rules.[15]

But then Hart goes on to suggest that it was 'perhaps optimistically' that we put such words 'into the mouth of an educated man'.[16] We cannot 'put an end to the persistent question "What is law?", simply by issuing a series of reminders of what is already familiar'.[17] The 'deep perplexity' that has kept that question alive springs from more than the conventional assertion that 'laws of various sorts go together'.[18] So Hart proceeds to give a general account of what has puzzled jurists in the past. But two points cannot be overemphasised, since they are basic to the whole approach of *The Concept of Law* – and have already been taken for granted. First, law is somehow connected with rules; and second, there are laws of various types.

As to *rules*, Hart tells us that whereas the idea that law is somehow explicable in terms of rules may seem indubitable, the notion of a rule is in fact the source of 'dissatisfaction, confusion, and uncertainty' underlying 'much of the perplex-

---

[12] HLA Hart, *The Concept of Law*, 3rd edn (Oxford, Oxford University Press, 2012) 3.
[13] ibid 5.
[14] ibid 49.
[15] On the educated man's list, rules in (i) and (ii) would count as 'primary', whereas those in (iii) would count as 'secondary'.
[16] ibid 5.
[17] ibid.
[18] ibid.

ity about the nature of law'.[19] Hereabouts Hart introduces the view that 'there are rules of many different types', an idea which he partially explains as follows:

(a) Rules which pertain to different 'spheres' of activity are different in type ('besides legal rules there are rules of etiquette and of language, rules of games and clubs');
(b) Rules which 'originate in different ways' are different in type ('even within the law some rules are made by legislation; others are not made by any such deliberate act');
(c) Rules which 'have different relationships to the conduct with which they are concerned' are different in type ('some rules are mandatory in the sense that they require people to behave in certain ways . . . [while] other rules . . . indicate what people should do to give effect to the wishes they have').[20]

The view expressed in (a) is Wittgensteinian. If the meaning of a word is in its use and if rules are used to define or constitute 'activities' or 'language games', then every 'language game' or 'form of life' has its own rules with their unique use and hence different meanings.[21] But as an argument for typological variety this is hardly persuasive. Rules pertaining to different activities could all be of the same type – certainly of the same *form*, which is really, as many passages in the book soon begin to reveal, what Hart means when he speaks of 'types' of rule.[22] It does not follow that the rules (or laws) that relate to marriage and those that relate to commerce are necessarily of different 'types' simply because they serve different social purposes or sustain very different 'activities'; and indeed the very same rule might well simultaneously serve more than one purpose, or pertain to more than one 'sphere' of activity.

The claim in (b) is similarly unconvincing. No one who holds that all rules are of the same type is thereby committed to the belief that they should all originate in the same way. It may be possible to regard rules of law as having the same form whether they originate in custom, from courts, or from the legislature; and one question for general jurisprudence is precisely whether the rich variety of legal phenomena can in some sense be 'reduced' to a single form. It may or may not be the case, for example, that statutory rules and common law rules are logically distinct and cannot be assimilated to one model. As we shall see in the final section, that is a big question within jurisprudence on

---

[19] ibid 8.
[20] ibid 9.
[21] See Wittgenstein, *Philosophical Investigations* (n 5) §§7, 43.
[22] See, eg, the passages at ibid 24 ('we shall have later [ie in chapter III] to consider the claim that these other varieties of law also . . . are really just complicated or disguised versions of [the] *same form*'), 36 ('all genuine laws, on this view . . . are *all of the* [*same*] *form*'; 'legal rules of every type . . . can be restated *in this . . . form*'), 38 ('Both versions of this theory attempt to reduce apparently distinct varieties of legal rule *to a single form*'), 41 ('But it would reduce all rules . . . to *a single form*'), or 49 ('the effort to *reduce to this single simple form* the variety of laws'); the italics are all mine.

which theorists differ. For example, Dworkin takes the view that 'much the same techniques of interpretation' are as appropriate to reading statutes as to deciding common law cases,[23] whereas Hart, though he does acknowledge that the dissimilarities can be exaggerated, nonetheless regards the difference as significant.[24] The important point of this discussion is whether or not it is possible to subsume both common law and statutory law under a common form even though they clearly do originate in different ways.

As to (c), quite what Hart means is unclear. Unless we have an idea of how rules relate to conduct we cannot suppose different 'types' of relation between rules and conduct. Something along the following lines may reconstruct Hart's position. The relation between rules and behaviour is *normative*; the behaviour is what *ought to be* according to the rule. But this 'ought' may be too coarse or general a term adequately to capture the relationship between rule and behaviour, because a rule might *command* behaviour or merely *authorise* it. Such a fundamental difference between 'must' and 'may' – that is, between normative modalities – should, it might well be thought, be clearly marked by a terminological distinction, rather than fudged by being merged into one general term such as 'ought'. The suggestion here, then, is that 'ought' should be further divided into different normative modalities such as commanding, that is, that which one 'must' do, and authorising, that is, that which one 'may' do. Any analysis of law which does not make such a distinction (as, for example, Austin's, and, arguably, Kelsen's[25]) might well be thought to be inadequate and distorting. Now, such a view would be extremely interesting and important. But though it is possible to read it into Hart, there is no corroborating evidence that this is what he meant. And at this preliminary stage there is no justification for the view that there are rules of different types. Yet this view is central to Hart's project. Chapter III of *The Concept of Law* is dedicated to defending it.

III. HART AND AUSTIN

In chapter III, under the rubric 'The Variety of Laws', Hart unleashes a full-scale attack on the Austinian position which he had built up, in the previous chapter, out of the artificially simplified 'gunman' situation. And his main claim – already announced at the end of chapter II – is that there are 'types of law' which the Austinian position appears not to fit:

---

[23] See R Dworkin, *Law's Empire* (Oxford, Hart, 1998) 313.

[24] *The Concept of Law* (n 12) 126ff.

[25] Kelsen gave his 'ought' four separate meanings: command, authorise, permit, and (added later) derogate: cf H Kelsen, *The Pure Theory of Law*, 2nd edn, M Knight (trans) (Berkeley, University of California Press, 1967 [1960]) 5; and 'Derogation', in O Weinberger (ed), *Essays in Legal and Moral Philosophy* (Dordrecht, Reidel, 1973 [1962]) 261.

The concept of general orders backed by threats given by one generally obeyed, which we have constructed by successive additions to the simple situation of the gunman case, plainly approximates closer to a penal statute enacted by the legislature of a modern state than to any other variety of law. For there are types of law which seem prima facie very unlike such penal statutes, and we shall have later to consider the claim that these other varieties of law also, in spite of appearances to the contrary, are really just complicated or disguised versions of this same form.[26]

'Not all laws', Hart now asserts, 'order people to do or not to do things'.[27] He isolates four main classes of phenomenon which do not square with Austin's position:

(1) Public and private power-conferring rules ('Laws which confer powers on private individuals to make wills, contracts, or marriages, and laws which give powers to officials, e.g. to a judge to try cases');
(2) 'Laws' or rules which are neither 'enacted nor . . . the expression of someone's desire' (for instance, customary rules);
(3) Laws which are not exclusively directed to others, ie which are self-binding ('Do not statutes often bind the legislators themselves?')
(4) Laws which are not the expression of a 'legislator's actual desires, intentions, or wishes' (often those voting do not know the content of the Bill and therefore cannot actually desire it or will it).

Note that Hart is not here concerned with the relatively trivial exceptions to the imperative theory which Austin admitted (namely, 'declaratory laws', 'laws abrogating or repealing existing positive law', and 'imperfect laws').[28] What Hart is arguing instead is that there are salient, central features of the law – and specifically the fact that legal systems 'contain' power-conferring laws – which are simply not accounted for by Austin's account. In order to accommodate these features, Hart believes, we would have to modify Austin's account out of all recognition.

Hart deals in this chapter with various defences which Austinian apologists might offer. His claim is, of course, that these defences are inadequate. He tends to some extent to run together the Austinian and the Kelsenian positions, and considers (or gives us to believe) that what counts against Austin counts also against Kelsen. I hope to convince you that while Hart succeeds in his attack on the Austinian position, he fails to make out an adequate case against Kelsen.

---

[26] *The Concept of Law* (n 12) 24.
[27] ibid 26.
[28] Austin's full passage reads: 'I assume, then, that the only laws which are not imperative . . . are the following – 1. Declaratory laws, or laws explaining the import of existing positive law. 2. Laws abrogating or repealing existing positive law. 3. Imperfect laws, or laws of imperfect obligation (with the sense wherein the expression is used by the Roman jurists).' See J Austin, *The Province of Jurisprudence Determined*, WE Rumble (ed) (Cambridge, Cambridge University Press 1995) 36.

It is important to stress from the outset that here, too, Hart asserts *but does not show* that there are laws of different 'types'. He does distinguish *uses* or *functions* of law which are different, and indeed different in important ways. But there is no reason to accept that we therefore have a case of 'different kinds'[29] or 'various sorts'[30] or 'different types'[31] or 'classes'[32] of laws – certainly not different 'forms'.[33] That there is a sociological or functional difference does not mean that there is a difference of logical form. Hart does, however, classify laws according to their 'social function':

> The social function which a criminal statute performs is that of setting up and defining certain kinds of conduct, as something to be avoided or done by those to whom it applies irrespective of their wishes. The punishment or 'sanction' which is attached by the law to breaches of violations of the criminal law is (whatever other purpose it may serve) intended to provide one motive for abstaining from these activities. In all these respects there is at least a strong analogy . . . between the criminal law and its sanctions and the general orders backed by threats of our model.[34]

It is *on the basis of social function*, then, that Hart admits that there is 'at least a strong analogy between the criminal law and its sanctions and the general orders backed by threats of our model'. He admits also, for the same reason, that there is 'some analogy . . . between such general orders and the law of torts'. He then says:

> But there are important classes of law where this analogy with orders backed by threats altogether fails, since they perform a quite different social function.[35]

Chief among such laws are those 'defining the ways in which valid wills or contracts or marriages are made', which 'do not require persons to act in certain ways whether they wish it or not':

> Such laws do not impose duties or obligations. Instead, they provide individuals with *facilities* for realizing their wishes, by conferring legal powers upon them to create, by certain specified procedures and subject to certain conditions, structures of rights and duties within the coercive framework of the law.[36]

The power of individuals 'to mould their legal relations', Hart says, 'is one of the great contributions of law to social life'.[37] And this very important characteristic of law is 'obscured', he argues, 'by [mis]representing all law[s] as

---

[29] *The Concept of Law* (n 12) 26.
[30] ibid 5.
[31] ibid 8.
[32] ibid 27.
[33] See n 22 above, and the corresponding text.
[34] *The Concept of Law* (n 12) 27.
[35] ibid.
[36] ibid 27f.
[37] ibid 28.

orders backed by threats': for there is a 'radical difference *in function* between laws that confer such powers and the criminal statute'.[38]

This argument is strengthened by reference to laws which confer 'public' as against 'private' powers. Rules of jurisdiction, of judicial appointment, and of judicial procedure, for example, are very different from orders backed by threats:

> [T]he concern of rules conferring such powers is not to deter judges from improprieties but to define the conditions and limits under which the court's decisions should be valid.[39]

Further, rules defining the competence of subordinate legislatures also cannot be fitted into the Austinian model:

> [T]here is a radical difference between rules conferring and defining the manner of exercise of legislative powers and the rules of criminal law which at least resemble orders backed by threats.
>
> In some cases it would be grotesque to assimilate these two broad types of rule. If a measure before a legislative body obtains the required majority of votes and is thus duly passed, the voters in favour of the measure have not 'obeyed' the law requiring a majority decision nor have those who voted against it either obeyed or disobeyed it: the same is of course true if the measure fails to obtain the required majority and so no law is passed.[40]

And to this Hart again adds that:

> The radical *difference in function* between such rules as these prevents the use here of the terminology appropriate to conduct in its relation to rules of the criminal law.[41]

This last point may be a bit unfair as against Austin, who specifically excluded constitutional law from his theory.[42] Nonetheless, Hart is clearly right that a general theory of law should be able to accommodate such obvious instances of 'law'.

Hart hints that a much fuller taxonomy of laws is possible once we are freed from 'the prejudice that all *must* be reducible to a single simple type':

> In distinguishing certain laws under the very rough head of laws that confer powers from those that impose duties and are analogous to orders backed by threats, we have made only a beginning.[43]

---

[38] ibid (emphasis added).
[39] ibid 29.
[40] ibid 31.
[41] ibid 32 (emphasis added).
[42] See Austin, *The Province of Jurisprudence Determined* (n 28) eg at 194f.
[43] *The Concept of Law* (n 12) 32.

His taxonomy, however, occupies a central place in *The Concept of Law*. Hart stresses it in the first endnote to chapter III:

> The pursuit of a general definition of law has obscured differences in form and function between different types of legal rules. The argument of this book is that the difference between rules which impose obligations, or duties, and rules which confer powers, is of crucial importance in jurisprudence. Law can best be understood as a union between these two diverse types of rule. This is, accordingly, the main distinction between types of legal rule stressed in this chapter but many other distinctions could, and for some purposes should, be drawn.[44]

'Nevertheless', he notes, 'the itch for uniformity in jurisprudence is strong: and . . . by no means disreputable'.[45] It is hard to see why Hart stigmatises the 'itch for uniformity' (which is my philosophical itch, as previously noted) as 'a prejudice'[46] if indeed it is 'by no means [intellectually] disreputable'. In resisting it, Hart is opposing a dominant and recurring trend in the history of jurisprudence; therefore he turns his attention to two arguments 'sponsored by great jurists',

> designed to show that the distinction between varieties of law which we have stressed is superficial, if not unreal, and that 'ultimately' the notion of orders backed by threats is adequate for the analysis of rules conferring powers as well as for the rules of criminal law.[47]

'As with most theories which have persisted long in jurisprudence,' he remarks, 'there is an element of truth in these arguments':

> There certainly are points of resemblance between the legal rules of the two sorts we have distinguished. . . . [i]t is important to realize that rules of the power-conferring sort, though different from rules which impose duties and so have some analogy to orders backed by threats, are always related to such rules; for the powers which they confer are powers to make general rules of the latter sort or to impose duties on particular persons who would otherwise not be subject to them.[48]

The question, then, is this: *can* all laws be assimilated to 'orders backed by threats'?

The two arguments or theories 'designed to show the fundamental identity of the two sorts of rule' are the nullity-as-sanction argument and the argument that power-conferring rules are 'fragments of laws'.[49] The first is an argument, as Hart notes, that 'Austin adopts but does not develop' in his *Lectures on*

---

[44] ibid 283.
[45] ibid 32.
[46] ibid.
[47] ibid.
[48] ibid 32f.
[49] ibid 33ff, 35ff.

Jurisprudence.⁵⁰ The second had been proposed, though in different versions, by Bentham in *On Laws in General*, by Kelsen in his *General Theory of Law and State*, and by Alf Ross in *On Law and Justice*.⁵¹

Hart needs to refute both arguments to succeed in his criticism of Austin's theory of law. If law is to be understood as a union of 'two *diverse types* of rules',⁵² neither argument can be sound.

IV. IS NULLITY A SANCTION?

The nullity-as-sanction argument, the first of the two arguments just listed, seeks to 'eliminate the distinction'⁵³ between rules which confer powers and rules which prescribe duties by holding that

> the 'nullity' which ensues when some essential condition for the exercise of the power is not fulfilled . . . is like the punishment attached to the criminal law, a threatened evil or sanction exacted by the law for the breach of the rule.⁵⁴

Hart's counter-argument? First, that nullity is not a sanction because nullity is not an evil:

> [T]he extension of the idea of a sanction to include nullity is a source (and a sign) of confusion . . . in many cases, nullity may not be an 'evil' to the person who has failed to satisfy some condition required for legal validity. A judge may have no material interest in and may be indifferent to the validity of his order; a party who finds that the contract on which he is sued is not binding on him, because he was under age or did not sign the memorandum in writing required for certain contracts, might not recognize here a 'threatened evil' or 'sanction'.⁵⁵

But this may be too swift. It assumes that a sanction is necessarily perceived as an evil by the individual against whom it is directed. Yet if a sanction is not always an evil, then it is (in this respect) no different from nullity, which *may* also be, according to circumstances, subjectively perceived as an evil. And Hart's assumption is indeed false. There are cases in which a 'sanction' is not an evil to the individual who does not obey a coercive order. Think, for example, of (1) the martyr or the masochist; (2) the rational criminal who seeks imprisonment to protect himself from vengeance; (3) vicarious liability: the 'evil' is not inflicted upon the individual whose behaviour does not conform to the coercive order, but inflicted upon another; the delinquent may not see this

---

⁵⁰ ibid 286.
⁵¹ *cf* ibid.
⁵² ibid 283.
⁵³ ibid 284.
⁵⁴ ibid 33.
⁵⁵ ibid 33f.

as an 'evil'; (4) collective liability: the 'evil' is inflicted upon a number of individuals which may or may not include the delinquent; again the delinquent may not perceive this as an 'evil'. Thus Hart requires 'nullity', in order conceivably to count as a sanction, to fulfil a test that 'sanction' does not fulfil.

Furthermore, it is non-juristic to define sanction as an 'evil' because what an 'evil' is, is a matter for individual psychology. All that a juristic definition can say is that a sanction is a legally determined consequence of a particular course of action, characterised as 'delict', 'tort', 'crime', or 'wrong'. So Hart's first objection to the nullity-as-sanction argument does not succeed. He is rightly diffident about it – he calls it a 'minor' and 'trivial' objection 'which might be accommodated with some ingenuity'.[56]

Hart's second objection, designed to show 'the confusion inherent in thinking of nullity as similar to the threatened evil or sanctions of the criminal law', is much more persuasive:

> In the case of the rules of the criminal law . . . we can distinguish clearly the rule prohibiting certain behaviour from the provision for penalties to be exacted if the rule is broken, and suppose the first to exist without the latter. We can, in a sense, subtract the sanction and still leave an intelligible standard of behaviour which it was designed to maintain. But we cannot logically make such a distinction between the rule requiring compliance with certain conditions, e.g. attestation for a valid will, and the so-called sanction of 'nullity'. In this case, if failure to comply with this essential condition did not entail nullity, the rule itself could not be intelligibly said to exist without sanctions . . . The provision for nullity is *part* of this type of rule itself in a way which punishment attached to a rule imposing duties is not.[57]

Nullity is not a sanction, then, Hart argues, because we cannot 'subtract' nullity from a rule and leave anything intelligible, whereas the removal of the sanction from its corresponding rule still leaves an intelligible standard of behaviour. But this argument, although sound, does not disprove the 'uniformity' thesis. Let us examine it more closely.

A coercive order is the expression of a command plus a threatened sanction; the sanction thus can be removed leaving a simple standard of behaviour. In turn, a rule providing individuals 'with *facilities* for realizing their wishes, by conferring legal powers upon them to create, by certain specified procedures and subject to procedures and subject to certain conditions, structures of rights and duties'[58] – which is, as we saw, the way Hart characterises a private power-conferring rule – is of the following form:

(P1) To make a valid will you must do *a*, *b*, *c*, and *d*.

---

[56] ibid 34.
[57] ibid 34f.
[58] ibid 27f.

But that is synonymous with:

(P2) In the absence of *a*, or b, or *c*, or *d*, there is no valid will.

Thus the expression of a facility-creating rule is simultaneously the expression, or at least the implication, of the conditions of nullity. Nullity is implicated in the notion of validity. Thus to subtract 'nullity' is to leave nothing. So Hart *has* shown that 'nullity' functions in a logically different way from 'sanction', and therefore that 'nullity' is not – or is not equivalent to – 'sanction'.

But this argument – sound though it is – does not prove that rules constituting facilities are logically different from rules imposing duties. For the argument that nullity is a sanction is not a necessary part of the thesis that all laws can be reduced to one logical form. Let us compare 'making a will' with 'committing an assault':

(W1) A valid will is made if and only if certain legally determined conditions (a, b, c, d) are satisfied.
(A1) An assault is committed if and only if certain legally determined conditions (p, q, r, s) are satisfied.

The two statements are formally similar. They are equivalent to:

(W2) VALID WILL if and only if (a and b and c and d).
(A2) ASSAULT if and only if (p and q and r and s).

In both cases, then, unless all the conditions are satisfied no legally determined consequence follows:

(W3) If (not-a or not-b or not-c or not-d), then no VALID WILL.
(A3) If (not-p or not-q or not-r or not-s), then no ASSAULT.

Now consider:

(W4) If there is a valid will, then the legally determined consequences ought to be implemented.
(A4) If an assault is proved to have occurred, then the legally determined consequences ought to be implemented.

In (W4) the legally determined consequences will typically not include a sanction. A valid will is only an *incomplete* condition of a sanction. In other words, if the will is valid, it justifies, *together with the satisfaction of other conditions*, the application of a coercive act. Those further conditions include interference with the property transferred under the will, and the initiation of legal action by the beneficiary. Thus the beneficiary can by his or her own motion bring about, as an *ultimate* legal consequence, a coercive act directed against any individuals who interfere with his rights under a will. In practice, the sanction is still a long way off. In the first instance, the court will direct that the interference cease, that the goods be restored to the beneficiary, or that damages be paid. Only if the interference continues, or if the goods are not restored, or the damages are not paid will forcible reaction be brought about.

In (A4), in contrast, the legally determined consequence typically is or includes a sanction. Assault is (or may be) a *complete* condition of a sanction. In other words, if an assault is proved to have occurred, it justifies, *by itself*, the application of a coercive act.

Thus the analogue of 'nullity' in a criminal law is the non-satisfaction of the legally determined conditions *a*, *b*, *c*, *d*, of the criminal act. Conversely, the analogue of 'sanction' in a facility-providing rule is the corresponding set of legally determined consequences – which establish *some* but not all of the conditions under which a coercive act is eventually stipulated as an ultimate legal consequence.

The cogency of Hart's second argument against the nullity-as-sanction argument, then, does not prove that there are different logical types of laws – for (W4) and (A4) display the same logical structure.

V. FRAGMENTATION

I turn now to Hart's objections to the argument that power-conferring rules are 'fragments of laws'. Hart identifies two forms of this argument. An 'extreme form' is the product of the more general view that

> [a]ll genuine laws . . . are conditional orders to officials to apply sanctions. They are all of the form, 'If anything of a kind X is done or omitted or happens, then apply sanction of a kind Y'.[59]

'On this view', then,

> what is ordinarily thought of as the content of law, designed to guide the conduct of ordinary citizens, is merely the antecedent or 'if-clause' in a rule which is directed not to them but to officials, and orders them to apply certain sanctions if certain conditions are satisfied.[60]

This is, Hart says, a 'formidable and interesting theory, purporting to disclose the true, uniform nature of law latent beneath a variety of common forms and expressions which obscure it':[61]

> By greater and greater elaboration of the antecedent or if-clauses, legal rules of every type, including the rules conferring and defining the manner of exercise of private or public powers, can be restated in this conditional form. Thus, the provi-

---

[59] ibid 36.
[60] ibid.
[61] ibid 37.

sions of the Wills Act requiring two witnesses would appear as a common part of many different directions to courts to apply sanctions to an executor who, in breach of the provisions of the will, refuses to pay the legacies . . . Similarly, a rule specifying the extent of a court's jurisdiction would appear as a common part of the conditions to be satisfied before it applies any sanctions.[62]

And so on: 'even the rules of criminal law', as Hart notes, would according to this argument not count as 'genuine laws':

> It is in this form that the argument is adopted by Kelsen: 'Law is the primary norm which stipulates the sanction.' There is no law prohibiting murder: there is only a law directing officials to apply certain sanctions in certain circumstances to those who do murder.[63]

Here is, in fuller context, the passage by Kelsen that Hart refers to:

> [If it is said that] the legal duty 'ought' to be performed, then this 'ought' is, so to speak, an epiphenomenon of the 'ought' of the sanction. . . . An example: One shall not steal; if somebody steals, he shall be punished. If it is assumed that the first norm which forbids theft is valid only if the second norm attaches a sanction to theft, then the first norm is certainly superfluous in an exact exposition of law. If at all existent, the first norm is contained in the second, which is the only genuine legal norm. . . . the first norm, which demands the omission of the delict, is dependent upon the second norm, which stipulates the sanction. We may express this dependence by designating the second norm as the primary norm, and the first norm as the secondary norm. . . . If one makes use of the auxiliary concept of secondary norms, then the opposite of the delict appears as 'lawful behavior' . . . and the delict as 'unlawful behavior' . . . When the delict is [so] defined simply as unlawful behaviour, law is regarded as a system of secondary norms. But this is not tenable if we have realized law's character of a coercive order which stipulates sanctions. Law is the primary norm, which stipulates the sanction, and this norm is not contradicted by the delict of the subject, which, on the contrary, is the specific condition of the sanction.[64]

The common-sense view that the criminal law is directed to ordinary citizens is here rejected (although the content of criminal law may yet be, inferentially, a source of guidance to ordinary citizens). Laws are understood as conditional directives to officials to apply sanctions, with a form along the lines of

'If X, then [you ought to] apply sanction Y'

where 'X' stands for the definitional elements of, say, murder, and 'Y' for the legally determined sanction for murder. The 'secondary' norm (in the sense which Kelsen stipulates for the adjective, which has nothing to do with Hart's

---

[62] ibid 36.
[63] ibid 35f.
[64] H Kelsen, *General Theory of Law and State*, A Wedberg (trans) (Cambridge, Mass, Harvard University Press, 1945) 60f.

own use of the 'primary'/'secondary' contrast) is implied from it. This 'secondary' norm is 'superfluous', Kelsen says, 'in an exact exposition of law' – in an exposition of law *from its point of view*, as it were – though it may be utilised as an 'auxiliary concept', helpful but not necessary in an exposition of the law.

Now this 'extreme' theory, Hart notes, 'involves a shift from the original conception of law as consisting of orders backed by threats' (that is, Austin's conception) to a different idea of law as 'orders to officials to apply sanctions' (that is, Kelsen's view):

> On this [Kelsen's] view it is not necessary that a sanction be prescribed for the *breach* of every law [that is, that every law be 'backed' by a sanction]; it is only necessary that every 'genuine' law shall direct the application of some sanction.[65]

Thus in Kelsen's view, as Hart notes 'it may well be the case that an official who disregards such directions will not be punishable'; and this is just as well for it is logically impossible for every (non-self-referential) directive to be backed by a sanction. Indeed Kelsen offers an argument against Austin's notion that every law is a command backed by a sanction: 'if it is necessary to guarantee the efficacy of a norm prescribing a certain behaviour by another norm prescribing a sanction', then 'a never-ending series of sanctions, a *regressus ad infinitum*, is inevitable'.[66] Kelsen holds instead that:

> A rule is a legal rule not because its efficacy is secured by another rule providing for a sanction; a rule is a legal rule because it provides for a sanction. . . . All the norms of a legal order are coercive norms, i.e. norms providing for sanctions; but among these norms there are norms the efficacy of which is not secured by other norms.[67]

As a consequence, as Kelsen notes, the sanction stipulated in a norm the efficacy of which is not itself secured by a higher, sanction-stipulating norm, is to be interpreted 'not as commanded but as authorised or positively permitted'.[68]

Alongside this 'extreme' version of the argument that power-conferring norms are 'really incomplete fragments of coercive rules which are the only "genuine" rules of law',[69] Hart identifies a more 'moderate view'. The 'only difference' is really that

> on the more moderate view the power-conferring rules are represented by the antecedents or if-clauses of rules ordering ordinary citizens, under threat of sanctions, to do things, and not merely (as in the more extreme theory) as the if-clauses of directions to officials to apply sanctions.[70]

---

[65] *The Concept of Law* (n 12) 37.
[66] Kelsen, *General Theory of Law and State* (n 64) 28.
[67] ibid 29. See also Kelsen, *The Pure Theory of Law* (n 25) 25 ('Since this regression cannot go on indefinitely, the last sanction in this chain can only be authorized, not commanded').
[68] *The Pure Theory of Law* (n 25) 51. Recall that Kelsen's broadly defined 'ought' encompasses not only commands, but also permissions, authorisations, and derogation: cf n 25 above.
[69] *The Concept of Law* (n 12) 35.
[70] ibid 38.

Thus in this 'less extreme' version of the argument, the conception of law 'as orders backed by threats directed to ordinary citizens, among others' is at least 'preserved', Hart notes, for 'those rules that, on a common-sense view, refer primarily to the conduct of ordinary citizens, and not merely to officials'. So the 'rules of the criminal law', for example, will count as laws 'as they stand', and 'need no recasting as fragments of other complete rules'.[71] But both 'rules which confer legal powers on private individuals' and 'rules conferring legislative powers' *will* be recast 'as specifying some of the conditions under which ultimately . . . a duty arises'. For example,

> provisions of such rules as those of the Wills Act, 1837, in relation to witnesses, and other rules conferring on individuals powers and defining the conditions for valid exercise of them . . . will appear as part of the antecedent or 'if-clause' of . . . rules imposing duties. 'If and only if a will has been signed by the testator and witnessed by the two witnesses in the specified manner and if . . . then the executor (or other legal representative) shall give effect to the provisions of the will'.[72]

It is Bentham's account of legal powers that Hart has here in mind.[73] For his critical purposes, however, the points of difference between the two versions of the 'fragment' view of power-conferring rules are less important than their points of similarity, since both versions 'attempt to reduce apparently distinct varieties of legal rule to a single form alleged to convey the quintessence of law'[74] – which is what Hart opposes.

Hart now offers a summary of his main objection to both versions:

> The specific criticism of both forms of the theory which we shall develop here is that they purchase the pleasing uniformity of pattern to which they reduce all laws at too high a price: that of distorting the different social functions which different types of legal rule perform. This is true of both forms of the theory.[75]

Note, however, that this is not – it cannot be – an argument against the *possibility* of presenting all law in a body of propositions of the same logical type. It is merely an argument against the *desirability* of doing so. Thus, in a sense, Hart admits that all law *can* be presented in a body of uniform propositions. His point must rather be that, in order to highlight different social functions, it should be presented in propositions of different types.

---

[71] ibid 37.

[72] ibid 37f.

[73] At ibid 286 (endnote to page 35) Hart quotes Bentham's *On Law in General*, which he himself had edited in 1970 as a volume in the series *The Collected Works of Jeremy Bentham* (his original 1961 endnote was accordingly updated), but Hart's edition has now been superseded by Philip Schofield's edition of *Of the Limits of the Penal Branch of Jurisprudence* (Oxford, Clarendon Press, 2010).

[74] *The Concept of Law* (n 12) 38.

[75] ibid 38.

But the same logical form can serve a multitude of social functions. And since logical form does not *reveal* social function, it cannot distort it either. And of course some theorists might also differ from Hart on whether there is 'distortion' at all; and if there is 'distortion', one might think it a price worth paying for such an elegant and insightful general conception of law.

Hart develops his 'distortion' point as follows. First, he rightly observes that

> The characteristic technique of the criminal law is to designate by rules certain types of behaviour as standards for the guidance either of the members of society or of special classes within it: they are expected without the aid or intervention of officials to understand the rules and to see that the rules apply to them and to conform to them. . . . What is distinctive of this technique . . . is that the members of society are left to discover the rules and conform their behaviour to them; in this sense they 'apply' the rules themselves to themselves.[76]

But this, contrary to Hart's argument, does not establish that rules about the conduct of ordinary citizens cannot be seen as derivative from rules about the conduct of officials. Note, first, that what Hart is saying here seems to be that the reason why citizens are 'left to discover' the rules that purport to govern their behaviour, and 'conform their behaviour to them', is that no such rules are issued as *individually addressed* to each citizen. This is but a repetition of a point on the 'generality' of law that Hart had already made in chapter II when he remarks that '[a] criminal statute . . . indicates a general type of conduct and applies to a general class of persons who are *expected to see that it applies to them and to comply with it*'.[77]

Now, this does certainly not imply that citizens are *not* generally – in modern legal systems – expected to infer such rules from rules about the conduct of officials. Indeed, it is not at all clear that they are not. At least it is not clear that citizens are generally able to acquire by themselves – without some intellectual guidance and assistance – an *exact* knowledge of what it is that the law does require them to do in all contexts. Moreover, however, and more importantly, the fact there may well exist positive laws designating 'certain types of behaviour as standards for the guidance . . . of the members of society' does not by itself undermine the thesis that the content of any such law *can* indeed be derived from the content of sanction-stipulating laws addressed to officials. If it can, then such laws may indeed be declared 'superfluous', as Kelsen says, 'in an exact exposition of law'.[78] For Kelsen's point, of course, is not that there can be no superfluous laws. What Hart would need to have shown against Kelsen is that such duty-imposing laws addressed to citizens are *not* superfluous in view of sanction-stipulating laws addressed to officials.

---

[76] ibid 38f.
[77] ibid 21.
[78] cf the passage quoted to n 64 above.

Secondly, Hart holds that 'a punishment for a crime, such as a fine' and 'a tax on a course of conduct' are different notions, and that the 'uniformity' thesis – which eliminates the idea that 'the substantive rules of the criminal law have as their function . . . the guidance not merely of officials operating a system of penalties, but of ordinary citizens' – distorts this, 'obscuring the specific character of law as a means of social control'.[79] Now, it is true that at a common-sense level there is a distinction which turns upon individual and/or collective value-judgments. The distinction to which Hart draws attention is a moral one – 'fines' are reactions to wrongful conduct, 'taxes' responses to acceptable conduct; fines involve compulsion, whereas taxes involve consent. Again, however, this is hardly persuasive as an argument against the 'uniformity' theory. As Hart himself notes, the distinction 'may in certain circumstances be blurred'.[80] Not all individuals regard conduct which is the condition of a fine as wrong; nor do all individuals consent to taxation. (For example, what is the difference, if any, between perhaps modest fines for possession or use of cannabis and heavy taxation on tobacco?) More to the point, Hart also admits that even if taxes and fines are different ideas, 'both involve directions to officials to inflict the same money loss'.[81] Does this then not concede that unity of *form* is quite compatible with diversity of *social function*?

Thirdly, Hart argues that the law ought not to be understood as being only concerned with the 'bad man' (the allusion is to Holmes[82]):

> Why should not law be equally if not more concerned with the 'puzzled man' or 'ignorant man' who is willing to do what is required, if only he can be told what it is? Or with the 'man who wishes to arrange his affairs' if only he can be told how to do it?[83]

To some extent, this begs the question: for *if* the law does in fact provide no clear, explicit statement of citizens' duties – leaving the content of such conduct rules to be inferred from the content of rules directing official behaviour – then the 'puzzled' man's puzzlement will persist no matter how one chooses to cast or 'recast' the law. At any rate, the emphasis on information seems misguided. It is the task of *legal science* – not of logical analysis – to state what the law requires of or permits to the ordinary citizen. Law itself does not primarily inform – it directs. Hobbes, Kelsen, and Ross all have apposite comments:

---

[79] *The Concept of Law* (n 12) 39.
[80] ibid.
[81] ibid.
[82] See Hart's endnote to page 39 at ibid 286.
[83] ibid 40.

> [I]t is manifest that law in general is not counsel, but command.[84]

> Legal norms . . . are commands; they may be also permissions and authorizations; but they are not instructions as is often maintained when law and jurisprudence [that is, legal science] are erroneously equated. The law commands, permits, or authorizes, but it does not 'teach'.[85]

> The law is not written in order to impart theoretical truths, but to direct people – judges and private citizens alike – to act in a certain desired manner. A parliament is not an information bureau, but a central organ for social direction.[86]

Note, moreover, that the secondary stage whereby the general propositions of legal science are translated into citizen-friendly propositions about what the law requires of or permits to citizens is arguably a matter of legal practice as much as a matter of legal science. In other words, it may not be the function or responsibility of legal science to assist the 'puzzled' or the 'ignorant', who may be better served by their local legal practitioners. In any case, however, the claim, which Hart opposes, that the legally relevant material can be reduced to a simplified and unified form is a *logical* claim – a claim about the logical analysis of law – rather than a claim of legal science; so whether or not it helps dissolve citizens' puzzlement and ignorance about the content of the law seems beside the point.

Fourthly, Hart finds some 'justification' – unsurprisingly, if you remember section I – in 'common usage':

> power-conferring rules are thought of, spoken of, and used in social life differently from rules which impose duties, and they are valued for different reasons. What other tests for difference in character could there be?[87]

This rhetorical question can be answered. There certainly are tests *other* than correspondence to actual usage by which intellectual theories may be assessed, some of which I mention in the closing section.

Fifthly, Hart is ambivalent. His criticism borders on a contradiction. He asserts at one point that a definition of law in terms of coercion excludes rules conferring public and private powers:

> Rules conferring private powers must, if they are to be understood, be looked at from the point of view of those who exercise them. They appear then as an additional element introduced by the law into social life over and above that of social control. . . . The reduction of rules conferring and defining legislative and judicial powers to statements of the conditions under which duties arise has, in the public sphere, a similar obscuring vice. Those who exercise these powers to make authoritative enactments and orders use these rules in a form of purposive

---

[84] T Hobbes, *Leviathan*, E Curley (ed) (Indianapolis, Hackett, 1994) 173 (ch xxvi [2]).
[85] Kelsen, *The Pure Theory of Law* (n 25) 71.
[86] A Ross, *On Law and Justice*, M Dutton (trans) (London, Stevens & Sons, 1958) 8.
[87] *The Concept of Law* (n 12) 41.

activity utterly different from performance of duty or submission to coercive control.[88]

But his objection is cancelled by an admission that power-conferring rules are after all not really excluded by all accounts of law in terms of coercion: they are really not excluded, Hart eventually grants, by Kelsen's definition.[89] So Hart's argument changes: coercion-based accounts are now declared inadequate because they do not distinguish sufficiently criminal law from civil law, fines from taxes, or power-conferring rules from duty-imposing rules. But in so far as a definition (of law) purports to be generic, Hart's objection cannot be valid. Hart's objection is that a generic definition does not accurately describe how laws operate: that it does not describe their 'social function'. But neither Hart nor anyone else would seriously argue that each and every law performs the same 'social function'. Questions about the 'function' of law are central both in jurisprudence and in the sociology of law but they cannot be answered, definitively, if at all, *a priori* through conceptual debates. A definition of law must be neutral as to social function; and for that reason no such definition can 'distort' social function.

I conclude therefore that Hart's central criticism of unifying theories fails.

VI. CUSTOM AND DEMOCRACY

Hart makes two other noteworthy points in this chapter. The first is that the coercive model is inadequate because laws can bind those who make them, which conflicts with the 'vertical or "top-to-bottom"'[90] model of the relation between sovereign commander and subject. This point, however, counts only against Austin, and not against Kelsen, for whom 'it is possible that a norm be created by the same individuals who are bound by this norm'.[91] Thus the theories of both Kelsen and Hart, unlike that of Austin, allow the possibility of a democratic legal system – that is, one in which laws are made by those subject to them rather than laid down by a political superior.

Indeed, one telling (and, in my view, fatal) criticism of Austin's theory is that it cannot without extensive modification, if at all, accommodate democratic law. One test of a theory of law is that it should help us 'understand' law. Other possible tests of a theory of law are that it should both (1) 'fit' the facts and (2) be normatively appealing. In other words, it is legitimate to ask of a theory of law if it necessitates something morally monstrous, or excludes something morally desirable. In any event, if the objective is to reach some

---
[88] ibid.
[89] See the endnote to page 35 at ibid 286.
[90] ibid 42.
[91] Kelsen, *General Theory of Law and State* (n 64) 36.

general truths about law, it cannot be a recommendation of a theory that it wholly excludes the possibility of democratic law. It seems to me that a theory which holds that only non-democratic arrangements can count as 'law' is a theory to be rejected on moral grounds.

The second noteworthy point that Hart makes in this chapter is that though it may be true that statutory law has 'one salient point of analogy with coercive orders' – for 'the enactment of a law, like the giving of an order, *is* a deliberate datable act'[92] – not all law can be seen in this way; custom, in particular (modest though its role in a modern legal system may be), is in this respect unlike legislation. Both Austin and Kelsen thought they could reconcile the apparently difficult nature of custom within their definitions of law. Austin's account in terms of 'tacit' orders, which is the focus of Hart's discussion,[93] may be an implausible (and *post hoc*) rationalisation, to shore up an unconvincing theory. For as Hart notes rules of law that 'originate in custom . . . do not owe their legal status to any . . . conscious law-creating act';[94] and hence

> to attribute the legal status of a custom to the fact that a court or sovereign has so 'ordered' is to adopt a theory which can only be carried through if a meaning is given to 'order' so extended as to rob the theory of its point.[95]

But Kelsen's account of custom as a constitutionally authorised source of law may seem acceptable, or at least as acceptable as any treatment of the subject offered by Hart. Indeed, the possibility of Hart's own 'fresh start' – which he begins to present in his chapter V – satisfactorily accommodating non-statutory law is open to serious question.[96]

---

[92] ibid 44.
[93] ibid 45f.
[94] ibid 48.
[95] ibid 45.
[96] AWB Simpson's well-known essay 'The Common Law and Legal Theory' in AWB Simpson (ed), *Oxford Essays in Jurisprudence. Second Series* (Oxford, Oxford University Press, 1973), even though it contains some serious misapprehensions about legal positivism in general and Hart's version in particular, makes some important and insightful points in this regard. Simpson claims that the common law cannot be properly represented as or reduced to a body of rules, and thus that Hart's theory – able to accommodate statute reasonably well, but inadequate as an account of common law – fares no better than Austin's.

4

Hart on Sovereignty

PAVLOS ELEFTHERIADIS

I. INTRODUCTION

IN CHAPTER IV Hart begins to introduce his own view of law, on the back of forceful criticisms of Austin's command theory. Nevertheless Hart's theory is not radically different from Austin's. Like Austin, Hart offers a simple view of law as the mundane creation of societies for practical purposes. And although the point is little noticed nowadays, this simple view of law was a major break with the history of the subject. Until Bentham's and Austin's works were published, law was not seen as something to be contrasted philosophically to other political institutions. All philosophers of note – including Thomas Hobbes, John Locke, Jean-Jacques Rousseau, and Immanuel Kant – had understood law and legislation by incorporating them into a more general view about organised power in the civil condition (an idea to which I return in section VI). Hart by and large ignores this tradition.[1] *The Concept of Law* takes Austin's and Bentham's jurisprudential views as its starting point.

This is a striking feature of the book, both because Hart was surely familiar with the works of Plato and Aristotle, which were widely studied at Oxford at the time, and because the leading classical philosophers (but many others too) offer clear and strikingly modern ideas of law that are still part of our legal heritage through the continuing influence of Roman law and Justinian's codification. Aristotle, for example, saw law as a combination of written rules and institutional roles that remove certain decisions from the unconditional consideration of virtue. He defended both the ideas of the rule of law and the separation of powers, and offered the following advice regarding the preservation of states:

> In all well-attempered governments there is nothing which should be more jealously maintained than the spirit of obedience to law, more especially in small matters; for transgression creeps in unperceived and at last ruins the state, just as the constant

[1] Hart briefly mentions Kant on p 301 of *The Concept of Law*, 3rd edn (Oxford, Oxford University Press, 2012) and Hobbes on pp 63, 191, 289, 299f, 303; *cf* also, on p 302, the endnote to p 185.

recurrence of small expenses in time eats up a fortune.[2]

So we should obey the law, in matters great and small, in well-attempered governments. Aristotle also tells us that laws are always imperfect; they cannot but miss the details of the particular circumstances:[3] 'the best man . . . must legislate, and laws must be passed, but these laws will have no authority when they miss the mark, though in all other cases retaining their authority'.[4] This does not change the principle, however. The rule of law is for him a constitutional principle concerning the appropriate function of offices and institutions. The imperfection of the laws becomes more agreeable if they are administered by appointed officers, appropriately trained in the law and suitably distant from the disputes they are called upon to resolve. The personal virtues of these officers are part of the ideal of the just city, for they are essential if the law is to be applied without passion or self-interest:

> The rule of the law, it is argued, is preferable to that of any individual. On the same principle, even if it be better for certain individuals to govern, they should be made only guardians and ministers of the law. For magistrates there must be – this is admitted; but then men say that to give authority to any one man when all are equal is unjust. Nay, there may be indeed be cases which the law seems unable to determine, but in such cases can a man? Nay, it will be replied, the law trains officers for this express purpose, and appoints them to determine matters which are left undecided by it, to the best of their judgment. Further, it permits them to make any amendment of the existing laws which experience suggests. . . . *The law is reason unaffected by desire.*[5]

This is not 'ideal' theory. The persons appointed can only work 'to the best of their judgment'. The statement implies that their judgment will not always be perfect and that their decisions will sometimes be flawed. The institutions of law are supposed to accommodate our human limitations, and indeed derive some of their force from them. Commitment to the rule of law requires us, to some extent at least, to forgive the officeholders' imperfections in judgment and strength of will. In Aristotle's version – endorsed by many others over the centuries – the rule of law is not just rule *by* law. It is not just the conscious organisation of human life according to rules. It is also our willing participation in a public system of government, whereby we recognise the

---

[2] Aristotle, *Politics*, 1307b, B Jowett (trans), in *The Basic Works of Aristotle*, Richard McKeon (ed) (New York, The Modern Library, 2001) 1246.

[3] Plato also writes that 'law could never accurately embrace what is best and most just for all at the same time, and so prescribe what is best. For the dissimilarities between human beings and their actions, and the fact that practically nothing in human affairs ever remains stable, prevent any sort of expertise whatsoever from making any simple decision in any sphere that covers all cases and will last for all time'; see Plato, *Statesman*, 294a, CJ Rowe (trans), in JM Cooper (ed), *The Complete Works* (Indianapolis, Hackett, 1997) 338.

[4] Aristotle, *Politics* (n 2) 1286a, 1200.

[5] ibid 1286b, 1202 (emphasis added).

authority of officeholders even when we happen to disagree with their decisions. We are ruled by law when we accept that we are ruled by people whose failures we accept, because we too can cause others injustice due to our own failures. Law here is intimately related to virtue, that is, to human excellence as a whole.[6]

II. AUSTIN'S SOVEREIGN AND THE CONTINUITY PROBLEM

Austin is not concerned with duties of virtue. His view of law is mundane through and through: it is solely based on the reality of commands. Sovereignty is for him the abstract idea that brings commands together into a system that amounts to law. Without the organising work of sovereignty, the various credible commands one encounters in social life would have just created a cacophony of apparent obligations.

Hart begins by outlining Austin's idea of sovereignty as merely a pattern of conduct marked by a 'habit of obedience':

> [Austin's] doctrine [of sovereignty] asserts that in every human society, where there is law, there is ultimately to be found latent beneath the variety of political forms, in a democracy as much as in an absolute monarchy, this simple relationship between subjects rendering habitual obedience and a sovereign who renders habitual obedience to no one. This vertical structure composed of sovereign and subjects is, according to the theory, as essential a part of a society which possesses law, as a backbone is of a man.[7]

Hart asks if the 'habit of obedience', on which Austin builds the idea of sovereignty, can sustain two 'salient' features of most legal systems, namely the '*continuity* of the authority to make law possessed by a succession of different legislators' and the '*persistence* of laws long after their maker and those who rendered him habitual obedience have perished'.[8] The test Hart applies here is one of correspondence. Can Austin's austere 'command' theory accommodate these salient features of legal systems? Hart's view is that Austin's theory cannot accommodate them and that for that reason it fails.

Hart's first argument, covering ten pages, concerns the continuity of law from one sovereign to the next. Hart examines Austin's argument by simplifying it. He begins by postulating an absolute monarch, Rex, who reigns 'for a very long time'.[9] The relationship between Rex and his subjects is, Hart notes,

---

[6] For one among many comments on these Aristotelian ideas see M Schofield, 'Sharing in the Constitution' in his *Saving the City: Philosopher-Kings and Other Classical Paradigms* (London, Routledge, 1998) 124.
[7] *The Concept of Law* (n 1) 50.
[8] ibid 51.
[9] ibid 52.

a 'personal' one.[10] And this is the problem. Because obedience is owed directly to the person of Rex, there is no one to whom obedience is necessarily owed when Rex inevitably dies:

> Let us now suppose that, after a successful reign, Rex dies leaving a son Rex II who then starts to issue general orders. The mere fact that there was a general habit of obedience to Rex I in his lifetime does not by itself even render probable that Rex II will be habitually obeyed. Hence if we have nothing more to go on than the fact of obedience to Rex I and the likelihood that *he* would continue to be obeyed, we shall not be able to say of Rex II's first order, as we could have said of Rex I's last order, that it was given by one who was sovereign and was therefore law.[11]

So Austin's theory would lead to the conclusion that the law disappears with Rex, only to be built again afresh by whoever takes over in the absence of law. Yet, as Hart points out, this is a great distortion of modern legal systems. We do have rules of succession, 'even in an absolute monarchy'. Thus 'if the rule provides for the succession of the eldest son', we would say that the new monarch, Rex II, 'has a *title* to succeed', or something to that effect:

> In explaining the continuity of law-making power through a changing succession of individual legislators, it is natural to use the expressions 'rule of succession', 'title', 'right to succeed', and 'right to make law'. It is plain, however, that with these expressions we have introduced a new set of elements, of which no account can be given in terms of habits of obedience to general orders, out of which, following the prescription of the theory of sovereignty, we constructed the simple legal world of Rex I. For in that world there were no rules, and so no rights or titles, and hence a fortiori no right or title to succeed: there were just the facts that orders were given by Rex I, and his orders were habitually obeyed.[12]

It follows that Austin's ideas of sovereignty and 'habitual obedience' do not account for the legal succession of sovereigns or, more generally, for the continuity of legal systems. It is obvious that a habit of obedience to the current sovereign cannot possibly 'confer on the new legislator any *right* to succeed the old and give orders in his place'.[13] If indeed Rex II is to *succeed* Rex I,

> there must have been somewhere in the society a general social practice more complex than any that can be described in terms of habits of obedience: there must have been the acceptance of the *rule* under which the new legislator is entitled to succeed.[14]

Here, then, Hart introduces his idea of a social rule, as something distinct from a habit of obedience to the commands of a sovereign. A *habit* involves

---

[10] ibid.
[11] ibid 53.
[12] ibid 54.
[13] ibid 55.
[14] ibid (emphasis added).

only a general convergence of behaviour. For a social *rule* to exist, however, mere convergence of behaviour is not enough. Involved in the notion of a social rule is also the idea that any deviations from the rule 'are generally regarded as lapses or faults open to criticism, and threatened deviations meet with pressure for conformity, though the forms of criticism and pressure differ with different types of rule'. 'Where there are such rules', says Hart, 'not only is such criticism in fact made but deviation from the standard is generally accepted as *good reason* for making it.'[15] Unlike habits, rules have an 'internal aspect', and not merely an 'external one':

> if a social rule is to exist some at least must look upon the behaviour in question as a general standard to be followed by the group as a whole. A social rule has an 'internal' aspect, in addition to the external aspect which it shares with a social habit and which consists in the regular uniform behaviour which an observer could record'.[16]

The internal aspect of rules – an idea that Hart develops more fully in chapter V – is not a matter of psychological 'feelings of compulsion', which are 'neither necessary nor sufficient for the existence of "binding" rules':

> What is necessary is that there should be a critical reflective attitude to certain patterns of behaviour as a common standard, and that this should display itself in criticism (including self-criticism), demands for conformity, and in acknowledgments that such criticism and demands are justified, all of which find their characteristic expression in the normative terminology of 'ought', 'must', and 'should', 'right' and 'wrong'.[17]

Perhaps this paves the way to restoring the idea of the 'normativity' of law. For if law is open to this type of 'normative' language, it opens itself to the full range of practical rationality, the prospective rationality of what we ought to do and the retrospective rational reflection on our responsibility for what we have done. But to solve the continuity problem faced by Austin's theory, argues Hart, we need not go that far. All we need to do, according to him, is to replace the habit of obedience with public 'acceptance' of the relevant rules. The rules here are not rules of conduct; they are rules about the holding of an office, the office of legislator:

> In order to see how such rules explain the continuity of legislative authority, we need only notice that in some cases, even before a new legislator has begun to legislate, it may be clear that there is a firmly established rule giving him, as one of a *class* or line of persons, the right to do this in his turn. Thus we may find it generally accepted by the group, during the lifetime of Rex I, that the person whose word is to be obeyed is not limited to the individual Rex I but is that person who, for the

---

[15] ibid 55.
[16] ibid 56.
[17] ibid 57.

time being, is qualified in a certain way, e.g. as the eldest living descendant in the direct line of a certain ancestor: Rex I is merely the particular person so qualified at a particular time.[18]

It may be useful to distinguish two rules here. The first rule is the construction of a particular office: the office of legislator. The second is the rule about who is qualified to occupy that office. Hart explains this in the next couple of pages, when he says that:

> the officials of the system may be said to acknowledge explicitly such fundamental rules conferring legislative authority: the legislators do this when they make laws in accordance with the rules which empower them to do so: the courts when they identify, as laws to be applied by them, the laws made by those thus qualified, and the experts when they guide the ordinary citizens by reference to the laws so made.[19]

This formulation takes us back to Aristotle's point that the rule of law requires not only abstract rules of conduct but also persons who must have the authority to occupy relevant offices and administer justice as best they can. But Hart is not interested in this aspect of the argument he has just made; he puts the point immediately to one side. All he takes from this discussion is the idea of a manifest fact of acceptance. He says that the 'ordinary citizen manifests his acceptance largely by acquiescence in the results of these official operations'.[20] But then where does this leave the 'critical reflective attitude'? 'Acquiescence' sounds like 'compliance', and 'compliance' sounds just like another way of describing the habit of obedience, which Hart has said is not sufficient. Hart does not pause here to ask what this manifest fact of acceptance may be, or if his answer is any different from Austin's.

III. THE ARGUMENT FROM PERSISTENCE

Hart identifies a second problem in Austin's theory: the problem of explaining the continuous effect of laws passed by earlier sovereigns. Hart illustrates this with the prosecution, in 1944, of a woman 'for telling fortunes under the Witchcraft Act 1735'.[21] How is it possible, he asks, for an earlier statute to have *any* effects after its actual author has long ceased being the sovereign? It is an obvious fact in every legal system that such continuity is common place; but Austin's theory is unable to account for it:

---

[18] ibid 58.
[19] ibid 61.
[20] ibid.
[21] *R v Duncan*, a Court of Appeal case that turned on whether the defendant was summoning 'evil spirits', and which also discussed whether a supernatural demonstration involving 'ectoplasm' might be acceptable as evidence before a jury.

We cannot . . . narrow our view of laws to the life-time of their makers, for the feature which we have to explain is just their obdurate capacity to survive their makers and those who habitually obeyed them. Why is the Witchcraft Act law still for us . . .? Surely, by no stretch of language can we, the English of the twentieth century, now be said habitually to obey George II and his Parliament'.[22]

The problem with Austin's theory is that the personal relationship he had assumed was at the heart of law cannot survive changes of personnel. His account implies that if the sovereign goes, so does the law he created. Hart considers, and rightly rejects, the idea that each new sovereign tacitly recognises or adopts the previous sovereigns' commands, in so far as he does not interfere with their enforcement by the courts and other agents, for this would implausibly assume that such laws were not laws until 'actually applied by the courts in the particular case, and enforced with the acquiescence of the present sovereign'.[23] He states emphatically that laws passed by the present Queen in Parliament and earlier ones are laws in exactly the same way:

> Victorian statutes and those passed by the Queen in Parliament today surely have precisely the same status in present-day England. Both are law even before cases to which they are applied arise in the courts and, when such cases do arise, the courts apply both Victorian and modern statute because they are already law. In neither case are these law only after they are applied by the courts; and in both cases alike their status as law is due to the fact that they were enacted by persons whose enactments are now authoritative under presently accepted rules, irrespective of the fact that these persons are alive or dead.[24]

Hart's own account of the persistence of law relies on the same thought that supported his earlier objection. As with continuity, 'unless the officials of the system and above all the courts accept the rule that certain legislative operations, *past or present*, are authoritative, something essential to their status as law will be lacking'.[25] Once again Hart uses the flaws in Austin's account to suggest the alternative explanation that:

> the courts (and with them any lawyer or ordinary citizen who understands the legal system) use as a criterion a fundamental rule or rules of what is to count as law which embraces past as well as present legislative operations.[26]

This 'fundamental rule' of 'what is to count as law' is what in chapter V Hart will call a 'rule of recognition': a 'secondary' social rule specifying 'some feature or features possession of which by a[nother] suggested rule is taken as a conclu-

---

[22] *The Concept of Law* (n 1) 62.
[23] ibid 64.
[24] ibid.
[25] ibid 65.
[26] ibid.

sive affirmative indication that it is a rule of the group'.[27] The rule of recognition plays in Hart's theory a similar foundational role to the habitually obeyed sovereign in Austin's:

> According to [Austin's] theory . . . the foundations of a legal system consist of the situation in which the majority of a social group habitually obey the orders backed by threats of the sovereign person or persons, who themselves habitually obey no one. . . . [This theory] does contain, though in a blurred and misleading form, certain truths about certain important aspects of law. These truths can, however, only be clearly presented . . . in terms of the more complex social situation where a secondary rule of recognition is accepted and used for the identification of primary rules of obligation. It is this situation which deserves, if anything does, to be called the foundations of a legal system.[28]

IV. LEGAL LIMITATIONS TO SOVEREIGNTY

These arguments lead Hart also to take issue with Austin's idea that there can be no *legal* limitations to sovereignty. Austin's idea, Hart notes, is not that 'there are no limits', namely political limits, 'on the sovereign's power', but only 'that there are no *legal* limits on it'.[29] In this respect, too, Hart argues, the command theory clashes with our ordinary understanding of law: 'the conception of the legally unlimited sovereign', he says, 'misrepresents the character of law in many modern states where no one would question that there is law.'[30] It is a commonplace fact that some legislators, like the US Congress, are not allowed by a written constitution to legislate in certain fields. These limitations are not duties to do or refrain from doing something; they are disabilities that prevent their actions from having the desired legal effects:

> A constitution which effectively restricts the legislative powers of the supreme legislature in the system does not do so by imposing (or at any rate need not impose) duties on the legislature not to attempt to legislate in certain ways; instead it provides that any such purported legislation shall be void. It imposes not legal duties but legal disabilities. 'Limits' here implies not the presence of *duty* but the absence of power.[31]

Such legal systems cannot be denied the character of law, although this is precisely what Austin's command theory implies. Austin was therefore wrong in supposing that 'in order to establish that a purported enactment is law' we must 'trace it back' to a 'sovereign' legislator whose authority is legally unre-

---

[27] ibid 94.
[28] ibid 100.
[29] ibid 66.
[30] ibid 68.
[31] ibid 69.

stricted or 'who obeys no one else habitually'. On the contrary, says Hart, what we have to show is only that the law was 'made by a legislator who was qualified to legislate under an existing rule and that either no restrictions are contained in the rule or there are none affecting this particular enactment.'[32] Finally, we must be able to distinguish between 'a legally unlimited legislative authority and one which, though limited, is supreme in the system'.[33]

Austin, however, may have a way out of these objections. For his view, as Hart observes, was that 'in any democracy it is not the elected representatives who constitute or form part of the sovereign body' – it is the *electorate*.[34] Hart devotes some of the best pages in *The Concept of Law* to assessing and ultimately dismissing this surprising doctrine.

Throughout the chapter Hart has been seeking ways of showing how the simple model of the habit of obedience to a sovereign is unable to account for salient features of law and legal systems. Austin's theory tells us that some ordinary such features are in fact incompatible with law. Now Hart turns his attention not to the structure of the theory, but to its judgements. This is more an *ad hominem* argument against Austin (as opposed to the command theory *in abstracto*). Hart begins by noting that many legislatures cannot amend the rules under which they operate:

> Whereas legal limitations on the normal operations of the supreme legislature are imposed by a constitution, these themselves may or may not be immune from certain forms of legal change. This depends on the nature of the provision made by the constitution for its amendment. Most constitutions contain a wide amending power to be exercised either by a body distinct from the ordinary legislature, or by the members of the ordinary legislature using a special procedure.[35]

Article V of the United States Constitution, for example, provides for amendments 'ratified by the legislatures of three-fourths of the States or by conventions in three-fourths thereof'.[36] This poses an obvious further difficulty for any theory that identifies the sovereign with the *legislature*, for it is obvious that the process of constitutional amendment is beyond the powers of the legislature alone. This is why Austin concludes that the sovereign must be the electorate: this move enables him to account for the fact that in many cases the ordinary legislator is indeed legally bound by constitutional rules that are made and amended according to separate procedures. Hart cites Austin's words that in England 'speaking accurately the members of the commons house are merely trustees for the body by which they are elected and appointed: and consequently the sovereignty always resides in the Kings Peers

[32] ibid 70.
[33] ibid.
[34] ibid 74.
[35] ibid 73.
[36] ibid.

and the electoral body of the commons'.[37] The problem, however, as Hart immediately notes, is that this is obviously inconsistent with the simple theory of law as command. We now need concepts and distinctions not envisaged by that theory:

> It is plain that in these further reaches of [Austin's] theory [according to which it is in the electorate that one is to find 'the sovereign free from all limitations'] the initial, simple conception of the sovereign has undergone a certain sophistication, if not a radical transformation. . . . [T]he present identification of the sovereign with the electorate of a democratic state has no plausibility whatsoever, unless we give to the key words 'habit of obedience' and 'person or persons' a meaning which is quite different from that which they had when applied to the simple case [that is, to the 'simplest form of society' with 'an absolute monarch']; and it is a meaning which can only be made clear if the notion of an accepted rule is surreptitiously introduced. The simple scheme of habits of obedience and orders cannot suffice for this.[38]

Hart notes that if the electorate is sovereign, then the hierarchical relationship of obedience and command disappears. Instead we are left with highly abstract distinctions between members of society 'in their private capacity as individuals' and 'in their official capacity as electors or legislators'.[39] This distinction requires a framework of offices and institutions organised according to public rules:

> For if we ask what is meant by saying of a group of persons that in electing a representative or in issuing an order, they have acted not 'as individuals' but 'in their official capacity', the answer can only be given in terms of their qualifications under certain rules and their compliance with other rules, which define what is to be done by them to make a valid election or a law. It is only by reference to such rules that we can identify something as an election or a law made by this body of persons. Such things are to be attributed to the body 'making' them not by the same simple natural test which we use in attributing an individual's spoken or written orders to him.[40]

So in Hart's hands the command theory is not only shown to be incompatible with ordinary assumptions about law, but is also internally inconsistent because the sovereign is both legally free and legally constituted. Hart concludes, already at the start of chapter V, that Austin's theory 'either distorted or altogether unrepresented some familiar features of municipal law in a modern state'.[41]

---

[37] ibid 74.
[38] ibid 75.
[39] ibid 76.
[40] ibid.
[41] ibid 79.

V. CAN THERE BE A TEST OF AN ULTIMATE RULE?

I know of very few commentators who think that Hart's critical arguments against Austin in chapters II, III, and IV go astray. I agree with the majority that Hart's points against Austin are correct and devastating for the command theory. But what do they actually show about what is to replace it? Hart's positive argument has a somewhat narrow focus: the single option pursued by him is that of a general social 'rule of recognition' specifying what counts as law.[42] Yet Hart (correctly, in my view) does not merely say that the supreme test for law is impersonal rather than personal. He does not simply put an abstract rule, as it were, in the place that was, in Austin's theory, held by a person (that is, by the sovereign). The change is far more substantial. Hart's attitude toward that rule (or set of rules) is entirely different from Austin's attitude toward the sovereign. What appears to be happening in chapter IV is that Hart's arguments are devastating not only for the Austinian sovereign but equally for *any* idea that there is an 'authorship' of law, personal *or* impersonal. In chapter IV, I believe, we find the undoing of Hart's own system.

In chapters V and VI, Hart explains more clearly that what replaces the Austinian sovereign in his theory of law is not just the 'rule of recognition' but also rules and practices of adjudication and legal change. In Hart's view a legal system must also include – alongside 'primary' rules of conduct – 'rules of change' enabling individuals to adapt existing law to changing circumstances 'by eliminating old rules or introducing new ones',[43] as well as 'rules of adjudication' conferring 'judicial powers' and enabling individuals authoritatively to settle disputes as to whether an admitted rule has been breached and to direct the application of penalties.[44] So just like Aristotle in the passage quoted at the start of this chapter,[45] Hart divides the law into *rules of conduct* and *offices* of law-making and law-application. Of course, the argument depends on what we mean by 'rules of adjudication'. It is evident, however, that if a rule of adjudication is to delegate the resolution of gaps and ambiguities to judges, then that rule does not *remedy* these gaps and ambiguities (nor could they be remedied, indeed, by any set of general rules; such rules would themselves generate gaps and ambiguities and require similar interpretation). So the rules of adjudication (so little discussed in Hart's book) must have a different structure. There is a balance between officials that issue decisions and the rules that define these decisions and give them their authority. And this aspect injects an element of *correctness* into the notion of an adjudicative judicial decision. Judges are not

---

[42] *cf* text to n 27 above.
[43] See *The Concept of Law* (n 1) 93, 95.
[44] See ibid 93f, 97f.
[45] *cf* passage quoted to n 5 above.

merely empowered to reach *some* decision, nor is a judicial decision given authority simply because it has been authored by an individual empowered to do so; judges are expected to decide correctly.

But what is this correctness? Hart points out in chapter V that

> a system which has rules of adjudication is necessarily also committed to a rule of recognition of an elementary and imperfect sort. This is so because, if courts are empowered to make authoritative determinations of the fact that a rule has been broken, these cannot avoid being taken as authoritative determinations of what the rules are. So the rule which confers jurisdiction will also be a rule of recognition, identifying the primary sources through the judgments of the courts and these judgments will become a 'source' of law.[46]

This means that any rule of adjudication that confers 'jurisdiction' must at the same time be itself a rule of recognition, identifying ways in which judgments may be correct or incorrect, and through which the judgments of the courts become 'authoritative determinations'. So the gaps are to be filled by the courts. But why does Hart say this? Why not say instead that it is up to the legislator, not the judge, to remedy the law's gaps and ambiguities – and indeed that until this has occurred judges must refrain from passing any judgment, on the grounds that there is *no law* about the case?

The answer is obvious once we grasp the relationship between courts and citizens in its political context. There cannot be cases where the courts say 'there is no law'. It is in the nature of what we normally call sovereignty but should more accurately call the political relationship itself that political institutions (including courts) are both coercive and comprehensive. This is not a logical point about sovereignty. It is a political requirement for the legitimacy of institutions.[47] And it is a point that Hart seems simply to presuppose in his account of a modern legal system.

So understood, Hart's theory is much closer to the Aristotelian model than appeared at first sight, because in addition to the first 'rule of recognition' of a legal system Hart adds that we also need rules setting out the architecture of legal institutions, including rules about the responsibilities of different offices and choice of office holders. Such persons will be legislators and judges, according to some institutional scheme. In Aristotle's language, we need appropriate 'magistrates'.

Hart acknowledges quite explicitly in chapter VII that even the ultimate rule of recognition, by which valid law is identified, can be uncertain, just like any other rule.[48] Hart does not rule out, therefore, that judges have jurisdiction

---

[46] *The Concept of Law* (n 1) 97.

[47] See eg J Waldron, 'Special Ties and Natural Duties' (1993) 22 *Philosophy and Public Affairs* 3 and P Eleftheriadis, 'Citizenship and Obligation' in J Dickson and P Eleftheriadis (eds), *Philosophical Foundations of European Union Law* (Oxford, Oxford University Press, 2012) 159–88.

[48] *The Concept of Law* (n 1) 147ff.

over the most fundamental matters of the law. He admits that the rule of recognition is not an area outside the law and its processes. The answers that courts give to the most fundamental constitutional questions, he says, will have a 'unique authoritative status among the answers which might be given'.[49] But does this not give rise to a paradox? The ultimate constitutional architecture seems to be both inside and outside the law. Here is Hart's account:

> At first sight the spectacle seems paradoxical: here are courts exercising creative powers which settle the ultimate criteria by which the validity of the very laws, which confer upon them jurisdiction as judges, must be tested. How can a constitution confer authority to say what the constitution is? But the paradox vanishes if we remember that though every rule may be doubtful at some points, it is indeed a necessary condition of a legal system existing, that not every rule is open to doubt on all points. The possibility of courts having authority at any given time to decide these limiting questions concerning the ultimate criteria of validity, depends merely on the fact that, at that time, the application of those criteria to a vast area of law, including the rules which confer that authority, raises no doubts, though their precise scope and ambit do.[50]

This argument sounds plausible to our ears, but how can it be so? As we saw above, Hart tells us, on the one hand, that a system's 'rule of recognition' is a social rule the existence of which is dependent on convergent practices, at least on the part of officials, and thus dependent on some measure of agreement. On the other hand, he tells us that disagreement about the rule of recognition is possible, and that courts are tasked with deciding such unclear cases. So the rule of recognition is the object of both *agreement* and *disagreement*. Thus Hart tells us that law is everywhere determined by the master rule of recognition, except when it is not. The law is both a matter of validity and a matter of judicial creativity.

Such paradoxical statements might perhaps have been dismissed out of hand if uttered by some less authoritative source. But Hart's voice makes us sit up and listen, and think about them again and find them plausible. How is that possible? Because anyone acquainted with constitutional law knows that Hart is right. Hart explains very well the way judges are supposed to argue in these cases: from the 'vast, central areas of the law' *upwards*, as it were.[51] Constitutional law is continuous with ordinary law. This is Hart's point. Understood in this way, Hart's account of constitutional disagreement is entirely reasonable and plausible. The argument is further strengthened by Hart's earlier account of the internal aspect of rules. This involves, remember, a 'critical reflective attitude' to certain 'patterns of behaviour', an attitude

---

[49] ibid 152.
[50] ibid 152.
[51] ibid 154.

which publicly displays itself in warranted criticism and demands for conformity.[52] So we conclude, with Hart, that judges on constitutional matters are doing exactly the same job that they are doing in ordinary cases. They are deliberating about the right standards, according to the available sources and precedents.

There is only one problem with this plausible account of adjudication in constitutional matters. The problem is that it contradicts Hart's theory of law. Hart replaced Austin's habit of obedience, as we saw above, with an entirely parallel analysis. For Austin's sovereign, Hart substituted the idea of an accepted, ultimate rule of recognition which serves as the foundation of legal validity.[53] One would therefore suppose that the rule of recognition would enable us to determine in advance what is and is not law without having to concern ourselves in any way with its merits. We see now, however, that Hart himself comes to acknowledge that no such rule can be satisfactorily formulated in advance. The rule of recognition is itself open to judicial scrutiny and elaboration – alongside the 'vast, central areas of the law' that we admittedly understand without controversy. But if the ultimate criteria of legal validity are themselves a matter for legal interpretation and deliberation, to be pursued by everyone and litigated in courts, then they cannot really be *foundational* in Hart's desired sense. They are continuous and internal to the law, part of its main preoccupations. They are constructs of law rather than its 'authors'. They lie at the same argumentative level as any other legal question. And if the rule of recognition thus emerges through the law, it cannot be prior to it.

In effect, Hart's own rule of recognition is prey to the very same criticisms to which Hart subjected Austin's sovereign. How can the continuity and persistence of the rule of recognition themselves be established? Is the rule of recognition not itself subject – just like sovereignty – to legal limitation and determination? If so, the rule of recognition – just like sovereignty – is not the determinant of law, but its result. If it is absurd to postulate a sovereign 'outside' the law, then it is equally absurd to postulate a rule of recognition 'outside' the law.

To put the matter another way, neither sovereignty nor any ultimate rule of recognition can ever even be described before we engage with them as law with the tools of legal reasoning and argument. There is no sense in which either sovereignty or recognition can possibly be a pre-legal social fact. Our views on these matters are always the result of many parallel deliberations and debates within law itself (and constitutional law in particular), about competence, offices, and duties.[54] Hart does not speak of sovereignty as the basis of

---

[52] *cf* passage quoted to n 17 above.
[53] *cf* text and passage quoted to n 28 above.
[54] I develop this point much more fully in P Eleftheriadis, *Legal Rights* (Oxford, Oxford University Press, 2008).

law. He speaks of questions regarding the 'legal competence of the supreme legislature itself' as questions concerning the 'ultimate criteria of legal validity'.[55] But neither sovereignty nor any ultimate rule of recognition can be 'ultimate' criteria in Hart's sense. Neither can provide the 'foundations' of a legal system, for they are its creations.

VI. PUZZLES OF SOVEREIGNTY, PUZZLES OF LAW

The idea of sovereignty as explained by Hart places law in a unique political and moral context. Law is, inescapably, a matter of force and a matter of remedies that change the way we relate to one another. Austin's view sets out law as a creation of a hierarchical political relation between those who rule and those who are ruled. Aristotle gives us a very different view of law, one which is equally political, but in which the hierarchies are different. Law is a moral idea that makes it possible to be both ruler and ruled at the same time, for it is only with law that you can be a co-legislator with everyone else. This is why your personal virtues are essential to the success of the joint project as a whole, namely the creation of a *politeia*. Austin sought to turn away from these matters of responsibility and practical reflection. Yet, as we saw, his determination to excise such matters from the theory of law ended up presenting something that cannot be law, namely the unlimited sovereign. His simple view is untenable and foreign to legal reasoning. It is not sovereignty that makes law possible. Instead, sovereignty, or rather, more accurately, the political relation, is itself, as we saw, a *creature* of the law, a creature, at least, of constitutional law and of the work of courts in public law.

Hart accepts this point and tries to accommodate it in his account of the rule of recognition. In the end, however, he ends up committing the same error. If the putative 'sovereign' is not obeyed by everyone and is in fact limited and defined by law, then he is not a sovereign. Similarly, if 'acceptance' of the master rule of recognition is not the *fact* of acceptance but a matter for creative disagreements *within* law, then the rule of recognition is not really a rule of recognition in Hart's sense of the word. It is not the author or proximate cause of the legal system. Because the major constitutional principles – the allocations of offices, the separation of powers, the major legislative tests – are themselves, permanently, matters for legal argument and deliberation, rather than a simple matter of 'foundational', pre-legal, social acceptance, then there is no relevant foundation to be found. We can only build a constitution by working from within the law.[56]

---

[55] *The Concept of Law* (n 1) 148.
[56] I explain this further in P Eleftheriadis, 'Law and Sovereignty' (2010) 29 *Law and Philosophy* 535.

I cannot argue for this position here, but my own view is that the only way to explain this self-referential nature of constitutional law is by accepting that law is, finally, an exercise in practical deliberation continuous with all other kinds of practical deliberation. And if the question about what the law is on any particular matter is an irreducibly deliberative question, then the authority of law cannot be settled by any factual, causal chain of events. This is the argument effectively made by Nigel Simmonds in *Law as Moral Idea*.[57] It is also the heart of John Finnis' assessment of Hart's legal philosophy.[58] Finnis writes that Hart's rule of recognition requires some kind of moral reasoning if it is to be of any use:

> What are they [judges] to *say to themselves*, one may ask, about their commitment? The plain fact that they made that commitment, publicly and no doubt privately, by itself settles nothing, nothing at all, about what they have sufficient reason to do, that is, about what is to be done, had better be done, and in any relevant sense ought to be done by them.[59]

Hart's arguments to the contrary, just like Austin's, fail to block this conclusion. Precisely because law and legal reasoning are deliberative in this sense, all legal ideas and arguments are practical ideas and arguments. This is the only plausible sense in the practices that Hart refers to when he speaks, as we saw, of the 'internal aspect' of rules.

It is not only the classical philosophers, then, who deploy a moral idea of law. Modern philosophers who explore more austere ideas of 'right' conduct (as opposed to the good life, or virtue) are equally committed to a complex idea of law as part of a broader moral ideal. The very idea of a 'social contract' is a metaphor conveying the message of a human union based on reciprocity. At the more abstract end of this tradition, Kant, for example, notes that law is connected to the idea of the 'civil condition' or the self-organised society of institutions that jointly make up the state. He tells us that 'a *state* (*civitas*) is a union of a multitude of men under laws of right'.[60] The multitude is united, not by power, but by its laws. A theory of law, in this tradition of thought, would therefore have things to say about motivation, the role of institutions, reciprocity and justice. None of these issues are addressed by Hart's theory. Indeed, Hart's vindication of the simple theory of law aims to sever such links between law and the ideal of a just state. Hart's view of the state is

---

[57] NE Simmonds, *Law as a Moral Idea* (Oxford, Oxford University Press, 2007) 123–43. For a discussion of Simmonds' arguments see J Finnis, 'Law as Idea, Ideal and Duty' (2010) 1 *Jurisprudence* 245; T Endicott, 'Morality and the Making of Law: Four Questions' (2010) 1 *Jurisprudence* 267; and NE Simmonds, 'Reply: The Nature and Virtue of Law' (2010) 1 *Jurisprudence* 277.

[58] J Finnis, 'On Hart's Ways: Law as Reason and as Fact' in his *Philosophy of Law: Collected Essays IV* (Oxford, Oxford University Press, 2011).

[59] ibid 250.

[60] *The Metaphysics of Morals*, AK6:313, in I Kant, *Practical Philosophy*, MJ Gregor (trans and ed) (Cambridge, Cambridge University Press, 1996) 456.

the direct opposite of the one we encounter in Aristotle's or Kant's works. Note how, describing the social situation of a population living in a territory in which Rex I reigns, Hart remarks in passing that

> the community under Rex has certainly some of the important marks of a society governed by law . . . It has even a certain unity, so that it may be called 'a state'. This unity is constituted by the fact that its members obey the same person, even though they may have no views as to the rightness of doing so.[61]

In this view, law is nothing nearly as exalted or moral or complex as Kant and Aristotle tell us. It is simply a mundane human arrangement.

I will now try to surprise you and argue that John Austin's considered view of law was much closer to the classical view, much as Hart's exposition of Austin's ideas may lead one to suppose otherwise. Austin was not really the consistent legal positivist portrayed in chapters II, III and IV of *The Concept of Law*. Austin's *The Province of Jurisprudence Determined* moves on, from the early chapters on which Hart concentrates, to offer a fuller account of law. In his little-read Lecture V, Austin ventures into matters of historical and political interest, and notes that the Roman Emperors or Princes 'did not succeed to the sovereignty of the Roman Empire or World by a given generic title: by a mode of acquisition given or preordained, and susceptible of generic description'.[62] Those pretenders to the throne relied instead on brute force. Austin finds this unacceptable, anomalous and inappropriate:

> Every successive Emperor acquired by a mode of acquisition which was purely anomalous or accidental: which had not been predetermined by any law or custom, or by any positive law or rule of positive morality. Every actual occupant of the Imperial office or dignity . . . was obeyed, for the time, by the bulk of the military class; was acknowledged, of course, by the impotent and trembling senate; and received submission, of course, from the inert and helpless mass which inhabited the city and provinces. By reason of this irregularity in the succession to the virtual sovereignty, the demise of an Emperor was not uncommonly followed by a shorter or longer dissolution of the general supreme government. Since no one could claim to succeed by a given generic title, or as answering for the time being to a given generic description, a contest for the prostrate sovereignty almost inevitably arose between the more influential of the actual military chiefs. . . . There was not, in the Roman World, any determinate person, whom positive law or morality had pointed out to its inhabitants as the exclusively appropriate object of general and habitual obedience.[63]

---

[61] *The Concept of Law* (n 1) 53.
[62] J Austin, *The Province of Jurisprudence Determined*, WE Rumble (ed) (Cambridge, Cambridge University Press, 1995) 132.
[63] ibid 133–34. I discuss Austin's views further in 'Austin and the Electors' (2011) 24 *Canadian Journal of Law and Jurisprudence* 441.

For Austin too, then, the major offices must be filled according to stable, public rules. So he would have *agreed* with Hart on the need for rules and titles of succession. Why? The answer must be that they both share a commonplace moral premise: that there are certain political goods that can only be achieved through stable rules and institutions. The task of constitutional laws everywhere is to deal with predictable political upheavals, brought about through normal passions and failings, in ways that are just and fair for all. This is why we need *public* standards of conduct. It is not a logical need, but a moral one. Austin agrees with that, too, when he writes that a command is a law or rule only if 'it obliges *generally* to acts or forbearances of a *class*'.[64] Why do commands need to be general? For the same reason given by Hart: so that they can operate as public tests of conduct and not merely as private guides to action.

I conclude, then, that although Austin and Hart both wished to defend the theory that law is a mundane creation, entirely a product of social facts not significantly connected to morality and somehow external and prior to law, they fail to do so. The idea of sovereignty invites questions of political and moral responsibility. Most obviously, it invites the question of who is to hold power over others. No one can be indifferent to that question.

Hart's supporters will rush to his defence. They will say something like this: 'You misunderstand the rule of recognition. Its indeterminateness is by no means fatal. All rules are indeterminate to some extent; it is always up to judges to deal with such indeterminacies and settle them by issuing authoritative decisions. The rule of recognition is a rule just like any other'. But my point is precisely that constitutional rules *are* just like any other rule. They are determined in exactly the same way. Hart thought that Austin's project was generally well founded, and that Austin was mistaken only in identifying the habitually obeyed sovereign as the appropriate foundational device. So all Hart did was to replace Austin's device with a different one, namely the idea of a *social rule* which is generally accepted as a matter of fact. My point, however, is that Hart's account fails because the idea of an accepted social fact cannot accommodate the deliberative nature of constitutional questions. Austin's inconsistencies have not been solved. The problems remain exactly the same.

The puzzles of sovereignty illustrate in the clearest possible way the deliberative nature of law. Constitutional questions are matters of great moment because they ultimately decide how power is distributed and how persons relate to one another. They are moral matters *par excellence*, in that they always invite practical reflection on how to distribute resources, how to shape institutions, how to allocate civic honour. Even Hart had to accept that such matters

---

[64] Austin, *The Province of Jurisprudence Determined* (n 62) 25.

were always open to judicial deliberation whenever they took the form of questions of constitutional law, even though formally they ought to have been pre-legal issues of the rule of recognition. But these constitutional matters are only one illustration of the more general point that legal questions are *always* questions of practical deliberation. If so, law is always to be addressed with the techniques and methods developed by practical reason as a whole.

Hart recognises in chapter VII (on 'Formalism and Rule-Scepticism') that rules by themselves can never do all the required work. There will always be scope for judges to interpret, determine, and apply the law in particular cases. The work they are invited to do is deliberative. This idea is already intimated, I think, although left incomplete, in Hart's elaboration of the 'internal aspect' of rules. As we have seen, neither the rules nor the judgments of courts are to be understood as mere communications, by the sovereign or anyone else, as to what we must do. They are to be understood, Hart tells us, as common, public standards of conduct.[65] But what does this really mean? Hart explains again and again that the internal aspect of rules involves a 'critical reflective attitude', and he further elaborates on this idea later in the book when he remarks that judges and other officials cannot look at the rule of recognition as a personal prudential guide for the avoidance of sanctions. He says that if the rule of recognition 'is to exist at all', it must be public and shared. In particular the rule of recognition:

> must be regarded from the internal point of view as a public, common standard of correct judicial decision, and not as something which each judge merely obeys for his part only. Individual courts of the system though they may, on occasion, deviate from these rules, must, in general, be critically concerned with such deviations as lapses from standards, which are essentially common or public. This is not merely a matter of the efficiency or health of the legal system, but is logically a necessary condition of our ability to speak of the existence of a single legal system . . . For [the characteristic unity and continuity of a legal system] depends on the acceptance, at this crucial point, of common standards of legal validity.[66]

On the basis of these thoughts Hart draws his famous conclusion that for a legal system to exist, two 'minimum conditions' are both necessary and sufficient:

> On the one hand, those rules of behaviour which are valid according to the system's ultimate criteria of validity must be generally obeyed, and, on the other hand, its rules of recognition specifying the criteria of legal validity and its rules of change and adjudication must be effectively accepted as common public standards of official behaviour by its officials.[67]

---

[65] *cf* text and passage quoted to n 16 above.
[66] *The Concept of Law* (n 1) 116.
[67] ibid.

The thinking behind this passage is exactly the same as that which forced Hart (and Austin) to say that the major constitutional matters of a state must be determined by public standards. This is the crucial point that Hart truly makes explicit in chapter IV. All legal questions must be decided by public standards, of which sovereignty is one – flawed – manifestation.

Chapter IV is at the epicentre of Hart's legal philosophy. It introduces some of its main ideas and contains all of its contradictions. Hart's idea of the rule of recognition plays a similar idea to that of Austin's 'sovereignty'. It provides a more or less causal foundation to a legal system that is to be empirically described. To be such a cause, the rule of recognition, just like sovereignty, must be free from legal deliberation. If it were not, the theory of law would be caught in a vicious circle, because the cause of legal reasoning cannot be legal reasoning itself. Hart exposed the inadequacy of 'sovereignty' in its role as a causal foundation by noticing the ways in which the power of law-making is normally subject to legal determination and therefore legal limitation. Yet the very idea of the rule of recognition, which Hart supposes can replace that of sovereignty, is open to exactly the same process of deliberative determination, and Hart's theory fails for the same reason. For the rule of recognition to succeed as a factual foundation of law and a legal system, it must stand, as it were, outside the law. Hart, like Austin, could not describe the rule of recognition in any way that could show it be outside the law. Any such insulation from the law would contradict our ordinary practices and assumptions of constitutional law *everywhere* in the world.[68]

What Hart ought to have said (but did not say) in chapter IV is that the reason Austin's sovereign is not the author of the law is that the law can *have* no such author (whether personal or impersonal). The authority of law is rather the result of practical reflection and is inextricably linked to an ever-present moral requirement that the exercise of political power be public and ultimately legitimate. This requirement finds expression in historical institutions; it is sometimes met, and sometimes is not. Because law is part of practical reason, its theory is also practical reason and cannot be accommodated by a causal, descriptive model. Hart failed to see this. Although he claimed that legal theory ought to adopt what he called the 'internal point of view',[69] he saw it as just another descriptive and explanatory attitude. As he famously put it in the Postscript, 'description may still be description, even when what is described is an evaluation'.[70] So, for Hart, instead of describing a habit of

---

[68] For reasons of this sort, HWR Wade – who had developed, a few years before Hart, a rather similar analysis of foundational norms – held that constitutional fundamentals must be always immune to any constitutional change. *cf* HWR Wade, 'The Basis of Legal Sovereignty' (1955) *Cambridge Law Journal* 172, and his *Constitutional Fundamentals* (London, Stevens, 1980).

[69] *The Concept of Law* (n 1) 89ff, 98ff.

[70] ibid 244.

obedience a legal theorist is tasked with accurately describing the 'acceptance' of the rule or rules of recognition, change and adjudication as a common public standard. But practical arguments are constructions of reason that reflect upon our practices and intuitions. Practical reason is in this sense constructive, not foundational.[71] When speaking of the 'internal point of view',[72] therefore, Hart ought to have been speaking instead of the practical, deliberative standpoint of the reflective agent who faces a first-person choice about action and remains situated in the common circumstances of social life. This standpoint is necessary both at the highest offices of state and the lowest matters of social interaction. That Hart did not see this in chapter IV is the origin of all the subsequent failures of the *Concept of Law*.

---

[71] CM Korsgaard, 'Realism and Constructivism in Twentieth-Century Moral Philosophy' in *The Constitution of Agency: Essays on Practical Reason and Moral* Psychology (Oxford, Oxford University Press, 2008) 302.
[72] *The Concept of Law* (n 1) 89ff, 98ff.

5

Why Law Might Emerge: Hart's Problematic Fable

JOHN GARDNER*

CHAPTER V IS the 'Eureka!' chapter of *The Concept of Law*. It reveals, in outline, Hart's proposed new 'key to the science of jurisprudence'.[1] By Hart's restrained standards, the chapter moves at a spirited pace. It covers a lot of ground and throws up numerous difficulties, to some of which Hart returns in later chapters but many of which lie where they fall. A vast and excellent critical literature has grown up around them. It would be impossible, within the confines of this essay, to trawl through all of the philosophical riches that chapter V has left in its wake. We need to focus, alas, on just a small part of its vast legacy.

In what follows I will focus on the final eight-page section of the chapter, which Hart calls 'The Elements of Law'.[2] This is where the chapter's title – 'Law as the Union of Primary and Secondary Rules' – crystallises into a thesis. In a legal system, claims Hart, 'primary rules of obligation' are conjoined with 'secondary rules of recognition, change, and adjudication'.[3] My focus here will not be on the thesis itself, tempting though it is to revisit some of its many intricacies and obscurities. My focus will instead be on the argument that Hart runs, in chapter V, to give the thesis its prima facie plausibility or appeal. I say 'prima facie' because Hart goes on, in chapter VI and beyond, to make arguments for the thesis that are of greater philosophical moment. Nevertheless it is the prima facie argument in chapter V that is the most engaging and the best known. It has caused a great deal of trouble. I hope to explain and perhaps mitigate some of the trouble.

---

* Many thanks to the editors of this volume for saving me from errors galore.
[1] HLA Hart, *The Concept of Law*, 3rd edn (Oxford, Oxford University Press, 2012 [1961]) 81.
[2] ibid 91–99.
[3] ibid 98.

I. HART'S FABLE OF LAW'S GENESIS

Hart's prima facie argument uses what Peter Hacker calls the 'genetic-analytic method'.[4] It attempts to alert us to some features that characterise a legal system by having us reflect on how and why such a system, meaning a system with such features, might emerge. It is important to emphasise the 'might'. Hart's story is a fable, an imaginary tale of the birth of a possible legal system. He does not care, and has no reason to care, whether this is how actual legal systems in general emerge, or whether even one legal system has ever so emerged. Nor does he care, or have reason to care, whether the 'pre-legal'[5] conditions that he presents as obtaining at the start of the story, before law emerges, have ever obtained anywhere. As Hacker says:

> [T]his revealing analysis is not a piece of armchair anthropology, but is conceptual analysis. We are asked to envisage a purely notional situation in order to perceive what crucial features characterize our own complex situation, and to understand the structure of the concepts with which we describe it.[6]

Hacker emphasises 'the key notions . . . of rules, reasons, and justifications' in terms of which Hart would have us understand the 'structure' of the concept of law. But one of the abiding attractions of Hart's book seems to be that it has many more 'key notions' than this, and perhaps none that are its master-keys. *The Concept of Law* might indeed be the exemplar that Peter Strawson has in mind when he commends the reorientation of philosophy from the 'reductive' to the 'connective':

> Let us abandon the notion of perfect simplicity in concepts; let us abandon even the notion that analysis must always be in the direction of greater simplicity. Let us imagine, instead, the model of an elaborate network, a system, of connected items, concepts, such that the function of each item, each concept, could . . . be properly understood only by grasping its connections with the others . . . If this becomes our model, then there will be no reason to be worried if, in the process of tracing connections from one point to another of the network, we find ourselves returning to, or passing through, our starting-point.[7]

Locating the idea of law in a network of other ideas (rule, reason, justification, obligation, power, official, practice, habit, sanction, attitude, system, and many more) is one way to understand Hart's 'elucidatory' ambition in *The*

---

[4] PMS Hacker, 'Hart's Philosophy of Law' in PMS Hacker and J Raz (eds), *Law, Morality, and Society: Essays in Honour of H.L.A. Hart* (Oxford, Clarendon Press, 1977) 11.
[5] *The Concept of Law* (n 1) 94.
[6] Hacker, 'Hart's Philosophy of Law' (n 4) 12.
[7] PF Strawson, *Analysis and Metaphysics* (Oxford, Oxford University Press 1992) 19.

Concept of Law.⁸ For this purpose, as Hacker says, the 'genetic-analytic method' offers 'great expository advantages'.⁹ Most obviously, we can exhibit the conceptual web by weaving it from small beginnings. There may no longer be a master-thread once the web exists. Everything may come to depend, in one way or another, on everything else. But one way to see how the web holds together is to imagine its inception, to look for a possible *first* thread.

Yet Hart also has a more specific reason for choosing the 'genetic-analytic method' to set up his thesis in chapter V. As revealed in his discussion of rulers Rex I and Rex II in chapter IV,¹⁰ there is a large metaphysical problem about law, a problem about the very possibility of law, which can reasonably be presented as a problem of genesis or poïesis. If law is made by human beings, then those human beings need to be somehow accredited as the ones who are qualified to do the law-making. Accrediting them as law-makers seems to be itself a job for the law and the law alone. Each law-maker is accredited by some law, which, ex hypothesi, must have been created by an already accredited law-maker, who must have been accredited by a further law, which must have been created by a further, already accredited law-maker, and so on until we reach constitutional law, where we find the accreditations for the top tier of law-makers. Or do we? Why stop there? There must surely be some human beings accredited as the ones qualified to make the constitution, and thus some even more ultimate law which accredits them to do so. And so it goes on. Each time we think we have reached the ultimate law accrediting the top tier of officials, we are faced with the thought that there must be some even more ultimate law accrediting an even higher tier of officials, or else the officials before us are unaccredited.

Although this problem is not strictly speaking one about how law came into being – it is strictly speaking a problem about the identification of *currently ultimate* laws rather than *historically first* laws – it can be vividly represented in genetic terms. That is how Scott Shapiro represents it in recent work when he calls it a 'chicken-egg' problem.¹¹ It is also how Hart represents the problem in his chapter V fable. He is using the 'genetic-analytic method' not only for its wider expository advantages, but also for the specific expository advantages it affords in foregrounding this metaphysical problem about law. How is law possible? How can it ever conceivably get off the ground?

The final pages of chapter V do not spell out Hart's solution to this problem. That comes only in chapter VI. But the solution is already more than

---

⁸ 'Elucidation' is the word that Hart often uses to describe what he is doing: eg *The Concept of Law* (n 1) 17, 123, 202. It is also the name that Strawson gives to his kind of 'connective' analysis: *Analysis and Metaphysics* (n 7) 19.
⁹ Hacker, 'Hart's Philosophy of Law' (n 4) 11.
¹⁰ Especially *The Concept of Law* (n 1) 58–66.
¹¹ SJ Shapiro, *Legality* (Cambridge, Mass, Harvard University Press, 2011) 39ff.

hinted at in his fable, so we are well-prepared for it when it comes. The solution will be found in the realm of custom, in the realm of rules that are made by their use over time and across a certain population.[12] In chapter VI it will turn out that the relevant custom, the one that endows a legal system with an ultimate 'rule of recognition' by which its highest tier of officials are accredited, is a custom of the same officials that it (the custom) accredits as officials, or at any rate of some of them. But from where we stand right now, all of that still lies ahead. In chapter V it is foreshadowed by Hart's tale of an imaginary world in which there are, at the outset, *only* customary rules. They are what he calls 'primary rules of obligation'. In time, 'secondary' rules emerge 'specify[ing] the ways in which the primary rules may be conclusively ascertained, introduced, eliminated, varied, and the fact of their violation conclusively determined'.[13] At this later stage custom cannot but anoint some people as proto-officials. They are the ones charged with doing the conclusive ascertaining, introducing, eliminating and so on. By their own customs of ascertainment, introduction, elimination, and so on, an emerging officialdom presides over what is by now beginning to take shape as a *system* of rules – giving us, says Hart, 'the heart of a legal system'.[14] In what sense a system? The rules no longer form 'just a discrete unconnected set'.[15] Mechanisms exist for identifying and using the rules of the set, themselves regulated, reflexively, by rules of the set.[16]

Hart brings all of this alive in his fable by telling us not only how, but also why, it takes place. How could he tell it as a story without filling in the whys as well as the hows? He portrays a population struggling with certain 'defects' that afflict their use of primary rules unsystematised by secondary rules. We are led to imagine the world that they inhabit getting more populous and more socially complicated. Under these conditions the primary rules become increasingly hard to ascertain (the problem of uncertainty) and increasingly in need of updating to deal with changing conditions of life (the problem of stasis). Increasingly they also give rise to wasteful struggles over their alleged

---

[12] Hart does not use the word 'custom' in telling his chapter V fable 'because it often implies that the ... rules are very old and supported with less social pressure than other rules', implications that he wants to avoid: *The Concept of Law* (n 1) 91.

[13] ibid 94. Hart's use of the labels 'primary rule' and 'secondary rule' is notoriously tricky. At the beginning of chapter V one has the impression that primary rules are obligation-imposing, whereas secondary rules are power-conferring (ibid 81). By the end of the chapter, however, it emerges that the contrast Hart has in mind must be more complex. All power-conferring rules are secondary rules, but not all secondary rules are power-conferring. The class of secondary rules also includes those obligation-imposing rules that share with all power-conferring rules the property that they regulate the operation of other rules. Hart's improved characterisation of a secondary rule is at ibid 94. A secondary rule, he says, is a rule 'about' other rules.

[14] ibid 98.

[15] ibid 95.

[16] cf ibid: Once there is a rule of recognition 'we have the germ of the idea of legal validity'.

violation and its consequences (the problem of inefficiency). Secondary rules of recognition emerge to tackle the uncertainty, rules of change to deal with the stasis, and rules of adjudication to mitigate the inefficiency. Hart emphasises that these three types of secondary rules interdepend in numerous ways, so that their social functions cannot be quite so neatly segmented as this summary suggests.[17] Nevertheless, secondary rules of all three types come into being, perhaps one by one. And they come into being for one and the same reason: because, in the changing conditions portrayed in the fable, regulation by primary rules alone 'must prove defective'.[18] The secondary rules between them 'provide a remedy for each defect'[19] and in doing so take us by stages 'from the pre-legal into the legal world'.[20]

It is thanks to this narratively inevitable excursus into the 'why?' question that Hart's philosophical woes stack up. Here is the first woe, as expressed by Nicola Lacey:

> The fable of secondary rules of recognition, adjudication and change as emerging to 'cure the defects' of a system composed exclusively of primary rules carries, it has been argued, an implicit evaluation of other sorts of . . . order . . . as less advanced or civilized.[21]

Why is this a problem for Hart? Mainly because it conflicts with his own conception of his project in *The Concept of Law*. Here is his own (later) summary of what he was trying to do in the book:

> My account . . . is morally neutral and has no justificatory aims: it does not seek to justify or commend on moral or other grounds the forms and structures which appear in my general account of law, though a clear understanding of these is, I think, an important preliminary to any useful moral criticism of law.[22]

Yet the chapter V fable does seem precisely to commend law as a step forward for 'primitive communities',[23] and it does so precisely by commending, if not on moral grounds then at any rate on 'other' grounds, certain 'forms and structures' that 'appear in [Hart's] general account of law'. As John Finnis explains:

> [In chapter V] Hart argued that law should be understood as, centrally, a union of primary with secondary rules. . . . The latter are, he said, to remedy the defects of a set-up in which rules of the primary kind were unaccompanied by rules conferring

---

[17] ibid 96f.
[18] ibid 92.
[19] ibid 94.
[20] ibid.
[21] N Lacey, 'H.L.A. Hart's Rule of Law: The Limits of Philosophy in Historical Perspective' (2007) 36 *Quaderni Fiorentini* 1209.
[22] *The Concept of Law* (n 1) 240 (in the posthumously published Postscript).
[23] ibid 91.

powers to change them and adjudicate about their application – rules which although logically secondary are so important to a society that their introduction 'is a step forward' comparable to 'the invention of the wheel.' Talk about valuable amenities and steps forward cannot reasonably be described as normatively inert[24] [ie as not commending the amenities and steps].[25]

Doesn't it follow, as Finnis joins many others in pressing, that Hart fails in his attempt to provide a value-neutral explanation of law's nature? Isn't his an ideological venture after all, a defence of law as an answer to certain social ills? Some say that things are even worse than that. His is ideological propaganda dressed up, in a classic hegemonic move, as dispassionate reporting of some ineluctable truths.[26] Hart pretends that he is remaining aloof from the question of law's desirability when in fact he is stealthily marketing law as 'a Good and Necessary Thing'.[27]

Perhaps this most cynical of criticisms could be repelled by insisting that Hart attests to law's value, such as it is, only as a side-effect of explaining law's nature. He does not provide 'a general account of law' that is tailored, in some sinister way, to establishing law's value. He provides a general account of law free of such tailoring, thanks to which the value of law is incidentally brought out. Law, it turns out, has value; but Hart's account of its nature, its distinguishing features, does not depend on its having that value. That is clearly a possible way for someone's thought about law, or indeed about anything, to unfold. But it seems unlikely to be the way that Hart's thought unfolds in *The Concept of Law*. For Hart goes beyond the mere repudiation of justificatory aims. He also writes that 'it is in no sense a necessary truth that laws reproduce or satisfy certain demands of morality'.[28] This is a claim, not about his own aims as an author, but about law itself. Those who idealise law by presenting it as a thing of value, even of just one value among many, get their 'general account of law' wrong.

This proposal only adds to Hart's woes where his chapter V fable is concerned. How can he avoid the claim that, in the fable, he is himself idealising

---

[24] J Finnis, 'Law and What I should Truly Decide' (2003) 48 *American Journal of Jurisprudence* 120. Finnis's mention of 'valuable amenities' is intended to echo Hart's talk of 'huge and distinct amenities': *The Concept of Law* (n 1) 41.

[25] I have added the words in square brackets because 'normatively inert' is a technical expression that Finnis is borrowing from my 'Legal Positivism: 5½ Myths' (2001) 46 *American Journal of Jurisprudence* 203. I hope my parenthetical does justice to what Finnis takes the expression to mean.

[26] See, eg, M Wood, 'Rule, Rules and Law' in P Leith and P Ingram (eds), *The Jurisprudence of Orthodoxy* (London, Routledge, 1988) 30f; B Edgeworth, 'H.L.A. Hart, Legal Positivism and Postwar British Labourism' (1989) 19 *University of Western Australia Law Review* 275; P Fitzpatrick, *The Mythology of Modern Law* (London, Routledge, 1992) ch 6; R Cotterrell, *The Politics of Jurisprudence*, 2nd edn (London, LexisNexis, 2003) 94f.

[27] AWB Simpson, *Reflections on* The Concept of Law (Oxford, Oxford University Press, 2011) 181.

[28] *The Concept of Law* (n 1) 185f.

law, and so, by his own lights, getting his general account of law wrong? Is it open to Hart, perhaps, to deny that the 'certain' values that his fable associates with law are moral ones, or at any rate that they add up to 'moral demands' of the kind that, as he puts it, laws need not 'reproduce or satisfy'?

Perhaps. The values ascribed to law in the chapter V fable seem to be, or at any rate to include, what are sometimes known as 'rule of law' or 'legality' values. In particular there is the value of certainty that is apparently embraced when Hart parades the rule of recognition as a rule for the mitigation of uncertainty (as establishing 'the proper way of disposing of doubts as to the existence of the rule').[29] There is also the value of finality that is apparently embraced, albeit in the name of efficiency, when Hart advertises the rule of adjudication as a way of curtailing dispute as to the application of the rules (as remedying the 'serious defect' which is 'the lack of official agencies to determine authoritatively the fact of violation of the rules').[30] Hart may well be reluctant to call such values 'moral' ones, or to think of them as making 'moral demands'. He has repeated and compound difficulties with the word 'moral' and its cognates.[31] Yet he has no apparent difficulty in referring to 'the requirements of justice which lawyers term principles of legality'.[32] And he agrees, it seems, that justice 'constitutes one segment of morality'.[33] So his chapter V fable does seem to commit him to embracing, as a 'necessary truth', that laws (or legal systems) automatically satisfy certain moral demands, namely at least some of the demands of justice that go to make up the ideal of the rule of law.

This is a very uncomfortable conclusion for Hart to reach, another woe heaped upon his woes. He famously resists Lon Fuller's arguments to the effect that, necessarily, a legal system substantially lives up to the ideal of the rule of law – or, putting it the other way round, that something that does not substantially live up to the ideal of the rule of law is not a legal system.[34] Yet in his fable in chapter V Hart appears to favour something like the Fullerian view. He appears to say that merely acquiring the three types of secondary rules by which to manage one's primary rules of obligation is both (a) necessary to acquire a legal system and (b) sufficient to meet certain (although not all) demands of the ideal of the rule of law. From which it follows – does it not? – that Fuller is on the right track: no legal system exists without the rule of law. Can this possibly be Hart's position? Does his fable leave him any space to avoid it?

---

[29] ibid 95, emphasis removed.
[30] ibid 93f.
[31] I documented some of them in 'Hart on Legality, Justice, and Morality' (2010) 1 *Jurisprudence* 261–65; a modified version of that essay now appears as chapter 9 of my *Law as a Leap of Faith* (Oxford, Oxford University Press, 2012).
[32] *The Concept of Law* (n 1) 207.
[33] ibid 167.
[34] LL Fuller, *The Morality of Law*, revised edn (New Haven, Yale University Press, 1969) 33–94.

The philosophical stakes here are high. Ronald Dworkin insists on reading Hart's 'general account of law' in *The Concept of Law* as an interpretation (he calls it a 'conventionalist' interpretation) of the ideal of legality.[35] Hart resists this reading, not because he dislikes the conventionalist interpretation of the ideal of legality, but because he denies that he is interpreting the ideal of legality at all.[36] But if what Hart thinks of as his 'general account of law' is actually a commendation of law, and if the features in virtue of which law is commended are classic 'legality' features, such as certainty and finality, then how is the Dworkinian reading to be resisted? How, to unpack a point that Hart makes in chapter IX, can we continue to distinguish between *lex, Gesetz, legge, loi* (law) and *ius, Recht, diritto, droit* (law that has something going for it *qua* law)?[37] If the chapter V fable is taken as most readers naturally take it, law according to Hart always has something going for it *qua* law, and the distinction between his project as he sees it, and his project as Dworkin sees it, seems to ebb away. What can Hart say to maintain the difference between the two?

II. SOME POSSIBLE WAYS OUT

Hart has a number of possible ways to extricate himself from this mess without abandoning the 'genetic-analytic method' of his fable. I am going to list four of them. They are not rivals. They all free up some space between the mere acquisition of a legal system and the achievement of legality, or (in other words) between *lex* and *ius* as I just defined them. Together, indeed, they free up a great deal of space. Yet, as we will see, they are not all equally comforting in their other implications.

(i) Change of narrative perspective. It is necessary for Hart's fable to do its genetic-analytic work that some people in the 'pre-legal' civilisation he describes should regard or experience their existing arrangements as defective. It is not necessary that they should be right to do so; maybe there are no such defects. It is also necessary that some people in the pre-legal civilisation should think of the emergence of secondary rules (of recognition, change, and adjudication) as a possible remedy for the perceived defects. But again it is not necessary that they should be right; maybe these rules offer no help. To make his

---

[35] R Dworkin, 'Hart's Postscript and the Character of Political Philosophy' (2004) 24 *Oxford Journal of Legal Studies* 28, summarising a position staked out at length in *Law's Empire* (Cambridge, Mass, Harvard University Press, 2006). The 'conventionalist' position is explained in chapter 4 of *Law's Empire* and associated with Hart at 429 n 3. This note in turn refers back to a passage in 'A Reply by Ronald Dworkin', in M Cohen (ed), *Ronald Dworkin and Contemporary Jurisprudence* (London, Duckworth, 1984) 255, where Dworkin relied on Hart's chapter V fable to assert 'the political basis of positivism'.

[36] *The Concept of Law* (n 1) 248ff (in the Postscript).

[37] ibid 208.

fable do its genetic-analytic work, Hart does not need to show that the development of a legal system is a *defensible* response to circumstances. He only needs to show that it is an *intelligible* response, that some people in the pre-legal world could conceivably come to think they have a problem to which the changes that Hart describes could conceivably be entertained as a possible solution. Hart could have pointed out at the end of the fable that, quite possibly, disappointment awaits. The new secondary rules do not end up giving people what they had hoped for, namely mitigation of uncertainty, stasis and inefficiency. But for better or for worse they do give them law.

(ii) Law is only the first step. Hart appears to say that the emergence of the secondary rules is both (a) necessary to acquire a legal system and (b) sufficient to meet certain demands of the ideal of the rule of law. But perhaps that is not what he is *trying* to say. Perhaps he is only trying to say that the emergence of the secondary rules in question is (a) necessary to acquire a legal system and (b') *necessary* to meet certain demands of the ideal of the rule of law. That would be an untroubling conjunction for Hart to embrace. On any plausible view, including Hart's, one can live under the rule of law only by having law. The first step is to acquire a legal system. The second is to make the legal system one has acquired conform to the ideal of the rule of law. Possibly Hart intended to leave open whether the inhabitants of his fable actually managed to get the rule of law advantages that they sought (greater certainty, less stasis, more efficiency). The point was merely that these were the advantages they sought, the ones they were after. When asked 'Why have a legal system?' they answer: 'In order to get the rule of law.' When asked: 'Did you get it?' they might well reply: 'We're still working on it. We have the secondary rules; we have a legal system. Now we need to work away at the secondary rules, hone them in certain ways, so as to secure the advertised advantages of legality.' If this is the true moral of Hart's fable then he is in no danger of violating the other precepts of his project. He has no need to deny (and indeed freely asserts[38]) that there is value in living under the rule of law. At most, to keep faith with the other precepts of his project, he has to deny that one gets that value automatically by having a legal system. This move grants him that denial.[39]

(iii) Sometimes, not always, valuable. Hart could also say this. He could point out that anything at all can be valuable in the right circumstances. Betraying one's comrades can sometimes put an end to one's torture. Murdering a witness can sometimes keep one safely out of gaol. Acquiring a legal system, likewise, can occasionally get a population out of deep water. Admitting this

---

[38] Consider especially his 'Legal Responsibility and Excuses' (first published in the same year as *The Concept of Law*) in *Punishment and Responsibility*, 2nd edn (Oxford, Oxford University Press, 2008) 43–50.

[39] He makes the denial later, at *The Concept of Law* (n 1) 207: for the rule of law to prevail, legal systems and legal rules must 'satisfy certain [obviously, additional] conditions'.

doesn't make Hart an enthusiast for law any more than admitting the occasional advantages of betrayal or murder would make him an enthusiast for betrayal or murder. When people 'seek to justify or commend [law] on moral or other grounds' they are usually looking for something less circumstantial than this. They are looking for a relatively general case for having law. This, Hart could say, is not what he is providing in chapter V. He is merely providing some reasons for having law in the narrow set of decidedly unfortunate, and imaginary, social circumstances that are specified in his fable – those in which (alas!) law becomes necessary because of (regrettable) changes in, say, population and social complexity. That is consistent with his saying that in many or even most other circumstances law is nothing but a curse or a burden or an evil. It is also consistent with his refusing to say anything general about the value of law.

(iv) Some legality, but not much. It is also open to Hart, perhaps most simply, to say that the mere fact of having a legal system gives one a little taste of the ideal of legality, or, as he himself puts it, a 'germ, at least, of justice',[40] but with a long way still to go before one fully, or even substantially, lives up to the ideal. The ideal of the rule of law demands, for example, that adjudicative bodies make their particular rulings on the basis of general rules. Not all rules are general to the extent, or in the respects, that make them conform adequately to this demand. Some people think, for example, that in order to conform adequately to this demand, the rule cannot pick on one person ('Jones must eat three meals a day'). It must apply more generally, meaning to an indefinite class of persons.[41] Nevertheless all rules including this one have a certain generality – this one applies to all days and all meals – in the absence of which they are not rules at all. All legal systems include rules, so all exhibit a certain measure of fidelity to the demand for generality. The point is merely that this can leave them falling a long way short of complying with the ideal of the rule of law, and in particular (Hart could reasonably argue) a long way shorter than Fuller or Dworkin would allow.

III. IS HART A 'LEGAL POSITIVIST'?

All of these ways out of his chapter V woes are open to Hart, and it is by no means clear which he takes and when. It is undeniable, however, that some of his remarks point to his favouring route (iv). Consider, for example, this remark in chapter IX, in which the fable from chapter V is recalled:

---

[40] ibid 206.
[41] See, eg, FA Hayek, *The Road to Serfdom* (London, Routledge, 1944) 62.

[T]he step from the simple form of society, where primary rules of obligation are the only means of social control, into the legal world with its centrally organized legislature, courts, officials, and sanctions brings its solid gains at a certain cost. The gains are those of adaptability to change, certainty, and efficiency, and these are immense; the cost is the risk that the centrally organized power may well be used for the oppression of numbers with whose support it can dispense, in a way that the simpler regime of primary rules could not.[42]

This shows that route (iv) is not an answer to all of Hart's woes. It certainly allows him to resist the idea that law is justified or commendable. It may be unjustified or damnable because its 'solid gains' are eclipsed, in some circumstances, by the oppression that it enables. But this still leaves Hart in trouble with respect to his remark, quoted above, that 'it is in no sense a necessary truth that laws reproduce or satisfy certain demands of morality'.[43] If law necessarily comports to some modest extent with the demands of the rule of law, and if the demands of the rule of law are demands of justice (and Hart, as we saw, agrees that they are), then law is necessarily to some modest extent just. It is then going much too far to say that it is *in no sense* a necessary truth that laws satisfy certain demands of morality. In some sense they do. In the sense in which demands of justice are moral demands, and in the sense in which minimal satisfaction is a kind of satisfaction, legal systems necessarily satisfy certain demands of morality. They are minimally moral. How is Hart to get away from that?

The answer may be that he doesn't want to. I presented the claim that 'it is in no sense a necessary truth that laws reproduce or satisfy certain demands of morality' as Hart's own claim. But on closer inspection it is offered by Hart, not as his own thesis, but as his working definition of the distinctive thesis of 'Legal Positivism'.[44] That he himself endorses the thesis is a conclusion drawn from his generally sympathetic mentions of legal positivism, which lead one to think that he regards it as his own creed. But maybe he does not, or not without reservation. Maybe his sympathy for it has its limits.

As Hart points out, the distinctive thesis of legal positivism has often been formulated a lot less cautiously, as the claim that there is 'there is no necessary connection between law and morals or [between] law as it is and law as it ought to be'.[45] Even in his earlier debate with Fuller, in which he is sometimes thought to have stood by this thesis, Hart rejected it.[46] In *The Concept of Law*

---

[42] *The Concept of Law* (n 1) 202.
[43] ibid 185–86, quoted above in text at n 28.
[44] 'Here we shall take Legal Positivism to mean the simple contention that it is no sense a necessary truth that laws reproduce or satisfy certain demands of morality, though in fact they have often done so': *The Concept of Law* (n 1) 185f.
[45] ibid 302, reproducing Hart, 'Positivism and the Separation of Law and Morals' (1958) 71 *Harvard Law Review* 601 n 25.
[46] Hart, 'Positivism and the Separation of Law and Morals' (n 45) 624.

Hart rejects it many times over. By now he has come to see how many possible necessary connections between law and morality there might be, and how few are worth denying.[47] One might well think, for example, that law necessarily calls for moral scrutiny. Or that law necessarily uses moral concepts. Or that law necessarily confronts moral problems. By the time of *The Concept of Law* Hart has come to think that 'Legal Positivism' is a broader church that does not exclude those who think these modest thoughts. It does not even exclude those philosophical anarchists who think that law is necessarily *immoral*. It only excludes those who think that there is some sense in which laws necessarily 'reproduce or satisfy certain demands of morality'.

Does it thereby exclude Hart himself? On the very same page on which Hart gives this more cautious characterisation of the legal positivist thesis, he nevertheless agrees that it 'may in some sense be true' that 'a legal system *must* exhibit some specific conformity with morality or justice'.[48] Surely he is knowingly distancing himself, with these words, from what he regards as the creed of the 'Legal Positivists'. In the process he signs up to a yet more cautious thesis, namely a thesis about *legal validity*. '[I]t does not follow,' he continues, 'that the criteria of legal validity of particular laws used in a legal system must include, tacitly if not explicitly, a reference to morality or justice.'[49] This thesis allows that there may be some necessary moral value in laws or legal systems. It only rules out one possible explanation of that value. One possible explanation for the value of law, such as it is, is that nothing qualifies as a law in any legal system – nothing is legally valid – except by virtue of some value that it exhibits. This explanation is what Hart sets himself against. To state his thesis very crudely: perhaps some things are valuable because they are law, but it does not follow (as a general truth about law)[50] that they are law because, even partly because, they are valuable.

I have elsewhere suggested, following Joseph Raz, that we should think of this thesis, and this thesis alone, as the distinctive thesis of legal positivism, thereby rehabilitating Hart as a torchbearer of that tradition.[51] But this was not the role, I think, that Hart envisaged for himself. From the start he saw

---

[47] Indeed at *The Concept of Law* (n 1) 207, Hart observes that 'few legal theorists classed as positivists would have been concerned to deny the forms of connection between law and morals discussed under the last five headings'.

[48] ibid 185 (emphasis in original).

[49] ibid.

[50] These parenthetical words are needed because Hart was what has since come to be known as an 'inclusive' or 'soft' legal positivist who thought that a particular legal system might have evaluative criteria for legal validity set by the system itself. He merely resisted the view that all legal systems by their nature have such evaluative criteria. See ibid 204, and, for more explicit later confirmation of his view, ibid 250 (in the Postscript).

[51] See my 'Legal Positivism: 5 ½ Myths' (n 25). I was mainly clarifying some implications of the 'sources thesis' advanced by Joseph Raz in his 'Legal Positivism and the Sources of Law' in Raz, *The Authority of Law* (Oxford, Oxford University Press, 1979) 37.

himself as a sympathetic critic of the tradition, defending elements of truth in its thesis while resisting some associated excesses. That is perhaps one reason why he did not go to great lengths, or indeed to any lengths at all, to craft his chapter V fable in such a way as to avoid the implication that acquiring a legal system is acquiring something valuable. He could have helped himself to options (i), (ii) or (iii) on our list of escape routes. They would have taken him to total safety. What he said was largely consistent, however, with route (iv). That was not because he was trying to defend the thesis in (iv), which endows law with a minimal but necessary moral value. As he later said, he had no 'justificatory aims'; he did not 'seek to justify or commend on moral or other grounds the forms and structures which appear in my general account of law'.[52] Nevertheless he sought to make space for the view that law by its nature has some 'moral or other' value. In doing so he was mainly trying to show that taking this view is compatible with holding that there are (or at any rate need be)[53] no moral (or otherwise evaluative) criteria of legal validity.

IV. HART V FULLER, HART V DWORKIN

Where does this leave Hart in his long debates with Fuller and Dworkin? Is it in either case a phony war?

Hart and Fuller certainly confused each other a great deal in their famous debates, and often spoke at cross-purposes. Some of the differences between them concerning the nature of law are routinely exaggerated, including by them.[54] Nevertheless there are differences. To Hart's way of thinking, Fuller overeggs the value of law, and in two ways: first, by overstating the extent to which law necessarily lives up to the ideal of the rule of law; and secondly, by being overoptimistic about the extent to which other kinds of moral upstandingness must go hand-in-hand with living up to the ideal of the rule of law. Yet Hart does not attack, and sometimes seems to support, Fuller's thesis that law by its nature exhibits some value in the rule-of-law dimensions of certainty, generality, and so on. Doesn't that put them on the same side so far as the *big* issue that was supposed to divide them is concerned? Doesn't it put them on the same side in the debate about the truth of 'Legal Positivism', with capital letters?

Not quite. When I introduced Fuller's position a few pages ago I characterised him as saying that 'necessarily, a legal system substantially lives up to the

---

[52] *The Concept of Law* (n 1) 240, quoted above in text at n 22.
[53] Again the parenthetical qualification is needed to accommodate Hart's leaning towards 'soft positivism': see n 50.
[54] See my discussion in 'The Supposed Formality of the Rule of Law' in *Law as a Leap of Faith* (n 31).

ideal of the rule of law – or, putting it the other way round, that something that does not substantially live up to the ideal of the rule of law is not a legal system'. We can now see that it really matters which way round one puts Fuller's position. The *umgekehrt* reformulation carries an undertone or subtext that the other does not, namely that what qualifies as law so qualifies partly *because* of its value. It is possible to hold this view without going on to embrace the view that there are always moral (or otherwise evaluative) criteria of legal validity, and hence without coming into conflict with what Hart says in chapter V. Imaginably, there are moral criteria for something to qualify as a legal system, even though legal systems need not set moral criteria for identifying the legal norms that belong to them. It is not clear whether Fuller embraced this two-level thesis. In fact, it is not clear which of several possible theses Fuller embraced in this neighbourhood. All we can say is that, inasmuch as Fuller thought that there are evaluative criteria for legal validity supplied by his 'internal morality of law', that drives a major wedge between him and Hart. Hart can accommodate the idea that what is legally valid is, for that reason, valuable in some respect. But he cannot accommodate the converse idea that what is valuable in that respect is for that reason – even if only partly for that reason – legally valid. Or at any rate, he cannot accommodate the idea, which he attributes rightly or wrongly to Fuller, that this is a necessary truth about legal validity.

Hart's disagreements with Dworkin range more widely. Some are more radical. At his most radical, Dworkin denies the intelligibility of the Hart–Fuller debate. He does not think it *makes sense* to ask whether some system qualifies as a legal system, or some norm qualifies as a norm of that system, even though it fails to exhibit the value of legality. He writes:

> [I]t would be nonsense to suppose that though the law, properly understood, grants [P] a right to recovery, the value of legality argues against it. Or that though the law, properly understood, denies [P] a right to recovery, legality would nevertheless be served by making [D] pay.[55]

This passage explains why Dworkin cannot but read Hart's 'general account of law' as an interpretation of the ideal of the rule of law. There is no conceptual space for anything else. It is not merely, as Hart might be willing to grant to Fuller, that law is necessarily a bringer of minimal clarity, openness, generality, etc and in that respect valuable. Nor is it merely, as Fuller might argue, that what is law is law only because it brings such value. It is that there is nothing but such value to discuss. The idea of law is simply the idea of whatever exhibits the value of legality. Being legal in the sense of being legally valid just is being legal in the sense of living up to the ideal of the rule of law. So the only work for a philosopher of law is the interpretation of that ideal.

[55] R Dworkin, 'Hart's Postscript' (n 35) 25.

Nothing in Hart's fable, or indeed in *The Concept of Law* more generally, even in its posthumous Postscript, suggests any kind of *rapprochement* with this radical claim about law, or the reductive view of legal philosophy that underlies it. Hart rightly resists it at every turn. He insists that, even though law may have value, the question of law's value remains an open one so far as his 'general account of law' is concerned. What he means, I think, is that one may understand what counts as law and identify instances of it without necessarily invoking or presupposing law's value. One may be an anarchist who thinks that law has no redeeming value, and yet agree with Hart's explanation of what law is. Hart's chapter V fable, even read so as to allow for what I called a 'route (iv)' escape from its woes, does not militate against this possibility. At most it goes to show that neither Hart nor the inhabitants of his 'primitive community' are anarchists.

That comes as no surprise. Hart was openly not an anarchist. He was openly a believer in the ideal of the rule of law, which he defended with vigour elsewhere.[56] The inhabitants of his 'primitive community' think, in this respect, much as he does. That is why they opt for, or maybe we should say drift into, having law. And Hart makes that perfectly clear. It does not follow, of course, that regarding what they drift into as law, or endorsing Hart's explanation of what makes it law (roughly: 'the union of primary and secondary rules'), commits one to sharing Hart's or any other positive judgment on its value.

V. THE FABLE IN ITS PLACE

As I said, the fable that occupies Hart at the climactic end of chapter V is not the whole of the chapter. Before it there comes Hart's discussion of the nature of obligation. In spite of its pace, and its feast of ideas, this discussion is unsatisfactory. The ideas do not work out. Hart is in a muddle.[57] Very little of his analysis of obligation (beyond the agreement that an analysis of obligation is needed) has survived into the thinking of Hart's successors. More generally, in *The Concept of Law*, Hart did not get very far in his attempts to understand what makes norms into norms, or rules into rules. His idea that such things have an 'internal aspect' gestures towards important truths but constantly pulls him and his readers in various competing directions. Hart's thinking on this point is fertile, but mainly because of the various ways in which it primed later writers to react against it and move off in their own directions. Hart's revolutionary positive contributions to our understanding of the nature of law

---

[56] Especially in *Punishment and Responsibility* (n 38).
[57] And he knows it: see the notebook entry quoted by Nicola Lacey in *A Life of H.L.A. Hart: The Nightmare and the Noble Dream* (Oxford, Oxford University Press 2004) 228.

lie mainly on two other fronts: first, in his grasp of how various kinds of norms (duty-imposing and power-conferring, primary and secondary, general and particular) interact to constitute legal systems; second, in his realisation that a legal system is (in a sense) a creature of custom. Although these thoughts gradually take shape through the earlier chapters of *The Concept of Law*, it is in the famous chapter V fable that they are explosively combined for the first time to reveal what Hart plausibly parades as 'the heart of a legal system'. Tony Honoré, who was Hart's collaborator on other work in the years when *The Concept of Law* was being written, reports[58] that Hart was in a state of some commotion when he came up with the idea of law as a 'union of primary and secondary rules'. 'I've got it!', he exclaimed to Honoré on return from the absence during which chapter V was drafted. Hart's excitement, as I said, comes across in the chapter itself. The last few pages, in particular, contain such highly reactive elements that much of the remainder of the book has to be devoted to post-explosion rebuilding work, often from the ground up. Not only that, but much of the philosophy of law in the 50 years since has been devoted to dealing with the fallout. Nothing in the way law is theorised has been the same afterwards. It is an authentic 'Eureka!' moment in the history of ideas.

---

[58] In conversation.

6

The Rule of Recognition and the Foundations of a Legal System

GRANT LAMOND*

CHAPTER VI OF *The Concept of Law* is devoted to an exposition and analysis of the rule of recognition. The rule of recognition forms the keystone in Hart's account of the law, playing a role comparable to Austin's sovereign and Kelsen's basic norm. Indeed, the rule of recognition grows out of a critical engagement with both Austin and Kelsen, and Hart sees it as a better solution to the problems which preoccupied his predecessors. The rule of recognition is one of the best known and most influential contributions in *The Concept of Law*, and a wide range of critical commentary on it has accumulated in the 50 years since the book's first publication. My aim in the present chapter is not to survey that literature, but to raise some new questions about the adequacy of the rule of recognition that do not depend upon existing lines of criticism.

The present chapter is divided into two sections: the first attempts to restate Hart's claims about the rule of recognition, while the second probes five issues to which that account gives rise. The first section is necessary because Hart's discussion of the rule of recognition is more elaborate and intricate than is often supposed, and his exposition is far from straightforward: he shifts from point to point in developing the details of the rule of recognition, and doubles back at times to fill in yet more detail. In addition, although chapter VI of *The Concept of Law* contains the most sustained discussion of the rule of recognition, it cannot be read in isolation from other parts of the book. Hart's analysis builds upon his account of 'social rules' in chapter IV and his preliminary account of a legal system in chapter V; the rule of recognition is considered further in chapter VII and is applied to the case of international law in chapter X. On some key issues, as shall be seen below, Hart's views are unclear, either because of what he says in different places or because of what he does not say at all.

* I would like to thank John Stanton-Ife and the editors of this volume for their comments on an earlier version of this paper.

In the second section of this chapter I raise five questions about Hart's analysis, two concerning the role of officials in the rule of recognition, and one each about Hart's conception of 'validity', legal duties, and the nature of sources of law. These questions raise some doubts about whether Hart's solutions to the problems that preoccupied Austin and Kelsen are satisfactory. But in so doing they also cast doubt on a key idea that Austin, Kelsen and Hart all shared: that there is one thing – be it sovereign, basic norm, or rule of recognition – that provides *the* foundations of a legal system. If these doubts are well placed, the rule of recognition occupies a more modest role in a legal system than Hart supposed.

I. THE RULE OF RECOGNITION

Hart opens chapter VI by noting the inadequacy of the claim, based on Austin's theory of law, that

> [t]he foundations of a legal system consist of the situation in which the majority of a social group habitually obey the orders backed by threats of the sovereign person or persons, who themselves habitually obey no one.[1]

Although the theory points to some important truths about the law, it fails to account for 'some of the salient features of a modern municipal legal system'.[2] These truths can only be properly understood

> in terms of the more complex social situation where a secondary rule of recognition is accepted and used for the identification of primary rules of obligation. It is this situation which deserves, if anything does, to be called the foundations of a legal system.[3]

The passage points to three important aspects of the rule of recognition: that it (1) identifies primary rules of obligation; (2) is a 'secondary rule'; and (3) is 'accepted and used'. I shall consider each in turn.

The rule of recognition is first introduced by name in chapter V, although the same idea is raised in the discussion of the continuity of law in chapter IV.[4] Hart notes in chapter V that many societies have existed without 'legislatures, courts, or officials of any kind',[5] where the only means of social control is by way of social custom or, as Hart prefers to put it, by way of 'primary rules of obligation'.[6] He points out that except for small, close-knit societies

---

[1] HLA Hart, *The Concept of Law*, 3rd edn (Oxford, Oxford University Press, 2012 [1961]) 100.
[2] ibid.
[3] ibid.
[4] ibid 57–61.
[5] ibid 91.
[6] ibid: 'A social structure of this kind is often referred to as one of "custom"; but we shall not use this term, because it often implies that the customary rules are very old and supported with less social pressure than other rules. To avoid these implications we shall refer to such a social structure as one of primary rules of obligation.'

living in relatively stable circumstances, exclusive reliance on such primary rules will have a number of drawbacks. One of the drawbacks is that there may be uncertainty over which rules count as primary rules, and uncertainty over the precise scope of some of the rules, since their existence rests on a widespread acceptance throughout the society and there is no procedure for settling these doubts.[7] The solution to this drawback is to supplement the primary rules with a secondary rule of a different kind – the rule of recognition – that will

> specify some feature or features possession of which by a suggested rule is taken as a conclusive affirmative indication that it is a rule of the group to be supported by the social pressure it exerts. The existence of such a rule of recognition may take any of a huge variety of forms, simple or complex. It may, as in the early law of many societies, be no more than that an authoritative list or text of the rules is to be found in a written document or carved on some public monument. . . . [W]hat is crucial is the acknowledgement of reference to the writing or inscription as *authoritative*, i.e. as the *proper* way of disposing of doubts as to the existence of the rule. Where there is such an acknowledgement there is a very simple form of secondary rule: a rule for conclusive identification of the primary rules of obligation.[8]

Hart says at the start of chapter VI that where there is a rule of recognition 'both private persons and officials are provided with authoritative criteria for identifying primary rules of obligation'.[9] This might naturally be thought to mean that the rule of recognition only identifies duty-imposing rules. But elsewhere in chapter VI Hart refers to the rule of recognition as identifying 'the law',[10] 'rules of law',[11] 'the rules',[12] 'the rules of the system',[13] 'valid law',[14] or as providing the criteria of validity of the rules of the system.[15] As one of Hart's own criticisms of the command theory of law is that not all legal rules are duty-imposing rules,[16] he is best understood as claiming that the rule of recognition identifies (or provides criteria for the identification of) all types of rules as rules (or 'members'[17]) of the system, not just rules of obligation.[18] What

---

[7] ibid 92.
[8] ibid 94f.
[9] ibid 100; see also 94, 95, 98 and 155.
[10] ibid 101, 102, 110, 111, 112, 116.
[11] ibid 114.
[12] ibid 101, 106.
[13] ibid 102, 103, 106, 111.
[14] ibid 113, 114.
[15] ibid 102–03, 105, 106, 107, 108, 108f, 110, 116.
[16] ibid 26–44.
[17] ibid 109, 110.
[18] Hart's preferred description of the function of the rule of recognition is in terms of 'identifying' rules as rules of the system, as can be appreciated from the number of times he uses it: ibid 95, 96, 97, 100, 101, 102, 105, 106, 108, 110, 111, 112, 113, 114, 115, 122, 148, 149, 150, 152, 170, 214, 292, 293, 294, 295.

makes a rule a legal rule, a rule in a particular legal system, is that it is identified by the criteria in the rule of recognition of that system.

In addition to its identifying function, Hart characterises the rule of recognition as a 'secondary rule'. What does he mean by this? Hart's discussion of 'primary' and 'secondary' rules begins in chapter V, where he says that to understand the complexity of a legal system, there is a need to discriminate between two different (though related) 'types' of rules:

> Under rules of the one type, which may well be considered the basic or primary type, human beings are required to do or abstain from certain actions, whether they wish to or not. Rules of the other type are in a sense parasitic upon or secondary to the first; for they provide that human beings may by doing or saying certain things introduce new rules of the primary type, extinguish or modify old ones, or in various ways determine their incidence or control their operations. Rules of the first type impose duties; rules of the second type confer powers, public or private. Rules of the first type concern actions involving physical movement or changes; rules of the second type provide for operations which lead not merely to physical movement or change, but to the creation or variation of duties or obligations.[19]

He adds the 'general claim' that

> in the combination of these two types of rule there lies what Austin wrongly claimed to have found in the notion of coercive orders, namely, 'the key to the science of jurisprudence'.[20]

When Hart comes to discuss the legal system in chapter V and introduce the idea of the rule of recognition, he discusses two further difficulties that a society living exclusively under a regime of primary rules of obligation would experience. One is the problem of changing the primary rules. Since these are solely duty-imposing rules there will be no mechanism for *deliberately* altering the rules. Such changes will rely instead on a general shift in the practices and beliefs of the population over what is required or permitted. The other difficulty relates to breaches of the primary rules: there will be no way to authoritatively determine if a rule has been breached, and remedial action will be left to the party who claims to be wronged. To address these difficulties a legal system needs two further secondary rules in addition to a rule of recognition – a rule of change and a rule of adjudication. The introduction of these three rules is 'enough to convert the regime of primary rules into what is indisputably a legal system'.[21]

It is notable that although Hart describes the rules of recognition, change and adjudication as 'secondary rules', he does not identify them with power-conferring rules. Instead they are said to be 'secondary' because

---

[19] ibid 81; see also, at 283, the endnote to p 26.
[20] ibid 81.
[21] ibid 94.

they have important features in common and are connected in various ways. Thus they may all be said to be on a different level from the primary rules, for they are all *about* such rules; in the sense that while primary rules are concerned with the actions that individuals must or must not do, these secondary rules are all concerned with the primary rules themselves. They specify the ways in which the primary rules may be conclusively ascertained, introduced, eliminated, varied, and the fact of their violation conclusively determined.[22]

Hart never says expressly that the rule of recognition is *not* power-conferring, but he never says it is, and he never refers to the three secondary rules collectively as power-conferring, whereas he does refer to both the rule of change and the rule of adjudication as power-conferring.[23] The better view would seem to be, then, that the rules of recognition, change and adjudication are 'secondary' rules not because they are power-conferring, but because they are 'second-order' rules, that is, they are rules *about* first-order (primary) rules.[24]

Finally, Hart says that the rule of recognition is 'accepted and used'. In saying this, Hart is referring to his discussion of 'social rules' in chapter IV. That discussion arose from Hart's argument that Austin's model of sovereignty, based as it is on a population being in a 'habit of obedience' to a sovereign person or persons, is unable to explain the *continuity* of legislative authority, that is, the transition from one sovereign to another.[25] Instead of a social *habit*, Hart argues that what is needed for such continuity is a social *rule* regulating the transition of authority, and making one sovereign the *lawful* successor to that position.[26] Both social rules and social habits involve a population exhibiting a general pattern of behaviour, eg baring heads in church, going to the cinema on Saturday nights.[27] But in addition to this general pattern of behaviour (or 'external aspect'[28]), social rules have an 'internal aspect', inasmuch as the pattern of behaviour is regarded as a general *standard* to be followed by the group as a whole.[29] The 'internal aspect' of a social rule also involves the population having

> a critical reflective attitude to certain patterns of behaviour as a common standard, and that this should display itself in criticism (including self-criticism), demands for

---

[22] ibid.
[23] ibid 96, 97.
[24] Hart uses the primary/secondary distinction in a range of ways: for criticism see PMS Hacker, 'Hart's Philosophy of Law' in PMS Hacker and J Raz (eds), *Law, Morality and Society. Essays in Honour of H.L.A. Hart* (Oxford, Clarendon Press, 1977) 18–22, J Raz, 'The Functions of Law' in his *The Authority of Law*, 2nd edn (Oxford, Oxford University Press, 2009) 177–79; and N MacCormick, *H.L.A. Hart*, 2nd edn (Stanford, Stanford University Press, 2008) 130–34.
[25] Hart, *The Concept of Law* (n 1) 51–61.
[26] ibid 54.
[27] ibid 55.
[28] ibid 56, and 88f, 98f.
[29] ibid 56f.

conformity, and in acknowledgements that such criticism and demands are justified, all of which find their characteristic expression in the normative terminology of 'ought', 'must', and 'should', 'right' and 'wrong'.[30]

To say that a social rule is 'accepted' is a short-hand way of referring to the 'internal aspect', that is, of indicating that members of the population in question do have the critical reflective attitude towards the pattern as a standard and display it in their criticism, demands, and acknowledgements, and in the vocabulary they use.[31]

Hart adds two clarifications to his analysis of social rules. First of all, a social rule of a group only requires that there be 'general' acceptance of a pattern of behaviour as a standard to be followed by a group: the acceptance need not be universal and is consistent with 'a minority who not only break the rule but refuse to look upon it as a standard either for themselves or others'.[32] Secondly, 'acceptance' is not to be equated with 'feelings' such as 'psychological experiences' of compulsion. Those who accept a social rule may have such psychological experiences, but they need not: they need only regard the pattern as a standard for all and manifest that view in the appropriate ways.[33] In chapter V Hart goes on to say that those members of a group who use and accept social rules may be described as possessing the 'internal point of view' towards those rules.[34]

To summarise, then, the rule of recognition:

(1) provides criteria for the authoritative identification of the (primary) rules of the system;
(2) is a secondary, or second-order rule: it is a rule about the primary rules in a legal system, and is on a different 'level' from those primary rules; and
(3) is a social rule that is accepted and practised.

Hart goes on to argue that the rule of recognition helps elucidate the idea of a 'source' of law and of legal 'validity', and to explain the significance of 'efficacy' for the law. I will briefly examine each of these.

---

[30] ibid 57.
[31] ibid 55ff. For criticisms of the completeness of this account of social rules (the 'practice theory of rules'), see R Dworkin, *Taking Rights Seriously* (Cambridge, Mass, Harvard University Press, 1978) 48–58; and J Raz, *Practical Reason and Norms*, 2nd edn (Oxford, Oxford University Press 1999 [1975]) 49–58. See also Hart's acknowledgement of this in the posthumously published Postscript: *The Concept of Law* (n 1) 254–59.
[32] *The Concept of Law* (n 1) 56.
[33] ibid 57.
[34] ibid 89.

A. Sources

The rule of recognition uses criteria to identify rules as rules of the system. A criterion may be simple and particular, such as the rules set up in the XII tables in the Forum in Roman Law. But it may be more complex than this, in (a) using *general* characteristics to identify rules (eg enactment by a specified body), and/or (b) having more than one characteristic or set of characteristics as a criterion of identification (eg enactment or long customary practice), and where (b) is the case, (c) by providing a method of reconciling conflicts between rules identified by different criteria.[35]

The existence of more than one criterion for identifying the rules of a system provides the explanation for the existence of separate 'sources' of law, such as statute and precedent. The sources are separate because one does not depend for its existence on the other.[36] So the law in England recognises enactment by Parliament as a source of law, but also the decisions of superior courts (precedent). Precedent is not derived from statute: there is no legislative basis for the doctrine of precedent. But there can be, as there are in English law, rules for resolving conflicts between rules from these different sources. In English law statute is a superior source to precedent because in a conflict between rules from these two sources, statutory rules prevail over common law rules.[37] But this relative superiority of statute as a source does not mean that precedent is derived from statute. Contrary to Austin's conception of law, where all laws necessarily had one source (the sovereign), there can be separate sources.

B. Validity

For Hart, a legal rule is valid when it satisfies some criterion provided by the rule of recognition for identification as part of the law. Hart also notes that some rules owe their validity not to the rule of recognition itself but to being identified by rules that owe *their* validity to the rule of recognition. So there can be *chains* of validity, connecting different rules; but all of the chains lead back, in the end, to the rule of recognition[38] (or, as Hart sometimes describes it, the 'ultimate' rule of recognition[39]). To be valid, then, is to be a member of a system of rules, and to be a member by virtue of being identified by the criteria in some other rule.[40] All

---

[35] ibid 95, 100–01.
[36] ibid 95, 98, 101, 106, 294.
[37] See ibid 106.
[38] ibid 107.
[39] ibid 106, 107, 109, 110, 112, 114, 115, 116, 120, 121, 149, 292.
[40] ibid 110.

the rules of a system eventually trace their identification back to the (ultimate) rule of recognition. (In the following discussion I will generally write as if all valid rules were identified directly by the ultimate rule of recognition itself, since the complication does not alter the basic analysis.)

What about the rule of recognition itself? Unlike other legal rules it is not identified by the criteria in some further rule:[41] it is the last link in the chain – the point where the chain of rules comes to an end. It is in this sense that the rule of recognition is 'ultimate': it provides the ultimate criteria of validity, the final basis for the identification of other rules in the system. It follows from this analysis that the rule of recognition, since it is not identified by the criteria in a further rule, is not itself a 'valid' legal rule.[42] But this does not mean that it is an 'invalid' legal rule: the concept of 'validity' is simply inapplicable to the ultimate rule in the system:

> We only need the word 'validity', and commonly only use it, to answer questions which arise *within* a system of rules where the status of a rule as a member of the system depends on its satisfying certain criteria provided by the rule of recognition. No such question can arise as to the validity of the very rule of recognition which provides the criteria; it can neither be valid nor invalid but is simply accepted as appropriate for use in this way.[43]

Hart claims it is a mistake to think, as others have, that the ultimate rule in a system is itself valid, since this mischaracterises the nature of the rule of recognition.[44] When someone makes a statement about the validity of a legal rule they are normally presupposing two background conditions: (a) that the rule is identified by the rule of recognition; and (b) that the rule of recognition is generally accepted and employed in the system.[45] Whether or not (b) is true is a matter of fact, that is, of the actual practice in the system.[46]

Hart caps his discussion of the rule of recognition by considering how it should be classified: is it part of the law?[47] In a sense it is, since it provides the criteria for the identification of the other rules of the system. On the other hand it is not a rule on the same 'level' as the legal rules it identifies, such as those found in statutes and precedents. Their existence (as valid legal rules) depends upon the existence of the rule of recognition, but its existence consists in an actual practice, and is a matter of fact. So:

> The case for calling the rule of recognition 'law' is that the rule providing criteria for the identification of other rules of the system may well be thought a defining

[41] ibid 107.
[42] ibid 107, 109.
[43] ibid 108f.
[44] ibid 108–10.
[45] ibid 108.
[46] ibid 109f.
[47] ibid 111f.

feature of a legal system, and so itself worth calling 'law'; the case for calling it 'fact' is that to assert that such a rule exists is indeed to make an external statement of an actual fact concerning the manner in which the rules of an 'efficacious' system are identified. Both these aspects claim attention but we cannot do justice to them both by choosing one of the labels 'law' or 'fact'. Instead, we need to remember that the ultimate rule of recognition may be regarded from two points of view: one is expressed in the external statement of fact that the rule exists in the actual practice of the system; the other is expressed in the internal statements of validity made by those who use it in identifying the law.[48]

So the rule of recognition can be regarded as a 'legal' rule, but not in the same sense as valid legal rules. It is *sui generis* in being ultimate and being a matter of fact.

C. Efficacy

The rule of recognition also helps, Hart argues, to explain the relationship between validity and efficacy. Briefly put, a particular rule's legal validity does not depend upon whether or not *it* is generally obeyed, unless the rule of recognition in that system requires obedience as a criterion of validity (eg through something like the doctrine of desuetude).[49] On the other hand, the ordinary context in which internal statements of law are made is one where the system *as a whole* is generally effective. It is a normal presupposition of assertions about the validity of law that the system as a whole is in force.[50] But it is not meaningless or senseless to assert the validity of a rule that belongs to a system that is not in force. A person can make assertions *as if* the system was in force even when it is not, eg as a pedagogic exercise (teaching Roman Law) or as an ideological act (evincing loyalty to an overthrown regime).[51]

This distinction also throws light on the idea that to say that a rule is legally valid is simply to say (or predict) that officials will act on it.[52] Such a view oversimplifies what is going on. Statements of validity are not equivalent to predictions that officials will act on a rule: instead, they indicate that the rule satisfies the tests for identification in the rule of recognition. This is most obvious if the judicial point of view is considered: for a judge to say that a rule is legally valid is not to *predict* her own conduct, but to provide a *reason* for her decision.[53] There is an important relationship between validity and official action, but it is more indirect than the predictive view allows. Given a functioning legal

[48] ibid.
[49] ibid 103.
[50] ibid 103f.
[51] ibid 104.
[52] ibid 104f.
[53] ibid 105.

system where officials accept and follow the rule of recognition, it will generally be the case that rules identified by the rule of recognition will be applied. Thus there will normally be a strong correlation between validity and enforcement. But this does not mean that assertions of validity simply amount to predictions of application.

On the other hand, one of the things that the introduction of the rule of recognition does is to create a new sense in which rules can 'exist'.[54] Social rules, as explained above, exist when they are actually followed and accepted. But valid rules 'exist' when they satisfy the criteria for identification provided by the rule of recognition, whether or not they are generally followed or accepted (unless the criteria for identification include being followed).

The points about sources, validity and efficacy add to the earlier summary the following:

(1*) The function of the rule of recognition is to provide criteria (often general criteria) for the authoritative identification of the (primary) rules of the system. It can use more than one criterion for the identification of the rules of the system, and each criterion constitutes a 'source' of law. If it uses more than one criterion, it may also provide rules for resolving conflicts between rules from different sources.

(2*) The rule of recognition is a secondary, or second-order rule: it is a rule about the (primary) rules in a legal system, and is on a different 'level' from those primary rules.

(3*) The rule of recognition is a social rule that is accepted and practised.

(4) Rules that are identified by the criteria provided by the rule of recognition (or that are identified by the criteria in a rule that is identified by the rule of recognition, and so on) are 'valid' legal rules.

(5) The legal validity of a rule consists in it being a rule (that is, a member) of the system in question.

(6) Valid legal rules 'exist' in the sense that they satisfy the criteria for identification as members of the system. Individual legal rules need not be obeyed (or practised) in order to exist (unless the criteria for identification require this), so long as the system to which they belong is generally efficacious.

It follows from this analysis that:

(7) the rule of recognition is not itself a 'valid' legal rule. Its existence does not depend upon satisfying criteria in another rule but consists instead in its actual use and acceptance (3* above);

(8) the rule of recognition is the ultimate rule in a legal system, as it is the rule containing the ultimate criteria of validity in a legal system;

---

[54] ibid 109f.

(9) the rule of recognition is a 'legal' rule in the sense that it provides the ultimate criteria for the identification of rules as legal rules, but in other respects is a matter of fact.

Finally:

(10) A legal system consists of a rule of recognition and all of the rules identified by it (and the rules identified by rules that are themselves identified by the rule of recognition, and so on), that is, all the rules that trace their validity back to the rule of recognition.
(11) A legal system exists when the rule of recognition is accepted and followed and the rules identified by it (etc) are sufficiently effective.

To this already complex conception, Hart adds one final complication.[55] In a simple society the rule of recognition might be followed and accepted by the population as a whole. But in a modern state this is not the case. In a modern state many, perhaps most, non-officials will be ignorant of the content of the rule of recognition, and may simply follow the rules that are part of the law. They may also 'accept' those rules (including the rule of recognition), that is, have the internal point of view towards them, but it is enough if they follow the rules, eg out of fear of sanctions, whether or not they accept them.[56] Officials, on the other hand, *must* follow and accept the rule of recognition.[57] The 'characteristic unity and continuity of a legal system' depends on official acceptance of 'common standards of legal validity'.[58] A legal system requires that:

> its rules of recognition specifying the criteria of legal validity and its rules of change and adjudication must be effectively accepted as common public standards of official behaviour by its officials. . . . They must regard these as common standards of official behaviour and appraise critically their own and each other's deviations as lapses.[59]

So in the case of a modern state, the 'minimum conditions necessary and sufficient for the existence of a legal system' are that officials must accept the rule of recognition as a common standard of official behaviour, while non-officials need only follow the rules that are identified by the rule of recognition (though they may also 'accept' those rules and the rule of recognition).[60] So to the summary above must be added:

---

[55] ibid 112–17 (foreshadowed at 60f).
[56] ibid 114.
[57] ibid 115–17.
[58] ibid 116.
[59] ibid 116f.
[60] ibid 116.

(12) Officials must follow and accept the rule of recognition, whereas non-officials need only follow the rules identified by the rule of recognition (though they may also accept these and the rule of recognition).

II. QUESTIONS

There are a number of well-known criticisms of the rule of recognition, in particular: (1) whether it must be accepted for moral, rather than other, reasons;[61] (2) whether it can accommodate the existence of legal 'principles';[62] and (3) whether legal practice exhibits the type of convergent behaviour necessary for the rule of recognition to exist.[63] But in this paper I want to focus on a number of interrelated questions about the adequacy of Hart's account on its own terms: (a) whose rule is the rule of recognition? (b) who are 'officials'? (c) Hart's account of validity; (d) the normative character and function(s) of the rule of recognition; and (e) the status of the ultimate criteria of validity.

A. Whose Rule is the Rule of Recognition?

Whose actions and beliefs constitute the rule of recognition? In a simple society it is clearly the actions and beliefs of the population generally. But in a modern legal system, where there is a differentiation in the roles of officials and non-officials, what is the position? Hart argues that the *minimum* conditions for the existence of a legal system involve officials alone accepting the rule of recognition, but what is the situation where non-officials also accept it, as Hart recognises will sometimes be the case?[64] Does the acceptance by non-officials turn the rule of recognition from a social rule of the officials into a general social rule? This is an important question for the existence conditions

---

[61] See J Finnis, *Natural Law and Natural Rights*, 2nd edn (Oxford, Oxford University Press, 2011), ch I (esp 11–18), A Duff, 'Legal Obligation and the Moral Nature of Law' (1980) 25 *Juridical Review* 61–73, 79–87. An alternative view is that the rule of recognition should be understood as a conventional rule: GJ Postema, 'Coordination and Convention at the Foundations of Law' (1982) 11 *Journal of Legal Studies* 165. For criticism see L Green, 'Positivism and Conventionalism' (1999) 12 *Canadian Journal of Law and Jurisprudence* 35.

[62] The stepping-off point is Ronald Dworkin's 'Model of Rules I' in his *Taking Rights Seriously* (n 31), to which Hart responds, in the Postscript, in *The Concept of Law* (n 1) 250–54, 259–68. See also WJ Waluchow, *Inclusive Legal Positivism* (Oxford, Clarendon Press, 1994) and J Coleman, *The Practice of Principle. In Defence of a Pragmatist Approach to Legal Theory* (Oxford, Oxford University Press, 2001). For a different approach to both Hart and Dworkin see J Raz, 'Authority, Law, and Morality' in his *Ethics in the Public Domain* (Oxford, Oxford University Press, 1994).

[63] R Dworkin, *Law's Empire* (Cambridge, Mass, Harvard University Press 1986). For discussion, see SJ Shapiro, 'The Hart-Dworkin Debate: A Short Guide for the Perplexed' in A Ripstein (ed), *Ronald Dworkin* (Cambridge, Cambridge University Press, 2007).

[64] *The Concept of Law* (n 1) 116f.

of the rule of recognition, and also for understanding its possible functions.[65] To answer this question, it is necessary to consider the application of social rules in more detail than Hart did.

When Hart introduces the idea of a social rule, he envisages a situation in which the standard of behaviour which is generally accepted by a social group is also generally practised by the members of the group.[66] But some general social rules are more specialised than this, in that they only apply to a subgroup within society, eg to parents, or males, or students. In these cases, so long as the members of society generally take the internal point of view towards the standard (by regarding it as a standard of behaviour, criticising deviations from it, demanding conformity to it, and using 'normative' terminology), it can still be a social rule of the society as a whole. In other cases, however, a social rule that is applicable to a sub-group within society is a rule of that sub-group alone, for example a social rule of those who subscribe to a particular religion, or practise a particular profession, or participate in particular pastimes.

What distinguishes a general social rule that applies to a sub-group from a social rule that is simply a rule of a sub-group? As a first approximation, it might be said that the rules that apply, for example, to parents, are general social rules because they apply to parents as members of society, whereas the rules that apply to the religious are rules of the sub-group alone because they apply to them as members of the religion in question. Why lies behind this contrast? In essence, it seems to turn on the views of the rule-subjects (those to whom the rule applies). Parents accept the relevance of the views of other members of society (including non-parents) to the expectations that are placed on them as parents. Members of a particular religion, by contrast, generally do not regard the views of non-believers as relevant to what they should do *qua* members of that religion. This is not because non-believers cannot have views about religious practice – they sometimes do – but because the views of non-believers are not regarded as relevant in determining what the religious practice requires.[67]

Now the rule of recognition is the rule that identifies rules as legal rules. In modern legal systems it seems to be a rule constituted by the practices of officials, since it is the rules identified by official practice that amount to legal rules. Non-officials can of course identify rules using the same criteria as officials use, but if there is a divergence between official and non-official practice, it would normally be thought that it was the official practice that was determinative of

---

[65] See section II.D below.
[66] *The Concept of Law* (n 1) 55–57.
[67] These alternatives are not mutually exclusive: there can be a conflict between a widely accepted and practised social rule and a contrary social rule accepted and practised by a subgroup. But this complication may be ignored here.

which rules were legal rules, and thus of the content of the rule of recognition. Still, non-officials *can* have the internal point of view towards the rule of recognition, that is, they can regard it as a standard of official behaviour, criticise official deviations from that standard, and demand that officials comply with it. So the rule of recognition *could* be a general social rule even if it applied only to officials. The crucial question is: do the views of non-officials count for officials, that is, are they regarded by officials as partly determinative of which criteria should be used by officials in identifying legal rules? If they are, then the rule of recognition is a general social rule. If not, it is a social rule of officials. This is a contingent question, and different legal systems could answer it in different ways. But in contemporary systems it would seem that the views of non-officials are not usually regarded by officials as partly determinative of what the criteria of recognition are in those systems. Instead, the rule of recognition is constituted exclusively by the practices and the beliefs of officials in these systems, and are social rules of officials.[68]

So the distinction that Hart draws between official and non-official roles in the law does not mark a difference in their contributions to the rule of recognition, at least in a typical modern system. What they mark is a difference in their contributions to the existence of a legal system. As Hart notes, what must be followed by non-officials are the rules of the system, that is, the rules identified by the rule of recognition. Many non-officials may also accept these rules, that is, they will not simply do as the rules require, but will have the internal point of view towards those rules in guiding themselves and criticising deviations by others, etc. What these non-officials accept, then, is the law, that is the body of standards that make up the law. Since the rule of recognition is what identifies the law, it might also be said that those non-officials also implicitly accept the rule of recognition. And some non-officials (such as lawyers) may know of the criteria of validity and explicitly accept the rule of recognition. But in neither case does non-official acceptance of the rule of recognition constitute part of the existence conditions of the rule of recognition (at least in a typical modern system). It is a social rule of the officials alone.

B. Who Is an 'Official'?

Hart never explains what makes someone an 'official' within a legal system, despite the fact that the distinction between officials and non-officials is invoked frequently through the text. Instead, Hart works with an intuitive

---

[68] One small exception to this is that officials may give consideration to the views of certain legal experts who are regarded as theoretical authorities on the criteria of recognition.

understanding of the distinction on the part of his readers. Officials are said to include tax inspectors,[69] ministers,[70] county councils,[71] the police,[72] judges,[73] courts,[74] and legislators.[75] He sometimes refers to courts (or judges) *and/or* officials,[76] and to courts, legislatures *and* officials,[77] which might suggest officials do not include courts or legislatures, but at other points he speaks of courts and/or *other* officials,[78] and in chapter IV refers to 'the officials of the system, and above all the courts'.[79] It is reasonably clear that Hart regards the officials of the system as including the courts and legislators, but extending beyond them to those like the police who enforce the law. The closest Hart comes to a general statement is in chapter II, when he is discussing the variety of laws, and considers:

> a further class of laws which also confer legal powers but, in contrast to those just discussed, the powers are of a public or official rather than a private nature. Examples of these are to be found in all the three departments, judicial, legislative, and administrative, into which government is customarily though vaguely divided.[80]

'Officials' seem to be identified with the state (or the 'government'), that is, with the bodies exercising public powers in a community. But Hart does not elaborate on these ideas.

Given the importance of 'officials' to Hart's conception of law and legal systems, it is a significant omission that he says so little about them. In his later work Hart followed the 'judicial' drift of his successors, associating the rule of recognition with the practices of judges rather than officials generally.[81] The thought here is that ultimately it is the practices of the judges that determine the criteria of validity of the rules of the system. Other officials must use the rules that the judicial practice identifies, but their practices are not constitutive of those criteria. And since judges constitute such a small sub-category of officials, the issue of their characterisation seems far more tractable.[82] Whatever the

---

[69] *The Concept of Law* (n 1) 21.
[70] ibid 25.
[71] ibid.
[72] ibid 38, 61.
[73] ibid 25.
[74] ibid 36, 39, 60, 61, 65, 122.
[75] ibid 61, 122.
[76] ibid 10, 67, 108, 110, 135, 286, 293.
[77] ibid 91, 106, 202.
[78] ibid 101, 114, 136, 137, 138.
[79] ibid 65.
[80] ibid 28f.
[81] The term 'official' does not appear at all in the Postscript, and the rule of recognition is consistently attributed to the practices of the courts or judges (ibid 250, 256, 258, 259, 263, 266, 266f, 267). See similarly HLA Hart, *Essays on Bentham* (Oxford, Oxford University Press, 1982) 155f, 160f.
[82] See eg Raz, *The Authority of Law* (n 24) 105–11; N MacCormick, *H.L.A. Hart* (n 24) 136–52.

appropriate analysis is, however, it is worth emphasising that the answer will not be given simply by a legal system's *own* characterisations of 'judges'. That may be relevant, but in the end what is needed is a characterisation of the role of certain individuals or bodies in the system that make their functions 'judicial'.

But even allowing for these points, there is still something to be said in favour of the rule of recognition being a social rule of the broader category of officials, both judicial and non-judicial, in light of the discussion of acceptance above (section II.A). It may be true that the criteria of recognition are constituted by the practices of the judiciary, but that does not dispose of the question of whose rule it is. It seems quite plausible that other officials have the internal point of view regarding the rule of recognition, regarding it as the correct standard of official (including judicial) behaviour, criticising deviations from it by officials, including the judiciary, and demanding that it be complied with by all officials, again including the judiciary. Hart himself discusses, in the third section of chapter VI, the situation where there is a breakdown in official unity over the content of the rule of recognition, including cases where the courts are pitted against other officials.[83] Unlike non-officials, whose views are not regarded as crucial to the rule of recognition itself, the views of other officials, particularly high officials in the legislature and executive, on the criteria in the rule of recognition do not seem to be ignored, but to be regarded as relevant. This is particularly the case in systems where judges can be removed from office by legislative or executive action. It would be one thing for a judge to come to a controversial or contentious decision on existing law, quite another for a judge or court to flout the rule of recognition.

C. Hart's Account of Validity

Hart claims that for a rule to be legally 'valid' it must satisfy some criterion in the rule of recognition (or some criterion in a rule that itself satisfies a criterion in the rule of recognition, and so on). To be a legally 'valid' rule is to be a member of the legal system. But this seems problematic on two counts. First of all, it is not clear that all legally valid rules are rules of a system. Secondly, the primary use of 'validity' is arguably to indicate that a law is legally effective, that is, that it has the normative force in the law that corresponds to its normative character (as duty-imposing, or power-conferring, or constitutive, etc).[84]

On the first point, Hart's account entails that every legally valid rule is, *ipso facto*, a rule of the system. But this overlooks the existence of legally valid rules that would not ordinarily be regarded as rules of the system, such as those

---

[83] *The Concept of Law* (n 1) 122f, discussing the 1954 South African constitutional dispute.
[84] J Raz, 'Legal Validity' in *The Authority of Law* (n 24).

foreign rules recognised and enforced under the doctrines of conflicts of laws. A contract or a marriage concluded under a foreign legal system may be recognised and enforced in domestic law even though such a contract or marriage would not be valid if concluded under domestic law. Such foreign arrangements are legally valid under domestic law, but are not, on any ordinary understanding, rules of the system.[85]

The second point helps to make sense of the first. The language of validity is ordinarily used – at least in common law jurisdictions – to make three types of claim about a legal rule: (i) that it is legally effective (has legal force); (ii) that it is a member of this legal system (a valid rule *of* English law); and (iii) that it is valid*ated* by another law (valid under the relevant primary legislation, not *ultra vires*).[86] There is an important relationship between the three, inasmuch as the standard explanation for why a rule has legal force is that it is a member of the system in question, and the most common basis for a rule being a member of the system is that it is validated by another rule of the system. Validation gives rise to membership, and membership qualifies a rule for normative force. But it is the normative force of rules – their legal effect – that is fundamentally associated with 'validity'.

Hart's focus, by contrast, is almost exclusively on membership and validation. Indeed, he makes the relationship between membership and validation axiomatic: to be a member of the system is to be validated by another rule.[87] And instead of the normative force of legal rules, Hart is preoccupied with the question of how a legal rule can 'exist'. In particular, he is concerned to show that the existence of legal rules does not boil down to either the risk of official action nor to their having some elusive non-empirical status.[88] Instead, for a rule to be 'valid' is simply for it to satisfy the criteria for membership in a system of rules, that is, that it is a rule belonging to that system.

In developing his views on validity, Hart explicitly distinguishes it from an account in terms of the prediction of official action, such as might be derived from Austin's views.[89] But he is equally concerned to distance it from Kelsen's account of validity. Kelsen's significance for Hart is clear from the many references to Kelsen in the endnotes to *The Concept of Law*, particularly the endnotes to chapter VI,[90] and validity is one of Kelsen's central theoretical

---

[85] ibid 146–50. Nor is it obvious that every rule of the system is *ipso facto* legally valid: statutes that are 'struck down' on constitutional grounds may be held to be 'invalid', but such a judicial declaration does not repeal the statute, which remains 'on the books'.

[86] See JW Harris, *Law and Legal Science. An Inquiry into the Concepts* Legal Rule *and* Legal System (Oxford, Clarendon Press, 1979) 107–31.

[87] *The Concept of Law* (n 1) 103.

[88] ibid 8–12, 103–05, 109f.

[89] ibid 104f.

[90] Although Kelsen is not mentioned by name in the text of chapter VI, he is discussed on every page of the chapter's endnotes: ibid 292–97.

concerns.[91] For Kelsen, if a rule of law is valid, then it is a valid norm. To say that a norm is valid is to say that it exists and that it ought to be obeyed.[92] The validity of a norm depends upon various empirical facts (eg whether it was created by certain acts, whether the system to which it belongs is efficacious), but is not itself a matter of empirical fact. Norms stipulate what ought to be done, not what is in fact done, nor what someone wants done. Norms are irreducible to empirical facts. For Kelsen, law is a coercive social order, a system of rules for human behaviour. But the law is also conceived of as a system of norms, that is, as binding requirements on action, and to attribute validity to a legal norm is to attribute this binding quality to it.

Hart, by contrast, emphasises that to attribute validity to a rule is simply to recognise that it is a member of a legal system, due to satisfying the criteria for membership. As a result, Hart says very little about the normative significance of legal validity. Instead, the focus of his thinking about the normative force of legal rules seems to lie in the rule of recognition, and it is to this that I will now turn.

D. The Normative Character and Function(s) of the Rule of Recognition

I noted in the discussion of the rule of recognition as a 'secondary' rule that Hart refrains from describing it as a power-conferring rule, despite the claims at the start of chapter V that secondary rules do confer powers. And in chapter VI, when discussing the minimum conditions for the existence of a legal system, he states that:

> If only some judges acted 'for their part only' on the footing that what the Queen in Parliament enacts is law, and made no criticisms of those who did not respect this rule of recognition, the characteristic unity and continuity of a legal system would have disappeared. For this depends on the acceptance, at this crucial point, of common standards of legal validity.[93]

What exactly is the normative character and function of the rule of recognition? Hart says that it 'identifies' rules as legal rules. Of course the language of 'recognition' and 'identification' is not entirely apt: what the rule of recognition does is to *constitute* the rules as rules of the system, that is, it *makes* them rules of the system. Its function is not simply epistemological, as if it were the

---

[91] H Kelsen, *General Theory of Law and State*, A Wedberg (trans) (Cambridge, Mass, Harvard University Press, 1945) 29–44. By contrast, Austin barely mentions validity at all.
[92] ibid 30.
[93] *The Concept of Law* (n 1) 116.

approved guide for knowing which rules were legal rules.[94] Instead, it confers on the rules their *status* as legal rules.[95]

This might suggest that the rule of recognition is purely a constitutive rule: it determines what is to count as a rule of the legal system, but nothing more. Whatever further significance the rule of recognition may have lies in its relationship to other rules, which make use of it or rely on it. Although this is a possible understanding of the rule of recognition,[96] it does not accord with what Hart says about the rule of recognition, in particular on its acceptance as a common public standard for official behaviour.[97] This suggests that the rule of recognition is a duty-imposing rule: it not only provides the criteria for the identification of the rules of the system but imposes a duty on officials to use those criteria in identifying the laws of the system.

But even if there is such a duty to use the rule of recognition in identifying rules, what of the rules that it identifies? These 'primary' rules are members of the system, and it seems are to be applied and followed by officials and non-officials. But what explains this use of the primary rules of the system? It might be thought that the answer to this question lies simply in the nature of the primary rules themselves: if they are duty-imposing rules then there is a duty to apply them. But there are two difficulties with this thought. The first is that not all primary rules *are* duty-imposing: some, like the rules on contract formation, are power-conferring. Secondly, that a rule is a 'valid' legal rule means, for Hart, simply that it is a member of a system of rules identified by the rule of recognition. Their membership in the system does not, in itself, explain their use by officials and non-officials. So what does explain their use? Is it the rule of recognition that directs the use of the rules it identifies? Or is the requirement to use them imposed in some other way?

Hart never clearly addresses this question in *The Concept of Law*,[98] but in later work he expressly embraced the view that the rule of recognition itself imposes a duty to follow and apply the rules that it identifies.[99] And this is consistent

---

[94] Though the way that Hart introduces the rule of recognition, in terms of addressing the *uncertainty* whether a rule is a primary rule, suggests a primarily evidentiary function: ibid 92, 94f.
[95] *The Concept of Law* (n 1) 101, 109, 110, 111.
[96] See A Marmor, *Social Conventions: From Language to Law* (Princeton, Princeton University Press, 2009) ch 7.
[97] *The Concept of Law* (n 1) 116 (and, generally, 115–17).
[98] The closest he comes to an explicit statement is in chapter X, in the course of discussing the idea that the rules of public international law form a set, rather than a system: 'In the simpler case we cannot ask: 'From what ultimate provision of the system do the separate rules derive their validity or "binding force"?': ibid 235. But this is in a context where he is discussing both the rule of recognition and Kelsen's basic norm, so it is unclear how much weight to attach to it.
[99] HLA Hart, 'Legal Duty and Obligation', in his *Essays on Bentham* (n 81) 155f, 160f: 'Rules of recognition accepted in the practice of the judges require them to apply the laws identified by the criteria which they provide and of course the laws so identified are the same as those which impose duties and confer rights on individuals' (ibid 156). Some early commentators on *The Concept of Law* had also taken this view: J Raz, *The Concept of a Legal System*, 2nd edn (Oxford, Oxford, Clarendon

with Hart's ambitions for the rule of recognition as a replacement for Austin's sovereign.[100] The sovereign provides the 'foundations of a legal system' because it accounts for three central features of a legal system. In the first place it explains what makes a law *part* (that is, a member) of the legal system – because it is the sovereign's command. Secondly, the sovereign explains the *unity* of a legal system: the laws form a single system because all of them are the commands of *this* sovereign. Finally, the sovereign accounts for the existence of the legal system: the system exists because there is a habit of obedience to the sovereign and its commands. For Hart, by contrast, it is the rule of recognition that accounts for membership, unity and existence: a rule is a rule of the system if it is identified by the rule of recognition; a system is distinct from other systems because all of its rules trace their membership back to its own rule of recognition;[101] and a system exists where the rule of recognition is practised and accepted, and thus the rules are generally followed.

But if this *is* Hart's conception of the rule of recognition, there is a crucial point of divergence between him and Austin. For Austin, a legal system exists where the bulk of the population has a general habit of obedience towards the sovereign and its commands. For Hart, a legal system exists where there is a social rule (the rule of recognition) that imposes a duty to follow the rules it identifies. The rule of recognition is substituted for the sovereign in accounting for the force of legal rules. Now if the rule of recognition is a social rule of the society as a whole, this parallel with Austin is complete: there is a general social obligation imposed by the rule of recognition to follow legal rules (that is, the rules identified by the rule of recognition). The normative force of legal rules would be derived from the normative force of the rule of recognition itself. To have a *legal* obligation would be to have a social obligation imposed by the rule of recognition to follow the rules it identifies.

But if, as argued in section II.A above, the rule of recognition in a modern legal system is typically a social rule of the officials alone, rather than the community as a whole, then it can only impose a duty on officials to follow and apply the rules it identifies. On Hart's conception of a social rule, the rule of a sub-group cannot create duties for the group as a whole. Non-officials can, of course, accept that they ought to follow legal rules (and that officials and non-

---

Press, 1980 [1970]) 197–200; *Practical Reason and Norms* (n 31) 146f; *The Authority of Law* (n 24) 93; PMS Hacker, 'Hart's Philosophy of Law' (n 24) 23; N MacCormick, *H.L.A. Hart*, 1st edn (London, Edward Arnold, 1981) 109; and it is now a common interpretation of the rule of recognition: see J Gardner, 'Can There Be a Written Constitution?' in his *Law as a Leap of Faith* (Oxford, Oxford University Press, 2013) 103f; L Green, 'Introduction' to *The Concept of Law* (n 1) xxiii. For some alternative views, see S Munzer, *Legal Validity* (The Hague, Martinus Nijhoff, 1972) 50–56; MD Bayles, *Hart's Legal Philosophy* (Dordrecht, Kluwer, 1992) 65–67; MH Kramer, *Where Law and Morality Meet* (Oxford, Oxford University Press, 2004) 104f, 110–14.

[100] *The Concept of Law* (n 1) 100.

[101] See ibid 92, 95 and 233–36 for Hart's comments on the difference between a 'set' of standards and a 'system'.

officials ought to follow the rule of recognition), but this would amount at most to a *separate* social rule that the law ought to be obeyed – that is, it would create a social obligation to obey the law, not a legal obligation to do so. A legal obligation, on this conception, is one imposed *by* the rule of recognition itself, and the rule of recognition is a social rule of the officials.

So the parallel with Austin's sovereign is incomplete. The rule of recognition in a typical modern system is a social rule of officials alone. At best it can account for the obligation for officials to follow and apply the law. Yet as Hart himself emphasised in chapter III of *The Concept of Law* in criticising Kelsen's theory, most of the law is primarily directed to non-officials, and much of it imposes legal duties on them, whether or not they accept the law.[102] This conception of the role of the rule of recognition leaves the application of the law to non-officials unanswered.

E. The Status of the Ultimate Criteria of Validity

Hart regards the rule of recognition as containing the ultimate criteria of validity in a legal system. His most common example in chapter VI is: 'what the Queen in Parliament enacts is law'.[103] The legal authority of parliamentary legislation in England does not rest on some further legal basis: there is no written constitution or other source of its authority. The same is true of precedent: the legal authority of the decisions of courts does not rest on legislation or any alternative source. So the rule of recognition in England would identify both enactments of Parliament and decisions of superior courts as (sources of) law.

Hart's conception of the rule of recognition is deeply influenced by Kelsen's basic norm.[104] Indeed, one of the book's longest endnotes is devoted to discussing the differences between the rule of recognition and the basic norm.[105] As noted above, Kelsen argued that the law is understood as a system of valid norms. For Kelsen, a norm can only be valid if its creation is authorised by another valid norm. This led to a conceptual conundrum: validity could be traced back through other norms; for example, an ordinance could be validly created according to secondary legislation, which had been appropriately created according to primary legislation, which had been enacted according to the Constitution. The Constitution itself might be the successor to earlier Constitutions which had been amended according to their terms. But sooner or later one must reach a Constitution – the historically first Constitution – whose validity does not rest on some authorisation, but was the result of a

---

[102] ibid 35–40 and 286 (criticising Kelsen's *General Theory of Law and State* (n 91) 58–63).
[103] *The Concept of Law* (n 1) 102, 107, 111, 115, 116, 120, 293 (and see also 145, 148).
[104] Kelsen, *General Theory of Law and State* (n 91) 110–23.
[105] *The Concept of Law* (n 1) 292f.

revolution or some similarly non-lawful act.[106] How can the historically first Constitution amount to a valid norm, given that *its* creation was not authorised by another valid norm? Kelsen's solution to this conundrum was that the legal order understood as a system of valid norms rests on the postulate, or presupposition, of the basic norm – a norm directing that the historically first Constitution (or those who created it) ought to be obeyed.[107] The intelligibility of the law as a system of valid norms rests on the presupposition of the basic norm, since without the presupposition the laws of the system could not constitute valid norms. For Kelsen, the basic norm was not an actual belief held by anyone, but a presupposition necessary for the coherence of the conception of law as a system of valid norms.

Hart's analysis creates the same regress problem, since a valid rule must be identified by the criteria in another rule. But his solution to the conundrum is different. Rather than arguing that the rule specifying the ultimate criteria of validity is itself valid, Hart argues that it is simply accepted, and is neither valid nor invalid. So the officials in England accept that what the Queen in Parliament enacts is law. The rule containing this criterion for the identification of the rules of the system (that is, the rule of recognition) is not a 'valid' law; instead it is the ultimate basis for legal validity.

From a common law perspective, however, this analysis is somewhat puzzling. That precedents of superior courts and parliamentary legislation are sources of law is a fundamental feature of the system of law in England. But it would normally be thought that both rest on legal doctrines – the doctrine of precedent and the doctrine of the sovereignty of Parliament – and that both of these are *legally* binding doctrines. They are ultimate doctrines, of course, because they are neither grounded in case law nor legislation: cases only create law because of the doctrine of precedent, and legislation only creates law because of the doctrine of parliamentary sovereignty. As Hart rightly observes:

> Even if it [sc. what the Queen in Parliament enacts is law] were enacted by statute, this would not reduce it to the level of a statute; for the legal status of such an enactment necessarily would depend on the fact that the rule existed antecedently to and independently of the enactment.[108]

But none of this rules out the possibility that the doctrine of parliamentary sovereignty and the doctrine of precedent amount to *customary* law. Bentham drew the useful distinction between custom *in foro* and custom *in pays*, that is, customary law of the officials themselves and customary law of the general community.[109] The doctrines of parliamentary sovereignty and precedent

---

[106] *General Theory of Law and State* (n 91) 115.
[107] ibid.
[108] *The Concept of Law* (n 1) 111.
[109] J Bentham, *A Comment on the Commentaries and a Fragment on Government*, JH Burns and HLA Hart eds (London, The Athlone Press, 1977) 182–84.

would belong to the first class, custom *in foro*. The only customary law that Hart discusses in *The Concept of Law* belongs to the second class, that is, customs of the general community that the law recognises as binding.[110] In his later Postscript to *The Concept of Law* Hart describes the rule of recognition as a 'a form of judicial customary rule'[111] but this overlooks the possibility that it is not just a judicial custom but constitutes a binding legal rule.

Does any of this matter, however? If the rule of recognition is a custom of officials (or judges) that they regard as binding and that they use to identify other rules of the system, does it really matter whether it is described as 'legally' binding or described as 'a law' (or even a 'valid' law) of the system? Hart himself allows, after all, that the rule of recognition can be seen from one perspective as part of the law.[112] What difference could it make if it were a law rather than just a judicial custom? The reason it matters has to do with the status and nature of the ultimate criteria of validity.

If the doctrine of precedent and the doctrine of parliamentary sovereignty are customary laws of the English legal system, that would explain why their content seems to be subject to deliberate legal change. Hart notes this in chapter VII, when he discusses uncertainty in the rule of recognition.[113] As he observes, it is not self-evident whether Parliament can bind its successors, and if so, how.[114] But he acknowledges that the doctrine of parliamentary sovereignty does seem to be amenable to deliberate legal change by both legislation and precedent. Similarly, the doctrine of precedent is subject to deliberate change, even by judicial decision itself (rather than the superior source of legislation).[115] The extent to which such changes are possible, and how, is regarded by officials as itself a question of law. But if the rule of recognition, containing the ultimate criteria of validity, is simply a social rule, it cannot, according to Hart's analysis of social rules, be amenable to such deliberate change. Perhaps the rule of recognition is a different sort of social rule which *is* subject to such alteration, but if so, Hart does not explain how.[116]

---

[110] *The Concept of Law* (n 1) 44–48, 100, 101.
[111] ibid 256.
[112] ibid 111f.
[113] ibid 147–54.
[114] ibid 148–52.
[115] Indeed in theory the doctrine of precedent could be abolished by statute.
[116] Could it be argued that the rule of recognition simply directs officials to follow and apply the ultimate criteria of validity (eg 'the doctrine of Parliamentary sovereignty'), and thus the *content* of the ultimate criteria may be altered by the rule of change? But then the rule of recognition becomes a rule *beyond* the ultimate criteria, parallel to Kelsen's basic norm, directing that the ultimate criteria (and the rules they validate) are to be followed and applied. The ultimate criteria of validity (eg 'what the Queen in Parliament enacts is law') would no longer be ultimate, since they would be identified by the rule of recognition. Hart expressly rejects this view at *The Concept of Law* (n 1) 293. If it is embraced, the question becomes whether the rule of recognition is needed (see below).

That the ultimate criteria of validity are customary law would also dispel the curiosity in the idea that the rules of recognition, change and adjudication are 'second-order' rules, on a different 'level' from primary rules of the system. There seems no reason why the rule(s) of change cannot be identified by the ultimate criteria of validity, for example that the rules governing legislating and judicial decision making cannot be 'ordinary' (primary) rules of the system.[117] So, too, the rules of adjudication, governing the effect of judicial decisions and the procedures for the enforcement of judgments. There is no *a priori* reason why the rules of recognition, change and adjudication cannot simply stand in an interdependent relationship to each other, and to the other laws of the system.

The status of the ultimate criteria of validity also bears on the question of official 'acceptance'. According to Hart's later view, the rule of recognition imposes a duty to follow the ultimate criteria of validity and the rules identified by them. It is the acceptance of the rule of recognition that generates official use and application of legal rules. But if we return to the idea that the ultimate criteria of validity are purely constitutive legal rules, 'identifying' other rules as rules of the system, alternative possibilities become available. One possibility is that what officials 'accept' is not the rule of recognition, but the legal system, that is, the system of rules of a particular jurisdiction. Judicial oaths, for example, standardly involve an undertaking to uphold the laws of the system, and it is often thought that the fundamental judicial and official responsibility is to obey and apply the law. On this approach, instead of the laws of the system being followed because the rule of recognition is accepted, the ultimate criteria of validity are followed because they are (customary) legal rules *of* the system, and it is the system that is accepted.

This alternative to Hart, of course, presupposes a satisfactory account of customary law *in foro*. This is a relatively unexplored branch of municipal law.[118] But one way in which Hart's analysis of the rule of recognition could be understood is as a contribution to such an account. One thing that distinguishes customary legal rules *in foro* from other (validated) legal rules is that their existence depends upon the rules being practised. It is a condition of their existence that they are practised. On the other hand, the grounds for their status as part of the law lies in their role in validating other legal rules.[119]

---

[117] Though they need not be: the rules governing Parliamentary procedures (and thus enactment) in England, for example, may only be subject to the jurisdiction of Parliament.

[118] Nor is customary international law a particularly close analogy, since it rests on state practice, not the practice of international adjudicative institutions.

[119] As Hart, in a sense, acknowledges: *The Concept of Law* (n 1) 111. I discuss this possibility in 'Legal Sources, the Rule of Recognition, and Customary Law' (2013), unpublished manuscript, on file with author.

III. CONCLUSION

The preceding criticisms raise some doubts about the idea that the rule of recognition provides the foundations of a legal system. But they also cast doubt on the idea Hart inherited from Austin and Kelsen that there are foundations of this kind in the first place. Both Austin's sovereign and Kelsen's basic norm were foundational because they addressed three central aspects of law: membership in a system, the unity of a system, and the existence of the system. Hart proposed an improved understanding of the foundations of the legal system, but he never questioned the idea that law has such foundations.

It is far from clear, however, that these three central aspects of law have a common explanation. Membership might rest on chains of validity, but that does not mean that the system requires that those chains have a common terminus (nor that the final link is not just as much part of the chain). The unity of a legal system may have more to do with the relationships between various legal institutions than with those institutions all using exactly the same criteria of validity.[120] And the existence of a legal system may rest on official acceptance of the system as a whole, rather than on the acceptance of its ultimate criteria. The legal system may have many foundations, rather than just one. Hart perceptively noted in chapter I that the instances of a general term may be linked together by different relationships to a central element:

> [H]ere perhaps we have a principle similar to that which unites the different types of rules which make up a legal system – the several instances may be different constituents of some complex activity. The use of the adjectival expression 'railway' not only of a train but also of the lines, of a station, of a porter, and of a limited company, is governed by this type of unifying principle.[121]

Hart could have drawn a further moral from this analogy. A railway requires many components – engines, carriages, track, staff, stops – in order to function, and it would be a mistake to single out any one of these as *the* foundations of the activity. The same may be true of the law.

Be that as it may, chapter VI of *The Concept of Law* brings together the many strands in Hart's analysis from the preceding chapters and weaves them into a forceful, arresting and absorbing theory of law. There are many loose ends, and many intriguing and tantalising ideas. Indeed, chapter VI often falls short of the clarity for which Hart is rightly praised. It is not just the truth of Hart's claims that is contestable, then, but also the precise nature of the claims he is making. This essay has sought to clarify some of Hart's central claims, and to

---

[120] See, eg, J Raz, 'The Identity of Legal Systems' in *The Authority of Law* (n 24).
[121] *The Concept of Law* (n 1) 16.

consider and question some of their possible interpretations. But whatever flaws it may have, Hart's work retains its power, half a century after it was written, to challenge and deepen our understanding of the nature of law.

7
Words and Obligations

NICOS STAVROPOULOS*

I. OBLIGATIONS, RULES AND LANGUAGE

BY THE END of chapter VI of the book, much of what Hart had set out to accomplish is done. He has argued that the explanation of the nature and content of obligations[1] in law is a primary task of legal theory, one at which other theories have failed. He has then set out and defended his own explanation of obligation in terms of a complex arrangement of rules of certain kinds. In chapter VII, he turns his attention to some challenges that take the explanation of obligation in terms of rules as given, and argue from the nature of rules to some disturbing conclusions.

As Hart presents the matter, on one side he faces the formalist, who argues that rules always constitute determinate obligations. On the other, he faces the sceptic, who thinks rules never determine any obligation. It is common ground among all three that cases in law are disputes about what obligations certain rules constitute. The implication of the formalist view is that the rules uniquely determine the correct outcome of cases such that the role of judges is simply mechanically to work out that outcome – to subsume the facts of the case under 'general classificatory heads' and draw 'a simple syllogistic conclusion'.[2] By contrast, the implication of the sceptical view is that rules never uniquely determine the outcome of cases, such that in deciding cases, judges are unconstrained by the rules. These challenges offer an opportunity for Hart to clarify and refine the explanation of the nature of rules set out earlier in the book, and draw out what he perceives as the correct implications

---

* This chapter draws on material presented at the Law and Philosophy Workshop at USC in December 2009. I am grateful to participants in the discussion, and to Andrei Marmor and Scott Soames for written comments in advance of the workshop. I am also indebted to the editors of this volume for extensive comments on an earlier draft.

[1] As well as rights, powers, privileges, and so on. I shall be speaking about obligation alone for simplicity. Notice that some legal theories, plausibly including Hart's, explain rights, powers, and the rest ultimately in terms of obligations; I do not take a view on this issue in the ensuing discussion.

[2] HLA Hart, *The Concept of Law*, 3rd edn (Oxford, Oxford University Press, 2012 [1961]) 125.

regarding the determinacy of obligation in law, including the role of judges deciding cases.

That is not quite how chapter VII unfolds. In the discussion of the challenges, Hart makes a number of striking new claims about what rules are and how they operate. The claims all involve the role of language in the explanation of rules and obligations. In some considerable part, the novelty of the claims is the consequence of a critical gap in the explanation of the nature of rules that precedes and forms the background of the discussion of the challenges. The gap concerns the mechanism through which Hart supposes that rules and obligations are created, eliminated, or modified, both in general and in law.

Much of Hart's discussion of the challenges revolves around the nature of language, particularly as it concerns communication that makes use of general terms. Hart says that the issue raised by both the formalist and the rule sceptic – the issue of the determinacy of obligation in law – is ultimately the issue of the determinacy of the content of certain language. This is so, Hart claims, because '*all rules*' involve classification under '*general terms*'.[3] The dependence of obligation on language includes obligations that follow from 'ordinary' legal rules,[4] which, according to Hart, are constituted by official linguistic action – by the production of legal texts (and utterances), such as statutes and judicial decisions, which, explicitly or by example, convey the rules to subjects.[5] It also includes those obligations that follow from rules whose existence and content Hart explains in terms of non-linguistic actions and attitudes, such as ordinary customs or the special judicial custom that constitutes the fundamental rule of a legal system (the 'rule of recognition').[6] In the first case, Hart's assumption is that to identify obligations is to classify facts under the general terms that occur in certain legal texts and utterances, which canonically formulate the rules, or those that occur in formulations of rules 'extracted' from such materials. In the second case, Hart appears to think that for every rule constituted by practice and attitude, there is a formulation that is contemplated and implicitly endorsed in the attitudes of the agents that participate in the relevant practice. If so, to identify obligations in this case is to classify facts under the general terms that occur in the implicit formulations.

Hart then reasons from certain assumptions about how language works to the conclusion that law is only partly determinate. In what Hart calls 'plain' cases, classification is certain and uncontroversial. In Hart's familiar example,

---

[3] ibid 123 (my emphasis).
[4] ibid.
[5] I discuss this claim in some detail in sections V and VI.
[6] Hart does not clearly explain what 'general terms' he has in mind for rules that he believes to be constituted by non-linguistic action and attitude. I discuss this immediately below and in section II.

some objects are vehicles and some others are not, certainly and uncontroversially. In cases that are plain in that sense, classification is for that reason determinate and, given Hart's assumption, so is obligation. But there is a further possibility: cases where classification is uncertain and controversial. In those cases, classification is for that reason indeterminate. There may be some object that possesses only some of the features through which we recognise something as a vehicle in the plain cases, but also certain other features which the plain cases lack, and we are for that reason uncertain and divided as to whether the object is properly classified as such. It follows, Hart thought, that there is no fact of the matter as to whether the object is a vehicle and therefore whether the rule that prohibits vehicles in the park prohibits the object. In those circumstances, classification requires a 'choice between open alternatives',[7] a judgment of whether the instant case sufficiently resembles the plain ones in relevant respects. Such cases are bound to arise in connection with any general term, and when they arise in connection with a term in official legal language, obligation is to that extent indeterminate. Judges called upon to resolve disputes that turn on correct application of the term must therefore make a discretionary, quasi-legislative choice that turns on non-linguistic factors such as the proper aims or purposes that may be attributed to some legislation or precedent.

Hart's claims about classification under general terms are based on a view of language that has long been known to be fundamentally problematic.[8] It is therefore unsurprising that many critics focused on the linguistic part of Hart's argument, and sought to replace Hart's linguistic philosophy with a better one.[9] By itself, however, criticism of Hart's linguistic claims is inconclusive. For it is not clear how an improved understanding of how language works might affect Hart's reasoning from linguistic uncertainty to indeterminacy of obligation in law. What conclusions to derive about the determinacy of obligation from truths about the nature of language depends on the *role* of language in the determination of obligation (and that is a question about the nature of law, not language). It is this more fundamental question that will be

---

[7] Hart, *The Concept of Law* (n 2) 127.

[8] For general criticism regarding the role of plain cases of application of expressions and the philosophical tendency to slide from claims that involve epistemic notions such as uncertainty to claims that involve metaphysical notions such as indeterminacy, see G Rey, 'Concepts and Stereotypes' (1983) 15 *Cognition* 237, reprinted in E Margolis and S Laurence (eds), *Concepts: Core Readings* (Cambridge, Mass, MIT Press, 1999).

[9] For criticism of Hart's claims about legal indeterminacy that focuses on Hart's views on language see M Moore, 'The Semantics of Judging' (1981) 54 *Southern California Law Review* 256; M Moore, 'A Natural Law Theory of Interpretation' (1985) 58 *Southern California Law Review* 277; D Brink, 'Legal Theory, Legal Interpretation, and Judicial Review' (1988) 17 *Philosophy & Public Affairs* 105; N Stavropoulos, *Objectivity in Law* (Oxford, Clarendon Press, 1996); and S Soames, 'Interpreting Legal Texts: What Is, and What Is Not, Special About the Law' *Philosophical Papers*, vol 1 (Princeton, Princeton University Press, 2008).

my focus in this chapter, with the question of how exactly language works kept in the background.

How did Hart come to think of the problem of legal determinacy as a problem of determinacy of the content of language? In what follows I shall examine the particular close relation that Hart believes to hold between obligation and language in the context of his explanation of obligation in the general case. I shall then consider the special case of law. In both cases I shall argue that the relation does not follow from Hart's analysis without additional implausible assumptions that Hart does not articulate or defend. If I am right, the particular problem of determinacy that Hart identifies and explores in chapter VII of the book does not arise. I shall conclude by considering where this leaves us regarding the issue of legal determinacy.

II. FROM PRACTICES TO OBLIGATIONS

Hart thought that a major task of legal theory was to explain the idea of obligation in law, and this made the notion of rules indispensable. He said that obligations were fundamentally connected with social practices:

> [T]he existence of [social] rules . . . is the normal, though unstated, background or proper context for [the] statement [that a person has an obligation]; and . . . the distinctive function of such statement is to apply such a general rule to a particular person . . .[10]

Hart regarded this connection as built into the very idea of obligation, and said that it was important in its own right, and also a necessary preliminary to understanding the special case of obligation in the legal domain.[11]

His explanation is familiar. Patterns of action, recognition, and censure together constitute social rules. We arrive at the departure lounge, there are dozens of us. There is only one person working behind the check-in counter. We form a line, waiting to be served roughly in the order in which we each arrived, and we react furiously to anyone's cutting in or drifting along, ahead of others who arrived before. This is not an isolated incident. It is our practice to act in this way in (actual and hypothetical) circumstances such as these. Our practice includes, in other words, a current settled disposition to act in this way if and when the circumstances arise. In addition, we regard the practice as a standard to which it is our duty to conform. In other words, we regard it as our duty, not simply to form a line in the circumstances, but to conform to the pattern of behaviour of forming a line in the circumstances,

---

[10] Hart, *The Concept of Law* (n 2) 85.
[11] ibid.

and so regard the *pattern* as a standard.[12] It follows that we take the existence of the pattern as reason for the action (whatever other reasons we might also think we have for so doing). According to Hart, these facts about us constitute and therefore explain the existence of a rule – the very standard that we accept in our attitudes – that requires that we act as we do. So such facts are what fundamentally make it the case that we are under an obligation so to act. For a person to be under an obligation, is for some such rule to apply to that person, where the pressure to conform exceeds some threshold of seriousness.[13] The obligation is specifically moral in character where such pressure is meant to induce shame, remorse, and guilt.[14]

As stated, this explanation of obligation is obviously flawed. For one thing, it is clearly not true that an obligation to take some action in certain circumstances exists only when a social practice of taking (or otherwise endorsing) the action exists.[15] It may seem that the flaw can be fixed by restricting the scope of

---

[12] ibid 57. A pattern of behaviour, in itself, is consistent with a different attitude: each accepts some reason other than, and not dependent on, the existence of the pattern. In that case, we coincide in our action and concur in our acceptance of a duty so to act, but do not meet Hart's conditions of an obligation constituted by the practice.

[13] ibid 86–87.

[14] ibid 86. In the relevant passages (ibid 86f), Hart is referring to 'the morality of the social group', which he elsewhere calls 'positive' morality (as distinct from 'critical' morality). That is not because he accepts that obligations of critical morality are otherwise constituted. While Hart accepts that critical morality includes ideals that transcend and may ground criticism of social practice, it is doubtful that he would accept that the ideals could give rise to *obligations*. He draws a distinction between considerations that give reasons and those that constitute obligations (ibid 85–86) and he says that whether some rule is backed up by serious social pressure is the test of whether it gives rise to obligations (ibid 87). He further distinguishes positive and critical morality in chapter VIII of the book, and says in an endnote that there is a need to distinguish 'the *obligation and duties* of social morality both from moral *ideals* and *personal morality*' (ibid 301, endnote to p 167, emphases added). The italicised words suggest a contrast. Obligation is associated only with the social side of the distinction. On the other side there are ideals and principles that one accepts in one's own life, which may give reasons but ground no obligations. In the discussion in chapter VIII, Hart discusses moral obligation (and compares it with legal obligation) *only* in connection with positive morality (ibid 167–80), and shifts to discussion of moral ideals rather than obligation thereafter: cf J Tasioulas, 'Hart on Justice and Morality', in this volume. That Hart would not allow for the existence of obligations of critical morality is further suggested by the fact that Hart offers no more basic account of obligation that might allow for a distinction between positive and critical moral *obligation*. In addition, the account I summarise in the text is clearly offered as an explanation of what it is for *any* obligation to exist, without qualification: see the passage quoted in the text. The view that obligation, in its nature, is constituted by social practice is of course consistent with the view that critical morality transcends social practice.

[15] Hart was surely wrong to say that a statement that one has an obligation to take some action implies the existence of a social practice that underwrites it. Such a statement is perfectly sensible in the absence of any practice or even in the face of a practice to the contrary. Reformers, social critics, and original moral thinkers who argued for the existence of certain moral obligations (rather than mere ideals that could be converted to obligations only on condition that they were taken up by the relevant social group) would all be out of business if it were not. In the end, rejecting the unqualified claim is not enough, for as I go on to say in the text even the restricted claim is false.

the explanation to conventional obligation. But this is an illusion, for the flaw is finally in the supposed ground of obligation rather than the explanation's scope. Practice may play a role, albeit a very different one, in the explanation of obligation. Where some (permissible) practice exists, there is often reason to conform, and the existence of the practice, including attitudes of recognition and censure, plays a role in the explanation of how it is that the reason obtains. Yet the explanation must include the considerations that assign to the practice that reason-giving role, which are therefore fundamental.

Familiar examples are usually drawn from our relatively trivial obligations. Conventions of politeness sharpen the distinction between respect and offence in our interaction with strangers. We have reason not to risk causing offence, which makes existing practices of polite behaviour, including the expectations they create and sustain, relevant to our action. The reason makes it the case that we have an obligation to conform to the practices, therefore to take the actions that are customary and expected, and is in turn explained by some values that make offence (and frustration of certain expectations) worth avoiding. Queuing is a way of sharing some resource in circumstances of congestion. Where queuing is practised, jumping or drifting along the line would intuitively assign to the jumper or drifter a smaller share of the cost of using the resource compared to others and at their expense. In these circumstances, antecedent reasons of fairness obligate us to join the line and wait for our turn.

The practices, in these examples, are relevant to the content of the relevant obligation, but do not ultimately determine it. Rather, the normative facts, which are independent of the practice and give some of its aspects normative relevance, do. The structure of these cases is reflected in other domains, where more is at stake: the reasons not to hurt others (and ourselves) make driving practices relevant to our action, indeed ground an obligation to conform, including an obligation to drive on the left in England. It is also reflected, mutatis mutandis, in many other domains where there is reason to coordinate or cooperate, where what others are disposed to do is relevant to the question what each one has reason to do.

As the examples illustrate, the fundamental facts are often obvious and hardly worth mentioning – of course we should not offend strangers or hurt anybody – which may make it seem that the explanation can work without them. But this is an illusion. The general point is simple. Social facts including patterns of action and attitudes towards such patterns do not constitute, but may be relevant to and affect, the content of our obligations, when and in virtue of the fact that some non-social normative facts, which ground the obligations, give the social facts some such role. So Hart's claim, even restricted to obligations whose existence depends on the existence of some practice, misrepresents their nature, crucially including the source of their force.

The background normative facts in these examples solve a problem that would be intractable if we tried to solve it using only the materials that Hart allows. For Hart is optimistic in thinking that to the extent that some practice is settled, it constitutes a determinate rule. For any practice, the facts about actual settled action and attitudes (including existing settled dispositions to act in hypothetical cases) of the agents that make it up, even together with further social facts (which are the only kinds of fact to which Hart's explanation appeals), cannot by themselves determine any standard.[16] For any action that an agent might now propose to take, we can always cook up some 'bent' standard that is consistent with the practice so understood, under which the action is precisely what the practice now requires. Suppose that Hart's men, who in their settled practice have been removing their hats upon entering the church and have been expecting everyone else to do likewise, all wore hats of a certain style prevalent in England in the 1950s. The rule that required that hats *of that style* be removed would be consistent with these facts, and would fail to require removing, say, a cattle baron hat never before seen in these parts. But if no contemplated action can count as a mistake by reference to the practice, there is no genuine standard that the practice constitutes.[17]

The difficulty is familiar from Saul Kripke's discussion of Wittgenstein's writings on rule following. The fundamental problem is one of relevance. Does style of hat matter? (We could go on. Does it matter that it was men, not women, who wore hats and removed them in church at the time? And so on, indefinitely.) If not, why not?[18] The general lesson is as simple as it is profound. For any action and attitude or other contingency to determine any standard, something other than these factors must determine the relevance of each. In the examples of conventional obligation just discussed, moral facts fill that role, by making certain aspects of some practice relevant to what one ought to do, and therefore ground and explain the content of the obligation. Their role is not to ratify some standard constituted by the practice alone – there is no standard so constituted. Rather, in determining what matters by giving reasons why it should, they thereby determine the standard and so what it is for some action to be consistent (in principle, rather than formally) with the practice.

---

[16] If so, there is no determinate standard that may give content to participants' attitude of regarding the relevant pattern 'as a standard'.

[17] See M Greenberg, 'How Facts Make Law' (2004) 10 *Legal Theory* 157. The description of the fundamental problem is in S Kripke, *Wittgenstein on Rules and Private Language: An Elementary Exposition* (Cambridge, Mass, Harvard University Press, 1982), and its elaboration in terms of the emptiness of formal consistency and the need for substantive constraints is in Susan Hurley, *Natural Reasons* (New York, Oxford University Press, 1989). Greenberg discusses the problem in detail, and draws implications for the explanation of the nature of law, including Hart's proposed explanation.

[18] See Greenberg, 'How Facts Make Law' (n 17) for discussion of attempts to solve the problem of relevance by appeal to more social facts.

We might consider another possible fix for Hart's account. Perhaps we can take it to be partial by design, aiming to explain what it is to accept some obligation, or how things look from the perspective of someone who accepts it. But Hart has no more basic account of what it is that one accepts when one accepts some obligation, which could serve to give content to the supposed partial or perspectival account, and is quite clear that he intends his account as an explanation of what it is to *be* under some obligation, not what it is to accept one as distinct and derivative from one's being under it.

The distinction between considerations that an agent regards as a reason to which he is disposed to conform and considerations that are in fact such reasons regardless of the agent's dispositions hardly makes sense in Hart's philosophy, and he explicitly rejects it. It is essential to his view that each distinct practice – each pattern of action and disposition to conform – independently constitutes a separate domain of obligation, just as genuine or robust as any other, possibly differing only in the character or means of pressure that backs the relevant group's expectation of conformity. Hart thought that legal practice constituted yet another domain of genuine, full-blooded obligation special to it, and he resisted to the end the suggestion that he reconceive acceptance within legal practice as the attitude, sincere or feigned, of assigning to the practice moral force.[19]

The idea that there exist many separate domains of genuine obligation each constitutively explained independently of each other, by the actions and attitudes internal to the relevant practice, makes sense within Hart's non-realist view of reasons. Hart saw that on the hypothesis that reasons existed independently of the agent's subjective motivation, it would be hard to maintain the distinctness of domains so understood, including in particular the thesis that legal duty and moral duty were so distinct. Given the hypothesis, someone anxious to maintain the distinctness would face a dilemma. He might accept the suggestion that legal duty was a *form* of moral duty – moral duty from the point of view of the practice. This would dilute the distinctness of legal and moral duty in a way that Hart's theory could not accommodate, for the explanation of legal duty would now have to be derived in part from the explanation of moral duty, even as it would still allow him to insist that legal duty was not moral duty *outright*. Alternatively, he might be led to accept the further, 'extravagant' hypothesis that there existed two independent domains of objective reasons, one legal and the other moral. That would allow him to preserve the constitutive independence of the two domains albeit at a high metaphysical price. Hart considered the latter alternative not viable for that reason. He also rejected the former since, in addition to his worries about dilution of the distinction between legal and moral duty, he was not

---

[19] See HLA Hart, *Essays on Bentham* (Oxford, Oxford University Press, 1982) 266f, 153–61.

persuaded that insiders must assign (sincerely or not) moral force to a practice if the practice is to give them reasons for action. He concluded that he did not need to abandon his own practice theory, which reduced obligation to patterns of action and settled dispositions to conform without reference to considerations external to the relevant practice. One lesson we learn from Hart's uneasy reflections on these matters is that that realist and non-realist strategies for keeping moral and legal obligation distinct (in the specified sense) do not mix.

III. RULES AND THE ORDER OF EXPLANATION

In the alternative account of obligation sketched above, indeterminacies in the language of rules (or, more accurately, in explicit or implicit formulations of rules) do not make for indeterminacies in obligation. That is because in that account rules cannot have the place that Hart assigns to them.[20]

Given the moral and social facts of the examples, and therefore the obligations they constitute, we would be justified in asserting rules that require eg certain forms of greeting, waiting for our turn, or keeping to the left in the relevant circumstances. Such rules would merely sum up the effect of the relevant considerations on obligations, and would be useful for presenting the normative situation and for reminding ourselves what we should normally do in certain familiar circumstances. Rules so understood would not occupy the intermediate place that Hart assigns to them in the fundamental explanation from social practices to obligations. They would neither be constituted by social practices, nor ground or explain in the constitutive sense the relevant obligations (so it would not be true that the obligations obtain in virtue of the existence of the rules). Obligations would be instead explained by the background moral and social facts that are merely summarised and reflected in the rules.[21]

This would remain so even if we all happened to share and endorse a particular formulation, which would not thereby become canonical. The suggestion that it is permissible for a heavily pregnant woman to go to the front of the queue would imply that a flat 'first come first served' formulation is an

---

[20] In 'The Standard Picture and Its Discontents' in L Green and B Leiter (eds), *Oxford Studies in Philosophy of Law*, vol 1 (Oxford, Oxford University Press 2011), Mark Greenberg articulates the theoretical significance of questions of order of explanation in accounts of obligation, including the place of rules in accounts such as Hart's. The point that I make in the text is suggested in an ancestor to that paper, and in the passages from Dworkin in the text.

[21] One might complain that 'rule' stands for a consideration that plays the explanatory role that Hart assigns to it: a standard that makes it the case that certain obligations obtain. If so, the right thing to say is that the alternative account has no place for rules. But it is instructive to see why not, and why it still makes sense to talk in terms of rules. Besides, it may not be wise to build a contentious thesis in the metaphysics of obligation into the idea of a rule.

inaccurate summary of the relevant considerations and should be qualified, not that that case is left open by the considerations that regulate the plain cases and must be regulated afresh. Since obligations are not explained by the rules, difficulties with applying the terms of some formulation have no consequences for the obligations that the formulation aims to capture.

The conception of rules (and other standards) as convenient devices of exposition that do not explain obligation, but instead summarise the effect of other considerations, which in fact explain it, is suggested in the following passages from Dworkin's early criticism of Hart's theory of rules:

> It is true that normative judgments often assume a social practice as an essential part of the case for that judgment; this is the hallmark, as I said, of conventional morality. But the social rule theory misconceives the connection. It believes that the social practice *constitutes* a rule which the normative judgment accepts; in fact the social practice helps to *justify* a rule which the normative judgment states. The fact that a practice of removing hats in church exists justifies asserting a normative rule to that effect – not because the practice constitutes a rule which the normative judgment describes and endorses, but because the practice creates ways of giving offense and gives rise to expectations of the sort that are good grounds for asserting a duty to take off one's hat in church or for asserting a normative rule that one must.[22]
>
> In the same way, lawyers use rules and principles to report legal information, and it is wrong to suppose that any particular statement of these is canonical. This is true even of what we call statutory rules, because it is a commonplace that lawyers will often misrepresent the rules that a statute enacted if they simply repeat the language that the statute used. Two lawyers might summarise the effect of a particular statute using different words, and one might use more rules than another; they might still both be saying the same thing.[23]

The second passage moves beyond the simple case of obligations which Hart believes to be constituted by social rules. The discussion so far has offered reasons to doubt that Hart's practice theory is a viable explanation of obligation, and therefore to doubt that the problem of determinacy that Hart identifies arises in respect of obligations insofar as these depend on the existence of social practices. Even if Hart is wrong, however, about the link between obligation and language in the general case, he may be right about the link in the

---

[22] R Dworkin, *Taking Rights Seriously* (Cambridge, Mass, Harvard University Press, 1978) 57.

[23] ibid 76. Dworkin goes on to say: 'My point was not that "the law" contains a fixed set of standards of any sort. My point was rather that an accurate summary of the considerations lawyers must take into account, in deciding a particular issue of legal rights and duties, would include propositions having the form and force of principles, and that judges and lawyers themselves, when justifying their conclusions, often use propositions which must be understood in that way.' In spite of this disclaimer, Dworkin is often credited with the view that the law contains both rules and principles, where rules are understood to be constitutive of some obligations (and principles of some further ones). The right thing to say is that in Dworkin's view rules (or principles) so understood do not exist.

special case of obligations that depend on considerations that are recognised as grounds of obligation in the special practice of officials. There might be independent reason to accept Hart's claim in that domain, so we must examine that case more closely.

IV. PROCURING OBLIGATIONS

The distinctive character of obligation in the legal domain does not ultimately lie, Hart thinks, in either its moral pretences or the way conformity is secured. Rather, it lies in the distinctive way in which, in that domain, social practice is leveraged into a far more powerful mode of shaping obligation.

In the general case, social practice is the sole mechanism involved in the shaping of a given obligation, and the obligation thereby produced mirrors the action that makes up the practice: it is an obligation to take the action that makes up the relevant pattern. Settled practices are not always easy to come by, or, once in place, to refine or adjust. As long as patterned action and attitude are the only means of production of obligation, variation in the content of the obligations that apply to a group will normally be possible only through the spontaneous, slow processes normally required to bring about a corresponding variation in the underlying practices and thereby to the rules that the practices constitute.[24]

But practices can turn into another, more powerful mode of shaping obligation through a kind of nesting. Social practice, as a source of obligation, can take as its object the production of obligation itself. It might come to be our practice to regard as binding something other than our own practice, such as the practice of some other group or the action of an individual, and to regard our practice of so regarding it as binding. If so, we would have thereby gained access to a new source of obligation. It may come to be our practice, for example, to recognise as binding on us the customs of the Romans, at least when in Rome, or the actual and hypothetical orders issued by one of us, Rex, whom we all admire and fear. In the first case, our practice would now be one of recognition, placing us under a corresponding obligation of recognition in conformity with our own practice, and, in virtue of that obligation, under the substantive obligations constituted by the outside practice that is thereby recognised. Our new practice would also permit for a new – if equally unwieldy – mode of change in our obligations: by virtue of change in the recognised rather than our own practice.

In the second example, our new practice would achieve something more spectacular. In addition to being a practice of recognition, it would confer upon Rex the power to modify our obligations by issuing orders. In that way,

[24] Hart, *The Concept of Law* (n 2) 92.

it would be possible for change in our obligations to come about deliberately, through action taken by Rex with the intention precisely to change our obligations.[25] This new possibility transforms the new structure into a truly powerful engine of obligation, one that can be used to procure obligations on demand, allowing us to tailor obligations to what we want to achieve through their existence. By the same token, it makes it possible easily to tell in advance whether an attempt to change obligations by introducing some new rule might be successful. Hart says that, where that facility exists, members of a community 'are committed to the acceptance in advance of general classes of rule, marked out by general criteria of validity. In the simpler form of society we must wait and see whether a rule gets accepted as a rule or not; in a system with a basic rule of recognition we can say before a rule is actually made, that it *will* be valid *if* it conforms to the requirements of the rule of recognition'.[26] The way Hart puts the point is somewhat misleading. Hart's practice theory implies that even in the simpler form of society we can say in advance that a putative rule *will* bind *if* it is 'accepted as a rule'. What is harder to say in advance is *how exactly we need to arrange things* so that the rule is indeed accepted (so it is hard to eliminate the risk that the putative rule will not catch or that a slightly different one will). By Hart's theory, *that* task is made easier by the new facility. Where it exists, we can say in advance exactly how we need to arrange things so that the putative rule binds: we need to see to it that it meets the tests of validity, and we can make that happen. So the purported advantage finally lies in the ease and precision with which we can procure obligations.

The new structure retains the role of social practice as constitutive of obligation, even as it decouples the content of the practice from the content of the obligation. It is no longer necessary for the existence of an obligation to take some action in some circumstances that it be our practice to take the action in the circumstances. It is now possible for the obligation to exist by virtue of the fact that others take the action as part of their own practice, or that somebody has issued an order that we do so, even if many of us fail to conform. It also retains the role of rules in the explanation of the production of obligation. The social practice at the foundation of the structure constitutes a rule that determines what factors other than the practice affect obligation. It does that by recognising the obtaining of such factors as constituting further valid rules and thereby obligations.

---

[25] Hart includes in his typology a third way in which practices of recognition may transform the domain of obligation. They can vest power in some individual or group to settle doubts and disagreements as to what obligations exist, thereby introducing adjudication into the picture. Hart is quite clear that in all three cases, rules constituted by practices of recognition at once directly impose an obligation to conform to the practice on those whose practice constitutes the rules, and confer power on others to create or change further obligations. See Hart, *Essays on Bentham* (n 19) 158f.

[26] cf Hart, *The Concept of Law* (n 2) 235.

This structure is essential to law, Hart famously thought, the true key to the science of jurisprudence.[27] In the legal case, the foundation is the recognition, as a matter of the settled practice of judges and other officials, of certain rules as binding, by reference to some characteristic possessed by them. The practice constitutes a rule of recognition and makes it the case that the further rules that meet the criteria of recognition used by judges and other officials are indeed valid rules that impose obligations[28] on their subjects.

Hart's question of determinacy of obligation arises in connection with both types of rule and its proper answer depends on the specifics of the constitutive determination of each, and of the obligations under it. It depends, in other words, on what exactly makes it the case that a rule and the obligations under it exist and have a certain content. Regarding the fundamental rule, Hart understands the question of determinacy as the question whether the action and attitudes of judges and other officials constitute a rule with determinate content.[29] To the extent that officials are united in their practice as to how valid rules are to be identified, the rule of recognition does have determinate content. Where the pattern breaks down such that officials are divided as to whether some actions are capable of constituting valid rules (Hart uses the example of Parliament attempting to reshuffle legislative and other powers in certain ways and to entrench the new arrangement) the fundamental rule is, to that extent, indeterminate.[30]

The picture is far less clear when it comes to the determination of substantive rules of law and the obligations under them. Such rules are the creatures of Hart's powerful new normative structure, which as we saw decouples the existence and content of obligation and of the rules that impose them from the content of the underlying practice. Given Hart's account, a given such rule's existence and content and therefore the obligations that follow from it must be explained in part by factors that happen to be officially recognised as rule-shaping and therefore by the contingencies of the local official practice that constitute the rule of recognition. It must further be explained, in part, by the nature of the factors that are capable of playing the role of determinants of legal rules and the way in which such factors can achieve their rule-creating and thereby obligation-shaping effect, under *any* rule of recognition.

The first part is the easy one. Hart illustrates the role of local official practice in determining the content of the law through a number of examples drawn mostly from English legal practice, which concern procedures through

---

[27] Hart, *The Concept of Law* (n 2) 81.
[28] As well as rights, powers, privileges, and so forth: see above, n 1.
[29] Hart, *The Concept of Law* (n 2) 109.
[30] ibid 147–54. As we saw, Hart is wrong to think that a settled judicial practice constitutes a determinate rule that matches it in content and imposes an obligation to conform. So his conclusion that to the extent that the practice is unsettled judges are under no determinate obligation does not follow.

which certain people and bodies may exercise power to change obligations. He also gives some abstract formulations of the role of local practice, the most famous of which is entirely open-ended: it says that the rule of recognition specifies some 'feature or features possession of which by a suggested rule is taken as conclusive affirmative indication that it is a rule of the group to be supported by the social pressure it exerts'.[31]

Formulations such as this indicate that there can be great variation in what may be a source of valid rules and therefore the content of legal obligations, and Hart would rightly consider this inclusiveness a strength of his theory. But their open-endedness may make it seem that the question of determination of the content of the law turns exclusively on the contingencies of local official practice which, alone, need figure in the fundamental explanation of how it is that the law has a certain content.

Hart's account treats, however, two important questions of determination as belonging to the necessary, not the contingent side of a complete explanation of a given legal obligation.[32] They are the questions, first, what sort of factor (other than local practice) could affect obligations (directly or through and in virtue of recognition of its obligation-shaping role in local official practice). And, second, how eligible factors can work to change the obligations (including, if Hart is right, how they might work to do so by constituting rules that are recognised as valid from which the obligations follow). For example, local practice may or may not include Hart's attitude of regarding certain tribal customs as contributing to the law valid rules and therefore obligations, or of so regarding customs that relate to marriage though not those that relate to inheritance. Or it may include that attitude towards the orders of one person but not another; or of one person on matters of safety of structures and of another person on matters of restaurant hygiene. It may include restrictions of subject matter, scope, or source. The questions I mentioned – what kinds of factor may change obligations in law and how exactly any such factor works to change the obligations – are not pre-empted by these contingencies. They are questions about the kind of eligible factors – eg customs, orders, or other considerations – and the role of such factors, if they happen to be recognised, in the determination of obligation (and are parallel to questions about the eligibility and role of aspects of social practices in the determination of obligation in Hart's basic explanation of obligation).

Some of what Hart says as he develops his conception of law speaks to these two fundamental questions as such. In Hart's picture, rules (or at least those in

---

[31] ibid 94.

[32] And he is right to do so. For reasons related to the problem of relevance discussed above, the matters raised by the questions in the text cannot be settled by the contingencies of local practice. The questions concern the *role* of different aspects of local practice, so they cannot be referred back to the very considerations whose role is at stake. Since Hart does not attempt to refer these particular questions to local practice, I will not pursue this argument further.

which Hart is interested) are always man-made, the product of human action and psychology. This is clearly so in the book as originally written. Much later, in the posthumously published Postscript to the book, Hart said that he saw no reason why moral standards could not be among those recognised by institutional practice as binding in law. This may seem to allow for the recognition and therefore validation of standards that are not man-made. It is not clear whether Hart's view had evolved by the time he wrote the Postscript. As we saw, in Hart's original account at least some obligation-imposing moral standards were also man-made, the product of settled practices and attitudes – a kind of custom – the only peculiarity being that conformity was normally secured by pressure meant to induce shame or remorse. On the other hand, obligation-imposing moral standards that are not man-made may of course be recognised but *cannot derive their validity* from recognition (or any other contingency). If such a standard exists at all, it exists and is relevant to the action of those it concerns, regardless of whether it is so recognised. The role of moral standards in dispute between Hart and his critics (primarily Dworkin), to whom Hart is responding in the Postscript, is anyway different: it is *the role of determining how institutional contingencies bear on the law*. If moral standards have that role, they have it of necessity, not in virtue of recognition.[33] Of course the contingencies might include the non-normative contingent fact that some agent or institution expressed belief or endorsement of some moral standard, and *that* fact could be recognised as relevant to the law. The question *how* any kind of contingency, including such an endorsement, may bear on the law would remain open. To simplify the discussion, I will set aside what Hart says in the Postscript.

The human source of Hartian rules is clear in respect of customary rules, which Hart thinks are the product of patterned action and attitude. These raise no important new issues in their guise as ordinary rules and therefore grounds of ordinary legal obligation. Hart has already given a fairly clear systematic (if flawed) account of what it is for some custom to exist and how it can constitute binding rules and thereby obligations – his practice theory of rules. We might assume that, in his view, when some custom comes to contribute to the law a valid rule through the custom's recognition, it contributes a rule that has the same content as the original, as that is determined by the patterned action and attitudes of the relevant group (except that it is now binding as valid rather than practised, and in some cases may have different scope).[34] In our earlier example, it would be a rule to take the actions that are customary in Rome. The new rule and therefore the obligations under it would be determinate to the extent that the original custom and the obligations under it, as well as any new scope or other qualifications, were determinate.

---

[33] See also J Raz, 'Incorporation by Law' (2004) 10 *Legal Theory* 1–17.

[34] There may be further consequences of the fact that the rule is now binding as valid, eg that the obligations under the rule may now be enforced through the apparatus of the law.

Hart is clear that the non-customary rules that can be validated by local official practice are also man-made. They are rules made deliberately, through linguistic or other action – by human beings saying or doing certain things[35] – such as the action involved in enacting a statute, adopting a regulation, or issuing an appellate judgment. So we need to consider how action of that kind might produce legal rules and thereby obligation (and thus to consider to what extent, if any, the rules and obligations so constituted might be determinate, which would allow us to assess Hart's position on the question of determinacy).

In the discussion that precedes chapter VII, Hart says little more, and only in passing, about how exactly such action, which he discusses under the rubric of change, is supposed to bring about changes in rules and obligations. Hart talks about *deliberately adapting* rules to changing circumstances[36] and about the power of an individual or body to *introduce new rules of conduct or eliminate old ones*, and he says that the ideas of legislative enactment and of repeal are to be understood in those terms. He also says that the judgments of courts *may be used as authoritative guides to the rules* through inferences drawn from particular judgments.[37]

Much of the action Hart mentions in these passages and wants us to understand as potential modifiers of rules and therefore obligations is linguistic. Legislation normally involves the production of texts, and court judgments are usually issued in writing or less often verbally. Is this essential to deliberately changing the law? (It is certainly not essential *to the law* – custom, which by Hart's own lights can contribute to the law, need not involve any linguistic transaction or record.) If so, must the rule that the relevant action might add to the law (or the modification that it may bring about) be expressed in the text or utterance produced by the relevant agents? The case of judicial decisions suggests that this is not so. Perhaps explicit formulation of the contributed rule is still a constraint on other law-shaping action such as the production of legislation. In the case of judicial decisions, is it enough that it should be possible to infer the rule from what the court said in the particular case, together with certain assumptions? Or is there a fundamental constraint that applies across the board – perhaps that, in all cases, no rule can be added to the law unless the rule is actually represented in thought and endorsed in attitude by some agent who purports to change the law? Finally, what explains the constraints, whatever they might be? Is it something about legal obligation, and if so what, that might place these constraints upon the character of the action that is supposed to be capable of changing it and upon the way such action might produce its effect?

---

[35] Hart, *The Concept of Law* (n 2) 81.
[36] ibid 92f.
[37] ibid 95–98.

These questions concern legal impact. Let us say, roughly, that legal impact is the change in legal obligations (rights, powers, and so on) that obtains as a result of some action (or of some psychological state, or a combination; for convenience, I will mostly omit this qualification). For short, legal impact is the difference that the action makes to the law. Let us say further that some action is legally relevant just in case taking the action could have legal impact.[38] A theory may also separate the impact of some action into its *specific* or *immediate* or *pro tanto* impact, that is, the effect on the law that can be attributed to the action, other things equal, and its *final* effect, which may further depend on the immediate effect of other action.

Hart's account postulates standards (rules) as intermediaries in the explanation of obligation that is ultimately in terms of action such as enacting a statute or issuing a decision. On his account, an action is legally relevant only when it is recognised as capable of having legal impact in settled official practice. The (specific) legal impact of such an action is the change in the set of valid legal rules that existed prior to and independent of the action, by way of creation, elimination, or modification of some such rule, and *thereby* the change in the antecedently existing domain of legal obligations, which obtain in virtue of the action's obtaining. Given Hart's thesis that all rules are partly indeterminate, the impact of an action that created a rule would be exhausted when the rule that it created, and thereby the obligations under it, reached the limits of determinacy. Our question, then, is this: how exactly can the linguistic and other action we described make it the case that some impact on obligations obtains? It is hard to say, without examining more closely the operation of rule production – without looking inside the great new engine of rapid, predictable, and effective modification of obligations that his structured social practices make possible – how exactly Hart supposes that the engine works.

V. DO INSTITUTIONS CHANGE OBLIGATIONS BY CONVEYING STANDARDS?

It might be tempting to suggest, at this point, that Hart did not need to say anything more than that the doings and sayings of humans are the sort of thing that can modify ordinary legal rules through the operation of the rule of recognition, leaving the rest, including the question what rules and obligations are thereby constituted, to the specifics of the rule of recognition. We should resist the temptation. If Hart took that view, he could not say anything general about whether legal rules and obligations under the rules were determinate to any

---

[38] A more accurate definition might restrict the notion of impact to the sort of change that political action of a given kind can reliably and systematically produce without further intervention.

extent. It would all depend on the mechanism through which rules were procured by people doing and saying things, which, on the current hypothesis, would be a matter of local contingency. But as we will see, Hart does have such general things to say. And in any event, the suggestion is not relevant, for Hart did not take the view that he need say no more. At the beginning of chapter VII, he indicates how he thinks the production of rules and thereby of obligations works:

> If it were not possible to communicate general standards of conduct, which multitudes of individuals could understand, without further direction, as requiring of them certain conduct when occasion arose, nothing that we now recognise as law could exist.[39]

Hart goes on to infer that law must predominantly refer to classes of persons and of acts, things, and circumstances, hence is bound to use general classifying words. But the prior, fundamental point is that (presumably, custom aside; I will omit this qualification hereafter), the special legal way in which one can change obligations in law is by communicating the standards that thereby come to belong to the set of valid standards and constitute the obligations.

The intended scope of the claim is probably wide, to include constitutions, statutes, regulations, judicial decisions, and other legal texts, understood as instruments that permit the rapid, predictable, and effective procurement of rules and thereby obligations that Hart has argued to be the hallmark of law. Could Hart think that it is enough for law to exist that *some* though not all of the statutes, regulations, and so on, convey the standards that their enactment adds to the law? For that to be possible there would have to be something other than communication of some standard, by virtue of which the enactment added the standard to the law – perhaps the enactment itself, whether or not accompanied by any communication and independently of it. If so, Hart would owe us an explanation of the other mechanism, including an account of which standard an enactment adds to the law through the mechanism. Of course, Hart's inference from situations 'in the nature of a crisis in communication'[40] to indeterminacies in the standards and the obligations would not hold. For these reasons we should reject this interpretation. (The analogies with teaching that I discuss below further reinforce the wide reading.) The more interesting question concerns the content of the claim and so the precise role that communication plays in Hart's view. I will focus on statutes, and mention Hart's discussion of judicial decisions only as evidence of the content of his claim.

---

[39] Hart, *The Concept of Law* (n 2) 124.
[40] ibid 127.

Consider action that is recognised as legally relevant in the practice of officials. The question now is: what is its specific legal impact? How does taking the action make it the case that some obligations in law are changed, at least in the first instance, subject to the impact of any further legally relevant action? At the weak end, there is the claim that action that characteristically changes obligations in law, such as enacting statutes or deciding cases, involves the use of language, which would imply that the explanation of how the action achieves its effect on obligations should include an account of the role played by language in producing it. Or even the claim that the use of language consists in communication of certain standards, and as a result of that action some impact on obligations obtains. These claims are both consistent in different ways with explanations that compete with Hart's. For example, consider the view that through an enactment government puts on record its commitment to act in a certain way, say to subsidise some industry through some tax break, leading people to expect it so to act and to plan on that basis, such that it would now be unfair for government to act otherwise; thereby making it the case that a certain impact on a range of rights and duties related to tax and accounting obtains. Or the view that, by enacting some statute, government announces a standard that requires that one of several alternative solutions to a coordination problem be taken, given background reasons to coordinate action in the relevant domain, which has the effect of making the alternative salient so likely to be taken by most everyone; thereby making it the case that a general obligation to take the alternative now obtains. Or that it records its intention to enforce participation in some scheme of cooperation, with the effect of giving each assurance that others will not defect; thereby making it the case that each is placed under an obligation to cooperate.[41]

None of these proposals, including the one that is in terms of announced standards, would be acceptable to Hart. We could present each of them in terms of rules, albeit not Hartian ones. We could say that, in each case, as a result of the enactment some rule obtained. Yet in every case, including the one in which a standard was formulated in the language of the statute, the relevant standard's obtaining is explained not by the enactment or the announcement in itself, but rather by some of its psychological, behavioural or other effects, together with certain moral considerations of fairness and justice, which also explain the obligations themselves. So in these cases too, as in those discussed earlier, the rules would merely sum up rather than explain the obligations.

---

[41] Some of these examples are similar to those used in M Greenberg, 'The Standard Picture and Its Discontents' (n 20), to illustrate explanations of obligation that break what he calls 'explanatory directness', the view that the obtaining of some authoritative pronouncement explains the obtaining of a norm without explanatory intermediaries. See also N Stavropoulos, 'The Relevance of Coercion' (2009) 22 *Ratio Juris* 339, about certain ways in which law's coerciveness could bear on the role of institutional practice in the explanation of obligation in law.

Hart needs the standards to play a substantial explanatory role, so he must think that a standard's obtaining is to be explained by the obtaining of some official action, rather than the factors just discussed. He also thinks that official action is linguistic in character and consists in communication of standards. Moreover, he maintains that to the extent that *communication* of a standard is indeterminate, the *standard* that the action adds to the law and the obligations under it are indeterminate. For the linguistic action, the conveying of a standard, to have the constitutive role in the obtaining of the obligation that Hart envisages, it is not enough that some standard is conveyed and in consequence of that action some (other?) standard obtains (under which some obligations obtain). It must be that the standard (and therefore obligation) that obtains does so by virtue of the fact that the standard was conveyed. It follows that the standard that the action adds to the law must be the content that was conveyed.

This is a variant of the familiar view that institutions change the law through communication, usually defended these days in terms of directives. On this view, laws are directives (orders, instructions) which convey an intention that subjects be placed, by that very act, under an obligation to take some action. What the institution says constitutes a norm that is thereby added to the law, and subjects are meant to comply, that is, conform for the reason that the institution said so.[42]

Hart draws an analogy with teaching of standards of conduct. Legislation is analogous to teaching by explicit definition; precedent, to teaching by example. Like a parent teaching a child how he ought to behave, the law guides conduct by conveying standards. It can therefore be deemed to have guided conduct only to the extent that it has effectively conveyed some standard. The test of effectiveness is not individualised success. Rather, it is the social test captured in Hart's distinction between certainty and agreement in judgment about the correct application of the terms of official language, on the one hand, and uncertainty and disagreement about application, on the other. If communication so conceived breaks down – if it is uncertain and controversial what standard the law has conveyed – so does the guidance that is achieved through it. The epistemic failure – the uncertainty about what one is supposed to do – constitutes a metaphysical one. The standard has reached its limits of determinacy, and there is no longer a fact of the matter as to what one is supposed to do:[43]

> In all fields of experience, not only that of rules, there is a limit, inherent in the nature of language, to the guidance which general language can provide. There

---

[42] See J Raz, *The Morality of Freedom* (Oxford, Oxford University Press, 1986), and his 'Authority, Law and Morality', in his *Ethics in the Public Domain* (Oxford, Oxford University Press, 1994).

[43] See n 8 and accompanying text.

will indeed be plain cases constantly recurring in similar contexts to which general expressions are clearly applicable . . . At this point, the authoritative general language in which a rule is expressed may guide only in an uncertain way . . . the sense that the language of the rule will enable us simply to pick out easily recognisable instances, at this point gives way . . . The discretion thus left to [the person called upon to apply the rule] by language may be very wide.[44]

Hart does not think, of course, that once that limit is reached there is no consideration on the basis of which 'the person concerned to classify', including a lawyer or a judge, can and must form the judgment called for. To say there is discretion at the borderline is not to say that anything goes. There may be other rules, both substantive and procedural, that constrain what a judge may do at the borderline. In addition, there are the similarities and differences between cases that become 'visible only when considered in the light of social aims' and can be dealt with 'by weighing up of social issues'.[45] It remains true that, for Hart, once the *linguistic* borderline is reached, the institutional action of producing the relevant text has exhausted its contribution to the law – its specific impact.

Having assumed that institutions create rules by conveying them, Hart proceeds to treat a rule and some linguistic formulation of a rule as interchangeable. This is particularly striking in his discussion of precedent. There, he explicitly accepts that, while it is often easy enough to identify the rule which a decision contributes to the law, there is no authoritative or uniquely correct formulation of any rule to be extracted from cases. He goes on to claim that, when a court deciding a later case narrows the 'rule extracted' from the precedent and admits some exception to it not before considered by finding some relevant difference between the previous and the present case, the court changes *the rule*. The identification of rule and formulation is even more conspicuous in the passage that follows:

> [In] following an earlier precedent, the courts may discard a restriction found in *the rule as formulated* from the earlier case, on the ground that it is not required by any rule established by statute or earlier precedent. To do this is to widen *the rule*.[46]

In both cases, a court thereby engages in legislative activity – it changes the *rule* – within the space left open by the binding force of precedent.[47] This reasoning completely erases the distinction between a rule and its formulation. There is no such thing as improving a *formulation of a rule* so that it more accurately represents *the rule*. There is no such thing as narrowing a previous formulation by finding a difference that is relevant to the *original* rule. To

---

[44] Hart, *The Concept of Law* (n 2) 126f.
[45] ibid 130.
[46] ibid 135 (emphases added).
[47] ibid.

tweak the formulation is to represent a different rule. And the absence of an authoritative or uniquely correct formulation of precedential rules, instead of reinforcing the distinction between formulation and rule, collapses it. Cases contribute the rules represented in the formulations lawyers actually extract from the cases: as the formulations change, so do the precedential rules. These results may seem counterintuitive – lawyers are after all trying to represent *something* in their attempts to formulate the rules in law reports and journals – but they are entirely sensible, given Hart's view that a rule exists to the extent that communication of its content is certain, and so is capable of providing certain guidance.

VI. THE LANGUAGE OF A STATUTE AND THE EFFECT OF ITS ENACTMENT

Whether or not Hart's treatment of precedent seems convincing, he may seem to be on firmer ground when it comes to legislation. In that case, legal texts are clearly of paramount importance. Lawyers seem to worry a lot about what words or sentences in the text mean. It may seem obvious that statutes *say* what change in the law they bring about: surely legislation largely consists in writing down what people are supposed to do. *Obviously* the meaning of the relevant texts determines the change in the law that their existence accomplishes. What else could determine it? Why should we expect Hart to belabour such a trivial point?

As we have already seen, Hart's claim is not in fact a truism that cannot coherently be doubted. It is a claim about the role of official language in the fundamental explanation of obligation in law, therefore a claim about the nature of law. We have already seen examples of competing claims: that the language of an enactment is relevant to the explanation of the effects of the enactment on certain attitudes and behaviour, which play some key role in the resolution of collective action problems or are otherwise relevant to matters of fairness and justice. Furthermore, the claim is not confirmed in legal practice, and has implausible implications.

Consider, first, the idea that the enactment of a statute is an act of communication. Philosophers of language work with a variety of theoretical notions, each of which represents some aspect or component of the information that may be reliably conveyed by some linguistic act. First, there is the semantic content of a text, roughly its literal or *sentence meaning*, as that is determined by the meaning of the words that make up the sentences and the words' grammatical arrangement. Second, there is the proposition a speaker or writer *uses a sentence to express*, that is, what he *says* or *states* by those means, something that an audience or reader may work out by exploiting pragmatically available information and which may go beyond or even be other than the text's literal meaning. (By using the sentence 'I am thirsty' I am stating that the author of this chapter is thirsty.) Third, there is what a producer merely *implicates*, also exploiting pragmatically available information. (One can use the sentence 'it is getting late' to state that it is getting late, and thereby to implicate that it is time to leave.)

As these distinctions suggest, semantic content is a vehicle through which a speaker or writer conveys information, which can go beyond the content of the sentences used (and, as Soames points out,[48] sometimes the semantic content of a sentence is not itself asserted, or even included in what the speaker is committed to). If all works well, what the speaker intends to convey and what a competent hearer grasps coincide. But, as Neale points out,[49] their positions are asymmetrical. The hearer's task is to grasp what the speaker intended to convey. The conventional meaning of words and principles of grammar (the elements of semantic content) constrain the formation of the speaker's intentions, and a variety of considerations (notably aspects of the context of an utterance) may provide evidence for the purpose of working out, but do not constitutively explain, what is conveyed. The speaker's linguistic intentions do that.

Linguistic intentions should be distinguished from achievement intentions. The object of the former is the information that one uses language to convey. The object of achievement intentions is what one is trying to accomplish in consequence of realising one's linguistic intentions. On the hypothesis that we are examining, we might say that in the case of law, achievement intentions are normative; what they take as their object is a change in people's obligations in consequence of realising linguistic intentions.[50]

On the hypothesis that the impact of a statute is determined by its linguistic content, the distinction between linguistic and achievement intentions will be notional. However, as has been pointed out, given how statutes are actually made, there is reason to expect that the two may diverge.[51] Legislators may fear or expect that, given the intended content of the language of a statute, its enactment will change the law in certain ways they do not approve – but they could not get the votes or bear the political cost of preventing that from happening. Or they may fail to appreciate some unintended legal effect that their

---

[48] S Soames, 'Interpreting Legal Texts' (n 9).

[49] S Neale, 'Textualism With Intent' (2008), unpublished manuscript, on file with author.

[50] Indirect achievement intentions may also exist. These concern political objectives met in consequence of realising the normative intentions, eg an indirect intention to prevent gay couples from adopting by directly intending to achieve a prohibition of adoption by unmarried couples (where gays cannot marry). Indirect political intentions are often the primary incentive of political action.

[51] R Dworkin, *A Matter of Principle* (Cambridge, Mass, Harvard University Press, 1985) ch 2; and *Law's Empire* (Cambridge, Mass, Harvard University Press 1986) ch 9.

enactment might be thought to have.⁵² In some such cases, there may be reason to suppose that, had they been aware of the effect, they would have modified the enactment's wording. If we thought that relevant to the enactment's actual effect, we would have to defend its relevance by appeal to considerations other than the information that the legislators actually intended to convey by using the language, which by hypothesis is different. In general, the distinction between linguistic and achievement intentions (and distinctions internal to each) present theoretical choices that must be made on grounds other than the considerations whose relevance is at stake. A range of considerations of political morality about the proper role of (aspects of) the action of institutions in the determination of obligations are eminently suitable for that purpose.⁵³

On the other hand, the notion of linguistic intention in discussion refers to actual psychological states. The idea is that what a speaker in fact wants to convey as such, not what he should want to convey under some ideal, or what a hearer may reasonably suppose that he wants to convey, determines what is conveyed by some linguistic act (and that it thereby determines legal impact). That is what gives rise to the asymmetry mentioned above. The asymmetry would not hold if the speaker could be held to have conveyed some information regardless of whether he actually intended to do so.

Finally, notice that philosophers of language normally study ordinary communication, paradigmatically conversation. Casual exchanges – gossip, traffic reports, chit-chat, setting up lunch appointments – exploit a deeply embedded psychological mechanism that can be relied upon to operate more or less uniformly, which generates and adjusts expectations, selectively directs and holds our attention, allows us rapidly to test hypotheses about each other's thoughts, and otherwise facilitates the transmission of information from one to another by improving the chances of harmony in intentions, expectations, and other attitudes among the relevant parties. And in verbal, face-to-face transactions, which are the principal focus of philosophical study, it is all helped in some ineffable way by direct experience. This kind of mechanism works to permit exposing our mental life for inspection by each other, in circumstances where we are (and there are excellent reasons why we should be) interested precisely in each other's attitudes, paradigmatically including each other's intentions to convey certain information.

None of this holds in the case of law. It is highly implausible that when a lawyer reads some statute he is interested in the mental life of its author. That is in part because of the familiar difficulties of identifying some person whose

---

⁵² M Greenberg, 'Legislation as Communication' in A Marmor and S Soames (eds), *Philosophical Foundations of Language in the Law* (Oxford, Oxford University Press, 2011), provides a nice illustration with a case that concerned diversity jurisdiction of US Federal courts.

⁵³ R Dworkin, *A Matter of Principle* (n 51) ch 2; and *Law's Empire* (n 51) ch 9.

mental life would count as the author in the relevant way.[54] It is also because it hardly seems to be the right interpretative target. As Greenberg points out, unlike in normal communication, it is not possible to ask the speaker for clarification – a standard tool for ascertaining intention. Moreover, it would not seem appropriate to do so, even if it were possible (say, where the assembly that enacted a problematic statute is still in session). It is not that the people who enacted a statute hold some relevant information that it is not permissible to consult, as in the case of googling some question in a game of knowledge. Rather, any information the authors might be able to offer after the fact does not seem *relevant* to the reader's task of working out the statute's legal impact. Lawyers seem to assume that, once the statute is enacted, the matter of its impact is out of its authors' hands. The assumption constitutes a claim about what determines legal impact, and competes with the thesis that legislators convey the standards that their enactment adds to the law (which entails that the assumption is false). Political considerations of procedural fairness including the proper role of legislatures in a democracy are obvious candidates for choosing between the two.[55]

Finally notice that, although judges spend much time arguing about what expressions and sentences of statutory and other texts mean, in the course of working that out they often appeal to considerations that are not obviously or even plausibly constitutive of the linguistic content conveyed by the production of the texts. A standard example is appeal to counterfactual intentions such as what some legislative body would have said under certain conditions, taken to be relevant to what it has actually said. Other examples include appeal to a constructive notion of legislative purpose – roughly, good reasons for passing a statute regardless of whether anyone actually accepted such reasons – taken to play a role in determining what the statute means. Or the claim that the meaning of any constitutional clause cannot be such that political practices known and considered lawful before and after the clause's enactment come out unconstitutional because of it.[56] In addition, courts regularly appeal to moral considerations as directly relevant to a statute's legal effect, not as subsidiary to linguistic ones and pertinent only when these are not decisive.[57]

With all this in mind, consider Hart's discussion of the problems surrounding the meaning of general terms in legal language. In the famous example

---

[54] ibid.
[55] cf M Greenberg, 'Legislation as Communication' (n 52), also appealing to rule of law considerations.
[56] This is Scalia's view. See Scalia J, dissenting, *Virginia Military Institute* (United States v Virginia), 518 US 515. See also A Scalia, *A Matter of Interpretation* (Princeton, Princeton University Press, 1997), which relies heavily on the political ideal of being ruled by law not men for the defence of a view about what determines the *meaning* of legal texts.
[57] Here is a famous example: 'all laws and all contracts may be controlled in their operation and effect' by 'fundamental maxims of the common law', which 'are dictated by public policy': *Riggs v Palmer*, 115 NY 506 (1889). The Affordable Care Act, discussed below, is a recent example.

about vehicles in the park, Hart imagines that legislators adopt the regulation in the service of some aim: to secure peace and quiet in the park, which they weigh up against the cost of inconvenience or unfreedom inflicted upon those who want to cut through the park in their cars or on their motorbikes. Legislators did not think, let us say, about kids' scooters. There may be a unique balance to be struck, but striking it takes fresh substantive judgment given the regulatory aims. Hart's claim here is that, once the regulation expressed in terms of vehicles is adopted, and insofar as exemplars are concerned, substance can be avoided. Substantive judgment is called for afresh only at the borderline, where objects that are arguably vehicles, though not exemplary ones, are involved.

It is doubtful that a unique rationale or aim need underlie, as a matter of psychological fact, institutional action. On the other hand, it does not follow from the fact that some objects are conventionally associated with some expression that users of the expression in fact associate the objects with it. Perhaps Hart's legislators in fact 'envisaged' less or more than is included in the conventional content of 'vehicle'.[58] To impute aims and extensions to legislators on grounds other than their actual psychological states may be sensible, but not part of identifying the linguistic content of their action. If so, we need some explanation of the grounds of constructive attribution that Hart does not provide.[59]

Another doubt is whether exemplary status exempts an object from being the subject of judicial judgment. Hart seems to suppose that the following two distinctions map onto each other: (a) between exemplars of general terms and objects related by similarity to exemplars in respects that are arguably relevant; (b) between classification without substantive judgment or weighing of aims and classification based on such judgment. But the distinctions may cut across each other. Examples abound. The municipal garbage truck is a pretty exemplary vehicle. But reasonable doubts may exist as to whether the impact of the regulation is to exclude it from the park. It may be suggested that we should read into the regulation an implied restriction to vehicles used by the general public. Alternatively, it may be suggested that, in spite of the clear language, the presence of doubt, by itself, may trigger the need for fresh discretionary judgment that appeals to the 'social aims' of the regulation. Whichever solution we choose, we will thereby abandon the view that the linguistic content of the regulation determines its impact. For there is nothing to indicate that the authors of the regulation actually meant to convey the

---

[58] If so, the hypothesis that the conventional meaning of the regulation determines its impact would make for unanticipated consequences; cp n 52.

[59] Notice that for the explanation to be generally consistent with Hart's approach, it could not appeal to any substantive normative considerations, eg of good public policy, which are the most promising for the purpose of constructing 'social aims'.

implied clause. Nor is there anything linguistically amiss so as to justify, by the lights of the theory, any doubt about what is being conveyed and so the exercise of discretion.[60]

Consider, next, some cases which seem to raise matters of meaning of statutory language, from the US Supreme Court, an institution especially promiscuous in its use of dictionaries for the purpose of deciding important cases.

In *Smith*,[61] much discussed among philosophers interested in the relation between language and law, one issue was the way a statute that stipulated additional penalties for using firearms during and in relation to drug trafficking affected the case of someone who offered to trade an automatic weapon for drugs. Majority and dissent (Justice Scalia) agreed that at stake is the ordinary, literal meaning of the relevant statutory sentence. Scalia seemed to claim (and majority to deny) that, ordinarily, 'use' extends only to non-deviant uses of the relevant object:

> To use an instrumentality ordinarily means to use it for its intended purpose. When someone asks, 'Do you use a cane?', he is not inquiring whether you have your grandfather's silver-handled walking stick on display in the hall; he wants to know whether you *walk* with a cane. . . . The ordinary meaning of 'uses a firearm' does *not* include using it as an article of commerce. I think it perfectly obvious, for example, that the objective falsity requirement for a perjury conviction would not be satisfied if a witness answered 'no' to a prosecutor's inquiry whether he had ever 'used a firearm,' even though he had once sold his grandfather's Enfield rifle to a collector.[62]

Philosophy of language teaches us that this is confused. 'I used my laptop to drive a nail into the wall' involves a deviant use of a laptop, not a deviant use of 'use'.[63] Being non-deviant, we have no reason from lack of linguistic clarity to hesitate to apply the additional penalty in the circumstances of the case. Here again, the source of the hardness of the case does not seem to be linguistic. How to explain the sense that something is amiss?

Soames suggests a solution under which Scalia's preferred result *can* be reached on linguistic grounds.[64] His argument is that since speakers use

---

[60] In 'Interpreting Legal Texts' (n 9), Scott Soames discusses a structurally similar example furnished by Fuller. Assuming a bylaw that says that 'to sleep in any railway station' is an offence, compare a commuter dozing off on a bench, and a homeless man settling down for the night. Hart's distinction implausibly treats the former as clearly covered by the prohibition, and the latter as clearly not covered. Soames claims that, because the linguistic content of the imaginary regulation leads to a legally wrong result, courts have discretion to depart from it. He is right that the result in question would be legally wrong. But his hypothesis that linguistic content constitutes impact cannot explain why it is.

[61] *Smith v United States* 508 US 223 (1993).

[62] ibid.

[63] The point is due to S Neale, 'Textualism With Intent' (49).

[64] S Soames, 'Interpreting Legal Texts' (n 9).

sentences to say things, the object of interpretation must be not what a sentence means, but the information the speaker in fact uses the sentence to convey. Someone who asks if you use a cane wants to know if you use a cane to walk, and someone who interrogates a witness about guns wants to know if the witness used a gun as a weapon. The restriction to the characteristic use of the instruments is located at the level of the question one uses a sentence to ask, not the level of the content of the sentence. The right argument for Scalia to make (and for the majority to reject) would therefore be that Congress *should be held to have intended to convey* that extra penalties apply only in case one uses guns as weapons.

Can such a sophisticated variant of the view that the meaning of the text constitutes its legal impact be defended? The proposed solution is analogous to the one discussed earlier involving imputing to legislators some implied restriction. First, recall that if it is to be germane to the content conveyed by the language, the appeal must be to intentions that legislators actually had.[65] Absent any evidence, why should we accept that they had those intentions? In fact, there is no reason to expect to find decisive evidence either way. Of course we might think that legislators *must* have had that intention because the only sensible goal of providing for the extra penalty would be to remove guns used as weapons from the drug business. But if so, we would be tainting the process of identifying the meaning of statutory language with extra-linguistic, normative matters of sensible public policy. Since, as Soames would be the first to note, language does not work that way – you have no reason to assume that I intend to convey what it would be good for me to convey – this line of reasoning is better understood as a disguised argument about the impact of the statute on the law as that is determined by considerations further to the meaning of the statutory language. For questions of sensible public policy *may* be among the (non-linguistic) considerations that are pertinent to impact.

The recent Affordable Care Act[66] gives an opportunity to examine the relations between the meaning of an enactment and the expectations that obtain in consequence of the enactment, and their respective roles in the explanation of the impact of the enactment. In that case, one issue was whether Congress could make continued Federal funding of the Medicaid programme conditional on the States agreeing to expand the programme in certain ways (with the expansion almost entirely Federally funded). Chief Justice Roberts noted that the

---

[65] Scalia would not be pleased: 'Men may intend what they will but it is only the laws that they enact which bind us'; *cf* A Scalia, *A Matter of Interpretation* (n 56) 92. As Greenberg points out in 'Legislation as Communication' (n 52), Scalia and other judges would be loath to rely on legislators' actual mental states. For some, doing so would be inappropriate because these are not public. For Scalia, it is so because we want to be ruled by law, not men. His textualism is ultimately founded on a doctrine of political morality. Soames's argument about the true constituents of linguistic content cannot engage this concern.

[66] See *National Federation of Independent Business et al v Sebelius*, 567 US_ (2012).

Social Security Act, which includes the original Medicaid provisions, contains a clause (§1304) that expressly 'reserved "[t]he right to alter, amend, or repeal any provision" of that statute', yet said that the new Act changes the character of Medicaid, from a programme 'designed to assist the neediest' to one designed to assist anyone who meets a low income condition such that Medicaid would now become 'an element of a national program of universal health care'. He continued: 'A state could hardly anticipate that Congress's reservation of the right to "alter" or "amend" the Medicaid program included the power to transform it so dramatically.' To the contrary, States have been expecting that the existing programme or some moderately modified variant would continue to be funded by the Federal government, such that the threatened loss of so much money in case a State declines the expansion introduced by the new Act 'is economic dragooning that leaves the States with no real option but to acquiesce in the Medicaid expansion'.

This claim is explicitly about the expectations the original enactment generated, which are meant to be germane to its impact by virtue of changing what government can permissibly now do. It therefore implies the rejection of the view that the meaning of the enactment constitutes its impact. The critical issue is therefore the kind and content of the expectations in play. Why could the States not anticipate that the relevant reservation included the contested power?

One possibility is that a State could not anticipate such a change because, as a linguistic matter, 'alter' or 'amend' does not (or not clearly) cover policy changes of the proposed magnitude such that, when the statute that announces the reservation of a power to alter or amend was enacted, States properly understood Congress to have conveyed that it reserved the power moderately to modify the programme and therefore to have given notice to that effect. Another is that, while a reservation to 'alter' or 'amend' extends to major changes such as the one envisaged in the new statute, such that States were put on notice that such changes might be made in the future, States could not imagine that it might someday become politically possible to expand coverage in the way proposed and therefore expected government not to alter the terms of the programme in a way that secures that expansion.

On the view that the impact of the critical section of the original statute is in part determined by the expectations that States were led to form on the basis of what the section means or what its production conveyed, only the first alternative would be relevant. But that alternative is incredible. There is nothing in the meaning of 'alter' or 'amend' (or in the propositions Congress plausibly used the sentence in which these expressions occur to express) to support understanding Congress to have conveyed a reservation of a power to alter or amend of a kind that rules out designing an expansion of the programme, and henceforth undertaking funding only of the expanded programme. There is thus nothing in the meaning of those words, or in the propositions they were used to express, which could itself lead States to form expectations about the future that reflect such a limitation.

Of course the enactment of any statute results in expectations about what government might do based on much else besides the information conveyed by the text of the statute, and for reasons of fairness expectations so formed may matter to the statute's impact, making it diverge from the content of the statute's language. It does not follow that all such expectations matter in that way. The political shift regarding the grounds and scope of health care provision, to which the Chief Justice appeals, was surely hard to anticipate in the 1960s. But it is doubtful that a failure to anticipate that the political winds may profoundly change – a conservative bias in the formation of expectations – would be relevant to the effect of an announced reservation of power precisely to change some arrangement, even a politically sensitive one. The point of such announcements is to shape expectations and constrain their effect. In this case, it would be to encourage expecting that the arrangements introduced by the Social Security Act may not persist, to discourage expecting that they will or counting on it, so to notify people that any expectations of persistence that they may nonetheless form may be frustrated, thus destroying the grounds on which the expectations might bear on permissibility. On the basis of the announced reservation, States could and should anticipate the possibility of 'dramatic' changes in the programme. As Justice Ginsburg pointed out, Congress explicitly announced that it retains power to do more than alter or amend, even dramatically so: it announced that it retains 'power to repeal Medicaid, wiping it out entirely', so no State could reasonably expect that the powers reserved to Congress were 'to make adjustments only if modestly sized'.

It further follows that States were on notice that Congress had power to repeal the original statute and enact a new one in which the comprehensive programme was the only one available. If Congress could permissibly accomplish what it now wants in this way, why could it not do so in the way it actually chose? If this is right, the effect of §1304 of the original Act closely tracks the content of its language – it makes it permissible to alter, amend, or eliminate the Medicaid programme – because considerations of fair notice and legitimate expectations so dictate.

VII. A NONEXISTENT PROBLEM

The explanation of the impact of statutes promised to be the most straightforward illustration of Hart's hypothesis that institutions create or change obligations by conveying rules. It turns out there are problems similar to those we encountered in connection with Hart's hypothesis that social practices constitute rules that impose obligations. For any consideration, including the content of the language of a statute, something must assign it some role in the explanation of its impact on obligation. It is not even the case that the hypothesis that the content conveyed by the text of a statute constitutes its impact smoothly explains cases that turn on the statute's impact, or the methods and arguments that lawyers employ to calculate impact. There is a variety of considerations, linguistic and other, which compete as candidates for a role in the fundamental explanation of the impact of such action, and assigning any of these some such role seems to require appeal to considerations of political morality (and lawyers and judges seem to suppose so). If this is right, the statutory rules that lawyers may cite, whether or not they track the text of the relevant statute, would at best sum up rather than explain statutes' effect on obligations, and difficulties surrounding the correct application of their terms would be of no consequence for the obligations the rules reflect.[67]

Hart formulated the problem of determinacy of legal obligation as the problem of determinacy of the rules that explain it, and that, in turn, as the problem of determinacy of correct application of the constituent expressions of certain formulations of the rules. If there are no rules that play that role, while the role of official language in the explanation of obligation is determined by considerations of political morality, Hart's problem does not arise. If so, there is no answer to the question whether Hart succeeded in steering a middle course between his two opponents, the formalist, whom he defined as someone who thinks that rules always constitute determinate obligations, and the sceptic, whom he defined as someone who thinks that they never do.

It does not follow, of course, that legal obligation is determinate to any degree. If there is a problem of determinacy of legal obligation, it must be a problem inherited from its determinants or the particular mechanism through which these constitute the obligation. The alternative sketched at various places above appeals to moral considerations as determining the role of social and linguistic factors in the fundamental explanation of obligation in law. This is an instance of the ordinary moral explanation of obligation, which would inherit the problems of determinacy, if any exist, of such explanations.

---

[67] *cf* n 23 above and accompanying text.

8

Hart on Justice and Morality

JOHN TASIOULAS*

CHAPTER VIII OF *The Concept of Law* is probably one of the least influential chapters in that enormously influential work. And perhaps because it is principally a contribution to moral philosophy embedded in a jurisprudential treatise, it has not attracted critical attention remotely comparable in quantity and quality to that received by certain other chapters.[1] However, in addressing the nature of morality and of its key constituent elements – primarily the idea of justice – it arguably ventures out onto some of the deepest philosophical waters traversed by *The Concept of Law*.

The chapter has a twofold ambition. The first is to explain the nature of justice as one specific moral value among others and, in the course of doing so, to assess the widely credited thought that justice has a peculiarly intimate connection with the law. The second is to identify what distinguishes moral standards from legal and other standards of conduct. In characterising this second task Hart apparently assumes (mistakenly, I believe) that all moral standards are obligation-imposing, a topic to which I shall return.[2] In any case, the first task is that of limning the contours of justice within the general structure of our moral thought, while the second task is that of distinguishing moral standards among the general class of practical standards. In keeping with the preoccupations of the Oxford philosophical environment of the 1950s, Hart conceives of both undertakings as aimed at conceptual clarification, a matter of achieving 'a separation of some long-entangled issues'.

---

* I am grateful to the editors for extensive feedback on a previous draft of this paper and regret that I have not been able to address all of the points that they made.

[1] Note, however, that on the 50th anniversary of the publication of *The Concept of Law*, Peter Cane devoted his illuminating British Academy Maccabaean Lecture in Jurisprudence largely to an evaluation of Hart's attempt to characterise the distinctive nature of moral standards as compared, especially, with legal standards: *cf* P Cane, 'Morality, Law and Conflicting Reasons for Action' (2012) 71 *Cambridge Law Journal* 59.

[2] Hart formulates the second aim as 'to characterize, in general terms, those principles, rules, and standards relating to the conduct of individuals which belong to morality and make conduct morally obligatory': HLA Hart, *The Concept of Law*, 3rd edn (Oxford, Oxford University Press, 2012) 168.

Moreover, he expresses the conviction that success in these undertakings is attainable without proceeding 'far into moral philosophy'.[3]

This latter conviction manifests itself in two main ways. First, although Hart occasionally expresses certain first-order views about the content of sound principles of justice and morality throughout this chapter, his primary objective is to elucidate the concepts of justice and morality. Conceptual analysis seeks to tell us what makes a standard of conduct a standard of justice or morality, whether sound or not, as opposed to a practical standard of some other kind. Secondly, Hart believes the work of conceptual analysis can proceed in a manner that evades the question whether morality, as a domain of thought, enjoys an 'objective' status. In other words, in line with his general policy in *The Concept of Law*, Hart purports to be officially neutral regarding the central questions of meta-ethics: whether moral judgments are properly interpreted as aiming at, and capable of achieving, a mind-independent form of truth, and also whether and how we are capable of acquiring knowledge of any such truths.[4] The project of giving an analysis of the concept of justice and morality, as conceived by Hart, seeks to abstain from both first-order normative judgments, on the one hand, and epistemological and metaphysical entanglements, on the other.

Now, Hart's execution of his two-pronged project is encumbered not only by the limited space made available by a single, not too-long chapter, but also by the fact that it is not always clear whether he is addressing critical morality or social (or positive) morality. There is, as Hart himself points out in an endnote, a 'very important distinction between a social morality and those moral principles which transcend it and are used in criticism of it'.[5] Indeed, Hart subsequently deployed this distinction in his celebrated critique of Patrick Devlin's case for the legal enforcement of social morality:

> I would revive the terminology much favoured by the Utilitarians of the last century, which distinguished 'positive morality', the morality actually accepted and shared by a given social group, from the general moral principles used in criticism of actual social institutions including positive morality. We may call such general principles 'critical morality.'[6]

However, there is a shift of focus from critical to social morality as we move from section 1 to section 2 of chapter VIII. Hart might reply that this is

---

[3] ibid 157.

[4] The policy of neutrality, or at least 'evasion', regarding meta-ethical questions is announced at ibid 168, and it is reiterated as a general constraint on legal theory in the Postscript at ibid 253f: 'I think legal theory should avoid commitment to controversial philosophical theories of the general status of moral judgments and should leave open, as I do in this book . . . the general question of whether they have what Dworkin calls "objective standing".'

[5] ibid 301.

[6] See HLA Hart, *Law, Liberty, and Morality* (Oxford, Oxford University Press, 1963) 20; and P Devlin, *The Enforcement of Morals* (Oxford, Oxford University Press, 1965).

unproblematic, since his analysis is intended to apply to critical and social moral standards alike. Principles of both social morality and critical morality are, for all their differences, equally 'moral' principles, and it is this latter quality that his conceptual analysis seeks to elucidate.

But this predictable response needs to reckon with the possibility that critical morality enjoys a certain primacy when it comes to the conceptual analysis of morality. This is because only in relation to the idea of such critical – or what are taken to be genuinely reason-giving – standards can we make sense of a given social morality *as* a morality. In particular, a social morality might be best understood as in some sense derivative from what individual members of the society espouse as critical moral standards. If so, the concept of critical morality has explanatory priority over that of social morality, since the latter must be understood in terms of the former.[7] Indeed, Hart eventually admitted that social morality is to be understood by reference to an intelligible conception of critical morality held by individual members of the social group whose morality it is. In the Postscript, he conceded Ronald Dworkin's point that social morality is constituted by a 'consensus of *independent conviction*' regarding justified standards of morality, rather than a 'consensus of convention' in which others' general conformity with a standard is taken by individuals as the reason for accepting that standard.[8] As this formulation of the contrast shows, even a consensus of convention characteristically reflects individuals' critical judgments as to the reasons they have to accept an existing practice as establishing a genuine standard of conduct.

It is a plausible conjecture that the failure to recognise the conceptual priority of critical morality explains why Hart's elucidations of the concepts of justice and morality are, as I shall try to explain below, unduly formalistic. The requirement of intelligibility as a critical morality, or as an element thereof, entails substantive constraints on both the content and the function of anything recognisable as a moral outlook, constraints that go well beyond anything countenanced by Hart. Moreover, I suspect a shadow is also cast at

---

[7] 'In Hart's own terminology – employing the fruits of his main analysis in *The Concept of Law* – the central case of morality understood from *the internal point of view* is (what the deliberating person takes to be) *critical*, that is, justified, morality. Conscientiously deliberating persons are deliberating about what they should count as *reasons* for action, and the bare fact that others count something a reason does not constitute something a reason (though it may be persuasive as ground for some evidentiary presumption that those other persons have some good reason for their belief)': see JM Finnis, 'Hart as a Political Philosopher' in *Philosophy of Law: Collected Essays of John Finnis*, vol IV (Oxford, Oxford University Press, 2011) 271.

[8] See RM Dworkin, 'The Model of Rules II', in his *Taking Rights Seriously* (London, Duckworth, 1977) 53. As Hart puts it, social morality is constituted by 'a consensus of independent *conviction* manifested in the concurrent practices of a group . . . by the fact that members of the group have and generally act on the same but independent reasons for behaving in certain ways': *cf The Concept of Law* (n 2) 255f.

this point by Hart's anti-objectivist sympathies in meta-ethics,[9] notwithstanding his official agnosticism about such questions in *The Concept of Law*. This is because anti-objectivism seriously diminishes the significance, even if it does not entirely erase the existence, of the distinction between critical and social morality. If there is no objective truth in morality, 'critical' standards will simply be moral standards, taken to be correct by some practical reasoner or other, in terms of which some existing social morality may be criticised, even if those standards are not themselves embodied in any existing social practices or traditions. But a vindication of the reasoner's claim to take these standards as 'objectively' correct will always be unavailable.[10]

I. THE IDEA OF JUSTICE

I begin with Hart's explication of the idea of justice. He starts off promisingly, rebuking those lawyers who write as if the ideas of justice and morality are 'co-extensive'. In reality, justice is a 'distinct segment of morality', one moral value among others which the law may possess or lack.[11] I am deeply sympathetic to this line of thought. It seems to me that considerable damage has been done in contemporary moral, political and legal philosophy by the failure to keep in mind that justice is one value among others.

The damage consists, on the one hand, in the watering-down of the category of justice, as it is stretched to encompass practically any consideration with a positive ethical valence. And, on the other hand, in the distortion or sidelining of important ethical ideas, such as those of charity and mercy, that cannot be subsumed within the rubric of justice. Both of these tendencies are manifest in the leading work of political philosophy of the last 50 years, John Rawls's *A Theory of Justice*. Although Rawls characterises justice as the 'first virtue' of social institutions, implying that there are others besides, the overall

---

[9] Hart's sympathy towards moral anti-objectivism, at least late in his career, is clearly expressed in a review of B Williams's *Ethics and the Limits of Philosophy* (London, Fontana, 1985): see HLA Hart, 'Who Can Tell Right from Wrong?' (1986) 33 (July 17) *New York Review of Books* 49–52. For an insightful discussion of these matters, see JM Finnis, 'On Hart's Ways: Law as Reason and as Fact' in *Philosophy of Law* (n 7) 249–56.

[10] Interestingly, towards the conclusion of the chapter, Hart appeals to the two 'formal conditions' that critical morality imposes on any social morality: one of *rationality* ('social arrangements should not rest on beliefs [presumably, non-moral beliefs] which can be shown to be mistaken'), the other of *generality* ('the protections from harm, which morality characteristically affords through the actions and forbearances it demands, should be extended at least to all men who are able and willing themselves to observe such restrictions'): see *The Concept of Law* (n 2) 183. It is not made clear either on what basis these standards form part of critical morality, or why other, more 'substantive' standards may not be added to them.

[11] ibid 157.

effect is undercut by his expansive interpretation of justice[12] and his failure to elucidate in any serious way the nature and content of political values other than justice. Justice, on this view, becomes equivalent to the moral principles that appropriately regulate the basic structure of society. One consequence of this trend is that we lose a perspicuous grasp of the diversity of moral concerns and of their relation to each other, including potential conflicts between justice and other values. This pluralistic concern is one that would have resonated strongly with Hart.[13]

Still, it should be acknowledged that there is a broad sense of justice, one with a venerable philosophical pedigree, that roughly equates it with inter-personal morality in general: morality insofar as it relates to our treatment of other people. Or, more narrowly, as that component of inter-personal morality that may in principle receive the backing of legal or social sanctions. Insofar as this latter constraint has been historically thought to be intrinsic to justice, as it probably was in different ways by philosophers as diverse as Aristotle, Locke and Kant, we have one comparatively straightforward explanation of the supposedly 'intimate' connection between justice and the law.[14] In any case, the idea that one understanding of justice comprehends the whole of interpersonal morality is to be found in Plato and persists to the present day. (Hence the title of Michael Sandel's recent book: *Justice: What's the Right Thing to Do?*[15])

Nonetheless, Hart is undoubtedly correct to argue that both ordinary and philosophical moral thought also recognise a more specific notion of justice, according to which it is a particular kind of standard of inter-personal morality. How, then, are principles of justice to be distinguished within this wider moral landscape? And how can this be done in such a way that even flawed

---

[12] For Rawls, the concept of justice, of which there can be competing specific conceptions, designates 'a characteristic set of principles for assessing basic rights and duties and for determining ... the proper distribution of the benefits and burdens of social cooperation': J Rawls, *A Theory of Justice* (Oxford, Oxford University Press, 1999) 5.

[13] Recall, in this connection, Hart's observations on the use of the principle that an extremely immoral law is no law at all in order to justify the punishment of those who had denounced others pursuant to wicked Nazi laws. Among the defects of this argument, he thought, is the way it masks the plural and conflicting moral concerns that bear on this issue: 'Surely if we have learned anything from the history of morals it is that the thing to do with a moral quandary is not to hide it. Like nettles, the occasions when life forces us to choose the lesser of two evils must be grasped with the consciousness that they are what they are. The vice of this use of the principle that, at certain limiting points, what is utterly immoral cannot be law or lawful is that it will serve to cloak the true nature of the problems with which we are faced and will encourage the romantic optimism that all the values we cherish ultimately will fit into a single system, that no one of them has to be sacrificed or compromised to accommodate another': see HLA Hart, 'Positivism and the Separation of Law and Morals' (1958), in his *Essays in Jurisprudence and Philosophy* (Oxford, Clarendon Press, 1983) 77.

[14] For a discussion of historical conceptions of justice, see J Tasioulas, 'Justice, Equality, and Rights' in R Crisp (ed), *The Oxford Handbook of the History of Ethics* (Oxford, Oxford University Press, 2013).

[15] M Sandel, *Justice: What's the Right Thing to Do?* (London, Allen Lane, 2009).

principles of justice can nonetheless count as principles of *justice*? The second question might be thought to pose a peculiar requirement, but it is one that can be justified. If two people are really disagreeing about justice, then they must have the same subject-matter in their sights, otherwise their dispute would be merely verbal, like two people arguing about the merits of 'fencing', when one has in mind a sport involving sword-fighting and the other the erection of structures for dividing plots of land. What we are after is the *concept* of justice, of which there can be competing specific *conceptions*, including erroneous conceptions.[16]

In seeking to answer this question, Hart departs from his usual procedure of elaborating his preferred view by means of a dialectical encounter with some of the leading positions in the history of the subject. This illuminating procedure is often a precursor to Hart's deployment of the beguiling strategy of presenting his own position as a sane middle course, one that captures and illuminates truths that are distorted in opposite directions by rival views. This is a strategy he famously adopts both in his critique of formalism and rule-scepticism, on the one hand, and of command theories of law and natural law theories, on the other hand. Instead, the analysis that he provides of the concept of justice, as the endnotes to the chapter attest,[17] is one deeply influenced by Aristotle's classic discussion in Book V of the *Nicomachean Ethics*, as modified by what Hart takes to be the most illuminating modern treatment, that presented in chapter 6 of Sidgwick's *The Method of Ethics*. This limited historical focus is unfortunate, since what Aristotle (as an ancient Greek philosopher) shares with Sidgwick (as a utilitarian), albeit for different reasons, is a tendency to eschew according the notion of moral rights any heavy-lifting explanatory role in moral philosophy. Yet, it is arguable that this very notion is central to at least the modern understanding of justice.

In any case, the concept of justice affirmed by Hart is that of a species of moral standard that enjoins some form of equality (or, perhaps, proportionality) in the allocation of benefits and burdens among a class of individuals. It is the focus on the treatment of classes of individuals, rather than on individual conduct as such, that explains the special relevance of justice to the evaluation of legal institutions.[18] So understood, justice is essentially a matter of fairness and is relevant to two main situations in social life.[19] The first is the distribu-

---

[16] The distinction between a concept and a conception of justice was made famous by John Rawls. 'It seems natural to think of the concept of justice as distinct from the various conceptions of justice and as being specified by the role which these different sets of principles, these different conceptions, have in common': see J Rawls, *A Theory of Justice*, 5. In a footnote to this sentence, Rawls credits this distinction to Hart ('Here I follow H.L.A. Hart, *The Concept of Law* . . . pp 155–159'.)
[17] Hart, *The Concept of Law* (n 2) 299–302.
[18] ibid 167.
[19] ibid 158.

tion of benefits or burdens among individuals who are classed in certain ways. The second is compensation, in which some injury done by one person to another is redressed. Justice in its primary signification relates to situations of distribution and compensation, and it involves a constant and a variable component. The constant feature is the maxim 'Treat like cases alike, and different cases differently' (the 'like cases maxim', as I shall call it). But, as Hart rightly points out, in the absence of some criterion for determining what shall count as the relevant point of likeness or unlikeness, this maxim will remain 'an empty formula'.[20] What the relevant criterion of resemblance is will often be controversial, implicating the deeper moral outlooks of the disputants, and will vary from case to case, depending among other things on the nature of the benefit or burden in question or the relations in which individuals stand. For example, in the distribution of health care, the relevant criterion of distribution might be need, whereas in the distribution of tertiary education, it might be some combination of individual merit and social utility.

But even at this stage, however, Hart thinks at least one sound principle of justice emerges fairly directly from his conceptual ground-clearing exercise. When it comes to assessing the *administration* of law, as opposed to its content, he believes that the like cases maxim yields a standard of justice: a law has been *pro tanto* justly administered if it has been impartially applied according to its terms. This, Hart believes, is one explanation of the intimate connection often asserted between law and justice: whatever the content of any particular law, some form of justice is achieved whenever it is applied according to its terms.

But this thesis is questionable. First of all, even if it is true, it would appear to hold for all rules concerned with inter-personal allocation. Consequently, it would not show that law, as opposed to any other rule-governed system of allocation, enjoys a special connection with justice. But the more telling point is that the supposed standard of assessment does not obviously count as a sound principle of justice. When, in a death camp scenario, a well-intentioned guard rescues some inmates, but not others, from a hideous fate to which they are consigned by genocidal laws, it seems grotesque to describe his breaches of the law as even *pro tanto* unjust simply on this basis. Conversely, it seems no less grotesque to insist that justice is served by the application of a law according to its terms irrespective of its content. For example, Hart claims that one may say, without absurdity, that a law forbidding the access of black people to parks has been justly administered, in that only persons guilty of breaking the law were punished under it.[21] Even if such a view is not patently unintelligible as a principle of justice, it nonetheless appears to be unsound. Hart's suggestion involves the implausible thought that there is a moral obligation, albeit a

[20] ibid 159.
[21] ibid 161.

defeasible one, to apply the law according to its terms, irrespective of its content. We appear, at best, to have a formal principle of rationality that applies to any rule-governed endeavour, not a sound (or even intelligible) principle of justice.

As I already mentioned, one difficulty in assessing Hart's analysis of justice as equality in interpersonal allocation is that he fails to do much by way of identifying, let alone motivating, any competitor analyses. However, the more than 2,000-year interlude between Aristotle and Sidgwick discloses a salient rival. This is a view of justice encapsulated in what might be called Justinian's maxim. In Justinian's *Digest*, it is affirmed that 'justice is a constant and unceasing determination to render everyone his due' ['ius suum'].[22] Of course, what counts as each person's 'due' is open to radically different formulations, but according to one powerfully formative tradition, it refers to that to which each person has a (moral) right. The basic idea is that some moral obligations are perfect and others imperfect. Perfect obligations are owed to some ascertainable individual, the right-holder, whereas imperfect obligations have no counterpart rights.[23] Hence, we can differentiate duties of justice, which are owed to people as a matter of right from, say, reasons, or even duties, of charity, which are not owed to anyone in particular.[24]

How, then, are moral rights themselves to be understood, at the level of conceptual analysis, one that prescinds as much as reasonably possible from controversies that divide the proponents of different theories of rights, preserving the sense that for all their disputes they are engaged with the self-same subject-matter? I think we can say that the following features are characteristic of moral rights. First, they have corresponding moral duties, so that A's right to X involves a duty on someone else not to interfere with A's enjoying X or to protect or promote his access to X.[25] Second, the possession of the

---

[22] Justinian, *The Digest*, CH Monro (trans) (Cambridge, Cambridge University Press, 1904) I.I.10.

[23] So, for example, Mill writes that 'the notion which we have found to be of the essence of the idea of justice, that of a right residing in an individual, implies and testifies to this more binding obligation': JS Mill, *Utilitarianism* (Oxford, Oxford University Press, 1998) 5.2. For Kant's similar view, see I Kant, *The Metaphysics of Morals* (Cambridge, Cambridge University Press, 1996) Part II. The distinction between perfect and imperfect obligations has also been drawn in other ways that don't necessarily map on to the distinction as I have interpreted it. In particular, perfect obligations are often characterised as those which are highly determinate in their requirements, leaving the duty-bearer with little or no discretion regarding the occasion and manner of their performance. I set these other senses aside.

[24] For two important discussions of the distinction between justice and charity, see O O'Neill, 'The Great Maxims of Justice and Charity' in her *Constructions of Reason: Explorations of Kant's Political Philosophy* (Cambridge, Cambridge University Press, 1989); and A Buchanan, 'Justice and Charity' (1987) 97 *Ethics* 558.

[25] To this extent, we are talking about 'claim-rights'; in a broader sense, 'right' also encompasses privileges, powers and immunities. See WN Hohfeld, *Fundamental Legal Conceptions as Applied in Judicial Reasoning and Other Essays* (New Haven, Yale University Press, 1923).

right typically secures to its holder something of benefit to them, eg freedom from attack or the ability to sell one's property. Third, moral rights that do not owe their existence to the law or some social practice are generally thought of as grounded in some quality of the right-holder. There is extensive philosophical disagreement about the nature of this quality: whether it is the right-holder's needs or interests, their capacity for autonomous choice, their membership of the moral community, or their likeness to God. Fourth, the obligations associated with moral rights have a 'directed' character: violations of them are not merely moral wrongs, but involve the *wronging* or *victimisation* of the specific individual in whose right the obligation originates. Finally, the duties corresponding to rights are in principle properly enforceable against their bearers, whether by law or informal social sanctions. This last condition is sometimes presented as characterising not rights in general but, as in Grotius and Locke, the sub-class of rights that constitutes the domain of justice in the strict sense.

I believe that the Justinian maxim, on some such rendering, encapsulates the dominant concept of justice at least in the modern period, but it is passed over in silence by Hart. However, it is endorsed in the work of Grotius, Locke, Smith, Kant and Mill as well as figuring in Roman law and the natural law tradition.[26] In contemporary philosophy, it is endorsed both by prominent Kantians, such as Onora O'Neill, and prominent Thomists, such as John Finnis.[27] As the diversity of the philosophers I have mentioned plainly testifies, the adoption of the concept of justice as rights does not correlate with any underlying philosophical fault-lines, such as the distinction between teleological and deontological approaches to morality. But it does help explain the special stringency of duties of justice, as opposed to those of charity or beneficence, because duties of the former sort are owed to someone in particular, who has a special standing to feel aggrieved in the event of their violation.

Now, one possibility is that we are confronted at this point with a stand-off between two rival analyses of a concept, a dispiritingly familiar scenario in philosophy. Is there any reason to suppose that the Justinian concept of justice is preferable to Hart's broadly Aristotelian one? Well, one question is whether the elements of Hart's concept of justice are sufficient to bring us within what we would normally take to be the domain of principles of justice. The answer, I think, is 'No', because the two elements he describes – the likeness maxim and the allocative criterion – can be satisfied by principles that are clearly not

---

[26] For an historically-informed, contemporary defence of the view, see N Wolterstorff, *Justice: Rights and Wrongs* (Princeton, New Jersey, Princeton University Press, 2008). For general discussion, see J Tasioulas, 'Justice, Equality, and Rights' (n 14).

[27] O O'Neill, *Towards Justice and Virtue: A Constructive Account of Practical Reasoning* (Cambridge, Cambridge University Press, 1996) 128–35; and JM Finnis, *Natural Law and Natural Rights*, 2nd edn (Oxford, Oxford University Press, 2011) ch VII.

principles of justice. Suppose a rich individual sets aside a portion of his wealth to promote academic excellence. He adopts the principle of using these resources to fund doctoral scholarships for outstanding students who are graduates of his beloved old primary school. Exceptional circumstances aside, this scheme of beneficence does not plausibly reflect a principle of justice, yet both the bare like cases maxim and the distribution of benefits and burdens are present in this case. And this is so in spite of the fact the philanthropist's scheme impacts on the interests of others, perhaps in quite radical ways. And the ready-to-hand explanation for that conclusion is that the allocation in question is not one that directly bears on anyone's rights. This suggests that a principle of distribution will be a principle of justice only if the basis of distribution, whether it be need, merit, desert or whatever, is (intelligibly) portrayed as one that generates a right to a certain allocation.

Now, one might try to interrupt the preceding line of thought by arguing that the additional element required here is not the notion of rights, but rather that of a moral duty or obligation, one which may or may not have a corresponding moral right.[28] But it is doubtful that the introduction of the notion of duty suffices to pick out justice as a specific value, in the absence of a requirement that the duties in play have corresponding rights. After all, the question of which charity to support is also one of allocation, and plausibly both a matter of obligation and subject to the like cases maxim. Yet to regard all principles addressed to such a question as principles of justice risks effacing the distinction between justice and charity.

Whether consciously or not, Hart himself is not immune to the lure of the idea of justice as rights. What looks like an incipient awareness of the centrality of rights to the discourse of justice breaks out in chapter VIII at various points. For example, he suggests that the general principle latent in the diverse applications of the idea of justice is that 'individuals are *entitled* in respect of each other to a certain position of equality or inequality'.[29] Now, one natural way of reading 'entitlement' here is in terms of the existence of a moral right. Later, he even provides what looks like a general basis for this entitlement: the idea that 'prima facie human beings should be treated alike', that they are prima facie 'entitled' to equal treatment, a principle that Hart says is 'deeply embedded in modern man'.[30] However, it seems to me that any such principle would have to be one of basic human equality, or equal human dignity, and

---

[28] According to Amartya Sen, principles of justice are distinguished by two general features: (a) they embody a norm of fairness, which requires the adoption of an impartial perspective that precludes biased evaluations (this is similar to Hart's 'like cases' maxim); and (b) they are a source of moral obligations. Like Hart, Sen conceives of justice as centrally concerned with issues of allocation. See A Sen, *The Idea of Justice* (Cambridge, Mass, Harvard University Press, 2009), and, for criticism, J Tasioulas, 'Flutes and Fairness' (2010) 23 April *Times Literary Supplement* 9f.

[29] *The Concept of Law* (n 2) 159.

[30] ibid 162; see also the reference to 'the right of all to equal consideration' at ibid 206.

this is a principle that, if anything, informs the whole of inter-personal morality, not just some particular segment of it, such as the principles of justice. Moreover, it is questionable that any such principle is itself aptly characterised in terms specifically of any sort of *right*, though it may give rise to some rights in conjunction with other premises.

The need for reference to rights in order to bring justice into view becomes even more evident in Hart's characterisation of the other context of justice, that of compensation (or, it might be best to say, more broadly, correction). In this case, Hart explicitly draws on the concept of a right in order to explain the bearing of justice on compensation for injury:

> The connection between the justice and injustice of the compensation for injury, and the principle 'Treat like cases alike and different cases differently', lies in the fact that outside the law there is a moral conviction that those with whom the law is concerned have a *right* to mutual forbearance from certain kinds of harmful conduct.[31]

People are equal insofar as they equally possess these rights, and corrective justice requires the restoration of the moral *status quo ante* in the aftermath of its disruption by the wrong-doer.

Now, let us suppose that Hart responds to the foregoing criticism by incorporating rights as a third element – alongside the like cases maxim and the focus on allocation – in his conceptualisation of principles of justice. Principles of justice would them be principles relating to allocative rights or rights addressed to problems of allocation. Are we now equipped with a compelling account of what makes principles of justice principles of *justice*?

I think this modified view would still face formidable obstacles, because the concerns of justice plausibly extend beyond the realm of allocation, however that slippery notion is to be plausibly construed. As always in philosophy, one tempting remedial measure in response to these obstacles is to subject the meaning of 'allocation' to a tremendous amount of stretching. But then the question will arise whether the thesis secures only a Pyrrhic victory, having been emptied of the determinate content that the introduction of the notion of 'allocation' promised to introduce.

Consider the case of corrective justice. Hart seems to be committed to the idea that the wrongs for which corrective justice provides redress are themselves injustices. Even if this is not so, he regards such wrongs as essentially cases of misallocation, whereby it is essential to their nature that their perpetrator deprives another of some benefit that belongs to him, or else imposes upon him a burden he should not be made to bear. But what sense can we make of this idea in the case of an assault?

---

[31] ibid 165 (my italics).

Hart's answer is that it is not too far-fetched to say that the person who commits the assault 'has profited at his victim's expense, even if it is only by indulging his wish to injure him or not sacrificing his ease to the duty of taking adequate precautions'.[32] Presumably, a similar analysis extends to the just punishment of someone who has committed an assault: they have arrogated to themselves greater liberty to indulge their will than the law-abiding members of their community, and the punishment seems to cancel the extra benefit they have gained. Yet, it is strongly arguable that the idea that just compensation or punishment essentially consists in a restoration of a just balance of advantages between the wrongdoer and the law-abiding involves a fundamentally misplaced focus. It fails to grasp that the victim is entitled to compensation, and the wrong-doer deserves punishment, because the latter has wronged the latter. And paradigmatically, the wrong will consist in the violation of the former's moral or legal rights. We do not need to take the further step, in all cases, of characterising the wrong as necessarily involving the disruption of some allocation of benefits and burdens, with a consequent gain on the part of the wrong-doer at his victim's or someone else's expense.

One possibility that emerges from this line of thought is that justice can be identified with the domain of moral rights, perhaps socially and legally enforceable moral rights, without any need to restrict those rights to contexts of allocation. It is a view to which I am sympathetic, though it also faces some difficulties. On the one hand, it might be judged over-inclusive, since we might not regard all rights-violations as injustices, and not simply for the reason that designating them as such seems to understate their gravity as moral wrongs. Regarding the man who shows gross cruelty to his child, Hart says it would be 'strange to criticise his conduct as *unjust*',[33] although it may involve a rights violation. On the other hand, the idea of justice as the domain of rights might be thought to be under-inclusive. Consider, for example, the case of justice in punishment. If we give up on the idea of offenders having a right to be punished, then it seems that the obligation must be seen as in some sense arising out of the rights violations perpetrated by offenders. But it is far from clear that all properly criminalisable wrongs are rights-violations. When someone is punished for despoiling the environment, for example, it is not obvious that his wrong consists in the violation of the rights of some person or other entity. So perhaps retributive desert has to be introduced as a possible ground for justice alongside rights or else we may have to say that in speaking of 'retributive justice' we are using justice in a looser sense.

In short, there is reason to regard Hart's analysis of the nature of justice as excessively formal. We cannot demarcate the principles of justice by reference to the combined operation of the like cases maxim and some principle of allo-

[32] ibid.
[33] ibid 158.

cation with variable, topic-dependent content. We also have to introduce the thought that the relevant sort of likeness must be intelligibly presentable as grounding ethical considerations of a characteristic kind – I have suggested that these are centrally, although perhaps not exclusively, considerations of moral rights. But once we have made these ethical considerations integral to principles of justice in the narrow sense, how can we resist the pressure to widen the scope of justice beyond the distributive and compensatory rubrics discussed by Hart? Questions of justice will then arise whenever the observance of duties corresponding to rights are implicated. An alternative possibility is simply to have a three-level view of justice: universal justice, construed as interpersonal morality in general; and a wider and a narrower interpretation of justice as a specific moral value. On the wider interpretation, it is the domain of (legally or socially enforceable) rights; on the narrower interpretation, it is such rights as they bear on allocative questions among a class of individuals – justice as fairness, as one might call it.

One advantage of adopting the construal of justice as the domain of rights is that it promises to furnish us with a sharper and more accurate grasp of justice within the domain of value. In particular, it enables us to differentiate principles of justice from other moral values, even obligation-imposing values, such as charity. When he comes to articulating how justice is one value among others, and how it may enter into conflict with those other values, Hart largely limits himself to the potentially confused idea that justice may conflict with the general welfare of society.[34] One problem here is that this idea seems to presuppose, or to make most sense on, a broadly utilitarian reading of the general welfare. On an alternative, Aristotelian construal of general welfare or the common good, the idea of such a conflict is problematic, because justice is itself a component of that common good.[35]

In one way, Hart agrees with this last point, because he states that it is a requirement of distributive justice that decisions for the common good must impartially consider the claims of all affected.[36] But this sounds like a reversion to the idea of justice in the universal sense, which fails to pick out justice as one moral value among others. This impression is confirmed when Hart cites the claim of SI Benn and RS Peters that 'the criterion for calling a rule a moral rule is that it is the product of reasoned and impartial consideration of the interests of those affected'.[37] Alternatively, Hart's point may be interpreted as identifying justice with the observance of duties arising out of the rights of others, which is in essence the view I have advocated in this section.

[34] ibid 166f.
[35] See JM Finnis, *Natural Law and Natural Rights* (n 27) 210–18, and J Raz, 'Rights and Individual Well-Being' in his *Ethics in the Public Domain* (Oxford, Oxford University Press, 1994).
[36] Hart, *The Concept of Law* (n 2) 167.
[37] ibid 302.

II. THE DISTINCTIVENESS OF MORAL STANDARDS

Let us now turn to Hart's second topic – the distinctiveness of moral standards, as compared to legal and other social standards. Hart characterises this distinctiveness in terms of four 'cardinal features which are constantly found together in those principles, rules, and standards of conduct which are most commonly accepted "moral"':[38]

(i) Moral standards are 'regarded as something of great importance to maintain'. This manifests itself in a variety of ways: moral standards are upheld against the drive of strong countervailing passions, and at considerable cost to personal self-interest; serious forms of social pressure are deployed to ensure not only conformity to the standards in individual cases, but also that they are communicated and inculcated in society as a whole; finally, there is a general recognition that without the acceptance of moral standards large and unwelcome changes in the life of individuals would ensue.[39]

(ii) Moral standards are immune from deliberate change, in that they cannot be established or abrogated through anything like a legislative process: '[s]tandards of conduct cannot be endowed with, or deprived of, moral status by human *fiat*, though the daily use of such concepts as enactment and repeal shows that the same is not true of law';[40] indeed, 'the idea of a moral legislature with competence to make and change morals . . . is repugnant to the whole notion of morality'.[41]

(iii) Moral offences have a voluntary character:

> If a person whose action, judged *ab extra*, has offended against moral rules or principles, succeeds in establishing that he did this unintentionally and in spite of every precaution that it was possible for him to take, he is excused from moral responsibility, and to blame him in these circumstances would itself be considered morally objectionable.[42]

Although many legal offences share this voluntary character, legal systems often qualify this feature by such means as the use of 'objective' tests that attribute to individuals the capacities of a hypothetical 'reasonable' person or even by creating strict liability offences.[43]

(iv) The characteristic form of moral pressure, which involves appeals to respect for rules as important in itself and the deployment of a panoply of

---

[38] ibid 168.
[39] ibid 173f.
[40] ibid 176.
[41] ibid 177.
[42] ibid 178.
[43] ibid.

characteristic responses, such as guilt and remorse, in the event of their breach.[44]

These four features are presented as at least necessary characteristics of the moral domain and as neutral with respect to the contending philosophical views about the fundamental nature and status of morality. Moreover, according to Hart, they are ways of articulating the truth in the theme, recurrent in the history of jurisprudential inquiry, that morality differs from law in that the latter only requires 'external' behaviour on the part of its subjects, whereas the former places great importance on the quality of an agent's will.[45] Rather than go into the details of these four features individually, I shall suggest two broad concerns triggered by them as a general account of the distinctiveness of moral standards among other practical standards.[46]

The first is that the resultant account of morality seems unduly formal. Hart stresses the formal nature of his four features by saying that they 'make no direct reference to any necessary content which rules or standards must have in order to be moral, nor even to any purpose which they must serve in social life'.[47] However, it seems plausible that there are substantive constraints on what may intelligibly count as the *content* of a moral standard, and indeed that such constraints are presupposed by some of Hart's four features. Consider the first and fourth: importance and the distinctive character of moral pressure. It is arguable that we cannot make sense of either of these unless we understand that moral standards have an essential connection with human interests, the satisfaction or frustration of which have a significant bearing on how well or ill individual human lives fare.

Now, Hart of course agrees that the characteristic importance attributed to moral standards can be explained, in part, by the way in which compliance with them secures interests shared by all alike.[48] However, he resists incorporating any such relation to interests into his specification of the nature of moral standards, and he does so by appealing to the existence of norms which virtually everyone agrees count as moral, but which are disconnected from enhancing the fulfilment, or preventing the impairment, of basic human interests. These moral norms have the character of social taboos, or as Hart calls them, 'social vetoes',[49] and he believes that only a formalist analysis of the sort he offers can bring them squarely within the category of the moral where they

---

[44] ibid 178f.
[45] ibid 173.
[46] For criticism of these four features as necessary markers of moral standards, see Peter Cane, 'Morality, Law and Conflicting Reasons for Action' (n 1) 71–79. Cane is especially effective in undermining the credentials of the third supposed distinguishing feature.
[47] Hart, *The Concept of Law* (n 2) 118.
[48] ibid 174.
[49] ibid 175.

evidently belong. Exhibit 1 here is the widespread prohibition on homosexual conduct. As Hart puts it:

> Even in a modern society which has ceased to look on its morality as divinely ordained, calculations of harmfulness to others do not account for the importance attached to moral regulation of sexual behaviour such as the common veto on homosexuality.[50]

By bringing such norms within the province of the moral, Hart thinks, we not only respect ordinary linguistic usage, we also avoid making unrealistic distinctions among social norms that function in an identical manner in the lives of those whom they regulate:

> We have ... intentionally taken a broader view of morality, so as to include in it all social rules and standards which, in the actual practice of a society, exhibit the four features we have mentioned. We have done this not merely because the weight of usage of the word 'moral' favours this broader meaning, but because to take the narrower restricted view, which would exclude these, would force us to divide in a very unrealistic manner elements in a social structure which function in an identical manner, in the lives of those who live by it. Moral prohibitions of conduct, which may not in fact harm others, are not only regarded with precisely the same instinctive respect as those that do; they enter together with the requirements of more rationally defensible rules into social estimates of character; and, with them, form part of the generally accepted picture of the life which individuals are expected and indeed are assumed to live.[51]

But this line of thought is flawed in virtue of falsely posing as exhaustive only two alternatives: a purely formal account of morality, on the one hand, and one that survives rational criticism by reference to basic human interests and needs, on the other. There is, instead, an intermediate position: a putative moral standard must be *intelligible* as a way of respecting or advancing human interests.

Consider, in the light of this suggestion, the above quotation from p 174.[52] There is an ambiguity in the assertion that concerns about harm to others do not 'account for' the importance accorded to the moral prohibition against homosexual conduct that, in some version or other, has been part of so many different social moralities throughout human history. An opponent of formalism is not committed to the belief that considerations of harm provide an adequate justification for that prohibition; after all, he may reject the prohibition as profoundly mistaken. The question is whether we can make sense of it as a *moral* prohibition, as evidently we can, without seeing it as bearing some intelligible connection to significant human interests. And, plainly, it does bear all manner of such connections, connections that seem to be essential to

---

[50] ibid 174.
[51] ibid 181f.
[52] Passage quoted to n 50.

its status as a moral standard. Sexual relations are a source of profound human fulfilment and also the object of powerful, and potentially highly destructive, emotions. Moreover, there is a manifest human interest in reproduction, the rearing of children and the maintenance of a community's life across generations. It is against these genuine background interests that a norm prohibiting homosexual relations – a norm, say, that confines sexual activity to contexts in which biological reproduction is in some sense a possibility – makes sense as precisely a *moral* norm, irrespective of whether or not ultimately we judge it to be sound.

Consider now, by contrast, a norm that really does have the character of a brute social veto or taboo, lacking even the remotest and most circuitous connection with human interests. This is the norm, famously introduced by Philippa Foot, that prohibits anyone staring at hedgehogs by the light of the moon.[53] Absent any connection with human interests – for example, disregarding the possibilities that this peculiar nocturnal activity has or is believed to have a propensity to induce insanity or cause earthquakes – we should be hard pressed to interpret this prohibition as a moral norm. If in a given society its violation was seemingly the object of the familiar panoply of moral responses, such as blame, guilt, shame, and so forth, we could at best regard it as an aberrant or marginal instance of a moral norm.

If the preceding line of thought has merit, there are constraints of substantive intelligibility on the proper delineation of the domain of moral standards. Often, although perhaps not always, these constraints will require some suitable connection to what are intelligibly regarded as human interests. And, indeed, such constraints look as though they form part of the explanation for Hart's second feature, ie immunity from deliberate change. For if morality could just consist of 'social vetoes' that float free from any connection with human well-being, then it is not at all clear why moral norms could not be the product of deliberate change. Now, in fact it is not quite true that each and every moral standard is immune to deliberate change. One reason Hart overlooks this is that the possibility of such change is perhaps clearest in the case of critical morality and, as I mentioned, Hart fails to keep the distinction between critical and social morality firmly in mind throughout this chapter. So, for example, the legal enactment of a speed limit can make it the case that conduct that was not morally wrong prior to that enactment immediately becomes wrong.[54] Still, it remains true that morality is not subject to change by *mere* fiat

---

[53] P Foot, 'Moral Arguments' in her *Virtues and Vices: and Other Essays in Moral Philosophy* (Oxford, Oxford University Press, 2002) 107.

[54] For a helpful discussion of a range of cases in which 'moral rules' – relatively cut-and-dried moral standards that incorporate some arbitrary element – can come into being through processes of social decision that vary in degree of formality from the emergence of a convention over time to explicit legislation, see N MacCormick, *H.L.A. Hart*, 2nd edn (Stanford, Stanford University Press, 2008) 68–71.

or veto; deliberate change can only be effected against the background of standards, not all of which are the product of human choice, that confer that sort of moral significance on the individual or collective decision, as in the speed limit case.

In this context, it is worth addressing the thesis propounded by Peter Cane in his recent Maccabaean Lecture.[55] Although Cane rightly doubts that Hart's four formal features clearly serve to distinguish morality from law, he contends that a fifth feature mentioned by Hart plays a pivotal role in doing so. Hart invokes this feature when he explains why the very notion of change by legislative fiat is 'repugnant to the idea of morality':

> This is so because we conceive of morality as the ultimate standard by which human actions (legislative or otherwise) are evaluated.[56]

This thought echoes the conclusion of the preceding paragraph, but it needs to be handled with some care. If the line of argument pursued in this section is correct, the ultimacy of moral standards cannot consist in their being *underived* from any other, background normative standards. On the contrary, my contention has been that moral standards are in significant part derivative from reasons reflecting human interests. But this is not how Cane interprets the 'ultimacy' of moral standards. Instead, for him, it consists in the fact that legal standards are always subject to moral assessment and, in any such assessment, moral reasons always trump any conflicting legal reasons: 'when a moral reason for action conflicts with a reason for action derived from the law, the moral reasons trumps the legal reason'.[57]

I think the first half of Cane's thesis is importantly correct, but that the second, trumping thesis, misconstrues its significance. The ultimacy of morality does not license an inference to its supremacy in practical reasoning. A motorist's reason to stop at a red traffic light is a reason derived from the law; specifically, it is a moral reason that exists in virtue of a law requiring motorists to stop at red traffic lights. Now, the motorist may well have a conflicting moral reason not to stop at the red light, say, because running the red light will enable him to arrive at his ailing mother's bedside sooner. However, it is extremely implausible that the independent moral reason must inevitably triumph in this conflict with the law-derived reason.[58] Nonetheless, the core of truth in Cane's argument is that the normative significance of the law is everywhere determined by background moral standards that are not themselves

---

[55] P Cane, 'Morality, Law and Conflicting Reasons for Action' (n 1).
[56] Hart, *The Concept of Law* (n 2) 230.
[57] Cane, 'Morality, Law and Conflicting Reasons for Action' (n 1) 80.
[58] Indeed, Cane himself seems to acknowledge this point, contrary to his general thesis that legal reasons are always trumped by conflicting moral reasons: 'In some situations, a reason to act generated by the law for the sake of maintaining and promoting successful social life may outweigh a reason for action recognised independently of the law and of the fact of disagreement': ibid 82.

the product of law. And this will be so even when law-derived reasons defeat independent moral reasons.

Let us advance now to the second general concern with the formalism of Hart's account of morality. I began by applauding Hart's project of registering the variegated character of the moral domain by articulating justice as one moral value among others. Unfortunately, we found reason to judge his articulation defective insofar as it does not accord proper significance to rights, and hence to the distinction between perfect and imperfect obligations, in constituting the domain of justice. Now, another valuable observation Hart makes is that moral standards are not simply to be equated with standards imposing moral obligations or duties (like Hart, I use these two expressions interchangeably). As he puts it: 'Moral obligation and duty are the bedrock of social morality but they are not the whole'.[59] The second half of this sentence, at least, is a valuable corrective to those who are prone to identify every moral 'ought' statement, or even every appeal to a moral reason, with the assertion of the existence of a moral obligation. But, unfortunately, as in the case with the concept of justice, Hart's follow-through on this extremely important insight is problematic.[60] This emerges in at least two ways.

First, Hart plausibly contends that there are moral ideals which, unlike moral obligations, are not regarded as a matter for censure when we fail to achieve them, but are a basis for praise and admiration when we succeed in realising them. However, I think he is too quick to characterise a whole series of moral virtues, such as bravery, charity, benevolence, as essentially supererogatory, as a matter of conformity with moral reasons for action that are not obligations. His analysis would have been more persuasive if we had kept in mind the distinction between perfect and imperfect obligations. Arguably, what distinguishes justice from charity is that any obligations associated with the latter are imperfect, rather than perfect. Hence, a person who never renders assistance to needy individuals who nonetheless have no right to his assistance, and a judge who never tempers justice with mercy in sentencing, are open to moral criticism, and potentially criticism in terms of non-compliance with certain obligations. It's just that the performance of the obligations in

---

[59] See Hart, *The Concept of Law* (n 2) 180, 182.
[60] Problematic, also, is Hart's conception of *obligation*, one that applies to legal and moral obligation alike. This is characterised by Hart in terms of three features (ibid 86–88): the *seriousness* of the pressure exerted to ensure conformity with the rule; the *importance* of the values its observance secures; and the possibility of *conflict* between the obligation-imposing standard and the agent's desires and self-interest. A better understanding of moral obligations would, at least, characterise them in terms of three other features: (a) they are reasons that are *categorical*, ie their existence and stringency are independent of the desires of the agent to whom they apply; (b) they are *exclusionary* in their force, depriving some otherwise countervailing considerations of their normative force; and (c) their violation justifies *pro tanto* a series of moral responses that include blame on the part of third parties and guilt (self-blame) on the part of the agent who perpetrates the violation.

question cannot be demanded as of right by anyone.⁶¹ Of course, this still leaves open the possibility that some of the reasons associated with these virtues are truly supererogatory.

Conversely, Hart is too quick to assimilate certain individual moral ideals – the examples he gives are 'the pursuit of heroic, romantic, aesthetic or scholarly ideals' – to the cardinal characteristics he takes to be exhibited by social morality. He argues that the analogy between such individual ideals, insofar as they are moral in character, and social morality, is one of form and function, rather than content. One supposed point of analogy is that

> [t]hey are ranked as supremely important, so that their pursuit is felt as duty to which other interests or desires are to be sacrificed.⁶²

Here, I think, we run up against the limitations of Hart's analysis of importance, which lapses into spelling out the idea of anything having moral importance in terms of its being a matter of duty or obligation. But this is clearly not so.

Consider someone whose life is inspired by the ideal of promoting human rights. Human rights, of course, involve counterpart duties. But the reasons generated by human rights, including the reasons we have to promote the fulfilment of counterpart duties, need not all themselves be duties. It is a travesty of human rights morality, one encouraged by certain consequentialist outlooks, to suppose that we have a duty to do whatever we can reasonably foresee will promote the observance by others of human rights duties. So, for example, the lover of human rights may, at great risk to her own life, publicly expose and condemn the rights-violating practices of an oppressive regime in the hope that this will help reduce the number of future violations. Yet she is not necessarily thereby acting in conformity with any *duty*: the reason she has to put her life at risk in this way does not exclude or outweigh her reasons of self-interest to preserve her own life, nor does the failure to comply with that reason render her an appropriate object of blame or self-blame, that is, guilt.

So Hart needed to articulate the character of moral ideals in such a way that their importance did not necessarily implicate the idea of an obligation to pursue them. And the natural thought here is that some kind of non-formal feature, for example, one relating moral ideals to the interests of others, is unavoidable. If so, this would be a source of importance that characteristically lies behind all three of the moral categories I have mentioned in this chapter: perfect obligations of justice, imperfect obligations and supererogatory moral ideals. To this extent, Hart is mistaken to say that moral obligation is the 'bedrock' of morality, even of social morality. That bedrock, instead, seems to consist, to a significant extent, in considerations relating to the human good and the reasons we have to respect, protect and advance it in other persons as

---

⁶¹ See, eg, J Tasioulas, 'Mercy' (2003) CIII *Proceedings of the Aristotelian Society* 101.
⁶² Hart, *The Concept of Law* (n 2) 184.

well as ourselves. However, any account of morality that is steadfastly committed to formalism, as is Hart's, is not well-adapted to penetrate down to the bedrock.

III. CONCLUSION

It is in some ways remarkable that, during a period in the history of philosophy when moral philosophy was in a parlous condition, Hart should have devoted an entire chapter of *The Concept of Law* to the nature of justice and morality. Perhaps we should be grateful that the book grew out of a lecture course on jurisprudence that Hart delivered to undergraduates at the University of Oxford, the chapter's presence reflecting exigencies quite other than those dictated by any prevailing philosophical fashion.

In any case, there is much in this chapter to admire and from which we still need to learn. The guiding ideas that moral standards are one species of practical standards among others, and that principles of justice in turn are only one kind of moral principle among others, seem to me important and fundamentally sound. Contemporary legal and political philosophy, in particular, stand to gain a lot even now by engaging more fully with that second idea.[63]

Unfortunately, Hart's pursuit of this doubly pluralistic agenda eventually runs aground. His meditation on justice fails in virtue of ignoring the historically resonant hypothesis that the scope of that value is importantly delineated by the concept of a right. Meanwhile, his attempt to articulate the nature of the moral domain as a whole suffers from an excessive formalism, something that was probably inevitable in light of his failure to give the notion of critical morality its central place when elucidating the nature of the moral.

---

[63] For a book that rightly takes contemporary political philosophy in the Rawlsian vein to task for failing to construe justice as one value among others, yet which itself offers self-confessedly meagre guidance as to what it is for a principle to be a principle of justice, see GA Cohen, *Rescuing Justice and Equality* (Oxford, Oxford University Press, 2008).

9

The Morality in Law

LESLIE GREEN

I. DRAWING LINES

THE SINGLE MOST important thing to know about the relationship between law and morality is that there is no single thing to know. 'There are many different types of relation between law and morals and there is nothing which can be profitably singled out for study as *the* relation between them': so HLA Hart reminds us in chapter IX of *The Concept of Law*.[1] There are, for instance, questions about how law is and should be created, and about how law is and should be regarded:

(A) How far is law influenced by a society's moral beliefs and attitudes?
(B) How harmful does an activity have to be, and to whom, before we have a moral justification for regulating or prohibiting it by law?
(C) Do most people believe the law is morally binding?
(D) How far do we owe the law a moral duty of respect or obedience?

There are also questions about the nature of law, including the demarcation between laws and other kinds of standards, and between legal systems and other kinds of institutions, for example:

(E) Where does ethics or decency end and legal duty begin?
(F) What are the differences between legal systems on the one hand, and markets, or systems of arbitration, or sets of social customs on the other?

These six questions are different, but they are inter-related. For one thing, until we know what law is, and thus have at least working answers to (E) and (F), we aren't likely to make headway with any of (A) through (D). If you didn't know, at least roughly, what law is, how could you know what sort of things shaped it historically, or how could you decide what policy would be the right one to take towards its demands? Of course, you don't need an explicit *theory* of (E) and (F): making explicit things we already know and revealing the connections among

---

[1] HLA Hart, *The Concept of Law*, 3rd edn (Oxford, Oxford University Press, 2012 [1961]) 185.

them is a job for philosophers, and with respect to these questions, for philosophers who work in general jurisprudence.

My interests here are mainly in (E) and especially in (F).[2] In particular, I try to answer a question posed by Hart:

> Must some reference to morality enter into an adequate definition of law or legal system? Or is it just a contingent fact that law and morals often overlap . . . and that they share a common vocabulary of rights, obligations, and duties?[3]

Hart's answer is that there is a third option. There are things that are not quite definitional elements of law but aren't contingent overlaps either. I think there is truth in that conclusion, but that Hart's arguments for it need repair. After attending to that, I explore some general worries about the project of demarcating law and morality, whether in Hart's way or in any other. But first, a comment on efforts at jurisprudential line-drawing, including this one.

Like all interesting social demarcations – the line between religion and conviction, or between pressure groups and political parties, or between rebellions and revolutions – jurisprudential distinctions are somewhat indeterminate. There are clear cases of legal systems, things that are clearly not legal systems, and things that are arguably legal systems.[4] The indeterminacy has two related sources. First, many social kinds are multi-criterial; they are made up of various features and properties. For example, political parties are social organisations; they recruit and socialise members; they shape and articulate interests; they compete for power. But there are no precise rules that combine these criteria, and there can be disagreement about whether each is necessary or about the weight it has in determining whether something does amount to a political party. Second, none of the criteria are themselves very precise. (How organised do people need to be before they are an organisation? What do they need to do to be actually competing for power?) Laws and legal systems are no different, and the definitions legal theorists offer are no sharper.

So we should not understand jurisprudential questions of the form 'Where does . . .?' as asking '*Exactly* where does . . . (a set of customs end and a legal system begin, a matter of moral obligation become a legal obligation, and so on)?' The correct answers will be inexact answers to the extent that the phenomena we are trying to understand are unclear.[5] But clear cases do not need

---

[2] I assume with Hans Kelsen that all laws are members of legal systems, and that 'legal system' has explanatory priority over 'law' and 'a law'. The question whether law must have a certain content is thus the question whether legal systems must, so (F) takes some priority over (E). I cannot defend these assumptions here.

[3] HLA Hart, *Law, Liberty, and Morality* (Oxford, Oxford University Press, 1963) 2.

[4] There are no borderlines between the clear and the arguable cases, for some cases are arguably arguable. And so on.

[5] This remark disavows, but does not disprove, 'epistemicism' about vagueness. Some philosophers believe there is no indeterminacy in the *phenomena*, there is only our lack of knowledge of where the dividing lines lie. Such philosophers do not think, for example, that they grew older in a

to be bounded by clear lines, and so such questions should be taken as invitations to specify, as best we can, the necessary features of the clearer, standard cases of law. I think that if one reads most legal theorists, if not charitably then at least without malicious intent, one will find their views consistent with this way of proceeding.[6] At any rate, that is how I try to proceed here.

II. CONTENT AND STRUCTURE

Our question is whether law has a necessary content as well as a necessary structure. The terms 'content' and 'structure' are not perspicuous and legal theorists have used them in various ways. Here, I use them in the following way. Laws that require, permit, or empower us to do things are norms. The content of a legal norm is the action that, according to it, must or must not, may or may not, can or cannot, be done. I will focus mostly on laws that require things of us – 'mandatory' norms – but much of what I say can be extended to other types as well. The content of a legal system at any given time is the sum total of the content of all the norms of that system at that time.[7] Every legal system contains norms that empower people to create and vary legal norms, for instance, by legislative enactment or by judicial decision. As these powers get used, the law is set in motion. Hovering between modesty and pretension, old textbooks used to say things like 'the law is stated as at 27 November 1956'. A perfect snapshot, taken on a still and sunny day? But every day a legal breeze is blowing and clouds are gathering, for even without statutory changes material is constantly being added to and subtracted from the law as judges make rulings, distinguish cases, reverse decisions, and so on. So 'the English legal system' is a dynamic entity that stays the same while changing. Explaining how that is so is as difficult as explaining how, or in what sense, an adult is the same person as the teenager she used to be. Luckily, we can bypass this problem here, for if law has a necessary content then it will appear in every snapshot.

In addition to whatever content they have, legal systems also have structural features, that is, ways their norms relate to each other and to other things

---

gradual, boundaryless way, but rather that at some moment briefer than a picosecond, they tumbled over an indiscernible, 90-degree cliff, at the top of which was middle age and the foot old age. I find such views unconvincing; but since they come packaged with the view that no one knows, or could ever know, where the supposed cliffs are, no analysis can be faulted for failing to locate them. For an accessible treatment of the issues see T Endicott, *Vagueness in Law* (Oxford, Oxford University Press, 2000) ch 6.

[6] Bentham, Austin, and Kelsen are often read as if they were utterly ignorant of this. A fair reading of their works will not bear this out.

[7] 'Sum total' is meant to be consistent with the fact that some norms derogate from other norms, and that some conflict with other norms.

in society. For example, it would be a structural feature of a legal system if all of its norms were created by the same people, or by using the same powers, or were mutually consistent. Many legal theorists think certain structural features are necessary if a collection of social norms is to constitute a legal system. Hart, for example, says that nothing is a legal system that does not have both norms regulating people's conduct ('primary rules') as well as other norms determining how the conduct-regulating norms are to be identified, changed, and applied ('secondary rules'). With reservations, I think that is correct.[8] At any rate, I shall assume that an adequate structural account of legal systems can be developed along such lines. But is that enough to constitute a legal system?

The Marylebone Cricket Club (MCC) has a collection of rules to guide the conduct of players and others. The rules are promulgated in a code called *The Laws of Cricket*, now in its 4th edition.[9] Being in that code is one of the tests for ascertaining whether a rule is in fact a rule of cricket. The rules can be and are changed from time to time, using rules of the MCC Laws Sub-committee. There are also are rules establishing officials – umpires – and empowering them to render binding applications of the rules. Does this show that the cricket-rules are laws or, to be clear, *legal* laws? It does not. As we shall see, some things are missing. This does not mean there is anything amiss in calling them 'the laws of cricket'. The Oxford English Dictionary reports that 'laws' are something cricket can grammatically have; also that there is a 'law of the jungle' and a 'law of honour'. The issue is one of theory, not vocabulary. Moreover, when I deny that cricket-rules are laws or are parts of a legal system, I do not mean they have nothing in common with laws, or that there is nothing to be learned about legal systems by studying the rules of games, or even that lawyers should not study them while on duty. All kinds of things, including games, folk 'law', soft 'law', etc cast some light on law even though they are not law.[10] Karl Llewellyn says that 'the social sciences are not staked out like real estate',[11] and that is correct if taken as a disciplinary comment. As far as legal studies go, we should let a thousand flowers – and even a hundred weeds – bloom, intermingled. Nonetheless, the question remains, *what is law*, if not just any sufficiently complex system of social rules?

---

[8] For some of the reservations, see L Green, 'Positivism and Conventionalism' (1999) 12 *Canadian Journal of Law and Jurisprudence* 35, and for some others see L Green, 'Introduction' to HLA Hart, *The Concept of Law* (n 1) xxxviii–xliv.

[9] Somewhat missing the point, the MCC has also begun to encode the 'spirit of cricket': http://www.lords.org/laws-and-spirit/laws-of-cricket/. It can only be a matter of time before they find a need to encode the *spirit* of the spirit of cricket.

[10] For reasons that are obscure to me, scholars in some areas of legal studies seem to grasp the functions '*counts as*' and '*is a kind of*' yet apparently cannot master, '*is quite a bit like*', or even '*can fruitfully be compared to*'. This produces a lot of bad jurisprudence.

[11] K Llewellyn, 'A Realistic Jurisprudence – The Next Step' (1930) 30 *Columbia Law Review* 431.

Intuitively,[12] the difference is this: cricket rules, even when highly systematised and institutionalised, are special-purpose norms that regulate a restricted aspect of social life. Legal systems are not special-purpose institutions; they contain norms that regulate all kinds of things. And the law claims authority to regulate, and actually does regulate, the Marylebone Cricket Club, whereas the MCC does not even claim authority to regulate the English legal system. John Rawls elaborates these intuitive differences thus:

> What distinguishes a legal system is its comprehensive scope and its regulative powers with respect to other associations. . . . the legal order exercises a final authority over a certain well-defined territory. It is also marked by the wide range of the interests it is designed to secure.[13]

Joseph Raz refines Rawls's idea. It is not so much the regulative powers that law actually *has*, but the regulative authority it *claims* that sets it apart from limited-purpose normative systems. A legal system can limit its own regulative powers, and limited governments do, by constitutions, bills of rights, and so forth. But, as Raz says, they claim comprehensive authority, that is, 'the *authority* to regulate all forms of behaviour'; 'they either contain norms which regulate it or norms conferring powers to enact norms which if enacted would regulate it.'[14] It follows from this that legal systems also claim a kind of supremacy, that is, the 'authority to prohibit, permit, or impose conditions on the institution and operation of all the normative organisations to which members of its subject-community belong'.[15] Raz also argues that legal systems are to some degree 'open': they contain norms whose purpose is to give effect *within* that legal system to norms that are not norms *of* that system.[16] Conflicts-of-laws rules do this by giving effect to the laws of foreign countries; contract law does this by giving effect to norms created by private parties, and so forth.

Notice that with one exception, the Rawls–Raz conditions are all what I am calling structural. The exception is Rawls's claim that legal systems are designed to secure a wide range of interests. That is not a matter of how legal norms relate to each other; it is a matter what they require, permit or authorise. Law is

---

[12] The adverb 'intuitively' at the beginning of this, and most other jurisprudential propositions, does not indicate that the remark that follows is presented as true or correct on the basis of appeal to a faculty called 'intuition', let alone to *my* appeal to *my* intuition, the errors of which might be cured by taking a wider sample of other people's 'intuitions'. (Which is why much 'experimental philosophy' is an iatrogenic illness.) See H Cappelen, *Philosophy without Intuitions* (Oxford, Oxford University Press, 2012).

[13] J Rawls, *A Theory of Justice* (Cambridge, Mass, Harvard University Press, 1971) 236 (§38). I have suppressed Rawls's remarks about law monopolising coercion, because I think there can be law without any coercion. Perhaps we could say that a monopoly of coercive force is a necessary feature of *state* law. But even that proposition is uncertain: see L Green, *The Authority of the State* (Oxford, Oxford University Press, 1990) 78–83.

[14] J Raz, *Practical Reason and Norms* 2nd edn (Oxford, Oxford University Press, 1999) 151.

[15] ibid 152–54.

[16] ibid.

designed to secure, or at any rate comes to have the function of securing, many important human interests.[17] The view I defend here is essentially a version of that claim.

III. MAY LAW NOT HAVE 'ANY KIND OF CONTENT'?

The claim that law has a necessary content is not novel. Aristotle and Aquinas advanced it; so too did Locke and Hume. We have just seen that Rawls holds it and so does Hart. One legal theorist who appears to deny it is Hans Kelsen: 'Legal norms may have any kind of content,' he says.[18] But what does he mean? One thing he does *not* mean is that any possible normative set-up could be a law. Quite the contrary. Kelsen thinks a norm could be a law only if it authorises someone or other to deploy coercive force – a 'sanction' – on the condition that a certain act (the 'delict') is performed or omitted. Every law therefore needs a coercive sanction for its breach, a power on someone's part to authoritatively determine whether there was a breach, and a power (and also generally a duty) to order that a sanction be applied. Hence, 'Love thy neighbour as thyself', which, in England, is not an actual law, taken by itself is not even a possible law. On the other hand, 'Honour thy father and thy mother: that thy days may be long upon the land which the LORD thy God giveth thee . . .' *is* a possible law and, on some metaphysical and jurisprudential views, is an actual law.[19]

Is the need for coercive norms in law a matter of structure or content? In favour of viewing it as content is the fact that Kelsen cannot define 'sanction' save by reference to matters that are substantive, and not merely by relations among norms. Sanctions have to be coercive acts, whether punishments or civil remedies, and must 'consist in the forcible infliction of an evil or, expressed negatively, in the forcible deprivation of a value'.[20] With near-Foucauldian relish, Kelsen lists as paradigms: killing, blinding, amputation, imprisonment,

---

[17] For an explanation for the parenthetic, see section VIII, below.

[18] H Kelsen, *General Theory of Law and State*, A Wedberg (trans) (Cambridge, Mass, Harvard University Press, 1945) 113.

[19] Interpreting the second clause as an implied threat, rather than an offer or prediction, and taking the reference to God as presupposing the existence of an adjudicative and punitive authority. Now, if the love-directive were indirectly backed by force – eternal hellfire, say – we could reconstruct it as part of the delict of a law, and that is in fact Kelsen's strategy for dealing with legal material that has the form of a legal directive but lacks an apparent sanction. (Whether that would be a sane way to think of the love-directive is another matter.)

[20] H Kelsen, *The Pure Theory of Law*, Max Knight (trans) (Berkeley, University of California Press, 1967 [1960]) 108. In contrast, the Kelsenian delict *is* a structural feature of law, for it is defined, *not* as conduct that the officials disapprove or want to repress, but simply as whatever stands in the logical position of coercion-trigger: 'The behavior which is "commanded" is not the behaviour which "ought" to be executed' (ibid 25).

deprivation of property or loss of an office or of political rights.[21] Since something of this sort is always present, the war-cry 'law may have any content' must be 'read down' to mean something like 'any sort of *coercive* content'. On the other hand, law *may* have 'any content' in the sense that the coercion-*triggers* (the 'delicts') can be anything at all. A sanction could be triggered by homosexual conduct, or by discriminating against those who engage in homosexual conduct. Neither trigger is a clearer example, or a more central case, of law than is the other. Obviously, the second law is morally better than the first, but it is not a better specimen of law. And as the law sees things, each of these, when valid, is equally entitled to obedience. The law presents its directives to its subjects, not as things they should do only on the merits, for example because that would be just, efficient, or noble, but as things they are *to do*. The reasons legal norms purport to provide are in this way 'content-independent', and this is one of their most interesting features.[22] Law holds itself out as, and is often used as, a standard for guidance and evaluation of conduct without regard to the merits of the acts it requires, permits, or prohibits.

Kelsen therefore thinks it is not to any particular ends we should look to understand the nature of law, but instead to its means:

> [W]e can contrast it sharply with other social orders which pursue in part the same purposes as law, but by quite different means. . . . Law, morality, and religion, all three forbid murder. But law does this by providing: if a man commits murder, then another man, designated by the legal order, shall apply against the murderer a certain measure of coercion, prescribed by the legal order.[23]

One striking feature of this passage is a fact it mentions only to pass over in silence: 'Law, morality, and religion, all three forbid murder.' Why? Is that some kind of coincidence? If it is, there are many others. Law, morality, and religion, all three enjoin the keeping of promises. Law, morality, and religion, all three provide powers to marry. Law, morality, and religion, all three command respect for the authorities. And on it goes. Kelsen seems to feel no need to explain this.[24]

---

[21] ibid 109.

[22] The idea of 'independence of content' was introduced in Hart's essay 'Legal and Moral Obligation' in AI Melden (ed), *Essays in Moral Philosophy* (Seattle, University of Washington Press, 1958) 82–107. It was later developed and supported in J Raz, *The Morality of Freedom* (Oxford, Oxford University Press, 1986), and in L Green, *The Authority of the State* (n 13) 36–42. It has also been criticised: P Markwick, 'Law and Content-Independent Reasons' (2000) 20 *Oxford Journal of Legal Studies* 579.

[23] H Kelsen, *General Theory of Law and State* (n 23) 20. We should read 'sharply' in light of my remarks in section I, above.

[24] Or perhaps Kelsen sees that it cannot be explained within the strictures of his 'pure' theory of law, for the most plausible explanations need to rely on either empirical facts about human nature or on claims about morality, or both.

It is tempting to object that, on Kelsen's own account, law does have a necessary purpose and in that sense a necessary content: it aims at social peace and must therefore contain norms suitable for that. By its features of supremacy and efficacy law is the ultimate coercive regulator of coercion. Hence, law of its nature limits the use of force in every society and brings a minimum of peace. Kelsen will not go even that far: 'the peace of law is only a relative peace.'[25] In principle, law could authorise only self-help as a coercive sanction, and it could authorise it very broadly. That might be no better than the war of all against all – it could be worse, given that vendetta and revenge would then be sanctified with a halo of authorisation. Whatever the empirical tendency of societies under law, 'the securing of peace, the pacification of the legal community, cannot be considered as an essential moral value common to all legal orders: it is not the "moral minimum" common to all law.'[26] Indeed, there *is* no 'moral minimum', no 'essential moral value' that law, as law, must embrace.

IV. THE MORAL MINIMUM

Hart dissents. There *is* a 'moral minimum' essential to law, in one sense of 'moral' and one sense of 'essential'. The pertinent sense of 'moral' is that there are essential moral *obligations* that every legal system must impose. The pertinent sense of 'essential' is that these norms must be part of any *humanly possible* legal system – not just every actual one. So here is a further reason why the rules of cricket are not legal laws. Not only do they lack some of law's structural features, they do not impose the wide range of obligations that law imposes. None of them individually nor all of them collectively regulate the range of human interests to which law orients itself. In short, the cricket rules are not *about* or *for* the right things.

Now, Hart is well known as one who takes a social view of law; in fact, he thinks law is *wholly* a social construction. There is no law or legal institution that was not made, whether deliberately or accidentally, as aim or as by-product, by actual human beings living and acting in groups.[27] It is not so well known that he also takes a social view of morality, or at least the part of morality that has to do with obligations or duties. And this is quite a lot of morality, since we cannot explain moral powers without reference to their capacity to create or vary duties, and we cannot explain moral rights without reference to their capacity to justify the imposition of duties.[28] According to Hart, to have

---

[25] Kelsen, *The Pure Theory of Law* (n 20) 38.
[26] ibid.
[27] See L Green, 'Introduction' (n 8) xv–xx.
[28] But it does not cover individual ideals, the virtues, or the sources of moral value.

a moral obligation is to be subject to a social rule requiring one to φ, where: (a) φ-ing is generally believed to be important to human life, or to some valued aspect of it; (b) breach of the φ-ing norm is met with serious, if diffuse, pressure to conform; and (c) there is a standing possibility that being required to φ may conflict with one's own interests, at least as one sees them.[29] This is a social theory of obligation because of the nature of the factual conditions: obligations are marked by a group's beliefs about the importance of certain norms, by its response to breach of those norms, and by the relation between what individuals value and what the group norm requires of them. So the morality of obligation is always a social morality, or 'positive morality' to use John Austin's term.[30] What then is correct, ideal, or valid morality? That can't be purely positive: no 'ought' from 'is' alone. I think Hart's answer is essentially Bentham's. Ideal morality is the social morality that we *ought* to practice. This second 'ought' cannot be the 'ought' of obligation, for obligation was the output of the preceding analysis. How then should we understand it? We never get from Hart an explicit account of what could make a social morality an ideal morality, but we get some examples and those, together with the general Humean tenor of Hart's argument on these issues, suggests that the relevant considerations are eudaimonistic: ideal morality is the social morality which, were we to practise it, would best promote human flourishing.[31]

With all this emphasis on groups and rules, it might seem that Hart's morality of obligation is starting to sound uncomfortably like law. In fact, he thinks there is a distinction between them that turns on four features:

(i) Morality involves only matters that are thought to be of great importance to human life; legal obligations can involve trivia. It is worth emphasising that the test is not whether moral obligations *actually are* important for human flourishing. Parts of social morality amount to little more than socially organised fears, hatreds, and superstitions. Hart is well aware that many common sexual prohibitions, for example, have no sound rationale: they make human life go worse, not better. 'Yet it would be absurd to deny the title of morality to emphatic social vetoes of this sort; indeed sexual morality is perhaps the most prominent aspect of what plain men think morality to be.'[32] It is a measure of how important the social view of

---

[29] Hart, *The Concept of Law* (n 1) 85–91.

[30] Hart has a late change of heart on this point: see the Postscript to *The Concept of Law* at ibid 255–56. Here, I treat only his earlier, more developed, theory of obligation. For discussion of the later version see L Green, 'Positivism and Conventionalism' (n 8).

[31] Hart sometimes uses the term 'utilitarian' when writing of the possible justifications for social morality, especially in his early work. But this does not fit with his explicit value-pluralism. It should probably be understood broadly, without any commitment to commensurability or aggregation, much as Hume flexibly uses the term 'public utility' to cover all human interests the security or promotion of which justifies institutions, practices, etc.

[32] Hart, *The Concept of Law* (n 1) 175.

morality is to Hart that he insists on it notwithstanding the fact that it puts him at a disadvantage in his argument with Patrick Devlin over whether it is permissible to criminalise sexual immorality 'as such'.[33] Having adopted a broad view of morality, Hart cannot help himself to a Dworkinian short cut against meddlesome moralists. He cannot say, 'Never mind whether it is permissible to criminalise morality "as such"; hatreds and phobias simply don't amount to *morality*.'[34]

(ii) Unlike law, morality is immune to deliberate change. We can repeal a legal prohibition on homosexual conduct or a legal permission to force sex on one's wife, but once supporting social attitudes have solidified around those norms, and especially once they become entrenched by religion and forms of ideology, we cannot just 'repeal' the gut feeling that gay sex is wrong, or that one's wife has a duty to submit to her husband's sexual advances and no right to refuse. Conventional moral attitudes such as these can change, sometimes quickly, and sometimes as a consequence of changes in the law, but not as a result of the deliberate exercise of a power to change morality.[35] This is a point of great frustration for legal reformers, since much reform cannot succeed without a tandem change in social conviction, or at least in social convention.

(iii) Offences against moral standards must be voluntary. The plea, 'But I couldn't help it' is, when true, always relevant and often excusatory in morality – but not necessarily in law. Some who truly could not have done otherwise are nonetheless called to legal account and required to pay damages or even punished. Many consider strict liability, certainly in criminal law, to be a bad idea or at least something that calls for a very special justification. In morality, Hart thinks strict liability would not just be a bad policy, it would be a conceptual absurdity.

(iv) Finally, when moral norms fail to motivate, Plan B is resort to a diffuse, decentralised, social pressure that appeals to the intrinsic rightness of conformity and tries to trigger self-criticism in the form of the shame and guilt that often adheres to breach. Law can sometimes help itself to analogues of these, but usually only among habitual law-abiders. For the rest, law has other plans, usually involving police, courts, prisons and so on. Indeed, a judge might not even think it necessary to remind an offender that his action was *morally* wrong – he is as likely to say that, 'rightly or

---

[33] See Hart, *Law, Liberty, and Morality* (n 3), and P Devlin, *The Enforcement of Morals* (Oxford, Oxford University Press, 1968).

[34] 'What is shocking and wrong is not [Devlin's] idea that the community's morality counts, but his idea of what counts as the community's morality': R Dworkin, *Taking Rights Seriously* (Cambridge, Mass, Harvard University Press, 1978) 113.

[35] This leaves it open that we can sometimes change morality as a result of intended changes to the law, including changes that are intended to bring about changes in morality. See Leslie Green, 'Should Law Improve Morality?' (2013) 7 *Criminal Law and Philosophy* 473.

wrongly' the law required abstention from the prohibited action and punishment will now be meted out for the reason that the law was violated.

If these four features demarcate legal and moral obligations then there are limits to the candidate explanations for the fact that some obligations turn up in both law and morality, in society after society. That is unlikely to be explained by the nature of morality, for the domain of morality is not marked off by its content.[36] The consequences of this are far-reaching. Suppose law mirrors morality. In every society, then, law would contain what its morality contains. But this will not produce a common content *across* all legal systems, until we have an argument to show that all *moralities* have a common content. The four features do not entail that. Yet Hart thinks it is true. He says, 'there are certain rules of conduct which any social organisation must contain if it is to be viable': rules that promote people's 'vital interests', including rules about 'persons, property, and promises'.[37] Hart never gives us a crisp list of these rules, but from his comments we can infer that it includes at least these:[38]

(N1) Do not murder anyone.
(N2) Do not lie.
(N3) Keep promises.
(N4) Establish a system of mutual forbearances and comply with it.
(N5) Establish a system of property and respect it.
(N6) Establish a system of for enforcing (N1) to (N5) and use it.

Taking my cue from Hart's suggestion that these could be understood as a sort of 'minimum content of natural law' – natural law 'lite', purged of wishful thinking and dubious metaphysics – I am going to label this set of norms 'N'. The following should be noted:

First, N is not a set of positive norms. These are abstract norm-types, identified by their content, tokens of which can turn up in various places: in social morality, in law, in a story, in religion, or elsewhere. Put another way, N is an *ideal* (for) morality, a set of norms that *ought* to be practised and, perhaps less directly, an ideal for law. (Less directly because law also has to answer to law-specific ideals including administrability and the rule of law, and these requirements affect the way, and perhaps the extent to which, N can be realised in law.) But Hart thinks it is an ideal that must be realised in all 'viable' social organisations.

---

[36] Hart says the four marks of morality are 'in a sense *formal* criteria': *The Concept of Law* (n 1) 180f. This contrasts with the view of someone like Warnock, who holds that morality *itself* has a necessary content: morality must contain ameliorative norms that improve the human condition by limiting the general tendency of things to go badly for us; *cf* G Warnock, *The Object of Morality* (London, Methuen, 1971).
[37] *The Concept of Law* (n 1) 193.
[38] ibid 181, 195–97.

Second, the norms of N fall into two groups.[39] (N1) to (N3) are mandatory norms directed at individuals (or groups acting as individuals) and are satisfied when individuals do as they require. (N4) to (N6) are different. They call for setting up systems of social cooperation that define, require and support the relevant norm-acts. Thus (N5) directs people to make arrangements to regulate the use and control of external resources, and then to conform to those arrangements. Individuals acting independently cannot set up such norms.

Third, N is incomplete. Some norms have been missed. Following David Hume,[40] Neil MacCormick plausibly suggests we should add some child-rearing norms (for example, natural parents have a duty to see to it that their infant children are fed).[41] Then there are norms not included but which are derivable from N.[42] Some can be obtained by what Kelsen would call 'static' derivation: roughly, they are norms entailed or justified by norms on the list.[43] 'Do not murder anyone' entails 'Do not murder (even) terrorists'. Whether a society needs a separate norm of that sort depends, inter alia, on how it tends to regard terrorists. (Are terrorists seen as human? Does it conceive that any terrorists could be morally innocent?) Further norms can be 'dynamically' derived, via the powers provided or presupposed by N: (N4) is a whirring engine of dynamic derivation. It can generate all sorts of obligations, depending on what schemes of cooperation and forbearances we need to set up. Some of these will not form part of the minimum content, since they are historically and socially variable. Our own legal system needs mechanisms to regulate access to and use of fossil fuels and radio frequencies; but it was not always so. On the other hand, there are forbearances that need to be organised everywhere. Every society needs rules for war that extend beyond the prohibition on murder but which are binding only on condition that they are defined and supported by an effective cooperative system. (For example: prohibitions on the sort of weapons that can be used in conducting wars.)

---

[39] The groupings are untidy because each of (N1) to (N3) has to be realised somehow or other, and that may involve some of the cooperative norms (N4) to (N6). Also, the classification is open to debate. Some philosophers, notably Hume, think that the promising norm belongs in the second group. Maybe there are even contractarians who think that the murder norm is agreement-dependent. I cannot explore these issues here.

[40] '[S]uppose the conjunction of the sexes to be established in nature, a family immediately arises; and particular rules being found requisite for its subsistence, these are immediately embraced': D Hume, *An Enquiry Concerning the Principles of Morals*, TL Beauchamp (ed) (Oxford, Oxford University Press, 1998 [1777]) III.1, at 19.

[41] N MacCormick, *H.L.A. Hart*, 2nd edn (Stanford, Stanford University Press, 2008) 117ff.

[42] Notice how many further 'laws of nature' Hobbes manages to generate from his big three in ch XV of *Leviathan*, E Curley (ed) (Indianapolis, Hackett, 1994 [1651]) 89ff.

[43] H Kelsen, *The Pure Theory of Law* (20) 195ff.

V. THE VIABILITY THESIS

The moral minimum, then, is a set of rules it would be good for anyone to have and practise. But the argument that this imposes a content condition on law has scarcely begun. Why are they rules that must be found *in the law*? Hart offers two lines of argument for that conclusion. Neither of them is compelling.

The first I'll call the 'viability thesis'. We have already met it: 'there are certain rules of conduct which any social organisation must contain if it is to be viable.'[44] Now viability, as Hart intends it, means providing for individual survival, and that is provided for when people can continue *to live* at some minimally adequate level (as Hobbes puts it, when they can persist 'in motion'; *perseverare in esse suo*).[45] Why does viability come into it? First, it is a contingent fact that (almost) everyone does value his own survival, and that is a fact that pervasively shapes concepts central to morality, including those of harm, benefit, need, and injury.[46] So survival is a common human aim that is conceptually entrenched at a deep level. Second, survival is a pragmatic presupposition of our inquiry: 'We are committed to it as something presupposed by the terms of the discussion; for our concern is with social arrangements for continued existence, not with those of a suicide club.'[47]

A few clarifications of this notion of survival may prove helpful. First, Hart is *not* saying that survival is the only thing that matters in life. He does not deny and, as a value pluralist, he is committed to accepting that there are other objectively good things.[48] John Finnis thus goes astray when he complains that Hart's 'list of universally recognised or "indisputable" ends contains only one entry: survival.'[49] That is not so. The minimum content thesis offers no such list. It maintains only that, beyond survival, any other indisputable or universally recognised final ends are either not necessarily compatible with each other, or not necessarily good for all who could recognise them as goods. This is obviously true with respect to various items on Finnis's own list, including 'religion' which, if it is a good at all, is good only for people with

---

[44] *The Concept of Law* (n 1) 193. I take the quoted passage at face value, and on its face 'any social organisation' includes law and other organisations as well. Could 'social organisation' just be literary variation for 'society', ie a complete human society? That is unlikely, and in any case the fact that a society needs such rules does not show that it needs them in its legal system. I pursue this point below.

[45] Hart is interested in the implicit teleology of *individual* human action, the elementary ends that people share with other animals, not in the survival of social forms or structures: *The Concept of Law* (n 1) 193f.

[46] ibid 192.

[47] ibid; I discuss suicide clubs below.

[48] *The Concept of Law* (n 1) 157, 204f. On Hart's (occasionally unnoticed) pluralism, see L Green, 'Jurisprudence for Foxes' (2012) 3 *Transnational Legal Theory* 150.

[49] J Finnis, *Natural Law and Natural Rights*, 2nd edn (Oxford, Oxford University Press, 2011) 82.

particular sensibilities and which, in its central cases, conflicts with other basic goods, including the pursuit of knowledge.[50] Hart's point, as he puts it perhaps more clearly in his Holmes lecture, is simply that

> above this minimum the purposes men have for living in society are too conflicting and varying to make possible much extension of the argument that some fuller overlap of legal rules and moral standards is 'necessary' in this sense.[51]

So survival is not the list of all the objectively good purposes there are, but the list of the non-conflicting common purposes *'that men have'*.

Second, the connection between individual survival and the viability of social organisations is indirect.[52] Consider Hart's remark that legal rules are not the rules of a 'suicide club'. Exactly what are a typical suicide club's rules? American readers may think of a phrase attributed to Abraham Lincoln. At the outset of the Civil War, Lincoln thought it better to suspend habeas corpus without the consent of Congress than to risk the future of the whole Constitution which, he supposedly said by way of justification, is 'not a suicide pact'.[53] But the viability Hart has in mind is not the continued existence of a constitution or even a country. It is the survival of individuals, and whether it attempts to provide for their survival is what determines whether a legal system satisfies the minimum content thesis. Remember that it is a mark of this presupposed aim that it is deeply entrenched in 'whole structures of our thought and language'.[54] That may be true of individual survival, but it is not true of constitutional or political continuity. There are constitutions that provide not only, as most do, for their own (repeated) amendment, but even for their own demise, and for the demise of the polity whose constitution they are.[55] It is true that Hart is concerned to identify the rules an organisation

---

[50] Finnis includes under the good of 'religion' inquiry into *whether* there is a god, *whether* there is an ultimate meaning to life, etc (ibid, ch 13). But that is not religion; it is philosophy. The central cases of religion are marked by commitment to, not merely inquiry about, the truth of theism, and this commitment is robust even in the absence of any ordinary reasons for belief in theism. The conflict between pursuit of religion and the pursuit of knowledge need not arise in non-theistic religions. (See, famously, the Buddha 'Kalama Sutta' (*Anguttara Nikaya*, 65).) But these are atypical cases of religion.

[51] HLA Hart, 'Positivism and the Separation of Law and Morals (1958) *71 Harvard Law Review* 592, 623.

[52] Finnis notices, without comment, the possible gap between individual and group survival when he describes Hart's view as being that 'Law must have a minimum content of primary rules and sanctions *in order to* ensure the survival of *the society or its members* . . .' (second emphasis added): *Natural Law and Natural Rights* (n 48) 7.

[53] There is no good source for the traditional attribution of this to Lincoln. A reliable, but less pertinent, source for the phrase is Justice Robert Jackson's dissent in *Terminiello*, maintaining that the Bill of Rights is 'not a suicide pact', and thus the First Amendment should not be interpreted to permit speech that might incite riot: *Terminiello v Chicago* 337 US 1 (1949). But killing someone in a riot is not 'suicide' and a pact that risks such killings is not a suicide pact.

[54] Hart, *The Concept of Law* (n 1) 192.

[55] See *Reference re Secession of Quebec*, [1998] 2 SCR 217 (Supreme Court of Canada).

must have if *it* is to be viable, but that concern is derivative of a concern for the conditions for individual survival.

Third, the contrast with 'suicide clubs' might suggest that members of such clubs have no interest *at all* in survival and thus that such clubs would not be expected to share any of the common normative content of law and morality. That is too sweeping. Setting aside the common moral prohibition on suicide (which, it is worth noting, is not included in N) such clubs and their members still have an interest in most of the fundamental moral rules Hart mentions. At any rate that is suggested by reflection on Robert Louis Stevenson's famous short story 'The Suicide Club'.[56] Stevenson's tale has it that, even in a club set up to organise suicide, elements of N prove necessary, including the now awful requirement that promises made are to be kept, and that once a system of cooperation has been set up its obligations are to be respected. There is even a version of (N1), for while the club's members include people who want others, in certain circumstances, to kill them; they do not want them to kill them *outside* those circumstances. That would not count as an (indirect) act of their own will; it would be murder. This broadens the reach of the viability thesis, for it turns out that the rules of N are rules, not only for those who can be supposed to want to survive, but also for those who want to be able to control the temporal extent of their own lives. We should interpret 'survival' accordingly.

With all that in mind, the viability argument might be rendered like this:

1. (We may presuppose that) each values his own survival.
2. On plausible assumptions about the world and human beings there is a set of rules N that conduce to individual survival.
3. Every viable social organisation provides for individual survival.
4. Therefore, every existing social morality must instantiate N.
5. And every existing legal system must instantiate N.
6. And thus every existing legal system must contain some of what morality contains.

The argument clearly needs elaboration and gap-filling: (3) is either doubtful or begs the question, and (4) and (5) can be derived from (3) and the other premises only with further claims about the character of law and morality. We could doubtless patch up, or give a better reconstruction of, the argument and avoid these problems. There is, however, a more architectural worry about the whole argument. The viability argument pictures the relations among law (L), morality (M) and the necessary content as being like those illustrated in Figure 1.

---

[56] RL Stevenson, *The Suicide Club* (Mineola, NY, Dover, 2000 [1878]).

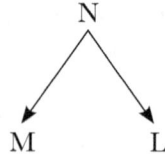

Figure 1

On this view, the fact that morality and law share something with each other is an artefact of the independent relation that each of them has with N. The fact that N is in L is not explained by the fact that it is in M; it is explained by a more general hypothesis, namely, that *any* viable social order requires N. But this cannot be correct. There are many existing sets of rules (social orders) practised by and among individuals who actually wish to survive, but whose rules do not contain N or anything like it: the MCC Rules of Cricket, or the rules of the Royal Scottish Country Dance Society, or of the Congregation of Oxford University. And the explanation is not far to seek. These rules and the institutions that implement them do not exist in an autonomous realm beyond law. They are rules *of* and *for* people who want to survive; but they aren't *survival rules*. As Hobbes says, when survival rules are not well implemented, many rule-governed activities cannot emerge, and there is 'no arts; no letters; no society'.[57] But when the survival rules are in place, other rule-governed activity can not only emerge secure in the knowledge that survival is under control, it can emerge without having to produce the requisites for survival.

So we cannot safely assume that because N is necessary to human life it will be realised in every viable form of social order, and thus in law as much as in morality. A quick fix would be to add something like the premise '*and law is a socially necessary institution without which these rules could not exist and we could not survive*'. But that is false. Homo sapiens may have emerged some 200,000 years ago, and other members of our genus, who had similar survival needs and at least some of our symbolic capacities, long before that. Yet we have no reason to think there were any legal systems at all before 3000 BCE, and for millennia after that lots of people survived without them. As Hart pointedly reminds us, although every human society needs rules, the special kind of rule-systems that characterise law are 'not a necessity, but a luxury'.[58]

VI. VOLUNTARY COMPLIANCE

Hart mentions a second consideration in favour of the minimum content thesis, and I am going to treat it as an independent argument. This one turns on

---

[57] T Hobbes, *Leviathan* (n 41) 76.
[58] Hart, *The Concept of Law* (n 1) 235.

institutional features of law. All legal systems contain norms that set up institutions like courts and tribunals. Indeed, this institutionalised division of normative labour is a mark of the emergence of law. One role these institutions have is to administer and, when necessary, order enforcement of the rules against individuals. How much enforcement goes on depends on how much voluntary compliance there is, but the power to enforce is always limited. Enforcement is slow and expensive, and at some level of non-compliance it is unaffordable. Moreover, some of the enforcers may themselves be recalcitrant, so there will need to be people to enforce the rules against them. But what about *those* enforcers? Coercion cannot rest on coercion, all the way down. So law needs to be able to count on some compliance without coercive back-up. This is the root of Hart's second idea: '[W]ithout a minimum of co-operation given voluntarily by those who find that it is in their interest to submit to and maintain the rules, coercion of others who would not voluntarily conform would be impossible.'[59] That suggests a second line of thought:

7. A legal system could not exist without a minimum of voluntary compliance of its subjects.
8. Subjects will comply voluntarily only if they believe it is in their interest to do so.
9. Only if a legal system contained N would enough subjects believe voluntary compliance to be in their interest.
10. So every (existing) legal system must contain N.

As with the viability thesis, the bracketed term in (10) suggests that a need for compliance goes to the existence rather than identification of law. A model legal system, for instance one newly drafted by a law commissioner, does not and may never exist so it is going to be tricky to figure out what sort of compliance it might need, and how that might be provided. But couldn't we still tell whether she has drafted rules for a model legal system or rules for a model train club? And might that not have something to do with what the rules are *about*?

That aside, the compliance argument is unconvincing. We might initially have doubts about (7). We are told by Hobbes that 'the weakest has strength enough to kill the strongest either by secret machination or by confederacy with others', for even the tyrant has to sleep.[60] Could a tyrant with a doomsday device and a secure redoubt not rule a whole population by terror alone, requiring the voluntary compliance of no one?[61] Offhand, it seems possible. Perhaps some would insist that such an arrangement would not amount to a legal system and the tyrant's orders would not amount to laws. Maybe not. But there is a more telling problem.

---

[59] ibid 193.
[60] T Hobbes, *Leviathan* (n 41) 72.
[61] As mooted in G Kavka, 'Rule by Fear' (1983) 17 *Nous* 601.

The case depends on the assumption that people will not *believe* it is in their interest to comply voluntarily unless *it is* in their interest to comply, which is what instantiating N supposedly achieves. This assumption neglects the complex, yet essential, distinction between what people believe to be in their interests and what is in fact in their (real) interests. It is the former, not the latter, that determines the prospects for their voluntary cooperation. There can be slippage between belief and reality in both directions. The fact that its norms satisfy N is not sufficient for people to believe their legal system serves their interests. Nothing is commoner than for people to be unaware how dependent they actually are on the effectiveness of a legal order they regularly disparage. (This is the truth behind some of David Hume's more conservative claims.) Some think, falsely, that they would be safer without the system of mutual forbearances provided by a civilised system of gun control: they fail to notice the n-person prisoner's dilemma. Some fail to see that legal constraints can make them less likely irrationally to discount their own future interests, for example, in health care or income support in their old age.

The slippage between subjective and objective interests goes the other way too. Social rules satisfying N may be unnecessary to secure the requisite degree of voluntary compliance. Ideology, in the pejorative sense of that term, can suffice.[62] Ideological beliefs are suspect in a variety of ways, but in ordinary cases they do not turn people into zombies or subject them to manipulation so severe as to call into question the voluntary character of their willingness to go along with the law. More typically, ideology leads people wrongly to discount certain options, to entertain fantasies about the feasible set, and to misidentify those who share their own interests. In the face of these elementary truths of political sociology, what jurisprudence has tended to offer is some version of Dicey's nostrum (quoting Stephen):

> [T]he power of imposing laws is dependent upon the instinct of subordination, which is itself limited. If a legislature decided that all blue-eyed babies should be murdered, the preservation of blue-eyed babies would be illegal; but legislators must go mad before they could pass such a law, and subjects be idiotic before they could submit to it.[63]

Dicey, it is true, did not live to see the Nazi holocaust; but had he never read of the Massacre of the Innocents?[64] And even if Dicey were correct it would show only that there are some things that all but the most 'idiotic' will recognise as meriting non-compliance. That may be enough to establish that the de

---

[62] R Geuss, *The Idea of a Critical Theory: Habermas and the Frankfurt School* (Cambridge, Cambridge University Press, 1981) 12ff.

[63] AV Dicey, *Introduction to the Study of the Law of the Constitution*, repr of the 8th (1915) edition, RE Michener (ed) (Indianapolis, Liberty Classics, 1982) 33. Dicey quotes from L Stephen, *The Science of Ethics*, 2nd edn (London, Smith Elder, 1907) 143.

[64] Matthew 2:16–18.

facto authority of law is always limited. But that is not our issue. A legal system can exist though there are things it could not get away with if it tried. It exists by learning not to try. It does not follow that the *other* things, all the things it *can* reliably get away with, actually serve the real interests of those whose voluntary compliance is needed.

The division of normative labour that characterises law may seem to abrade this thesis. Isn't ideology what holds the loyalty or acquiescence of the broad mass of subjects who could, anyway, have been coerced? Hart sets a low compliance baseline. Officially, he holds that the fraction of willing co-operators need only be non-zero: 'Only if the rules failed to provide these essential benefits and protections *for anyone* . . . would the minimum be unsatisfied and the system sink to the status of a set of meaningless taboos.'[65] Now, a set of meaningless taboos can exist, but laws are not like that. They are meaningful norms that at least some people use as guides to conduct. Ideology reduces enforcement costs, but it does not explain the voluntary compliance of those officials at the centre of the system, or so one might argue. Hart affirms that conceivable, and actual, legal systems can manage with the 'acceptance' and voluntary compliance of a *very* small group. So what about them? I see no reason to doubt that even their allegiance could be secured by ideology rather than by security for their real interests. The Inner Ring may itself be attached to the law only by an illusion of its sanctity, or by the idea that it is somehow an expression of their own personality: *l'état, c'est nous*. Perhaps compliance can't rest on coercion all the way down; but compliance can rest on ideology all the way down.

Against this argument one sometimes hears that law couldn't get *that* far adrift, except on the extravagant supposition that the whole population is confused or deluded. Sometimes that is a good form of argument. Native English speakers can't all be mistaken about how to form the regular plural of a noun in English. The currency markets can't all be mistaken that sterling is legal tender in the UK. But the question whether a given legal system serves any of its subjects' interests, whether defined by some function of individual survival or otherwise, is an inquiry of a different sort. These interests are (mostly) not convention-constituted in the way grammar and money are. And this is consistent, by the way, with the popular but narrower thesis advanced by EP Thompson in his attack on Marxist instrumentalism. Thompson thinks that the ideological power of law depends on its at least occasionally living up

---

[65] Hart, 'Positivism and the Separation of Law and Morals' (n 50) 624, emphasis added. Hart here assumes what he elsewhere argues, namely, that a legal system cannot exist unless at least some people, including some of the officials, take 'the internal point of view' towards its rules and thus 'accept' them in his special sense of that term (*The Concept of Law* (n 1) 55–57). It is, admittedly, hard to tell how far he thinks the class of real beneficiaries and the class of voluntary compliers coincide. But he is clear that one can 'accept' a rule without benefiting from it.

to its own declared standards of justice (and maybe also to *sound* standards of justice). He denies that the pomp and flummery of the English courts and the supporting apparatus of church and state could have been enough to distract people from the ferocity of eighteenth-century law: 'The essential precondition for the effectiveness of law, in its function as ideology, is that it shall seem to be just. It cannot seem to be so without upholding its own logic and criteria of equity; indeed, on occasion, by actually *being* just.'[66] If that is correct, there may be a lower boundary of so-called 'formal' justice, and maybe even a little substantive justice, that ideologically effective law must always meet.[67] It does not prove that every legal system must satisfy the minimum content thesis.

VII. THE INSTITUTIONAL SUPPORT THESIS

Neither the viability argument nor the compliance argument succeeds in establishing a common content amongst morality and all legal systems. But the ways they fail suggest an alternative argument that does. Law and morality share content because conforming to the norms of N is universally valuable, M instantiates N, and L is a kind of instrument *that can support M* and is used to do so. People have generic reasons to support M – the reasons given by Hobbes, Hume, Hart and many others – and where there is law they have reasons to use law to support it. A common content is shared across legal systems because, and to the extent that, the human predicament in all societies is similar, similar remedies can help with that predicament, and law is such a remedy. Indeed, it is a remedy whose features make it especially apt for helping with these predicaments.

The revised picture I have in mind is, in relevant part,[68] like Figure 2:

Figure 2

[66] EP Thompson, *Whigs and Hunters* (Middlesex, Penguin, 1975) 263.
[67] Why 'so-called'? See L Green, 'The Germ of Justice' (2010) *Oxford Legal Studies Research Paper No 60/2010* (http://ssrn.com/abstract=1703008).
[68] I am omitting a possible direct connection between N and L in order to focus on the mediating role of M, which law supports. In fact, the direct connection is much less important than the one via M: references and appeals to morality in law are overwhelmingly appeals to social morality.

Unlike the morality-law correlation produced by Hart's viability thesis this one is non-spurious: it exists because law aims to, or is standardly used to, support morality. Nor does it rest on any assumption about the sources of compliance with law. Like both of Hart's theses it yields a 'natural necessity' (although I note in passing that in socially constituted areas the distinction between what is naturally, or humanly, necessary and what is conceptually necessary is not as clear as some imagine).

It is tempting to summarise the institutional support thesis by saying that law and morality have a common content because securing that content is what law *is for*. That is acceptable only if we interpret it with caution. Aquinas famously compared law to a saw: a saw is for cutting, and the fact is has that function or purpose explains why saws have the structures they do: thin blades, jagged teeth, and so on.[69] These are design features that serve the purpose of saws, which purpose partly constitutes what it *is* to be a saw. This offers a tempting analogy. Law is an instrument. And many instruments do have constitutive purposes or aims: coffee grinders are for grinding coffee. So do some institutions: universities are for the broad pursuit and preservation of knowledge and culture. (That is why things which lack those constitutive aims – for example training schools or seminaries – are not universities, not even when they help themselves to the title.[70]) Although a few jurisprudential traditions regard laws and legal systems as being aim-constituted in this strong way, this is misguided, for law is not like a saw or even a university.[71] There is no function common to all legal systems that explains why legal systems have the structural features they have, and no function unique to legal systems.[72] The minimum content thesis does not depend on the idea that supporting morality is what law *is for* in the sense of 'constitutively for'. Law's structural features of institutionalisation, systematicity, comprehensive authority, etc are not design features that exist *in order* to enable law to support morality. The connection runs the other way round. It is law's having such features that explains why law is so apt for supporting morality (among other things). Law's comprehensive claim to authority means that it claims power to regulate whatever needs to be regulated; its openness to other norms means that it can

---

[69] Aquinas, *Summa Theologica*, vol 1, Fathers of the English Dominican Province (trans) (New York, Benziger Brothers, 1947) Pt I-II, Q 90, art 3, 995.

[70] 'Since its inception, training at Hamburger University has emphasized consistent restaurant operations procedures, service, quality and cleanliness. It has become the company's global center of excellence for McDonald's operations training and leadership development': <http://www.aboutmcdonalds.com/mcd/corporate_careers/training_and_development/hamburger_university.html> accessed 20 January 2013.

[71] See L Green, 'Law as a Means' in P Cane (ed), *The Hart–Fuller Debate in the Twenty-First Century* (Oxford, Hart Publishing, 2010).

[72] Hart says 'I think it quite vain to seek any more specific purpose which law as such serves beyond providing guides to human conduct and standards of criticism of such conduct': *The Concept of Law* (n 1) 249.

give effect to the moral requirements that people behave honestly and reasonably when in cooperative associations, and so forth. Where law exists and is effective, it is apt for supporting moral norms, which norms instantiate (perhaps imperfectly) the minimum content.

When I say that law and morality have a common content because law supports morality, I am not suggesting that the generic problems of the human condition somehow call law into being *in order that* they should be solved. We are not looking for an explanation of how it is that societies come to have law that shares a common content with morality. We are looking for an explanation of how it is, in societies that do have law, that there comes to be a significant overlap between law and morality.

But what is it to 'support' morality, and how does law do it? Law supports morality, first, by making it more effective at guiding conduct. And it does that in two main ways: by authoritative communication, by informing people of what is required, and also non-communicatively, by changing their decision-environment and options so that, whether or not they recognise what morality requires, they will tend to conform to it anyway. We often associate these two modalities with just two ways of acting: the issuing of general directives and the imposition of penalties. But law has many other techniques, including giving authoritative examples of how to 'go on' (the typical case-law method), and also by modelling desirable behaviour.[73] We should often treat others with impartiality: legal institutions contain not just directions for, but also models of, impartial conduct, as in (ideal) judicial decision-making. We should treat others as our moral equals: as in (an ideal) jury of peers. And so on.

It is worth stressing that the institutional support thesis does not make *success* at supporting morality constitutive of law. A degree of success may be among the legitimacy conditions for law.[74] Making and applying law is a way of governing, and governing is an activity no one should undertake if they are bound to fail at it. Even those who are not bound to fail are in some areas at predictably high risk of failure, and there they should govern cautiously and alert to their own fallibility.[75] But what about law's failed efforts to support morality? Do they, if pervasive, show that the legal system in question is only a marginal, ersatz member of the kind, in the way that one might hold that an

---

[73] As far as I know, only Kimberly Brownlee and Richard Child have noticed this important feature. See their helpful paper 'Can the Law Help us to be Moral?' (2012) *Warwick School of Law Research Paper No 2012/7*, online at http://ssrn.com/abstract=2091080.

[74] Why only 'may be'? Bear in mind that M, on the analysis here entertained, is the morality of obligation, understood as a social morality.

[75] See L Green, 'The Nature of Limited Government,' in R George and J Keown (eds), *Reason, Morality, and the Law: The Jurisprudence of John Finnis* (Oxford, Oxford University Press, 2013) 186–203.

'invalid proof' is no proof at all?[76] It depends on why it fails. Consider the difference between a jammed, disabled, or ill-engineered rifle on the one hand and a picture of a rifle on the other. The first three are rifles because they have enough of the structural and functional features of rifles (here reflected in the fact that their dysfunctions are among the species-typical ways that rifles can fail.)[77] The second is not a rifle; it is just a picture. A system of primary and secondary social rules, oriented to securing the wide range of human interests proper to law, can fail in dramatic ways. The rules can be pointless and inefficient; they can be unjust and ignoble. Such failures are common as dirt. If pervasive they will undermine the legitimacy of the legal system; but they do not call into question the fact that it is a legal system. That would take more exotic kinds of failure, ones resulting from a dramatic undermining of the structural features of law, which would in turn render the institution utterly inapt for doing any of the things it characteristically does, including supporting morality.

VIII. STRICTLY NECESSARY?

I now ascend, or possibly descend, to a methodological issue. I have been treating Hart's discussion as an effort to explain the nature of law by specifying its necessary and sufficient features, including its necessary content. Necessity poses problems for any empiricist. Sense experience, with or without the help of instruments, will fail to turn up what is strictly necessary. It must fail, because our experience, individual and collective, is finite while the features necessary to law are those found not only in all existing and historical legal systems, but in all possible ones – or all humanly possible ones – and those are numberless and unobservable. So how to proceed? The only way we can. We begin with the most reliable knowledge we have of actual legal systems, then we test conjectures about which of their universal features are necessary features by seeing whether they can resist contrived but intelligible counter-examples. There is no denying the fallibility of the method. Our conceptual powers are among our evolved capacities, and it may be that we just do not have the power to imagine all pertinent and intelligible counter-examples. The only ground for hope here is Giambattista Vico's: in the realms of human artefact and history, we may have a better chance of truly understanding what we have ourselves made than we do in the world of fundamental physics which began and will go on without us, as indifferent as the stars.

The necessity of law's minimum content is a point on which Hart himself

---

[76] This seems to be John Finnis's view: cf *Natural Law and Natural Rights* (n 48) 9–19.
[77] Law too has characteristic ways of failing at its aims. See L Green, 'Positivism and the Inseparability of Law and Morals' (2008) 83 *New York University Law Review* 1035.

seems uneasy. He sometimes says these 'points of contact' between law and morality are 'excuses'[78] for calling the connections in question necessary; sometimes he says they are not conceptually necessary, but rather matters of 'natural' necessity. Why so coy? One possibility is that Hart does not really mean what he says when he says law has a necessary minimum content. I return to that idea in section IX. Or maybe he is trying to steer a middle path between conceptual necessity and mere contingency in order to avoid colliding with another of his theses. For if the minimum content is *conceptually* necessary, then it is simply false that, as he also asserts, 'there are no necessary or conceptual connections between the content of law and morality'.[79] If that is Hart's worry, the remedy is at hand: we should reject the so-called 'separability thesis', for it is demonstrably false.[80]

Brian Leiter offers a different diagnosis, not as a criticism of Hart's arguments in particular, but as a broader strike against the methodology of 'analytic' legal philosophy that Hart employs. Leiter thinks anything heading in the direction of 'necessary' features of law is heading the wrong way down the one-way street of science:[81]

> [E]ven at the dawn of the 21st century, legal philosophers set conditions for a successful analysis of the Demarcation Problem – to identify the 'necessary' and 'essential' properties of law that distinguish it from morality in all cases – that would strike most philosophers in other fields, even 30 years ago, as wholly incredible.[82]

It is incredible, Leiter thinks, because laws and legal systems are artefacts, and anyone who is up to date knows that artefacts cannot be identified in terms of necessary and sufficient conditions: they have no essential attributes.[83] Informed people came to that view years ago, with the collapse or exhaustion of the so-called 'demarcation problem' in the philosophy of science.

I have reservations about the analogy to that demarcation problem, at least as Leiter deploys it. Whatever the state of play in the philosophy of science, no sensible legal philosopher, today or 30 years ago, is looking for properties of law that will 'distinguish it from morality in all cases'. That is because they know that law cannot be distinguished from morality in all cases. As I explained in section I, the demarcation lines around law and legal systems are not bright ones. So let us read Leiter charitably in conformity with my admonition in that section. But that is not the end of it. Leiter also thinks that artefacts – which he

---

[78] Hart, 'Positivism and the Separation of Law and Morals' (n 50) 624.
[79] *The Concept of Law* (n 1) 268; this seems to be what is at stake at 199, for example. See also 'Positivism and the Separation of Law and Morals' (n 50) 601 n 25.
[80] L Green, 'Positivism and the Inseparability of Law and Morals' (n 76).
[81] For an earlier critique, see B Leiter, *Naturalizing Jurisprudence: Essays on American Legal Realism and Naturalism in Legal Philosophy* (Oxford, Oxford University Press, 2007).
[82] B Leiter, 'The Demarcation Problem in Jurisprudence: A New Case for Scepticism' (2012) 32 *Oxford Journal of Legal Studies* 4.
[83] ibid 5.

takes law to be – have no natures. Things like micrometers and mousetraps, theatres and theodolites, do not have features necessary or sufficient for them to be what they are. I am not wholly confident on this point, but it seems that Leiter even holds that it is a necessary feature of something being an artefact that it has no (other) necessary features. This is puzzling. A printer-driver is an artefact. But no string of code is a printer-driver unless it is written in order to, or has or could have some capacity to, drive a printer. If all it is designed to do, and all it could be capable of doing, is regulate the fan, then it is *not* a printer-driver, and this is not a generalisation based on a study of millions of fans and printers (let alone a sample survey of college students' 'intuitions' about fans and printers).

What Leiter counts as an artefact is set out in this passage: 'The concept of law is the concept of an artefact, that is, something that necessarily owes its existence to human activities intended to create that artefact.'[84] It follows then that, necessarily, something that does *not* owe its existence to human activities intended to create that artefact is not law. Now for the blow-back: it also therefore follows, contrary to Leiter's claim, that law does have a nature at least partly specifiable by conceptually necessary conditions. Things that aren't intentionally created artefacts cannot, on his definition, be laws. Hence there is a line of demarcation between law and morality. For morality does *not* owe its existence to human activities intended to create morality. Ideal or correct morality is not intentionally created; but neither is social or customary morality: 'Standards of conduct cannot be endowed with, or deprived of, moral status by human *fiat*, though the daily use of such concepts as enactment and repeal shows that the same is not true of law.'[85]

So far from debunking the demarcation between law and morality, Leiter has bunked it. And I think a requirement of artefactuality puts law in the correct bunk, snuggled up with custom, money, language, etiquette, and so on. Nor is this truth trivial or obvious. Cicero, Aquinas and Locke firmly believed there is at least one kind of (legal) law that is not an artefact of any human activity: the unchanging and unchangeable law of nature. Ronald Dworkin goes further, for he thinks there is *wholly* non-artefactual law, law that no artificer – not even a god – has created: law that no one has ever made, used, applied, obeyed, or even heard of; law that may remain forever unknown.[86]

---

[84] ibid.

[85] Hart, *The Concept of Law* (n 1) 176. This is, by the way, consistent with thinking morality is a social, or even naturalistic, phenomenon. It is certainly consistent with Hart's Humean sympathies. Perhaps it is not consistent with some forms of actual-consent contractarianism, according to which all moral obligations are intentionally created. Those are the least plausible forms of contractarianism on offer.

[86] Dworkin holds that something can be law provided that it is the best *justification* for something that is artefactual law. A justification is an argument, not an action or event, and the best moral justification for something may be unknown; it may even be unknowable. See L Green, 'Introduction' (n 8) xvii–xviii.

Like all sensible lawyers, Leiter rejects that. But on the way he rejects too much ordinary law, for his version of the artefactuality thesis is too strong. He is right to say that law, unlike morality, is necessarily an artefact; but law is only contingently an artefact created with the intention to create an artefact, let alone with the intention to create a *legal* artefact. There are lots of laws that people created accidentally and even counter-intentionally, in an act that was not aimed at making that law, and possibly aimed at making a law inconsistent with the one they ended up making. The contribution of a legislative (or law-applying) act to the legal system often depends on its uptake: how it is received and used by courts and others. Customary law is thoroughly accidental; but so too are parts of the common law, and even some parts of statute and constitutional law, as judicially construed. At the broad systemic level, the role of intention is even more dilute. The King's judges went out intending to discipline local courts and subject them to Henry's will; but they did not go out trying to make a new legal system – the common law – though that is what emerged as the unintended and unforeseen upshot of their activities.

One last point on demarcation: what Karl Popper and others hoped for was not merely a criterion that would enable us to tell science from not-science, but one that would also enable us to tell science from *pseudo-science*. They wanted one criterion to do two jobs. But a pseudo-science is not merely a classificatory error, it is a fraud. Popper hoped the 'falsifiability criterion' could be both classifier and fraud-detector. But why should one demarcation be able to do both a conceptual job and a normative job? After all, there is nothing wrong or deficient with something being not-science; but there is something wrong with it being pseudo-science. Music is not-science and neither is formal logic, yet both are wonderful and valuable. (Logic is even valuable *to science*.) On the other hand, polygraph analysis, homeopathy, and graphology are pseudo-sciences, and dangerous ones. Sailing under false colours, they mislead people about their cargo. They pretend to bear techniques that can show which witnesses are lying, or how to cure diseases, or how to predict people's characters. They can't do any of these things. Yet pseudo-sciences hold themselves out as sciences; they invite others to use them as sciences; they try to get their adherents qualified, and paid, as expert witnesses, and so on. The demarcation criterion alone is not going to explain that, or what is wrong with it.

Possibly the philosophy of science will never come up with a single criterion for science-hood that succeeds at the classificatory task as well as the normative task. Be that as it may, there is no analogous pair of tasks waiting to be solved by jurisprudence. What distinguishes legal systems from non-legal systems is a matter for legal philosophy, and, since law is a mind-dependent artefact, explaining the concept of a legal system will go hand in glove with explaining legal systems (and, therefore, laws). But there is another, different, distinction to be drawn between law and *pseudo-law*. In every jurisdiction there are invalid statutes, false precedents, and people impersonating police. These can be as dangerous as any pseudo-science. We don't want our courts enforcing pseudo-laws; nor do we want people impersonating police officers then arresting people on suspicion of pseudo-offences. But it is not the task of legal philosophy to distinguish law from pseudo-law. *That is the task of the rule of recognition.* And, unlike philosophical 'demarcation criteria' for science, which must uniformly apply to all sciences, recognition rules vary enormously amongst legal systems. That is because the recognition rules that identify the fundamental sources of law aren't philosophical theories: they are actually practised, implicit, dynamic, and somewhat vague, social rules. They are among the most important unintended artefacts in a legal system, and they normally arise as a by-product of judges and others doing, not legal philosophy, but something much more mundane: settling legal disputes.

IX. OR JUST A GOOD IDEA?

I conclude with an interpretive point. I have treated Hart's arguments as theoretical efforts to understand the relations between law and morality. I have assumed that when he argues that legal systems have a necessary structure and content, he does so because he thinks that true, and when he argues that legal systems can be evil, not only in part but in essence, he also thinks *that* true. Some read Hart, not in this straight-up way, but more subtly and they discover a different message beneath, or alongside, his overt one. They say his supposedly theoretical efforts at understanding law are actually practical efforts at improving law, by improving the concept of law.[87] They are lessons in moral hygiene. I cannot here assess whether such arguments are intelligible, let alone correct. It is, however, easy to show that they draw no support from anything in chapter IX of *The Concept of Law*. But if you have no interest in that question, this would be a good place to stop.[88]

This esoteric, juris-Straussian, 'reading' of Hart as a philosopher with a secret message rests on a sentence in chapter IX which, for ease of reference,

[87] For a sample of the sort of doctrines I have in mind, drawing in varying degrees on Hart's own arguments, see N MacCormick, 'A Moralistic Case for A-Moralistic Law' (1985) 20 *Valparaiso Law Review* 1; T Campbell, *The Legal Theory of Ethical Positivism* (Dartmouth, Aldershot, 1996); J Waldron, 'Normative (or Ethical) Positivism', and L Murphy, 'The Political Question about the Concept of Law', both in J Coleman (ed), *Hart's Postscript: Essays on the Postscript to the Concept of* Law (Oxford, Oxford University Press, 2001).

[88] And, just in case, this may be a good moment to thank the Oxford Jurisprudence Discussion Group for the invitation to give the talk from which this paper descends, John Gardner and Brian Leiter for many instructive discussions of these issues, and especially Thomas Adams and Luís Duarte d'Almeida, who greatly improved an earlier draft of this paper, and prevented some unwarranted backsliding on my part.

I shall call 'The Sentence'. Its context is this. Hart is trying to tackle the claims of Gustav Radbruch and others who think that legal positivism, whatever its merits, is politically dangerous. Having lived through Nazism, Radbruch came to think its rise was caused by a reverse *trahison des clercs*, and that had German legal theory only been *more* moralistic and *less* dispassionate the Germans would have been better immunised against fascism. On this view, a 'narrow' concept of law, one that excludes evil laws from the category of full-blooded laws, is supposedly safer than the positivists' 'broad' concept, which puts good laws and evil laws in the same column conceptually (though not, of course, morally). After some exposition and clarification, we then get The Sentence: 'If we are to make a reasoned choice between these concepts, it must be because one is superior to the other in the way in which it will assist our theoretical inquiries, or advance and clarify our moral deliberations, or both.'[89] Hart's answer is 'both': the broad concept of law is theoretically correct and, contrary to the views of the Radbruchites, it is morally benign.

No other passage in Hart's oeuvre has been so productive of confusion. Let's begin with an elementary point. Hart never says the moral hygiene argument is *needed* to make or complete his case that something is law if and only if it satisfies the ultimate recognition rules that prevail in an effective normative system that conforms to the minimum content thesis. Indeed, in his 1962 Harry Camp lectures, he frames the methodological issue without so much as mentioning the possibility that moral-pragmatic considerations could play a role in the analysis of law.

> [T]oo little has been said about the criteria for judging the adequacy of a definition of law. Should such a definition state what, if anything, the plain man intends to convey when he uses the expressions 'law' or 'legal system'? Or should it rather aim to provide, by marking off certain social phenomena from others, a classification useful or illuminating for theoretical purposes?[90]

Here, the choice is not between a theory that shows law as it is versus a theory that improves moral deliberation, but between a theory based in *ordinary language* and one based in *theoretical utility*. Hart favours the latter, and in *The Concept of Law* makes this explicit: 'we cannot grapple adequately with this issue if we see it as one concerning the proprieties of linguistic usage.'[91] That is the methodological news Hart has for us. Contrary to what you may have heard, his view is that linguistic analysis bears 'only on a relatively small and unimportant part of the most famous and controversial theories of law',[92] and that for jurisprudence to leave everything as it is, and merely remind us of 'the

---

[89] Hart, *The Concept of Law* (n 1) 209.
[90] Hart, *Law, Liberty, and Morality* (n 3) 2f.
[91] *The Concept of Law* (n 1) 209.
[92] ibid 4.

existing conventions governing the use of the words "law" and "legal system" is . . . useless'.[93]

So The Sentence reiterates Hart's trademark view that substantive problems of jurisprudence cannot be resolved by lexicography or even by stand-alone techniques of 'ordinary language' philosophy. But it is doing something else as well, and to grasp that we need to understand its dialectical role in the dispute between Hart and his interlocutor. Hart says Radbruch began as a crude and somewhat muddled legal positivist then, convinced of the dangers of that view, revised his account of law and recommended others do the same. So The Sentence is pre-eminently a *reply* to a particular case for conceptual reform. Conceptual reform is not impossible, not unusual, and is sometimes in order. Our ordinary concept of 'race', for example, should obviously go. But take a more complex example. Think of the recurrent proposals to reform the concept of 'sex', also sometimes judged to be morally hazardous. It has been alleged that 'sex' inspires false binary thinking; it entrenches the power of men over women; it undermines human equality – so we need a more supple, more social, classification of human bodies, or maybe none at all. To such pleas for conceptual reform two sorts of response may be given. Response (A) insists on holding on to the concept while we deflect but do not refute the argument for reform. It may reply, for instance, 'But this is what sex actually is, throughout the world of animals and plants; it is a distinction with scientific value and, in the case of humans, it picks out morally salient capacities.' Response (B) instead meets the would-be reformer on his own ground, saying, perhaps, 'Reform is not necessary: the concept of 'sex' does not bring those hazards – 'gender' does; but let's not start confusing sex with gender.' What sort of reply is Hart offering Radbruch, (A)-type or (B)-type? The answer is both. What's more, Hart's (B)-type argument gilds the lily: he says not only is the Radbruchite wrong to think the positivist's theory is dangerous, it is actually morally *superior*! The whole point of the (B) argument is to meet the reformist's political plea, and when that plea is not being pressed, as is it not in the Harry Camp lectures, (B) drops out of sight and the action is all about (A). Hart's fundamental case is that (A) is correct and theoretically useful. Like everyone else, Hart thinks a correct understanding of law is a better foundation for moral deliberation than a confused or mistaken one. But he does not think it correct *because* it is more useful to moral deliberation.

There may seem to be an objection. If (B) is, as I claim, so unimportant, and if it is to be understood only as a response to a misguided proposal for conceptual reform, then why does (A) take just 16 lines of text (209–10) whereas (B) runs on for 80 lines (210–12)? Doesn't this alone suggest that Hart

---

[93] ibid 5. How *The Concept of Law* got its reputation as one of the bravura performances of Oxford linguistic philosophy is, in light of these passages and the structure of the whole book, something of a mystery. Perhaps it was the title.

thought that the moral hygiene argument, if not exactly five times weightier than the theoretical superiority argument, then at least a critical part of his positive case? It does nothing of the kind.

First this accounting is wrong. The demonstration that law has the structure and content that Hart defends does *not* take place on page 209. *It takes place over the preceding 208 pages.* By the end of chapter IX, the case for legal positivism is complete, apart from two residual issues – explaining law's relations to morality, then, in chapter X, testing how far the theory helps us understand international law. Second, the discussion at page 209 involves a very special context, one that Hart earlier refers to as a 'pathology' of a legal system: the problem of how to make sense of legality 'after revolution or major upheavals'.[94] During such a revolution, the connection to the old rule of recognition is broken. At its nadir there is not much, legally speaking, for anyone to go on, and to the extent that lawyers and judges remain socially active it is as ordinary political agents applying (or misapplying) ordinary moral standards. Law comes back to life only later, after the revolution or putsch has ended, whether successfully or in failure, and tolerably stable tests for law have re-emerged. Third, this whole discussion is one of Hart's attempts to find a kernel of good sense in a case he regards as flawed but which he knows others endorse. In treating it as a proposal for reform, he is doing the best he can for an argument he finds radically defective. (It is ironic that Hart's effort at a charitable interpretation of someone *else's* theory should be held up as evidence that he did not endorse his *own* theory.) Finally, Hart is deeply sceptical of the power of *any* moral-pragmatic argument as a prophylactic against evil, *including his own*: 'So long as human beings can gain sufficient co-operation from some to enable them to dominate others, they will use the forms of law as one of their instruments.'[95] Whether that is bleak or merely realistic, it is not the view of someone who thinks legal philosophers can do much to improve the world by improving the concept of law.

I conclude that Hart meant what he said about the relations between law and morality. There are no necessary moral tests for legal validity, but law does have necessary features, some of them structural and some of them matters of content, and the content features involve morality. Hart's main arguments for why the minimum moral content is in law are unconvincing; but his conclusion is broadly sound. To have law, we need social rules structured in a particular way and oriented to a wide range of morally important concerns. Law may fail at the aim of addressing those concerns without failing to be law. The aims are not specific to law – they are shared by many other social institutions, and they are not law's only aims – but law pursues them by means of a special sort. That set-up is good for giving institutional support to morality,

[94] ibid 208.
[95] ibid 210.

and the human predicament being what it is, that is how law is characteristically used. This is the route by which, and the extent to which, there must be morality in law.

10

International Law: 'A Relatively Small and Unimportant' Part of Jurisprudence?

JEREMY WALDRON

I. AN EMBARRASSING CHAPTER

CHAPTER X OF Hart's book, devoted to the subject of international law, presents a frustrating combination of insight and obtuseness. The insights are to be found in Hart's discussion of national sovereignty and in his consideration of the significance of the absence of organised sanctions to support law in the international realm. The obtuseness – some of it perhaps more obvious to us now, 50 years after the publication of *The Concept of Law*, than it was in 1961 – has to do with Hart's attempt to apply the apparatus of secondary rules and, in particular, the idea of a rule of recognition to the international realm, and, as a consequence, his characterisation of international law as, in many respects, more like a system of 'primitive' law than like a municipal legal system.[1] Hart is not prepared to dismiss out of hand the question of whether international 'law' really is law. He thinks it is an open question whether international law is sufficiently like the standard case of law to be described as law, and his comments have led a number of international jurists to suppose that Hart must have been a sceptic about this subject. Maybe that judgment is made too quickly. But it is clear that theorists of international law have not found much in this chapter to help them with their enterprise.

Nor have Hart's followers found much here to discuss or elaborate. One can't help thinking that the feel of this chapter – it seems like an afterthought, it departs quite markedly from the flow of the main argument of the book's later chapters, and it is not revisited at all in the 1994 Postscript[2] – has contributed to

---

[1] I use 'municipal legal system' as a term for the legal system of a particular state, like France or New Zealand.
[2] The editors of this volume have suggested to me that the best explanation of this is that no prominent objections to Hart's account of international law had been put forth by the time the Postscript was written. I do not think this is so. The book's approach to international law had been

a sense among analytic jurists in the positivist tradition that jurisprudential issues associated with international law are issues of marginal significance, mostly not worth the attention of serious legal philosophers.[3] Hart notes at the beginning of *The Concept of Law* that 'only a relatively small and unimportant part of the most famous and controversial theories of law' are concerned with issues about the propriety of using the term 'law' to describe normative arrangements in the international realm.[4] And both Hart and his supporters seem happy to follow his famous predecessors in that regard.

The agenda set out at the beginning of *The Concept of Law* was 'to advance legal theory by providing an improved analysis of the distinctive structure of a municipal legal system'.[5] Analysis of issues involving international law was always going to be a distraction from this task, and Hart did not venture in the chapter to consider the possibility that we would regard international law as a paradigm of law along with the law of a familiar municipal system; he was unwilling to raise that possibility and unwilling to consider how different our philosophical analysis would have to be if both of these were treated as paradigms instead of only one. So international law was treated from the outset as a borderline case. And although Hart acknowledged that such borderline cases generate not only semantic hesitations (about the proper use of the word 'law') but also challenging problems, he announced pretty firmly that his discussion of these problems 'at various points' is at best 'only a secondary concern of the book'.[6] Little wonder that his followers seem to have been encouraged to infer the instruction – if encouragement were needed – 'Don't waste your time on these topics'.

All of this is a great pity, because in recent decades the nature and status of international law has emerged as one of the issues in jurisprudence with greatest importance for real-world political debates. Responses to the terrorist attacks on the United States in 2011 and events at the United Nations leading up to the American-led invasion of Iraq led many American lawyers and

discussed several times in the critical literature; see, eg, R Dworkin, 'The Model of Rules' (1967–68) 35 *University of Chicago Law Review* 43f; R Falk, 'The Adequacy of Contemporary Theories of International Law – Gaps in Legal Thinking' (1964) 50 *Virginia Law Review* 234f; and DM McRae, 'Sovereignty and the International Legal Order' (1971) 10 *Western Ontario Law Review* 81f.

[3] This sense is discernible from the paucity of writing about international law by the best and most recognised analytic legal theorists. For example, the journal *Legal Theory* has had in the past 10 years at most one article on the central questions of international law jurisprudence – I mean central questions as opposed to discussions of the basis of human rights or Rawls's *Law of Peoples*. (And even that article is more an instance of political theory; see P Capps and J Rivers, 'Kant's Concept of International Law' (2010) 16 *Legal Theory* 229.) This is despite the fact that one of the most discussed jurisprudential questions among legal scholars who are *not* specialist philosophers in this period (particularly after 11 September 2001) has been the status of international law as law. See, eg, J Goldsmith and E Posner, *The Limits of International Law* (Oxford, Oxford University Press, 2006).

[4] See HLA Hart, *The Concept of Law*, 3rd edn (Oxford, Oxford University Press, 2012 [1961]) 4.
[5] ibid 17.
[6] ibid.

politicians to question the significance and sometimes even the existence as law of what was called 'international law'.[7] Very few of the legal philosophers working in the field defined by Hart's *The Concept of Law* saw fit to participate in this debate. No leading modern positivist saw fit to try to map onto these controversies what Hart had said in chapter X of the book. Whether this has been due to embarrassment at the chapter's inadequacies or to a broader indifference would be difficult to say. (The former explanation is probably implausible, for it would presume a degree of alertness to the detail of Hart's account, and a knowledge of international law, sufficient to be able to identify the inadequacies of the chapter that positivist jurisprudence has seldom disclosed.) Either way the silence is deafening. Analytic legal philosophy has been disgracefully bereft of good writing on international law, and on adjacent issues such as the rise of global law and global standards (such as human rights) for the legitimacy of national law. That is beginning to change,[8] though it has to be said that there is still no leadership in this regard from Hart's most prominent followers.

II. HART'S INSIGHTS

Let me begin – as one should – with the insightful aspects of Hart's discussion. The most important points he makes concern the nature of sovereignty and the role of sanctions in the international order, and their bearing (or the bearing of their absence) on the question of whether the international order can really be described as 'law'.

The argument about sovereignty involves the transposition of Hart's argument about Austinian sovereignty in chapter IV of *The Concept of Law*. In that chapter, Hart argued that sovereignty within a legal system must be understood as a construction of rules, not as the precondition for rules. The same is true in the international realm: sovereignty is not something external to international law that limits its operation; it is itself an artefact of international law. There is, says Hart, 'no way of knowing what sovereignty states have, till we know what the forms of international law are'.[9] This is a helpful insight, no less important for being quite familiar.

The argument about sanctions also involves the sophisticated application of elements developed earlier in Hart's jurisprudence. The argument is often heard – both today and in Hart's time – that the norms embodied in the international order cannot really be described as law because they are

---

[7] See, eg, J Goldsmith and E Posner, *The Limits of International Law* (n 3).
[8] See, eg, S Besson and J Tasioulas (eds), *The Philosophy of International Law* (Oxford, Oxford University Press, 2010).
[9] *The Concept of Law* (n 4) 224.

not backed up with organised sanctions, regularly enforced and imposed. To these jurists, the absence of 'centrally organised sanctions' suggests that the obligations of the international order are not really binding and, as Hart states the objection,

> if for this reason the rules of international law are not 'binding', it is surely indefensible to take seriously their classification as law; for however tolerant the modes of common speech may be, this is too great a difference to be overlooked.[10]

Hart does not himself assert that there are no sanctions in the international order; he just accepts for the sake of argument that the critic's premise is correct. But he puts to good use the arguments made in chapters II and III against John Austin's jurisprudence. Obligation is not to be understood in terms of command-plus-threat, nor is it to be understood in terms of the predicted imposition of sanctions. Hart's alternative analysis in terms of standards guiding behaviour understood from the internal point of view will do as well in the international realm as in the realm of municipal law.

I don't know why, but some of Hart's critics get this exactly the wrong way round. Alice Ristroph, for example, says that '[a]t the time he wrote *The Concept of Law*, Hart believed that the difference between international law and municipal law was that states could not be said to take the internal point of view toward international obligations'.[11] But Hart says exactly the opposite: he says there is evidently 'general pressure for conformity' to the rules of the international order, 'claims and admissions are based on them', and 'when they are disregarded, it is not on the footing that they are not binding; instead efforts are made to conceal the facts'.[12] These are exactly the behaviours and attitudes one expects so far as the internal aspect of obligation is concerned.

Is this enough to rebut those who are sceptical about international law? Apart from purely conceptual considerations Hart appreciates that our understanding of the minimum content that any system of municipal law must exhibit comprises the availability of organised sanctions to oppose and suppress the human tendency to violence, and he wonders whether this is true also of international law.[13] But in an extremely interesting argument, he distinguishes the two cases. Among natural individuals living in close proximity to each other, 'opportunities for injuring others, by guile, if not by open attack, are so great, and the chances of escape so considerable',[14] that mere natural deterrents are seldom adequate to restrain interpersonal violence. However,

---

[10] ibid 217.
[11] A Ristroph, 'Is Law? Constitutional Crisis and Existential Anxiety' (2009) 25 *Constitutional Commentary* 450f. For a similar mistake, see also HH Koh, 'Why do Nations Obey International Law?' (1997) 106 *Yale Law Journal* 2616.
[12] *The Concept of Law* (n 4) 220.
[13] ibid 218.
[14] ibid 213.

aggression between states is very unlike that between individuals. The use of violence between states must be public, and though there is no international police force, there can be very little certainty that it will remain a matter between aggressor and victim, as a murder or theft, in the absence of a police force, might.... In a population of a modern state, if there were no organised repression and punishment of crime, violence and theft would be hourly expected; but for states, long years of peace have intervened between disastrous wars.[15]

This difference means that the international order has been able to evolve on a different basis, and the long periods of peace that Hart mentions have been ordered by rules which do not have the endemic need for centrally imposed sanctions to maintain the peace that municipal laws have.

III. THE ABSENCE OF SECONDARY RULES?

Given the sophisticated character of the arguments just outlined, one might have expected Hart to cast some original light also on the institutional aspect of international law. But here, unfortunately, it is as though his interest in the subject has just run out. His arguments become careless and their application thoughtless in regard to law in this area.

Hart thinks it is helpful for our understanding of 'law' in the international realm to note 'the absence of an international legislature [and] courts with compulsory jurisdiction'.[16] He says that these differences between international law and ordinary municipal legal systems are striking and that they help explain the scepticism that many jurists entertain concerning the 'legal' character of international norms. Hart says that he is not himself a fully paid-up subscriber to that scepticism – '[W]e shall neither dismiss the doubts, which many feel . . . nor shall we simply confirm them'[17] – but his comments in this regard are so supportive of the sceptics' position as to leave precious little daylight between Hart's view and theirs. Certainly most working international lawyers who are not philosophers but who have looked at the tenth chapter of Hart's book come away with the impression that his view is that 'international law could not be admitted to the law club'.[18]

Yet Hart's reasoning in this regard is very poor. Let us concede the point that there is no international legislature, that is, nothing in the international order comparable (say) to the Queen-in-Parliament in the English legal system. Let us concede too that international courts do not have compulsory jurisdiction – though, with the rise of the International Criminal Court and

---

[15] ibid 218f.
[16] ibid 214.
[17] ibid.
[18] J Van Doren, 'McDougal-Lasswell Policy Science: Death and Transfiguration' (2012) 11 *Richmond Journal of Global Law and Business* 153.

other such tribunals, this is less so now than it was in 1961. Hart makes a series of fallacious inferences from these facts. His first inference is that 'international law . . . lacks the secondary rules of change and adjudication which provide for legislature and courts'.[19]

The inference goes through if Hart is interpreted as saying that international law lacks exactly the kind of secondary rules of change and adjudication that are required to set up institutions exactly analogous to municipal legislatures and courts. It will not go through if it is supposed to imply that international law lacks secondary rules of change and adjudication of any kind. On the first reading the inference is trivial. On the second reading, the inference is fallacious, and egregiously so. And Hart makes it plain that he intends the second reading when he goes on to say, in exactly the same passage, that

> [t]he absence of these institutions means that the rules for states resemble that simple form of social structure, consisting only of primary rules of obligation, which, when we find it among societies of individuals, we are accustomed to contrast with a developed legal system.[20]

In other words, because it doesn't have courts and legislatures exactly like those of a modern state, international 'law' is to be understood in terms of its resemblance to a primitive legal system.[21]

In chapter V of *The Concept of Law*, Hart had presented a model of the development of full-blooded legal systems out of 'primitive legal communities' that had social rules but no accepted let alone institutionalised mechanisms for changing them or for interpreting and applying them. A primitive legal community, on his model, had primary rules of conduct, but no secondary rules of change and adjudication. And the story he told of the development of a legal system involved the coming into existence of secondary rules of this kind to solve problems of conflict and inflexibility in these primitive communities. Others have commented on the character and plausibility of Hart's model.[22] For our purposes, the important point is that the relevant kinds of secondary rules are characterised very abstractly at this stage of Hart's account. For example, to solve problems of conflict and inefficiency of enforcement, Hart

---

[19] *The Concept of Law* (n 4) 214.
[20] ibid.
[21] I have heard Hart's defenders protest that he did not use the term 'primitive' in chapter X. This is true: the more delicate phrase Hart uses in the context of his sustained discussion of international law is 'that simple form of social structure, consisting only of primary rules of obligation, which when we find it among societies of individuals, we are accustomed to contrast with a developed legal system' (see ibid 214). But the connection to his earlier use of the term 'primitive', applied to legal systems and the societies in which they exist (see, eg, ibid 3, 4, 91, 156, 291) is unmistakeable and it has been noted by some of the most prominent international jurists. See especially TM Franck, 'Legitimacy in the International System' (1988) 82 *American Journal of International Law* 751f.
[22] See, eg, L Green, 'The Concept of Law Revisited' (1997) 94 *Michigan Law Review* 1687.

imagines the development of 'secondary rules empowering individuals to make authoritative determinations of the question whether, on a particular occasion, a primary rule has been broken'.[23] These rules define, in effect, the institution of courts and the role of judge. But they do so quite abstractly: a number of different kinds of institution and role can be fitted under this abstract heading.[24] It is not part of the abstract understanding of this kind of secondary rule, for example, that the institution in question must have compulsory jurisdiction. There is nothing about that in Hart's discussion in chapter V. And so an institution like the International Court of Justice, which doesn't have compulsory jurisdiction, but which can nevertheless issue authoritative determinations of the kind Hart mentioned in chapter V, does seem to satisfy the description Hart gives in that chapter.

I believe Hart thinks he can meet this point in the following way. Towards the end of chapter X, he writes:

> The fact that in almost all cases the judgment of the International Court . . . have been duly carried out by the parties, has often been emphasized as if this somehow offset the fact that, in contrast with municipal courts, no state can be brought before these international tribunals without its prior consent. . . . That there is some analogy is plain; but its significance must be assessed in the light of the equally plain fact that, whereas a municipal court has a compulsory jurisdiction to investigate the rights and wrongs of 'self help', and to punish a wrongful resort to it, no international court has a similar jurisdiction.[25]

'Significance' here seems to indicate the convincingness of the overall analogy between the courts of the international order and the courts of a municipal system. We can grant Hart's point about the significance of the analogy (though the last few lines of this excerpt seem question-begging). However, whether the overall analogy is significant or not, the fact remains that international courts *do*

---

[23] *The Concept of Law* (n 4) 96.

[24] This functional approach to an understanding of secondary rules in Hart's jurisprudence is argued for in M Payandeh, 'The Concept of International Law in the Jurisprudence of H.L.A. Hart' (2010) 21 *European Journal of International Law* 981:

> If the main distinction between the social rules of a primitive society and a more sophisticated legal system lies in the ability of the latter to address the problems of uncertainty, of the static character of the social rules, and of the inefficiency of the system in enforcing the rules, than there is no compelling reason why an international legal order needs to resemble the domestic legal order in form . . . It seems more convincing to evaluate the nature of the international legal system on the basis of whether it contains rules and mechanisms which perform the three functions which Hart deems necessary for the existence of a legal system.

So, Payandeh suggests, we shouldn't be asking 'whether international law encompasses legislative, judicative, and executive structures comparable to the municipal system in form', we should be asking how it performs these functions of recognition, change, and administration. 'In order for international law to qualify as a legal system it needs to be able to perform these fundamental functions attributed to the law. If it fulfils this requirement there are no grounds to deny international law the status of a legal system': see ibid 981f.

[25] *The Concept of Law* (n 4) 232f.

make determinations of whether rules of the international order have been broken and these determinations *are* by and large accepted and acted on. And this could not be the case if there were no secondary rules of adjudication. Remember that at this stage we are evaluating only Hart's claim that the international order is a primitive legal system, consisting of *nothing but primary rules*.

I have heard it said that Hart must have thought the relevant distinction here was between institutions that are public or official, in the sense that they have compulsory jurisdiction, and institutions that are private, in the sense that their jurisdiction – like that of an arbitrator – is dependent on consent.[26] In fact there is no evidence of Hart's having entertained any such thesis. And generally it is remarkable that the International Court of Justice is thought of as something much more than an arbitrator, notwithstanding its lack of compulsory jurisdiction. It is still thought of as a public body, if only because its continued presence and availability differentiates it sharply from arbitration tribunals which are usually set up on an ad hoc basis. Its prestige in the international community, the significance accorded to its decisions, and the basis of appointment of its personnel (the judges of the ICJ) are all indicators of this.

So: the criticism of Hart's account stands. The constitution of the International Court of Justice as a court is definitely an instance of a secondary rule as Hart understands this category of rule earlier in the book. The operation of such a court, with or without compulsory jurisdiction, cannot be understood except in terms of secondary rules. Since this is undeniable, Hart is not entitled to infer, from the fact that the international order lacks courts of compulsory jurisdiction, that therefore the international order can only be a 'primitive' system of primary rules so far as conflict resolution is concerned. To adapt a phrase from David Kennedy, Hart's logic here is an example of 'primitive legal scholarship'.[27]

I am afraid much the same has to be said about the alleged lack of a legislature. It is true that the international order lacks any institution that looks like a Parliament. It is true that it lacks exactly the kind of secondary rules that are necessary to constitute an institution of that sort. But again we cannot infer from this – as Hart does – that it lacks secondary rules of change altogether. For there may be other modes of legal change besides legislation. Hart is happy to acknowledge this in other contexts. For example, he insists that rules regarding the formation of contracts and the writing of wills must be regarded as secondary rules. He says, when he is not talking about international law, that 'the kinship of these rules with the rules of change involved in the notion of legislation is clear'.[28] But patently, the international order includes secondary rules of change of at least this kind. Hart's point cannot possibly be that there are no secondary rules – in the sense of rules providing that 'human

---

[26] This hypothesis was put to me by the editors of this volume.
[27] D Kennedy, 'Primitive Legal Scholarship' (1986) 27 *Harvard International Law Journal* 1.
[28] *The Concept of Law* (n 4) 96.

beings may by doing or saying certain things introduce new rules of the primary type, extinguish or modify old ones, or in various ways determine their incidence or control their operations'.[29] As individuals in a municipal order may enter into contracts, so states in the international order may enter into treaties and vary their obligations to one another accordingly. Such powers would be unintelligible if the international order were just a system of primary rules. So Hart is not entitled to infer – as he does – that the international order is just a system of primary rules (so far as legal change is concerned) from the fact that it has no parliament.

Not only that, but the international order has well-established norms about treaty-making like those set out in the Vienna Convention on the Law of Treaties. The 85 articles of that convention are all secondary rules: they cannot be understood in any other way. True, the convention is dated 1969, ten years after Hart wrote *The Concept of Law*. But it is widely accepted that the Convention codified existing customary norms on the subject, many of which had endured for centuries,[30] and such customary norms were themselves secondary rules of the international order, in much the same way as secondary rules are represented (as practices) in Hart's broader account.[31]

Hart, I think, would want to respond that a treaty is unlike legislation in many respects. Many treaties are bilateral – affecting the legal position of the relevant parties only – whereas legislation changes the law for the entire community. That is true, though it does not mean that the primitive law hypothesis is correct or that the rules empowering states to enter into treaties are not secondary rules. In any case, it ignores the importance of multilateral treaties, often involving almost every state in the world: the International Covenant on Civil and Political Rights is a good example. The closest Hart comes to conceding this point comes at the very end of chapter X, where he acknowledges that

> on many important matters, the relations between states are regulated by multilateral treaties, and it is sometimes argued that these may bind states that are not parties. If this were generally recognized, such treaties would in fact be legislative enactments and international law would have distinct criteria of validity for its rules.[32]

But it is not clear why the point about 'binding states that are not parties' should be jurisprudentially so important. Of course there are important differences between law-making in the international order and law-making at the municipal level. The fact remains that the international order *has* evolved

---

[29] ibid 81.
[30] See I Brownlie (ed), *Basic Documents in International Law*, 4th edn (Oxford, Oxford University Press, 1995) 388.
[31] See *The Concept of Law* (n 4) 110–17.
[32] ibid 236.

secondary rules which envisage ways of changing the law for the international community on a broad front.[33] The change is done in a different way and on a different basis than legislative change in a modern municipal system: it is plenary rather than representative and it works through a principle of voluntary accession rather than majority-decision. The relevant secondary rules of change are markedly different then from the secondary rules implicated in municipal legislation. They are secondary rules nonetheless and I think it would be a brave legal philosopher who would insist on an analytic link between secondary rules of change *as such* and principles of representation or majoritarianism.

As I said, to the extent that Hart addresses these issues – which is not very much – he focuses insistently on the point that treaty law is not imposed involuntarily in the way that municipal legislation is imposed. In a rather bewildering passage, he addresses what he imagines would be a way of responding to that point:

> [I]t has been claimed that war, ending with a treaty whereby the defeated power cedes territory, or assumes obligations, or accepts some diminished form of independence, is essentially a legislative act; for, like legislation, it is an imposed legal change. Few would now be impressed by this analogy, or think that it helped to show that international law had an equal title with municipal law to be called 'law'; for one of the salient differences between municipal and international law is that the former usually does not, and the latter does, recognize the validity of agreements extorted by violence.[34]

The last point in this extract is no doubt an interesting one, but again it does not establish – it does not even tend to establish – that the international order is a zone bereft of secondary rules.

Hart knew perfectly well that the modes of legal change in developed municipal legal systems are many and various. As well as the two examples we have considered – the exercise of individual or bilateral powers of contract or testamentary disposition and explicit legislation by a body like a parliament – there is also judge-made law to be considered, a mode of law-making for all the members of a legal system which is quite unlike legislation. There are secondary rules that empower judges to make law. I don't mean to raise here the question of judge-made law in the international system, but just to stress that the absence of a legislature doesn't necessarily preclude other secondary rules for law-making organised in a quite different way.

---

[33] At ibid 306 there is an endnote which says: 'For criticism of the common description of general treaties as "international legislation" see Jennings, "The Progressive Development of International Law and its Codification", 24 *BYBIL* (1947) at p. 303'. But Jennings' point is only that the multilateral treaty is a mode of general legal change quite different in character from municipal legislation; he does not deny that it is a mode of general legal change.

[34] ibid 232.

IV. NO RULE OF RECOGNITION?

As if the fallacious arguments we have just examined were not enough, Hart introduces another. He writes:

> It is . . . arguable . . . that international law not only lacks the secondary rules of change and adjudication which provide for legislature and courts, but also a unifying rule of recognition specifying 'sources' of law and providing general criteria for the identification of its rules.[35]

I find it harder to evaluate this contention, partly because I am still unsure after all these years what the idea of a rule of recognition is supposed to add to other secondary rules, such as rules of (recognisable) change and rules of adjudication, oriented to the application of rules that are recognised as already existing.[36] It is also unclear what the balance is supposed to be, in Hart's contention, between the importance of the recognition function of the particular kind of secondary rule that is in question here and the unifying function on which he appears to lay great emphasis in the passage excerpted above. (In the chapter on international law, Hart veers towards a Kelsenian view of the rule of recognition that is really quite different from the essential view of its 'recognition' function that accompanies its introduction in chapter V.[37]) Also, whatever its function, it is unclear how important it is for Hart that a legal system have a rule of recognition which is hard and fast and definitely rule-like as opposed to vague and standard-like and tattered around the edges. We will have to address all these points.

The recognition function – a practice shared among practitioners and judges in the international realm that identifies sources of law for that realm – is performed partly by the rules relating to treaties (including those codified in the Vienna Convention) and partly by rules emerging out of judicial practice in institutions like the International Court of Justice. So far as treaty-based law is concerned, the recognition of norms for the international realm is pretty straightforward. Hart's own general observation that '[f]or the most part the rule of recognition is not stated, but its existence is shown in the way in which particular rules are identified, either by courts or other officials or private persons or their advisers' seems entirely apposite here.[38]

Customary international law has always posed something more of a problem, at least for jurists who are seeking a precise statement of the relevant rule of recognition. But, again, acceptance of the point that Hart is willing to concede

---

[35] ibid 214.
[36] See J Waldron, 'Who Needs Rules of Recognition?' in M Adler and K Himma (eds), *The Rule of Recognition and the U.S. Constitution* (Oxford, Oxford University Press, 2009) 327.
[37] See *The Concept of Law* (n 4) 94f.
[38] See ibid 101.

when international law is not being discussed – namely, that courts mostly use *'unstated* rules of recognition' – helps greatly here.[39] And anyway, we are not dealing with anything like complete indeterminacy. The situation is comparable to the problems surrounding precedent as a source of law. We all know that in common law systems there are problems such as 'When are precedents binding?', 'When is it permissible to depart from them?', 'How exactly are the terms of their application settled when they are binding?', and so on. The contentious character of jurists' answers to these questions – something conceded by Hart,[40] again when those who want to talk of international law may not be listening – does not and should not lead us to deny that the municipal order lacks a rule of recognition. And it is not clear why similar problems about customary international law should lead to similar conclusions as far as the international order is concerned.

My point is that, so far as recognition is concerned, Hart should not be making greater demands on international law than he makes on municipal law. Any differences here are, I think, differences of degree, not differences of kind as between the various systems in question. As Ronald Dworkin has stressed with regard to precedent in municipal law and as John Finnis has shown with regard to custom in international law, we know how to argue our way through these issues, even if we don't have a precisely formulated and mechanically applicable meta-rule at our fingertips.[41]

One point that Hart seems anxious to insist on is that the international order lacks a single rule of recognition to perform a 'unifying' function,[42] providing not only the criteria we use to identify valid, binding treaties and valid customary norms, but ordering them into a structural unity whereby it is clear which ones have priority over others. He says that '[t]he rules of international law are indeed . . . conflicting on many points',[43] and he seems to imply that this is the upshot of the absence of a *unifying* rule of recognition. Hart says:

> [I]t is submitted that there is no basic rule providing general criteria of validity for the rules of international law, and that the rules which are in fact operative constitute not a system but a set of rules.[44]

Systematicity is no doubt important, but it has to be acknowledged that almost all legal systems lack it to some degree or other. The tensions and priorities between rules of different provenance are never fully worked out. In Anglo-American systems, we say that statute law prevails over common law and

---

[39] My emphasis. For 'unstated' rules of recognition, see ibid 102, 103, and 110.
[40] See ibid 134.
[41] See R Dworkin, *Law's Empire* (Cambridge, Mass, Harvard University Press, 1986), ch 6; and J Finnis, *Natural Law and Natural Rights*, 2nd edn (Oxford, Oxford University Press, 2011) 238–45.
[42] See *The Concept of Law* (n 4) 214.
[43] ibid 223.
[44] ibid 236.

there are some rules for resolving apparent conflicts among statutes themselves. But the matter is not fully settled.⁴⁵ And other jurists working in the wake of Hart's positivism have not thought it necessary to insist on the singularity of a unifying rule of recognition. As Joseph Raz puts it, 'there is no reason . . . to assume that a legal system can contain only one rule of recognition'; and 'there is no reason to believe that valid norms belonging to one system cannot conflict'.⁴⁶ On Raz's account, the unity of a legal system does not depend on a unifying rule of recognition, but on its containing 'only rules which certain primary organs are bound to apply'.⁴⁷ I don't mean to suggest that the norm-applying institutions of the internal system (like the International Court of Justice) perform exactly the function that primary organs fulfil on Raz's account.⁴⁸ But they may come close, particularly if attention is paid to them by all states whether they are willing in particular cases to submit to their jurisdiction or not.

Hart's preoccupation with singularity and the unifying character of rules of recognition seems connected with the fact that some jurists working in the Kelsenian tradition have tried to identify a single 'basic norm' for the international system. Hart spends a page or two in chapter X making fun of these efforts.⁴⁹ But he seems to want us to forget that it was never part of the philosophical agenda set out in *The Concept of Law* that a rule of recognition should perform the function that the basic norm was supposed to fulfil in Kelsen's jurisprudence. To the extent that Hart made a case for a rule of recognition at all, it was in regard to the function of identifying and keeping track of which rules counted as rules of a system given the various dynamics for the making and unmaking of rules.⁵⁰ As Raz notes, that might be done in many different ways in one and the same legal system, and it is no reflection on the international order that there too there are several ways in which this recognition function is performed.⁵¹

One last point: Hart thinks it is important that, in a fully operating legal system, norms can be identified by the rule of recognition as valid norms of

---

⁴⁵ Cf A Ross, '[Review of] *The Concept of Law* by H.L.A. Hart' (1962) 71 *Yale Law Journal* 1186: 'The much cherished logical unity of a legal order, in my opinion, is more a fiction or a postulate than a reality. The various sources in actual fact do not make out a logical hierarchy but a set of co-operating factors. Custom and precedents, says Hart, in the British system are subordinate to legislation. I believe that Hart, if he tried to verify this assertion, would find that it squares better with a confessed, official ideology than with facts. International law, according to Hart, is no system but a set of rules. . . . Why is it tacitly assumed that municipal law is a systematic unity?'
⁴⁶ J Raz, *Practical Reason and Norms* (Oxford, Oxford University Press, 1999 [1975]) 147.
⁴⁷ ibid.
⁴⁸ ibid 132–37.
⁴⁹ See *The Concept of Law* (n 4) 233–36.
⁵⁰ Again I draw here on the functionalist approach to secondary rules set out by Payandeh in 'The Concept of International Law in the Jurisprudence of H.L.A. Hart' (n 24).
⁵¹ See also the powerful argument of S Besson, 'Theorizing the Sources of International Law' in *The Philosophy of International Law* (n 8) 181.

the system even in advance of seeing whether they are followed. This is something that is supposed to distinguish a legal system in the full sense from a 'primitive' system consisting only of primary rules:

> In the simpler form of society we must wait and see whether a rule gets accepted as a rule or not; in a system with a basic rule of recognition we can say before a rule is actually made, that it *will* be valid *if* it conforms to the requirements of the rule of recognition.[52]

He seems to think that this cannot be said of the international system and that therefore the international system is simple or primitive in this regard. However, as a matter of practice in the international system, this characterisation by Hart is simply preposterous. It does not correspond either to the way that states or international lawyers or international organisations behave or to the attitudes exhibited in the judgements of validity that they form.

Someone committed to defending Hart's account at all costs might say that the so-called secondary rules of the international system are just packaging for the primary rules, that they don't do any independent work. But this too would be false. As Pierre-Marie Dupuy has pointed out, the secondary rules of change and recognition in the international legal system are fully detached from the primary rules that they concern:

> These international secondary norms are fundamentally the same whatever the object of the international primary rules. For instance, the negotiation, adoption, and implementation of a treaty is the same regardless of the treaty's aim and content.[53]

V. EXAGGERATED DIFFERENCES

I have emphasised throughout this discussion that there are important differences between the way municipal legal systems operate and the way international legal systems operate. Hart was right to that extent. But, it seems to me, he grotesquely exaggerated those differences in his characterisation of international law as a primitive system of primary rules.

This exaggeration has done no great harm in itself: international lawyers quickly recognised that Hart's account could be safely put aside or cited only as an example of the ignorance of analytic legal philosophers. The real harm lies in the opportunity costs of Hart's negligence. What we miss is what might have been done. It would have been good if Hart had analysed and explicated

---

[52] *The Concept of Law* (n 4) 235.
[53] PM Dupuy, 'The Danger of Fragmentation or Unification of the International Legal System and the International Court of Justice' (1999) 31 *New York University Journal of International Law & Politics* 793.

these differences in the sophisticated way in which he analysed and explained the different role that sanctions play in the international order: I mean the explication that I outlined in section II above. It is a pity that the author of *The Concept of Law* ran out of steam or inclination before doing this in his final chapter, for it deprived us not only of comparable insights, but of an example that might have inspired some of Hart's followers in jurisprudence to take up and pursue this challenge.

Part II

Hart's 'Persistent Questions'

11

How Persistent are Hart's 'Persistent Questions'?

JOHN FINNIS

I. THE THREE QUESTIONS UNDER 'WHAT IS LAW?'

ONE OF THE most important merits, and legacies, of *The Concept of Law* is the priority it gives to questions – those movements of the human spirit that invite us towards truth about reality and value. The titling of the book's first chapter, 'Persistent Questions', sets a good example to all students of theory, and indeed of history.[1] Of course, the question most frequently identified in the chapter is 'What is law?' But the chapter title's reference is directly to the three questions stated at the beginning of the chapter's last section:

> How does law differ from and how is it related to orders backed by threats? How does legal obligation differ from, and how is it related to, moral obligation? What are rules and to what extent is law an affair of rules?[2]

'Recurrent issues' is in fact the phrase Hart uses more often (and it appears in the title of the chapter's second section). But three paragraphs from the chapter's end he makes two moves, one linguistic, the other substantive. He brings together the talk of issues and the talk of questions by calling 'the three issues' 'the three questions'. And he says that they each or all 'underlie the recurrent question "What is law?"', and that therefore 'the instinct which has often brought these three questions together under a single question or request for definition ["What is law?"] has not been misguided'.

This substantive observation is in line with what he had said in the first section's last paragraph, just before identifying the three recurrent issues/questions (there called 'recurrent main themes' of the 'argument and counter-argument about the nature of law'): 'the best course is to defer giving any answer to the

---

[1] The strategic, indispensable role and priority of questions is thematic in the work of RG Collingwood on history: see, eg, his *An Autobiography* (Oxford, Oxford University Press, 1939), chs V and X.

[2] *The Concept of Law*, 3rd edn (Oxford, Oxford University Press, 2012) 13.

query "What is law?" until we have found out what it is about law that has in fact puzzled those who have asked or attempted to answer it.' In short, the chapter taken as a whole identifies four persistent questions, three of which 'underlie' the fourth, which is the question usually put first but best answered last, *by* answering the other three. Thus the three recurrent issues/questions 'come together in the form of'[3] the fourth, all-embracing question 'What is law?'

II. OVERLOOKING THE CLASSIC THESES ABOUT LAW AND MORALITY

The first question is introduced *along with the second* as, each of them, a 'sense' of what Hart calls 'the most prominent general feature of law at all times and places', namely, 'that its [law's] existence means that certain kinds of human conduct are no longer optional, but in *some* sense obligatory.'[4] This 'first, simplest sense' in which one's conduct is made non-optional is that one is told what to do and threatened with unpleasant consequences if one refuses, and 'there is . . . no doubt that a legal system', as in its penal statutes, 'often presents this aspect'.[5] So the first recurrent or persistent question or issue or theme is 'How do law and legal obligation differ from, and how are they related to orders backed by threats?'[6]

Correspondingly, the second recurrent/persistent question/issue/theme is introduced as 'aris[ing] from' a 'second way in which conduct may be not optional but obligatory'.[7] 'Moral rules impose obligations and withdraw certain areas from the free option of the individual to do as he likes.' Hart goes on to talk of 'the coincidence between the prohibitions of law and morals', and how it gives rise to views exaggerated in opposite ways: one exaggeration is 'the view that law is best understood as *a "branch" of morality* . . . and that its congruence with the principles of morality . . . rather than its incorporation of orders and threats is of its "essence"';[8] the second exaggeration, rather ambiguously set out by Hart, is or includes treating the first as 'nothing more than a mistaken inference from the fact that law and morals share a common vocabulary of rights and duties'.[9] In any event, Hart does not *formulate* the second

---

[3] ibid 6. In short, the three recurrent questions are summarised at the beginning of section 3, having been set up in section 2, the first in two paragraphs (on 6f), the second in two paragraphs (on 7f), and the third in eight paragraphs (on 8–13).

[4] ibid.

[5] ibid 6f.

[6] ibid 7; the formulation used on p 13 omits the reference to legal obligation.

[7] ibid 7.

[8] ibid 7f (emphasis added).

[9] ibid 8. Here Hart treats Holmesian 'Realism' (law is nothing more than prophecies of judicial action) as a paradoxical form of this exaggerated protest against the 'close assimilation of law to morality' made, as the first form of exaggeration, by for example (according to Hart) 'scholastic theories of natural law'.

question in these two paragraphs; he does so for the first time at the beginning of the third section, where it is articulated as: 'How does legal obligation differ from, and how is it related to, moral obligation?'

What is striking is this. At no point has he mentioned the actual views and theses about *that question* that have been primary in Western law and in legal theory down to the end of the eighteenth century: that law is positive, *not* a branch of morality, and is related to morality in three ways: morality requires (1) that each people equip itself with positive laws and back them up with sanctions and threats of sanctions; (2) that a small but crucial segment of such a positive legal system be a direct enforcement of certain basic moral principles and rules (or human rights), and that the remaining, much larger part of its positive law have *some rational relation to* the morally significant values of respect for life, for legitimate expectations and promises and established positive rights, and so forth; and (3) that a legal system's particular positive laws, even when (as is true of most such legal rules) they do not reproduce any moral rule and could reasonably have been significantly different, should all be morally decent,[10] and are to be *presumed* (defeasibly presumed) to be morally obligatory when and because they are legally obligatory.[11] If Hart had noticed these classic theses, he would have been able to establish the proper parallel between his first question and his second, by noticing (as he completely fails to do) that all this amounts to a second way, a second 'sense', in which *the law itself* (our law) makes conduct non-optional – morally non-optional – parallel to the way in which the law itself (our law) makes conduct non-optional by (as Hart puts it in this chapter) issuing orders and backing them up with threats and coercion. But he did not notice those classic theses, and the book's treatment of the relations between law and morality never recovers from the second section's mishandling of the data, and of the question.

III. OVERLOOKING MORAL RULES

The bulk of the three-issues discussion, as I said, is reserved for the third issue, which occupies by far the longest part of that same second section. Everyone agrees that law contains, if not largely consists of, rules; but, Hart goes on, 'What *are* rules? What does it mean to say that a rule *exists*?'[12] The discussion soon moves off onto the interesting, successful and important critique of

---

[10] That is, ought to be such, in both the manner of their making and their content, that they are morally fit to be treated as imposing (*qua* legally valid) a moral obligation of compliance defeasible only by sufficiently serious competing *moral* obligation(s).

[11] See Aquinas, *Summa Theologiae* I–II qq 95–96; C St German, *Doctor and Student* (1528, 1530/1), I cc 4–5; R Hooker, *Laws of Ecclesiastical Polity* (1594) I c 10; W Blackstone, *Commentaries on the Laws of England* ([1765] 8th edn 1778) I 38–62 (introduction, section 2).

[12] *The Concept of Law* (n 2) 8.

Austin-like reductions of rules to habits, and of 'Realist' theories unrealistically claiming that rules are predictions of what courts or officials will do. These paragraphs anticipate, perhaps a bit prematurely, the decisive critiques of both those kinds of explanation of rules in chapters IV and VII.[13] But notice that when he sets out[14] to explain (not answer) the question or questions 'What *are* rules and how do they *exist*?' by pointing to the 'many different types of rules', he completely omits to mention, here or anywhere in these pages, a kind of rule he had already mentioned: moral rules. Rather he says: '[B]esides legal rules there are rules of etiquette and of language, rules of games and clubs';[15] and there are 'non-legal rules like that requiring men to bare their head in church',[16] social customs. But this key section makes no mention, even as recollection, of moral rules – nor, indeed, of any of the other kinds of rule that are, so to speak, internal to rational thought in its activity as a practical engagement with real life, rules such as the rules of logic that we all need and use to keep our thinking straight, or rules of scientific inquiry or historical inquiry or textual criticism, or of techniques such as skydiving, seamanship, rocket-building, and so forth.

In relation to rules of these many kinds, just as in relation to moral rules, there is no temptation to think that they are merely habits, or merely or essentially predictions, and there is no sensible and urgent question about what it means to say that they exist. They are rules because they are true propositions about what you *need* if you are to get what you need or reasonably value: what you need if your thinking in general or your scientific or historical or text-critical inquiries are to give you coherent and *accurate* answers, or if you are to survive as a parachutist or sailor, or if you are to get to the Moon and back. And moral rules state what you rationally *need* to choose and do if you are to flourish in a flourishing community in which you treat people as what they are, fundamentally your equals but also different in many ways. (Hart himself will back into a sort of acknowledgement of this when, in his chapter on justice, he puts on display the rationality of thinking that wrongdoers, who have used their strength and cunning to rob or have lazily and negligently caused injury, need to be treated *differently* until they have paid the compensation needed to restore equality with those they have injured.[17])

In other words, the distinction between the second and the third question becomes in Hart's discussion a gappy separation between them. This spoils Hart's articulation, specification and discussion of each of them, both in chapter I and later on. So, in that important sense, two of Hart's three recurrent

---

[13] See ibid 55–59, 65, and 137f.
[14] ibid 9, at the top.
[15] ibid 9.
[16] ibid 10.
[17] ibid 165.

'underlying questions', as he meant them, are not well-framed, and do not deserve to persist.

IV. SOCIAL PHENOMENA OR REASONS FOR ACTION?

We should attend carefully to the sense Hart himself attributes to his questions, his own authoritative interpretation of them. This he gives us when he restates them in summary and non-interrogative form in the chapter's last paragraph: ' [the book's] purpose is . . . to advance legal theory by providing . . . a better understanding of the resemblances and differences between law, coercion, and morality, *as types of social phenomena*.'[18] The key words are those last five, which parallel the last six words of the very similar sentence with which the Preface, and thus the book, began: 'My aim in this book has been to further the understanding of law, coercion, and morality *as different but related social phenomena*.'[19] The phrases I have italicised have a double significance.

First: they misdescribe the book's own project, and achievement, which in large measure is, precisely, the consideration and understanding of law as a kind of reason for action.[20]

Second: the purpose of considering law *and morality* 'as social phenomena' pulls Hart away from any sound consideration of morality. For if you think of morality as a social phenomenon, you are not considering it precisely as *morality*, but just as *mores*, a set of beliefs out there. You may give some sort of priority of attention to the *mores* of your own people or culture, with which you have a familiarity amounting to a kind of inwardness which is not, however, the true inwardness and normativity of reasons understood as reasons. And in describing the *mores* with which you and your readers have such familiarity, you may find in them an interesting shape of a kind such as Hart depicts – indeed, illuminatingly – in his account of morality (as a 'social phenomenon'![21]) in the second and third sections of chapter VIII.[22] But, as beliefs out there,

---

[18] ibid 17.

[19] ibid v.

[20] On the centrality of understanding law as reasons for action in the Hartian jurisprudential project, see 'On Hart's Ways: Law as Reason and as Fact', essay 10 in *Collected Essays of John Finnis* vol IV *Philosophy of Law* (Oxford, Oxford University Press, 2011) 231–32, 235; on the limitations in his understanding of law as reasons, and on the complexity of such reasons, see ibid 239–46, 248–56.

[21] 'We shall consider first the social phenomenon often referred to as "*the* morality" of a given society or the "accepted" or "conventional" morality of an actual social group': *The Concept of Law* (n 2) 169. On the preceding page, Hart made a methodological statement vital to an understanding of his work as a whole: 'In what follows we shall seek to evade these philosophical difficulties' – that is, the 'great philosophical disagreement as to [the] *status* or relation [of rules or principles of morality] to the rest of human knowledge and experience': ibid 168, reaffirmed (in the Postscript) at ibid 253–54.

[22] ibid 167–84.

these *mores*, however familiar and (in a sense) well understood, give you no reason to judge that you *ought* to do something or *refrain* from something else. One can't rationally get an *Ought* from a social *Is*, from what Hart following Austin called positive morality, or morality as a social phenomenon. For one doesn't capture the sense and force of moral normativity (and thus of morality as distinct from *mores*) until one realises that it could be true that treating people in a certain way (say torturing them to death for fun) would be immoral – ruled out, something you need to refrain from if you're to be a decent human being – *even if* there were no corresponding social phenomenon at all (because no-one else in the world accepted that proposition and everyone else was willing to torture other people to death for fun).

Years later, in his Postscript, Hart took some steps towards acknowledging the profound flaws in *The Concept of Law*'s account of social rules, an account which he says needs 'considerable modifications', being

> defective in ignoring the important difference between a consensus of convention manifested in a group's conventional rules and a consensus of independent conviction manifested in the concurrent practices of a group. Rules are conventional social practices if the general conformity of a group to them is part of the reasons which its individual members have for acceptance; by contrast merely concurrent practices such as the shared morality of a group are constituted not by convention but by the fact that members of the group have and generally act on the same but independent reasons for behaving in specific ways.[23]

The last sentence (beginning 'by contrast') states in the manner of an external observer the way moral rules are regarded from the internal point of view by those who regard them as morally true, that is, as giving one a decisive reason to act (or abstain from acting), decisive not because other members of one's group recognise or adhere to the same rule(s), but for 'independent reasons' (concerning the conditions for respecting and promoting human well-being, and so forth).

But in the book's original and influential form, Hart's thinking of morality mainly as a social phenomenon meant that *The Concept of Law* says not very much of interest about morality, or the relation between law and morality. And this way of thinking had the further, disastrous consequence that Hart (in *Law, Liberty and Morality*, a couple of years after *The Concept of Law*) agreed with Devlin that it is sensible to debate about whether it is morally right to enforce other people's moral beliefs just because they are strongly held and even when they are in truth immoral beliefs.[24] That was an essentially absurd debate, because in the real world almost everyone rejects – and rightly rejects – the

---

[23] ibid 255–56.
[24] See 'Hart as a Political Philosopher', essay 11 in *Philosophy of Law: Collected Essays of John Finnis* (n 20) at 267–71.

view that it is right to enforce beliefs about conduct *because* they are strongly held (a social phenomenon). People who want to enforce certain beliefs about human conduct usually have this purpose because they think these are true beliefs, accurate propositions about what people need to do, or not to do, if they (and the rest of us) are to have satisfactory lives. Then the important debate is about whether those beliefs about right and wrong ways of life are sound, and if so, whether they are within the proper coercive jurisdiction of state government and law or, rather, are so far a matter of private, non-public concern that a decent state will be concerned with them only in relation to the protection and education of children.[25]

V. OVERLOOKING THE EXPLANATORY SIGNIFICANCE OF THE MORAL NEED FOR LAW

Back finally to the bad consequences of Hart's misidentification of the third question. I said just now that it entailed misdescribing – an oversight, not a deception – his own project of considering law as a reason for action. For of course, despite this misdescription, he did (as I have already stated in an initial way)[26] consider and explicate law as a reason for action – a reason fully intelligible (though not yet, perhaps, obligatory) even apart from its acceptance in social practice (if not from the need for such acceptance). That is the book's historic and lasting value: identifying the pervasive relevance of the internal point of view, and 'reproducing'[27] it as the point of view of those who treat something, eg a legal rule, as a reason for them[28] *and everyone like them* to act in accordance with it *as a common standard*,[29] and accordingly as reason for criticising those who don't so act, and so forth. But the misdescription foreshadowed, in Hart's execution of his own project, a foreshortening or truncation of, or even a pull away from, the reproducing of law as a kind of reason. Thus the book's value, as an inward illuminating of what law is all about, is much less than it could have been. And despite its author's salutary aversion to textbooks,[30] Hart's book perpetuated such essentially futile discussions as lie in

---

[25] Of course there can also be a residual issue about the prudence of attempting morally and politically justifiable enforcement in the face of widespread recalcitrance and/or abuse.
[26] Above, at n 20.
[27] *The Concept of Law* (n 2) 90, 98f.
[28] ibid 90: for persons with an 'internal point of view' of the rules of the road, 'the red light is not merely a sign that others will stop; they look upon it as a *signal for* them to stop, and so as a reason for stopping in conformity to rules which make stopping when the light is red a standard of behavior and an obligation'. 'For them the violation of a rule is not merely a basis for the prediction that a hostile reaction will follow but a *reason* for hostility.' Here at ibid 90 Hart italicises 'reason', as he does also at ibid 11, 55, 105, 193, and 194.
[29] ibid 116–17.
[30] See ibid vi.

wait in the textbook categories 'natural law versus positivism' and 'exclusive versus inclusive positivism'.

Consider for example the book's great central argument, that law and legal systems emerge as remedies for the defects of pre-legal social rules. It is a permanent acquisition for legal philosophy. But Hart's articulation of it is needlessly confused in the ways we should by now expect. I shall pick out two. (1) So-called social rules have been explained by him without reference to their character as – at least primarily and in their central-case forms – rational and moral rules widely held by people who believe that these rules should be followed not because they are widely held but because they are true guides to important distinctions between good and bad, right and wrong, ways of choosing, acting and living.[31] The nearest the main part of *The Concept of Law* gets to considering social rules as they are paradigmatically understood by those who view them 'internally' (namely, as moral rules) is when, after setting out[32] three features distinguishing social rules from habits, and after stating that 'rules are conceived and spoken of as imposing obligations when the general demand for conformity is insistent and the social pressure brought to bear upon those who deviate . . . is great',[33] Hart finally states two other 'characteristics' of such a rule which 'go naturally together with this primary one':

> The rules supported by this serious pressure are thought important because they are believed to be necessary to the maintenance of social life or some highly prized feature of it. Characteristically, rules so obviously essential as those which restrict the free use of violence are thought of in terms of obligation. So too rules which require honesty or truth or require the keeping of promises, or specify what is to be done by one who performs a distinctive role or function in the social group. . . . Secondly, it is generally recognized that the conduct required by these rules may, while benefiting others, conflict with what the person who owes the duty may wish to do . . . and the standing possibility of conflict between obligation or duty and interest is, in all societies, among the truisms of both the lawyer and the moralist.[34]

The last word is far too vague and distanced to make the point that Hart is determined not to make until the chapters on morality (chapters VIII and IX), long after the book's main theory of law has been articulated – namely, the point that social rules are, paradigmatically, conceived of, by those who acknowledge them, as moral truths, obligatory by reason of their truth about, and importance for, human flourishing and harm, justice and injustice, rightness and wrongness in choosing.

(2) The *defects* Hart points to in his great central argument are kept clear, by him, from being described as what they primarily are: defects that create *moral*

---

[31] See also n 23 above.
[32] ibid 55-57.
[33] ibid. 86.
[34] ibid 87.

obligations for the community or its elites to *move to* truly *legal* order by instituting *both* regular legislative powers and institutions (so that people can know in advance what their community expects of them and social problems and injustices be tackled in timely and coherent ways), *and* courts that can resolve disputes about the meaning and application of legally recognisable rules in an impartial and truth-seeking way. The book never recovers from considering the third 'recurrent question' before the second, shoving morality off to chapters VIII and IX, after the theoretical heavy lifting has been done.

Much of jurisprudence since 1961 has been an effort, by almost everyone, to get back to a due recognition that one cannot adequately understand how law *counts* (and operates) as a distinctive kind of reason for action unless one considers it as a reason which, even when (as most often) it is not part of the set of obligations everyone has by virtue of being a human person (morality), one nonetheless has a moral duty as a legislator to 'get right' (morally right, fair, for the *common* good) and, as a judge or citizen, has a moral duty, albeit only presumptive and defeasible, to comply with or apply. Such a fully and critically normative sense of 'reasons', and exploration of reasons, is the solid foundation for an adequately illuminating and explanatory account of law. And (despite Hart's fears and claim[35]) it has no tendency to obscure the fact that some or many laws are iniquitous (and motivated by iniquity). Deploying a fully and critically normative sense of 'arguments', and exploring arguments as structured by criteria of logical validity, has no tendency to obscure the fact that some or many arguments are logically invalid (unsound). Nor is there any need to fear that deploying and exploring the relevant fully and critically normative reasons for introducing and maintaining law and legal system may come to damage one's description of the various institutional and linguistic or propositional phenomena, or distort one's theorising (whether with descriptive-explanatory or critically normative intent) in response to the questions they raise.

VI. THREE TRULY RECURRENT QUESTIONS UNDER 'WHAT IS LAW?'

Which, then, *are* the recurrent questions underlying, or opaquely reflected in, the persistent master question 'What is law?'? Or at least, what should Hart have said they are? Granting, without conceding, that there are three, and accepting that there is merit in Hart's project of building up an explanatory

---

[35] ibid 210; see my reply in *Philosophy of Law: Collected Essays of John Finnis* (n 20), essay 1 ('Describing Law Normatively') at 30 and essay 10 ('On Hart's Ways: Law as Reason and as Fact') at 241–42 with 248 n 66; and *Natural Law and Natural Rights*, 2nd edn (Oxford, Oxford University Press, 2011) 364–66.

account of law through critique of his recent predecessors, I suggest[36] something like these:

How and why do laws differ from orders backed by threats, and how are they related to coercion?

On what conditions do a political community's members have a moral obligation to introduce, maintain and support a system of legal institutions and corresponding reasons for action comprising not only general principles common to all civilised peoples but also rules made (posited) for that particular community?

How are the legal obligations introduced by law-creating acts or facts related to the standing moral obligations of those laws' makers and subjects?

---

[36] Behind the suggestions lie various theses about the proper form of questions seeking explanation in fields shaped by human choices, attitudes, and conduct. Among these is the thesis that 'What?' questions can fruitfully be transposed into 'Why?' questions (in a number of the senses of 'Why?'): see 'Describing Law Normatively' (n 32) esp 23–32. There is also the thesis, largely shared with Hart but more resolutely developed than his version, that the proper direct object of the 'What?' question will be the *central case* of the subject-matter in question, with non-central cases being understood largely in relation to the central case: see, eg, essay 5 section V in *Philosophy of Law: Collected Essays of John Finnis* (n 20). Hart's discussion of definition in the final pages of chapter I of *The Concept of Law* gets close to articulating this methodology, but despite the obvious dependence of those pages (esp 13f) on Aristotle's account of (what we call) analogy, they miss the relevant central case of analogy, expounded by Aristotle as *pros hen* homonymy: see *Natural Law and Natural Rights* (n 35) 9–11, 429–31.

12
Hart's Anti-Essentialism

FREDERICK SCHAUER

I. THE PERSISTENCE (OR NOT) OF HART'S PERSISTENT QUESTIONS

CHAPTER I OF HLA Hart's *The Concept of Law*,[1] published 50 years ago, is tellingly entitled 'Persistent Questions'. In so characterising his opening chapter, Hart was plainly attempting to situate his analysis within a long jurisprudential tradition, while at the same time trying to take that tradition in a markedly different direction. And there can be little doubt that he was successful in both of these tasks, for not only is *The Concept of Law* considered a major component of a legal positivist tradition going back at least as far as Hobbes,[2] and perhaps further, but also much of jurisprudence since the publication of *The Concept of Law*, at least in the English-language analytic tradition, has taken Hart's work as both its starting point and its dominant focus.[3]

In his opening chapter, Hart refines his observation about 'persistent questions' to list 'three recurrent issues'.[4] One of the three pertains to the connection between law and morality, and thus focuses on the differences and similarities between legal and moral obligation, and between the commands of morality and the commands of law. And in identifying this relationship (or the lack of it) as a recurring and thus persistent issue in jurisprudence, Hart is plainly correct. Concern with the nature of a connection between law and

---

[1] HLA Hart, *The Concept of Law*, 3rd edn (Oxford, Oxford University Press, 2012 [1961]).
[2] See J Boyle, 'Thomas Hobbes and the Invented Tradition of Positivism: Reflections on Language, Power, and Essentialism' (1987) 135 *University of Pennsylvania Law Review* 383; S Coyle, 'Thomas Hobbes and the Intellectual Origins of Legal Positivism' (2003) 16 *Canadian Journal of Law and Jurisprudence* 243.
[3] Consider, for example, the following: 'HLA Hart's *The Concept of Law* is the most important and influential book in the legal positivist tradition. Though its importance is undisputed, there is a good deal less consensus regarding its core commitments, both methodological and substantive'; Jules Coleman, 'Incorporationism, Conventionality, and the Practical Difference Thesis' in J Coleman (ed), *Hart's Postscript: Essays on the Postscript to the* Concept of Law (Oxford, Oxford University Press, 2001) 99.
[4] *The Concept of Law* (n 1) 6.

morality is a hallmark of the natural law tradition, dating at least as far back as Cicero,[5] most prominent in the thinking of Aquinas,[6] dominant in Blackstone,[7] and exemplified, albeit in an idiosyncratic procedural form, in the writings of Hart's contemporary and adversary, Lon Fuller.[8] The conclusions of legal positivism about the relationship of law to morality of course differ, to a greater or lesser degree, from those of the theorists of natural law,[9] yet nevertheless the very question of the connection, if any, between law and morality was the preoccupation of such leading lights of the positivist tradition as Thomas Hobbes,[10] Jeremy Bentham,[11] John Austin,[12] and Hans Kelsen.[13] Indeed, although the Scandinavian Realists were moral sceptics, this very fact led them to be highly interested in morality's connection with law as well.[14] Thus, there can be little doubt that the relationship of law to morality was indeed a recurrent question when Hart was writing, and is one which persists to this day.

Although the question of the relationship of law to morality was and is a recurring and persistent question, Hart's characterisations of the other two issues as recurring and persistent are best understood more as rhetorical devices than accurate descriptions. Consider first the question of rules. Here Hart notes that there has been a degree of 'dissatisfaction, confusion, and uncertainty'[15] about the nature of rules and the relation of rules to the nature of law. Yet to describe such attitudes as either recurrent or persistent at the time that Hart was writing appears inaccurate. The American Legal Realists, Hart's foil in chapter VII of *The Concept of Law*, had, to be sure, put questions about rules

---

[5] See E Asmis, 'Cicero on Natural Law and the Laws of the State' (2008) 27 *Classical Antiquity* 1.

[6] See J Finnis, *Natural Law and Natural Rights*, 2nd edn (Oxford, Oxford University Press, 2011).

[7] W Blackstone, *Commentaries on the Laws of England*, vol 1 (London, 1765), Section the Second (38–62). See also J Finnis, 'Blackstone's Theoretical Intentions', in his *Philosophy of Law: Collected Essays*, vol IV (Oxford, Oxford University Press, 2011) 189.

[8] See, eg, LL Fuller, *The Morality of Law*, revised edn (New Haven, Yale University Press, 1969); 'Positivism and Fidelity to Law – A Reply to Professor Hart' (1958) 71 *Harvard Law Review* 630.

[9] An important analytical overview is L Green, 'Positivism and the Inseparability of Law and Morals' (2008) *New York University Law Review* 1035.

[10] In interesting, important, and complex ways, Hobbes straddles both the positivist and natural law traditions. See P Zagorin, *Hobbes and the Law of Nature* (Princeton, Princeton University Press, 2009).

[11] J Bentham, *Of the Limits of the Penal Branch of Jurisprudence*, P Schofield (ed) (Oxford, Clarendon Press, 2010).

[12] J Austin, *The Province of Jurisprudence Determined*, WE Rumble (ed) (Cambridge, Cambridge University Press, 1995).

[13] See J Bjarup, 'Kelsen's Theory of Law and Philosophy of Justice' in R Tur and W Twining (eds), *Essays on Kelsen* (Oxford, Clarendon Press, 1986).

[14] See JL Coleman, 'Methodology' in J Coleman and S Shapiro (eds), *Oxford Handbook of Jurisprudence and Philosophy of Law* (Oxford, Oxford University Press, 2002) 338–39. Of particular interest is V Lundstedt, *Legal Thinking Revised: My Views on Law* (Stockholm, Almqvist & Wiksell, 1956), maintaining that law played a causal role in determining the views that people held about morality.

[15] *The Concept of Law* (n 1) 8.

somewhat on the jurisprudential agenda,[16] at least if one assumes, correctly in my view but not necessarily in everyone's view, that the American Realists were part of (or interested in) the jurisprudential agenda at all.[17] But if one accepts that to be the case, then the close attention to what rules are and how they operate in the writings of Jerome Frank, Karl Llewellyn, and some number of other Realists would justify the claim that the issue was a live one in the 1950s. But prior to the Realists and a few of their precursors – François Gény,[18] the *Freirechtsschule*,[19] and snippets here and there in Holmes,[20] Gray,[21] and the like – issues about what rules were, what they did, and how they did it were not much of a concern of jurisprudence. To be sure, Austin had distinguished general rules from particular commands,[22] but apart from the Realists there is little indication that thinking about the nature of rules had been a central concern of the field prior to Hart making it so. Hart indeed made it so, and his distinctions between primary and secondary rules, his analogies between the rules of law and the rules of games, his development of the internal point of view largely in the context of the analysis of rules, and his response to the Realists (and, *en passant*, to Fuller) in chapter VII have made the topic of rules a central topic of jurisprudence ever since. So although Hart may have been inaccurate in describing questions about the nature of rules as recurring or persistent, and although he may have described them as such in order to put them on the jurisprudential agenda, the only charge that we can level against him here might be excessive modesty in not fully owning up to having repositioned, and valuably so, at least part of the focus of the domain of jurisprudence.

Hart's treatment of the topic of legal compulsion – the role of sanctions in law and the related but not identical ideas of force and coercion – might again be understood as a largely rhetorical device, but it has a more curious history. Bentham and Austin had of course treated the threat of formal state-imposed sanctions as central to the very idea of law and legal obligation, but Hart surely knew when he was writing that their claims to this effect were so widely

---

[16] See J Frank, *Law and the Modern Mind* (New York, Brentanos, Inc, 1930) 127–58, 283–306; KN Llewellyn, *The Theory of Rules*, F Schauer (ed) (Chicago, University of Chicago Press, 2011); W Twining, *Karl Llewellyn and the Realist Movement* (London, Weidenfeld & Nicolson, 1973). See also D Marcus, 'The Federal Rules of Civil Procedure and Legal Realism as a Jurisprudence of Law Reform' (2010) 44 *Georgia Law Review* 434.
[17] On the theory of law implicit in the core claims of Legal Realism, see B Leiter, *Naturalizing Jurisprudence: Essays on American Legal Realism and Naturalism in Legal Philosophy* (Oxford, Oxford University Press, 2007). For a decidedly different view of the Realists' legal theory, see MS Green, 'Legal Realism as a Theory of Law' (2005) 46 *William and Mary Law Review* 1915.
[18] See J Mayda, *Francois Gény and Modern Jurisprudence* (Baton Rouge, Louisiana, Louisiana State University Press, 1978).
[19] See JE Herget and S Wallace, 'The German Free Law Movement as the Source of American Legal Realism' (1987) 73 *Virginia Law Review* 399.
[20] OW Holmes, 'The Path of the Law' (1897) 10 *Harvard Law Review* 457.
[21] JC Gray, *The Nature and Sources of Law* (New York, Columbia University Press, 1909).
[22] Austin, *The Province of Jurisprudence Determined* (n 12) 25–28.

treated as sound that they could hardly be considered even as issues or as open questions.[23] Many dimensions of the Austinian picture were discussed and debated, and Arthur Goodhart, Hart's predecessor in the Chair of Jurisprudence at Oxford, had, prior to Hart, questioned Austin's willingness to reduce legal obligation to the threat of sanctions,[24] but the dependence both of law and of the very idea of law on the threat of sanctions or other forms of coercion was so accepted prior to Hart that it would have been more accurate to describe it as the conventional wisdom than as a persistent or recurrent question. The view that law was characterised by its ultimate coerciveness was held not only by Bentham and Austin, but also by Hans Kelsen,[25] the legal anthropologist Adamson Hoebel,[26] the philosopher Elizabeth Anscombe,[27] and countless others, such that thinking of this even as a question would have been surprising by the middle of the twentieth century.

Hart, of course, changed all of that, and the central focus of much of his book is well known as both a challenge to Austin and as an alternative to the Austin-inspired and subsequently prevalent sanction-centred account of the nature of law. But in an interesting way this question – the question of the relation between law and sanctions – is still not a persistent one. One answer to the question – law is of course necessarily based on its use of credible threats of sanctions – had been taken widely as a given prior to Hart, and a different answer – one seeing the concepts of law and legal obligation as sanction-independent – has been taken as a given in the wake of Hart's book.[28] Intriguingly, therefore, the questions of sanctions and coercion were treated

---

[23] Thus Gerald Postema observes that, especially outside of the United States, the 'Austinian orthodoxy' dominated the common law world before the late 1950s, and that there was hardly 'even any desire to challenge it': GJ Postema, 'Analytic Jurisprudence Established' in GJ Postema and E Pattaro (eds), *Legal Philosophy in the Twentieth Century: The Common Law World* (Dordrecht, Springer, 2011) 1.

[24] 'It is because a rule is regarded as obligatory that a measure of coercion may be attached to it; it is not obligatory because there is coercion': AL Goodhart, *English Law and Moral Law* (London, Stevens & Sons, 1953) 17.

[25] See H Kelsen, 'The Law as a Specific Social Technique' in his *What is Justice? Justice, Law, and Politics in the Mirror of Science* (Berkeley, California, University of California Press, 1957).

[26] EA Hoebel, *The Law of Primitive Man: A Study in Comparative Legal Dynamics* (Cambridge, Mass, Harvard University Press, 1954) 28.

[27] GEM Anscombe, 'On the Source of Authority of the State' in J Raz (ed), *Authority* (New York, New York University Press, 1990) 148. Anscombe's paper was originally delivered in the 1970s, and I suspect and assume that it reflected her thinking, and that of other philosophers, going back at least several decades earlier.

[28] Thus, by 2002 Leslie Green was able to describe the Austinian picture as 'friendless': L Green, 'Law and Obligations' in Coleman and Shapiro, *Oxford Handbook of Jurisprudence and Philosophy of Law* (n 14) 517. To the same effect are J Coleman, *The Practice of Principle: In Defence of a Pragmatic Approach to Legal Theory* (Oxford, Oxford University Press, 2001) 72, 203f; S Shapiro, *Legality* (Cambridge, Mass: Harvard University Press, 2010); N MacCormick, 'Legal Obligation and the Imperative Fallacy' in AWB Simpson (ed), *Oxford Essays in Jurisprudence: Second Series* (Oxford, Clarendon Press, 1973).

as beyond question both before and after Hart, although beyond question in diametrically opposed ways.

But have we been right to take Hart's argument as being so conclusive? The question of coercion is now neither persistent nor recurring, but it is worth considering whether it should be. Perhaps Hart's attack on Austin is more open to question and debate than he and his numerous followers have supposed. If that is so, then perhaps what has not been a persistent question should be treated as one now. But in order to see what and how that might be so, it is necessary to spend some time on a vital methodological issue, and it is to that that I now turn.

II. CONCEPTUAL NECESSITY AND THE CONCEPT OF LAW

In order to analyse and evaluate Hart's claims about sanctions and coercion, both in the opening chapter of *The Concept of Law* and throughout the book, we must confront an important methodological question: Was Hart seeking to locate the necessary and sufficient conditions for the concept of law? Many theorists have assumed that the answer to this question is in the affirmative, or have assumed at least that Hart was looking for necessary even if not sufficient conditions.[29] This assumption is arguably supported by some of the language in the Postscript,[30] and indeed by Hart's occasional use of the word 'necessary',[31] as well as by his reference in the principal text to the union of primary and secondary rules as being the 'key to the science of jurisprudence',[32] and as something located at the 'heart of a legal system',[33] the understanding of which could give us a 'powerful tool for analysis'.[34]

Yet although what some might interpret as an essentialist flavour crops up here and there through the book and in the Postscript, one of the intriguing aspects of chapter I is its decidedly anti-essentialist tone. At the very least, Hart is hardly clear at any place in the book about just what a 'concept' is, or about how we would locate one, or how we would analyse one even if we did locate it.[35] But on the basis of chapter I alone, one might reach an even stronger conclusion. Thus, even on the first page Hart appears to scorn those who

---

[29] See, most recently, T Endicott, 'The Generality of Law' in this volume.

[30] *The Concept of Law* (n 1) 239 (the aim of the book 'was to provide a theory of what law is that is both general and descriptive').

[31] ibid 23, 154.

[32] ibid 81.

[33] ibid 98.

[34] ibid.

[35] This conclusion is consistent with that in J Finnis, 'HLA Hart: A Twentieth Century Oxford Political Philosopher: Reflections by a Former Student and Colleague' (2009) 54 *American Journal of Jurisprudence* 164. See also J Finnis, 'On Hart's Ways: Law as Reason and Fact' (2007) 52 *American Journal of Jurisprudence* 25.

had sought 'revelations of truths about law' and insights into law's 'essential nature'.[36] Later he makes much of the existence of 'borderline cases', distinguishing them from 'standard cases', and emphasising that even the standard cases sometimes (and surely he was thinking of law at this point) consist of 'a complex of normally concomitant but distinct elements'.[37] Indeed, although this phrase possibly stops short of reiterating Wittgenstein's idea of a family resemblance[38] or of Searle's somewhat related idea of a 'cluster concept',[39] it does not stop much short, and the phrase is susceptible to the interpretation that the Hart of chapter I did not think that law had individually necessary properties at all.

Moreover, when Hart later in chapter I turned even more explicitly to the question of definition, and argued that definition *per genus et differentiam* might be inapplicable to attempts to define law – indeed, his words were even stronger, characterising that form of definition as 'useless' for law – he came even closer to the family resemblance or cluster concept view about law's properties. He suggested not only that law had borderline as well as clear cases, but also that the term 'law' might be 'open', in the sense 'that it does not *forbid* the extension of the term to cases where only some of the normally concomitant characteristics are present'.[40] In making this claim, it is noteworthy that Hart described the concomitant characteristics as 'normally' and not essentially present, suggesting a non-universal empirical concentration. This reading is confirmed but a few lines later, where he goes on to say that, even 'apart from . . . borderline cases',

> the several instances of a general term are often linked together on quite different ways from that postulated by the simple form of definition. They may be linked by analogy . . . [or] by *different* relationships to a central element, [or] the several instances may be different constituents of some complex activity.[41]

And much of this is reinforced in the final sentence of the chapter, where Hart previews what is to come in terms of identifying 'the central elements in the concept of law'.[42] Perhaps the distinction between 'central' and 'essential'

---

[36] *The Concept of Law* (n 1) 1.

[37] ibid 4.

[38] In fact, Hart makes explicit reference to Wittgenstein in the notes (see ibid 280), and in the text (ibid 4) he makes reference, but without attribution at that point, to Wittgenstein's famous example, 'Is it chess without the queen?' See J Holloway, 'Can You Play Chess Without the Queen?' (1954) 6 *The Hudson Review* 620; J Wisdom, 'Ludwig Wittgenstein, 1934–1937' (1952) 61 *Mind* 258. Hart uses the aphorism, however, to make a point about central and borderline cases, although Wittgenstein was almost certainly using it to make the even stronger claim about family resemblance.

[39] JR Searle, 'Proper Names' (1958) 67 *Mind* 166.

[40] *The Concept of Law* (n 1) 15.

[41] ibid 16.

[42] ibid 17. I believe that my reading of Hart is largely consistent with that in D Lyons, 'Book Review [of N MacCormick, *H.L.A. Hart*]' (1983) 68 *Cornell Law Review* 257. And note that Hart again refers to 'central' rather than necessary or essential elements at *The Concept of Law* (n 1) 81 and 110.

(or 'necessary') is too nice, but much in the flavour of the entire chapter supports the reading that Hart did not understand 'central' to be synonymous with 'necessary', and that nothing in his project was intended, when he wrote chapter I, to be an identification of the essential or necessary properties of law or legality as opposed to the analysis of those properties that were ordinary or typical. Indeed, when Hart says much later in the book that 'this book is offered as an elucidation of the concept of law, rather than a definition of "law"',[43] he appears to reinforce the anti-essentialist character of the opening chapter.

That chapter I had such an anti-essentialist flavour should come as no surprise. Its beginnings go back to 1952,[44] when Hart was very much in the middle of Oxford philosophical discussions in which JL Austin was a major figure and in which his and Wittgenstein's ideas were the normal fare.[45] Moreover, the general approach to language and definition appearing in chapter I has a close affinity with similar views at the centre of Hart's 1949 'The Ascription of Responsibility and Rights'[46] and of his 1952 inaugural lecture, 'Definition and Theory in Jurisprudence'.[47] Indeed, for the Hart of 1952 (and arguably even the Hart of 1961) to have concluded that concepts had essential or necessary properties would have been, if not heresy, at least at odds with the philosophical climate of the times, a climate in which he was a participant, and in fact very much of a creator.

At least for purposes of this chapter, I do not wish to argue that Hart's (or Searle's or JL Austin's or Wittgenstein's or anyone else's) anti-essentialism was necessarily correct, although I do not deny my own anti-essentialist sympathies.[48] Rather, my point here is only that some of the essentialism in contemporary jurisprudential debate[49] can only with difficulty claim to be continuing the Hartian project, at least methodologically. At least from chapter I, Hart's anti-essentialist commitments seem clear, and, for the times, not surprising.

[43] *The Concept of Law* (n 1) 211.
[44] Nicola Lacey, *A Life of H.L.A. Hart: The Nightmare and the Noble Dream* (Oxford, Oxford University Press, 2004) 155f.
[45] ibid 133–37.
[46] HLA Hart, 'The Ascription of Responsibility and Rights' (1949) 49 *Proceedings of the Aristotelian Society* 171.
[47] HLA Hart, 'Definition and Theory in Jurisprudence' (1954) 70 *Law Quarterly* Review 37; reprinted in Hart's *Essays on Jurisprudence and Philosophy* (Oxford, Clarendon Press, 1983).
[48] See my papers 'The Best Laid Plans' (2010) 120 *Yale Law Journal* 586; 'On the Nature of the Nature of Law' (2012) 98 *Archiv für Rechts- und Sozialphilosophie* 457; 'Necessity, Importance, and the Nature of Law' in J Ferrer Beltrán, JJ Moreso and DM Papayannis (ed), *Neutrality and Theory of Law* (Dordrecht, Springer, 2013). An important anti-essentialist argument in jurisprudence is B Leiter, 'The Demarcation Problem in Jurisprudence: A New Case for Skepticism' (2011) 31 *Oxford Journal of Legal Studies* 663.
[49] See, eg, S Shapiro, *Legality* (n 28); J Raz, 'Can There Be a Theory of Law?' in MP Golding and WA Edmundson (eds), *Blackwell Guide to the Philosophy of Law and Legal Theory* (Oxford, Blackwell, 2005).

And thus Hart can be understood as engaging in an enterprise in which he sought to identify illuminating and (empirically) central aspects of the concept of law, which were to be understood as important but unidentified features of law ordinarily present in modern municipal legal systems. This is, to be sure, some distance away from the more explicitly particular jurisprudence espoused by Ronald Dworkin,[50] but it is also some distance away from a search for essential or necessary properties of our concept of law, that would apply to all possible legal systems in all possible worlds. If we seek to understand Hart and understand *The Concept of Law*, therefore, we would do well to understand, appreciate, and possibly even agree with its decidedly (JL) Austinian character.

III. RECAPTURING COERCION

Part of the significance of the foregoing methodological discussion lies in how it might situate Hart's discussion of sanctions and force and coercion in the balance of *The Concept of Law*. It is true, of course, that one of the enduring contributions of the book lies in Hart's argument against (John) Austin,[51] and in Hart's demonstrations that, first, legal obligation cannot be *defined* in terms of the threat of sanctions,[52] and, second, that one could, in theory, have a legal system in which sanctions were absent. And thus if one embraces an essentialist view of concepts, and therefore of the concept of law, one can say that sanctions are simply not part of the concept of law at all.

It is interesting, however, that Hart himself admits that sanctions are normally – indeed, almost universally – an important part of all actual legal systems, even though legal systems might in theory exist without them.[53] And thus we might ask what role examining the place of such ubiquitous but not strictly essential components of actual legal systems should play in the enterprise of jurisprudence. One view would say that it should play no role at all, precisely because jurisprudence is a branch of philosophy, and philosophy is concerned – of necessity – with the examination of conceptually necessary properties and not with an inquiry into empirically contingent properties.[54]

---

[50] See especially R Dworkin, *Justice in Robes* (Cambridge, Mass: Belknap Press, 2006).

[51] Or at least against the John Austin described in *The Concept of Law*, which is a John Austin hardly identical to the John Austin of *The Province of Jurisprudence Determined*.

[52] As noted above, this argument did not originate with Hart, although he undoubtedly developed it at greater length and in greater depth than his predecessors; see text to n 24.

[53] *The Concept of Law* (n 1) 198–200. Hart's description of sanctions as constituting a 'natural necessity' (ibid 199) should be tempered by his description of sanction-free systems of adjudication in the endnote at 291f.

[54] Thus, J Raz writes that '[s]ociology of law provides a wealth of detailed information and analysis of the functions of law in some particular societies. Legal philosophy has to be content with those few features which all legal systems necessarily possess': J Raz, *The Authority of Law:*

And if this is an accurate characterisation of the nature of the enterprise, whether that enterprise be considered a branch of philosophy or a branch of legal theory, then Hart's demonstration of the non-necessity of sanctions to a legal system is sufficient to cast an inquiry into sanctions and coercion out of the boundaries of the enterprise of jurisprudence.

Two conceptions of jurisprudence would reject this move, however. One is the conception I have been concerned with here, a conception that recognises that even conceptual analysis in jurisprudence should acknowledge the lack of essential properties either generally, or at least in artefacts or social constructions[55] such as the concept of law. For if that conception of jurisprudence is correct, then it may well be that sanctions and coercion, like the other components of a family resemblance or cluster concept, may be vital in understanding the concept even if they are not present in every instantiation of it.[56] And thus we might conclude that the presence of the threat of officially imposed sanctions might under some circumstances be a characteristic of law, and part of proper application of the concept, when other characteristics may not be present.

Alternatively, and even if Hart (in chapter I) and I (here) are wrong about family resemblances, cluster concepts, and the structure of the concept of law, it may be that it is valuable to have a more capacious understanding of the enterprise of jurisprudence. That is, perhaps jurisprudence should be as concerned (and not exclusively concerned) with what is typically present as with what is necessarily present, with what is ordinarily part of a legal system even if it is not essentially part of a legal system. If this is so, and if some of these typical but not essential properties are usefully illuminated by philosophical analysis, and if that philosophical analysis might also give us a 'powerful tool' for understanding the phenomenon of law (almost) wherever it exists and

---

Essays on Law and Morality (Oxford, Clarendon Press, 1979) 104f. For commentary on precisely this point, see Brian Bix, 'Raz on Necessity' (2003) 22 *Law and Philosophy* 537; D Priel, 'Jurisprudence and Necessity' (2007) 20 *Canadian Journal of Law and Jurisprudence* 173. To the same effect as Raz, see Shapiro, *Legality* (n 28); RHS Tur, 'What is Jurisprudence?' (1978) 28 *Philosophical Quarterly* 149; A Marmor, *Interpretation and Legal Theory*, 2nd edn (Oxford, Oxford University Press, 2005) 27.

[55] See F Schauer, 'The Social Construction of the Concept of Law' (2005) 25 *Oxford Journal of Legal Studies* 493. Although there are active philosophical debates, largely inspired by the work of Saul Kripke and Hilary Putnam, about whether natural kinds can have essences, an implicit assumption of many of these debates is that only with respect to natural kinds is it even worth entertaining the possibility of essentialism. See J Almog, 'Nature Without Essence' (2010) 107 *Journal of Philosophy* 360; T Dumsday, 'Natural Kinds and the Problem of Complex Essences' (2010) 88 *Australasian Journal of Philosophy* 619.

[56] Indeed, this may be true of philosophy as well, as potentially supported by the increasing philosophical interest in generics – sentences (or words) that express generalisations that tolerate exceptions. See KY Cheng, 'A New Look at the Problem of Rule-Following: A Generic Perspective' (2011) 155 *Philosophical Studies* 1; SJ Leslie, 'Generics: Cognition and Acquisition' (2008) 117 *Philosophical Review* 1. See also F Schauer, 'Legal Fictions Revisited' in J Cerdio (ed), *Truth in Law* (Madrid, Marcial Pons, forthcoming 2013).

(almost) whenever it exists, then perhaps this better understanding of what Hart was up to, especially, chapter I, will help us along in this endeavour.

It is not my purpose here to offer this previewed analysis of the role of force, sanctions, and coercion in understanding the phenomenon of law. But it should be of some interest that an increasingly large number of theorists have become interested in law's coerciveness, and of the role that coercion might play in understanding the nature of law.[57] And in that sense, the present chapter might be understood as sort of a prolegomenon. If we take Hart's main points against Austin, as we should, then putting coercion, sanctions, and force back on the agenda of the philosophy of law will require that we understand the philosophy of law as being involved with things other than, or at least in addition to, the search for the strictly essential properties of law. Perhaps surprisingly to some, Hart, or at the very least the Hart of chapter I of *The Concept of Law*, is a strong ally in pursuing this task.

---

[57] See, eg, MH Kramer, *In Defense of Legal Positivism: Law Without Trimmings* (Oxford, Oxford University Press, 1999); G Lamond, 'Coercion and the Nature of Law' (2001) 7 *Legal Theory* 35; H Oberdiek, 'The Role of Sanctions and Coercion in Understanding Law and Legal Systems' (1976) 71 *American Journal of Jurisprudence* 71; D Priel, 'Sanction and Obligation in Hart's Theory of Law' (2008) 21 *Ratio Juris* 404; N Stavropoulos, 'The Relevance of Coercion: Some Preliminaries' (2009) 22 *Ratio Juris* 339; F Schauer, 'Was Austin Right After All? On the Role of Sanctions in a Theory of Law' (2010) 23 *Ratio Juris* 1; EN Yankah, 'The Force of Law: The Role of Coercion in Legal Norms' (2008) 42 *University of Richmond Law Review* 1195. There are, of course, distinctions among the concepts of sanctions, coercion, punishment, and force, but exploring them is far beyond the focus of this chapter.

13

The Model of Ordinary Analysis

PIERLUIGI CHIASSONI

[Analytic philosophy] is suspicious of grand theory if it comes along too soon and obscures valuable distinctions.

HLA Hart[1]

I. THE FOURTH ISSUE

BENEATH THE ELUSIVE 'What is law?' question, Hart suggests in chapter I, lie three 'persistent' issues. One is whether, and to what extent, law is 'a matter of rules'; another concerns the relation between law and coercion; a third, the relation between law and morality.[2] These issues are all addressed in *The Concept of Law*. Nonetheless, the book – and indeed Hart's entire body of work, from its beginnings in the early 1950s – is also concerned with a fourth and equally persistent issue: a meta-philosophical one, regarding the point, the subject-matter, and the method of legal theory.[3] This issue is in fact paramount: it made *The Concept of Law* the cornerstone of a revolutionary view – the new 'analytical jurisprudence' – on how philosophical inquiries about law are to be carried out.

Hart's philosophy of legal theory – his theses about legal theory's point, subject-matter, and method – has met with some prominent objections. Among the early critics, the late Ronald Dworkin was perhaps the most radical. Yet further work has more recently emerged pressing the suggestion that Hart's approach has not only become outdated, but may even from its outset

---

[1] D Sugarman, 'Hart Interviewed: H.L.A. Hart in Conversation with David Sugarman' (2005) 32 *Journal of Law and Society* 290.

[2] HLA Hart, *The Concept of Law*, 3rd edn (Oxford, Clarendon Press, 2012) 13.

[3] This issue is clearly set out in the opening words of Hart's 1953 inaugural lecture: 'In law as elsewhere, we can know and yet not understand. Shadows often obscure our knowledge, which not only vary in intensity but are cast by different obstacles to light. These cannot all be removed by the same methods, and till the precise character of our perplexity is determined we cannot tell what tools shall we need'; *cf* HLA Hart, 'Definition and Theory in Jurisprudence', in his *Essays in Jurisprudence and Philosophy* (Oxford, Clarendon Press, 1983) 21.

have constituted a wrong-headed detour from more venerable and valuable traditional approaches.

My purpose in this chapter is as far as possible to vindicate Hart's philosophy of legal theory. His view, I shall claim, is valuable still, here and now, in connection both with a particular way of posing questions (which Hart's account suggests), and with a particular way of answering them (which it promotes). I begin, in section II, by reconstructing and surveying the central tenets of Hart's model of legal theory, and by then recalling, in section III, some of the related theoretical claims that he can safely be said to have endorsed. In sections IV to VII I then address the main objections raised against Hart's model by endorsers of hermeneutic conceptual analysis (Joseph Raz), 'naturalized jurisprudence' (Brian Leiter), and interpretivism (Ronald Dworkin). Such objections, I will argue, can be overcome.

II. THE MODEL OF ORDINARY ANALYSIS

Hart's philosophy of legal theory turns on five core tenets: A) the Clarification Principle; B) the Conceptual Analysis principle; C) the Not-On-Other-Books Principle; D) the No-Mystery principle; E) the Nirvana Principle. The first tenet concerns the purpose and basic features of legal theory: the core, so to speak, of its disciplinary charter. The other four tenets complement the former by identifying the tools, the standpoints and the attitudes that legal theory must adopt in its inquiries. Together, the five principles build up a model of general expository jurisprudence that is simultaneously aligned with two distinguished traditions: Bentham's and Austin's analytical jurisprudence, on the one hand, and modern 'linguistic' (or 'ordinary language') philosophy, on the other.[4] I shall call it 'the Model of Ordinary Analysis'.

A. The Clarification Principle

According to the Clarification Principle, the proper purpose of legal theory is the clarification of the general framework of legal thought. This is to be done by focusing not only on the concept of law – which is the centrepiece of legal thought – but also on the related concepts of legal obligation, legal right, legal duty, legal power, legal rule, legal validity, legal sanction, nullity, etc, and on their connections with the more general concepts of rule, obligation, coercion,

---

[4] These philosophical allegiances are clearly avowed in many passages of Hart's work. See, eg, *The Concept of Law* (n 2) vi–vii, 1–17, 277–80; 'Jhering's Heaven of Concepts and Modern Analytical Jurisprudence' (1972), in his *Essays in Jurisprudence and Philosophy* (n 3) 271ff; and the 'Introduction', also in the *Essays* (n 3) 1ff.

morality, and so forth. Such clarification, Hart suggests, can only be brought about by way of speculation – Socratic-like speculation, one might say – on the conceptual webs (that is, the frameworks and structures) revealed by both ordinary and specialist usages of legal words. It can only be brought about, that is, if nothing is taken for granted. The philosophers' task is not to cast light on unknown worlds, nor to create new conceptual structures by definitional *fiat*, nor to indoctrinate other people on the 'correct' way of using legal words (as therapeutic lexicography would do), but to procure greater awareness and deeper insights about 'our' everyday, familiar, legal reality; and to do it primarily by solving the manifold puzzles arising from 'our' shared beliefs about phenomena which are non-controversially perceived and classified as belonging to law.[5]

Legal theory, in Hart's view, is one of two branches of jurisprudence (understood as the philosophical study of law). The other branch, 'legal policy', concerns itself with 'the criticism of law'.[6] (In turn, legal theory and legal policy are complementary enterprises to the doctrinal study of law, to legal history, and to legal sociology.)

Legal policy, to take the latter branch first, is an evaluative, prescriptive venture. It is, roughly speaking, the correlate, in Hart's theory, of Bentham's 'censorial jurisprudence'[7] or Austin's 'science of legislation'.[8] Hart's view on the matter can be fairly reconstructed, I suggest, as follows. Hart sees the evaluation of law as a two-level process. At the first level, any positive legal system is to be assessed from the standpoint of its being 'acceptable to any rational person'.[9] Acceptability depends on two main conditions: (1) the legal system must contain 'certain rules concerning the basic conditions of social life', namely 'rules restricting the use of violence, protecting certain forms of property, and enforcing certain forms of contract';[10] and (2) these rules must satisfy the 'procedural requirements' imposed by 'the rule of law', that is, 'the principles of legality' (rules must be general, fairly determinate, publicly promulgated, easily accessible to knowledge, not *ex post facto*), as well as the principles of 'natural justice' (rules must be applied by impartial judges through fair trials).[11] At the second level, evaluation of existing legal systems

---

[5] See Hart, 'Definition and Theory in Jurisprudence' (n 3) 21ff; *The Concept of Law* (n 2) 4f, 207ff, 214ff; and 'Problems of the Philosophy of Law' (1967) in *Essays in Jurisprudence and Philosophy* (n 5) 90–92. I return to this point in the following subsection.

[6] See *The Concept of Law* (n 2) vi; 'Problems of the Philosophy of Law' (n 5) 88f, 109ff.

[7] See J Bentham, *A Fragment on Government*, JH Burns and HLA Hart (eds) (Cambridge, Cambridge University Press, 1988 [1776]) 7f; *Introduction to the Principles of Morals and Legislation*, JH Burns and HLA Hart (eds) (London, The Athlone Press, 1970 [1789]) 298ff.

[8] J Austin, *The Province of Jurisprudence Determined*, HLA Hart (ed) (New York, The Noonday Press, 1954 [1832]) 6f, 33ff, 365f, 372f.

[9] Hart, 'Problems of the Philosophy of Law' (n 3) 113.

[10] ibid 112.

[11] ibid 114.

(or parts thereof) is guided by 'more ambitious' principles concerning what is good and just for members of a society to be granted by law. Such principles will usually be drawn from some previously selected moral or political philosophy (utilitarianism, liberalism, moral-majority perfectionism, free-market Darwinism, catholic natural law theory, etc). In any case, the evaluation of law has a practical import; it is a necessary preliminary step with regard to, say, recommending the preservation of the legal *status quo*, promoting legal reform, deciding unconditionally to obey existing law, preaching disobedience or even open rebellion, and so on.[12]

Legal theory, in contrast, is to adhere to three basic standards. The first is generality of scope. Legal theory should be about, and seek to elucidate, law in general, law as a widespread social and historical phenomenon. A concern with structure is the second standard: legal theory should be a structural inquiry about law. It should occupy itself, not with the peculiar contents of the legal rules in this or that legal system (which is a matter for doctrinal legal study), but with the conceptual apparatus and institutional arrangement common to developed legal systems and legal cultures. It should concern itself, that is, with what Hart calls 'the general framework of legal thought',[13] with the 'distinctive structure of a municipal legal system'.[14] Legal theory should also be descriptive – this is the third standard – in two different senses. In a negative sense, legal theory is descriptive if, but only if, it is *not* a justificatory, morally laden enterprise. Legal theory, accordingly, is to guide itself by a Weberian ideal of scientific *Wertfreiheit* (that is, the ideal of value-neutrality as freedom from practical evaluations or commitments).[15] It ought to be transparently committed to certain *epistemic* values (truth, clarity, reliance on evidence, logical and terminological consistency, empiricism); and it ought also to refuse to pass any kind of judgment on positive law on the basis of *practical* (moral) values. Only then, Hart suggests,[16] is legal theory to provide, as it should, a clear and honest prologue to any informed (rational) criticism of law.

In a further, positive sense, legal theory is descriptive if, but only if, it *is* a venture of 'explanatory elucidation' (as Hart puts it) of law's conceptual apparatus,

---

[12] ibid 116–19. As Hart suggests, *moral* criticism is not the only form of criticism directed to positive laws, though it is widely regarded as the most important one; instrumental (means-to-end) and efficiency criticisms are also in order; see *The Concept of Law* (n 2) 167f, 193ff, 205f.

[13] *The Concept of Law* (n 2) vi.

[14] ibid 17.

[15] See M Weber, 'The Meaning of "Ethical Neutrality" in Sociology and Economics' (1917), in his *The Methodology of the Social Sciences*, EA Shils and HA Finch (eds and trans) (Illinois, The Free Press, 1949) 1ff. The meaning of 'Wertfreiheit' is made clear from the very beginning of this essay of Weber's. Obviously, freedom from *practical* evaluations ('ethical', 'aesthetical', grounded on 'cultural ideals' or on some 'intuition of the world', etc) does not mean freedom from *any* evaluation whatsoever.

[16] *The Concept of Law* (n 2) 240.

promoting 'clear thought' in its province.[17] I have just said something about the way Hart conceives of this task. I should add that it seems also to be his view that this task is to be carried out along the lines of what Strawson dubbed 'descriptive metaphysics': namely, by combining therapeutic (ie puzzle-solving) and systematic (that is, re-constructive) analysis with thought-experiments (designed to explain, for instance, why 'our' law has – and why it *must* have – *certain* constant features and not others).[18] Descriptive metaphysics relies on cultural sociology ('descriptive sociology', in Hart's phrase[19]), and vice versa: the latter supplies data which the former takes as *explicanda*; and in turn descriptive metaphysics turns out a framework of elucidated concepts and tools – its *explicata* – which can then be used in fresh sociological inquiries.[20]

There is a further claim involved in the clarification principle: a claim about the subject-matter of legal theory. In a trivial sense, of course, legal theory is about law. But the clarification principle carries the further non-trivial suggestion that, for the purposes of philosophical inquiry, law is to be regarded as a linguistic phenomenon: as a matter of sentences, words, and concepts, variously connected to institutional structures, collective practices, and psychological attitudes. This linguistic conception of law is fully in tune with Hart's double philosophical allegiance – to Bentham's analytic jurisprudence and to ordinary language philosophy. It also paves the way to the second tenet of the Model of Ordinary Analysis, to which I now turn.

B. The Conceptual Analysis Principle

This second tenet of Hart's model holds that clarification of the general framework of legal thought is to be carried out by careful analysis of legal language and legal concepts.

I have already mentioned how the process of clarification should avoid definitional *fiat* and therapeutic lexicography (seeking to establish the 'correct' or

---

[17] Hart, 'Introduction' (n 4) 12.
[18] See PF Strawson, 'Construction and Analysis', in AJ Ayer and others, *The Revolution in Philosophy* (London, Macmillan, 1956) 97–110; his *Individuals. An Essay in Descriptive Metaphysics* (London, Routledge, 1959) 9: 'The idea of descriptive metaphysics is liable to be met with scepticism. How should it differ from what is called philosophical, or logical, or conceptual analysis? It does not differ in kind of intention, but only in scope and generality. Aiming to lay bare the most general features of our conceptual structure, it can take far less for granted than a more limited and partial conceptual analysis'. See also Strawson's 'Analyse, Science et Métaphysique' in J Wahl (ed), *La philosophie analytique* (Paris, Les Éditions de Minuit, 1962) 105–18; his *Analyse et Métaphysique* (Paris, Vrin, 1985) ch I; and GJ Warnock, 'Analysis and Imagination', in *The Revolution in Philosophy* (London, Macmillan, 1956) 111–26. One of the clearest examples of explanatory imagination provided by Hart concerns his 'empirical' theory of the minimum content of natural law: see *The Concept of Law* (n 2) 193ff, 303.
[19] Hart, *The Concept of Law* (n 2) vi.
[20] The point is made clear by Hart in D Sugarman, 'Hart Interviewed' (n 1) 289ff.

'proper' use of words and expressions), and devote itself instead to solving what might be called 'familiarity puzzles'. For '[i]n law as elsewhere, we can know and yet not understand'.[21] We may be puzzled by what we (assume we) know. We may not be fully aware of the complexities of the legal phenomena we (assume we) know. We need something that helps us to bridge the gap between (superficial) knowing and (thoughtful) understanding. We need something that can deliver the blessings of that elusive form of philosophical knowledge that consists, so to speak, in bringing our mind *into* the very things we are familiar with, so as to be able to 'read' them in a clear light. To be sure, we may conceive of that helpful 'something' as tantamount to 'conceptual analysis' – provided, as Hart repeatedly warns us, that we do not take it to be merely a matter of playing, and staying, with words.[22] Indeed, again to stress a point made in the previous subsection, conceptual analysis *à la* Hart is more properly to be seen as an exercise in Strawsonian descriptive metaphysics applied to the province of law. This point finds evidentiary support in the varied and sophisticated tool-box Hart makes use of in his essays. Hart's tool-box includes three kinds of tools: linguistic, hermeneutic, and metaphysical. These are all philosophical tools; the tripartite classification reflects the different uses or purposes which they may serve. Let us take a closer look at them.

i. Linguistic Tools

Hart's chosen tools for the analysis of discourse in natural languages – that is, non-artificial spoken languages, such as English, Spanish or Swahili – are, again, the combined reflection of his familiarity with the achievements of ordinary language philosophy and of his pioneer awareness of the powerful insights embodied in Jeremy Bentham's jurisprudential works. Three items can be isolated: a theory of natural languages; a theory of definition; and a theory of concepts.

Among the building blocks of Hart's theory of natural languages are some important ideas, which can be summarised as follows. The meaning of words and sentences is determined by their use. It is wrong to assume that when a general term or concept is applied to many different instances all the instances must share a single set of necessary and sufficient properties. It is wrong to assume that meaningful discourse is either descriptive of some empirical state of affairs, or dependent on previously stipulated axioms and definitions (and thus analytically, or logically, true or false): to describe is only one among several functions which language may be used to perform; language may also be used to prescribe, to congratulate, to bring about certain changes within rule-governed (or convention-governed) contexts by means of 'performative'

---

[21] Hart, 'Definition and Theory in Jurisprudence' (n 3) 21.
[22] Hart, *The Concept of Law* (n 2) 13f; 'Introduction' (n 4) 4ff.

utterances (such as those employed in christening babies, making promises, bequeathing objects, enacting statutes, convicting somebody of an offence), and so on. There are 'levels' of sentences in natural languages: one should distinguish between first-order sentences (for instance, about actions or states of affairs) and higher-order, meta-linguistic sentences about words or other sentences. It is wrong to assume that substantive nouns must always refer to some real object (or set of objects). It is wrong to assume that deduction and induction are the only proper forms of reasoning. It is wrong to assume that, for any given sentence in a natural language, its grammatical form will exactly correspond to its logical form (that is, the form that reflects the sentence's actual syntactic structure, its full meaning and its pragmatic force in a communicative context).[23] At the core of these views, furthermore, there lies the thought that natural languages are fairly efficient tools of human communication, even if their words and sentences are characterised by a fringe of indeterminacy – the product of both ambiguity and several forms of vagueness (ranging from ordinary vagueness to 'open texture' or *Porosität der Begriffe*).[24]

Hart's theory of definition, in turn, while profiting from the insights of modern linguistic philosophy,[25] was also developed very much along the lines of two of Bentham's path-breaking contributions: Bentham's account of 'fictitious' entities (such as rights, duties, responsibility, and so on) and his method of 'paraphrasis' (which is a specific method of definition in use).[26] Hart's own account of definition revolves around three ideas. The first is that there are several forms of definition, and, particularly, that there are forms of definition other than definition *per genus et differentiam specificam* – to wit, contextual definition ('definition in use') and central-case definition – which may be more suitable to define legal terms. For there are legal terms, such as 'right', 'duty', or 'corporation', for example, which do not (differently from terms like 'elephant', 'triangle', 'gold', etc) refer to any definite object in reality; and there are also legal terms (such as 'punishment') that have no clear *genus*, or no closed set of common necessary and sufficient properties, as their reference.[27] Hart's second idea is that a good definition – when dealing with legal terms – will be an *explanatory* definition: it will instruct us both about how the term being defined is (or may be) used, and

[23] See Hart, 'Definition and Theory in Jurisprudence' (n 3) 21ff; 'Theory and Definition in Jurisprudence' (1955) 29 *Proceedings of the Aristotelian Society* 258ff; *The Concept of Law* (n 2) ch I; 'Problems of the Philosophy of Law' (n 5) 89ff; 'Jhering's Heaven of Concepts and Modern Analytical Jurisprudence' (n 4) 269–77; 'Introduction' (n 4) 1–6.

[24] See Hart, *The Concept of Law* (n 2) chs I, VII; 'Definition and Theory in Jurisprudence' (n 3) 26ff; 'Jhering's Heaven of Concepts and Modern Analytical Jurisprudence' (n 4) 269–71, 274f.

[25] See Hart, *The Concept of Law* (n 2) 279f.

[26] See Bentham, *A Fragment on Government* (n 7) ch V, §6, n 1; 'Jhering's Heaven of Concepts and Modern Analytical Jurisprudence' (n 4) 272.

[27] See *The Concept of Law* (n 2) 15; Hart, 'Prolegomenon to the Principles of Punishment' (1959), in his *Punishment and Responsibility. Essays in the Philosophy of Law*, 2nd edn (Oxford, Clarendon Press, 2008 [1968]) 4f.

about the things to which the term refers. Definitions, then, are not – thinks Hart, following JL Austin – just 'about words'; definitions, rather, 'may make explicit the latent principle which guides our use of a word, and may exhibit relationships between the type of phenomena to which we apply the word and other phenomena'.[28] As for the third idea of Hart's theory of definitions, it could already be found in John Austin's 'The Uses of the Study of Jurisprudence' (which Hart had edited in 1954).[29] It amounts to the rejection of what might well be dubbed the 'definitional fallacy': the methodological blunder of pretending to have solved some complex theoretical problem (such as the long-standing problem 'What is law?') by having identified the sentences that make up the definition of a term (such as by providing a strictly therapeutic-regulatory definition of the term 'law').[30] At the heart of every theory, of course, there will be definitions of key terms;[31] but no theory can be superseded by – nor should any theory be 'built on the back' of – definitions.[32]

As for Hart's theory of concepts, it too can be characterised by three backbone ideas. First, concepts are a matter of either convention or stipulation. Outside of the realm of common uses of words (whether by ordinary speakers or by experts), there are no true concepts; differently from what had been maintained by the adherents of *Begriffsjurisprudenz* (the 'Jurisprudence of Concepts'), concepts are not to be found in some rarefied dimension of 'real essences'.[33] Second, stipulated concepts are neither true nor false. Stipulations are to be assessed instead in terms of whether they are pragmatically justified; their value, if any, depends on the goal(s) they are meant to serve, and on how they have been worked out in view of those goals. Third, theoretical concepts – like those worked out by legal theory – should be stipulated concepts

---

[28] Hart, *The Concept of Law* (n 2) 13f, 214f.

[29] J Austin, 'The Uses of the Study of Jurisprudence', in *The Province of Jurisprudence Determined* (n 8) 365ff.

[30] See ibid 370f; and cf also Hart, 'Definition and Theory in Jurisprudence' (n 3) 25ff, 47 fn 28; *The Concept of Law* (n 2) 16, 213f; and *Law, Liberty and Morality* (London, Oxford University Press, 1963) 2–3. In this latter work, Hart recalls the importance of reflexion upon 'the criteria for judging the adequacy of a definition of law', and considers definitions aiming 'to provide, by marking off certain social phenomena from others, a classification useful or illuminating for theoretical purposes'. The passage, however, must be read against other passages in *The Concept of Law* (pp 15, 213f), where Hart insists on the difference between providing a *concept* of law and providing a *definition* of law: 'It is because we make no such claim to identify or regulate in this way the use of words like 'law' or 'legal', that this book is offered as an elucidation of the concept of law, rather than a definition of 'law' which might naturally be expected to provide a rule or rules for the use of these expressions' (ibid 213).

[31] According to Hart, adequate descriptive theories of social phenomena like law are made of three basic ingredients: definitions; empirical statements about passing features of the world ('ordinary statements of fact'); and empirical statements about constant features of human beings and their world (statements 'the truth of which is contingent on human beings and the world they live in retaining the salient characteristics they have'): *The Concept of Law* (n 2) 199f.

[32] See Hart, 'Definition and Theory in Jurisprudence' (n 3) 23ff; *The Concept of Law* (n 2) 13ff, 279f.

[33] See Hart, 'Jhering's Heaven of Concepts and Modern Analytical Jurisprudence' (n 4) 265–77.

informed by an overall explanatory goal; they should, accordingly, be 'weak' stipulations: meant not to depart altogether from ordinary concepts, but to provide improved, puzzle-solving, versions thereof.[34]

ii. Hermeneutic Tools

Hart's hermeneutic tools reflect his interest not only in sociology, but also in anthropological philosophy, as we might call it (the use of anthropological tools in philosophical enquiries), and in philosophical anthropology (the converse use of philosophical methods to construct and sharpen anthropological tools).[35] It is at this crossroads of perspectives that Hart lays down his well-known distinction between the 'internal' and the 'external' points of view as to social systems of norms. He is careful to reject a purely behaviouristic conception of the external point of view, favouring a 'hermeneutic' conception instead. A wise 'observer' of some group's rule-based practice, as Hart sees it, will not limit herself to recording the non-linguistic behaviour of the participants in that practice. Crucially, she will also take into account the participants' normative concepts and *use* of normative language; and she will even – by a process of identification – put herself, as it were, in the participants' own shoes, in order fully to understand their normative structures as *they* themselves understand them.[36]

The observer/user contrast is connected to another key distinction: that between descriptive statements *about* a normative system (that is, 'external', factual statements about the rules and about the rule-oriented actions and attitudes of a normative system's officials and subjects), and *normative* statements *grounded on* (what is taken to be) the content of the system ('internal' statements of what duties, rights, liabilities, etc one has under that system: statements which, 'assessing' situations 'by reference to rules' assumed to be valid legal rules of the system, can only be made by *users* of the system's rules).[37]

---

[34] See Hart, *The Concept of Law* (n 2) 213f; 'Jhering's Heaven of Concepts and Modern Analytical Jurisprudence' (n 4) 269–71.

[35] See *The Concept of Law* (n 2) 289 (where, besides P Winch, Hart also quotes an essay by R Piddington on B Malinoswki's theory of needs) and 291 (where works by Malinowski, AS Diamond, KN Llewellyn and EA Hoebel are quoted).

[36] ibid 88ff, 239ff; see also Hart's 'Theory and Definition in Jurisprudence' (n 22) 247–49; his *Essays on Bentham. Jurisprudence and Political Theory* (Oxford, Clarendon Press, 1982) 106–61; and his 'Introduction' (n 4) 13ff. Kant draws a similar distinction between '*know*[*ing*] the world' and '*hav*[*ing*] the world': the former amounts to '*understand*[*ing*] the play that one has watched'; the latter amounts instead to '*participat*[*ing*] in it': see I Kant, *Anthropology From a Pragmatic Point of View*, RB Louden (trans) (Cambridge, Cambridge University Press, 2006) 4.

[37] Hart, 'Theory and Definition in Jurisprudence' (n 22) 248: 'We can contrast the "external" standpoint of the observer of a legal system who is thinking about its rules and their present and future operation with the "internal" standpoint of one who is using the rules of the system either as an official or private person in various ways'. See also Hart, 'Definition and Theory in Jurisprudence' (n 3) 27; *The Concept of Law* (n 2) 56f, 88f, 102–05, 109f, 115–17, 291; and 'Introduction' (n 4) 13ff.

iii. Metaphysical tools

This last set of tools in Hart's tool-box expresses his commitment to re-establishing jurisprudence as a genuinely philosophical enterprise: one concerned with the elucidation of the structure of legal thought and legal institutions (in the line, as explained above, of Strawson's 'descriptive metaphysics'), not with writing down linguistic *spicilèges*. In this regard three principles stand out from Hart's approach: methodical distrust, anti-reductionism principle, and resort to philosophical imagination.

The principle of methodical distrust had already been advocated by Austin as a basic methodological tenet.[38] It is a safety device against the risks surrounding knowledge by acquaintance. Familiarity with words and objects often goes along with confusion and delusion. 'Common sense' views about the law must therefore be subject to relentless critical scrutiny if they are to serve as adequate starting points for fruitful philosophical inquiries.[39]

Anti-reductionism is also a safety device, against unwarranted theoretical reductionism. It resists the tendency, in the process of seeking (as far as possible) to present legal systems as structurally simple phenomena, to overlook, disregard, or underappreciate their actual complexity. The anti-reductionist is not on the lookout for 'pleasing uniformit[ies] of pattern'.[40] She strives instead to retain and display the complexity of legal systems by means of a network of adequately articulated concepts.

As for philosophical imagination, I have already pointed out that it is one of Hart's main tools. Suitably devised thought-experiments may throw much light on our actual conceptual and institutional structures, by comparing them to alternative imaginary situations. The use of thought-experiments is manifest in at least three points in Hart's theory: in his reconstruction of the simple model of law as a coercive order; in his idealised picture of a primitive, pre-legal, society governed only by a set of unconnected primary rules (a prelude of sorts to Nozick's invisible-hand explanation of the emergence of state out of a Lockean state of nature[41]); and in his account of the 'minimum content of natural law' (the 'empirical theory of natural law' which Hart sets against both traditional natural law theory and Kelsenian positivism).[42]

So much, then, for the principle of conceptual analysis. The remaining three tenets of the Model of Ordinary Analysis can be more rapidly described.

---

[38] Austin, 'The Uses of the Study of Jurisprudence' (n 28) 370.

[39] Remember: 'In law as elsewhere, we can *know* and yet *not understand*' (Hart, 'Definition and Theory in Jurisprudence' (n 3) 21, italics added).

[40] *The Concept of Law* (n 2) 38ff.

[41] See R Nozick, *Anarchy, State and Utopia* (Oxford, Blackwell, 1974).

[42] Hart, *The Concept of Law* (n 2) 18ff, 91ff, 193ff. See also, eg, Hart's 'Jhering's Heaven of Concepts and Modern Analytical Jurisprudence' (n 4) 270f; and 'Introduction' (n 4) 12, 13–14.

C. The Not-On-Other-Books Principle

There are two sides to the pedagogically minded not-on-other-books principle,[43] the third tenet of the Model of Ordinary Analysis. On its 'positive' side, it prescribes that legal theorists concern themselves directly with the law and related social phenomena – not with legal theory books. On its corresponding 'negative' side, it rules out that way of doing legal philosophy – 'jurisprudential theology', as it might be called – which proceeds by first identifying some broadly formulated 'truth' about the law ('law is fact', 'law is convention', 'law is force', 'law is norm', 'law is morality', 'law depends on social sources', 'law is interpretation', etc) and by then spending time discussing competing interpretations of such putative 'truths', in a never-ending series of arguments, counter-arguments, counter-counter-arguments, and so on.

D. The No-Mystery Principle

Due mostly to the influence of natural law theory, jurisprudence is sometimes thought of as an investigation about the 'nature', or the 'essence', of law. This assumes that the law does in fact have one true 'nature', one true 'essence', which adequate inquiries will succeed in unveiling. Hart finds such conceptions of jurisprudence metaphysically suspect. They misleadingly surround law with a needless halo of mystery (as reflected in the very way in which such driving questions as 'What is *the nature of* law?' or 'What is *the essence of* law?' are phrased). For there is no such thing, thinks Hart, as the one true nature or essence of law. All we have is a general social phenomenon that we call 'law' ('*derecho*', '*diritto*', '*droit*', '*Recht*'), and any philosophical inquiry into such a phenomenon is to be conceived simply as purporting to answer plainer (and metaphysically safer) questions like 'What is law?' or 'What is the concept of law?' (These questions, of course, are in turn to be understood against the background of Hart's clarification and conceptual analysis principles, discussed above). If we do nonetheless go on using such phrases as 'the nature of law' or 'the essence of law', we should at least be sure to surround them, as Hart does,[44] with a *cordon sanitaire* of scare quotes. Things do have properties; outside some determinate conceptual frame, however, they do not have any *essential* property – and law is no exception.

---

[43] *The Concept of Law* (n 2) vi.
[44] See, eg, ibid 155.

E. The Nirvana Principle

Legal philosophers are sometimes less than rhetorically moderate when presenting their alleged findings about law. *Pour épater les juristes*, perhaps, they are somewhat prone to exaggeration. As a result, puzzlement and even paradox can unnecessarily emerge among both jurists and the educated general public; and the need arises for adequate deflationary analyses. Hart recommends a softer tone. In his view, legal theorists should adopt a more modest, craftsman-like approach; they should aim at the formulation of (tentative and revisable) 'cool definitions'.[45] And Hart's own body of work provides abundant evidence of his unflinching abiding to this 'Nirvana' principle, as it may be called.[46]

III. THEORETICAL CLAIMS: HART'S THREE 'PERSISTENT QUESTIONS'

So far we have been concentrating on Hart's philosophy of legal theory. It is now time to recall the answers that he (putting to use the methodological apparatus of his Model of Ordinary Analysis) gives to legal theory's 'persistent questions'. Such answers are well known; a swift account will do.

A. Law and Rules

Hart sets forth a paradigm-case definition of the concept of law: law as 'the union of primary and secondary rules'.[47] This, he warns, should not be understood as a strict definition of expressions such as 'law', 'legal', or 'legal system'. His is a definition, not of linguistic uses or terms, but of a theoretical device – of 'a concept'[48] – and its value must be assessed on the rod of its ability to promote clearer theoretical understanding and more informed moral deliberation. There is nothing odd or self-contradictory in the fact that the title of Hart's book is '*The Concept of Law*'.[49]

---

[45] ibid 2.
[46] Consider, for instance, the way Hart deals with the relations between law and morality in chapters VIII and IX.
[47] See chapters V and VI in *The Concept of Law* (n 2).
[48] ibid 207ff, 213ff.
[49] Hart also defended, on this issue, a normativistic conception of law: he held, against radical rule-sceptics, that law *is* made of rules. His view of rules, however, laid down in seemingly exclusive linguistic, natural language terms, was accused of overlooking the actual practice of written-law interpretation. Hart appears to have accepted this objection; he conceded that interpretive methods may cast doubt on the idea that rules *pre-exist* their judicial application: see Hart, 'Introduction' (n 4) 7f. With this concession, nevertheless, it seems that his views about rules (and about law being made of rules) become terribly similar to Kelsen's (and the soft realists') 'frame-theory' of general norms – on which *cf*, eg, H Kelsen, *The Pure Theory of Law*, 2nd edn, M Knight (trans) (Berkeley, University of California Press, 1967 [1960]) 350ff.

B. Law and Coercion

In order to outline an explanation of why coercive sanctions are a constant feature of the social phenomenon we call 'law' – a feature to be taken into account if we are concerned, as Hart is, with the concept of 'our' law, *here and now* – Hart appeals to a Hobbesian/Humean model of the human condition: a model in which sanctions are needed as a means of guaranteeing voluntary cooperation and preventing free-riding.[50]

C. Law and Morality

Hart's sophisticated views on this issue have been somewhat obscured by the familiar 'no necessary connexion between law and morality' shibboleth. In effect, Hart makes three main claims on the relationship of law and morality. We may label them the 'multiple contingent connexions' claim, the 'conceptual neutrality' claim, and the 'no-commitment' claim. (To these three claims, jointly considered, there is, incidentally, a pedagogical bent. Hart's account makes clear that 'the' *law and morality* issue is in fact a heterogeneous set of problems which – though often dealt with in a wholesale, confused manner – are really to be separately discussed, possibly from different standpoints and by means of distinct approaches. This way of characterising 'the' issue is itself a valuable pay-off of the Model of Ordinary Analysis.) Let us take a quick look at each of these claims.[51]

---

[50] *The Concept of Law* (n 2) 191ff.
[51] The claim that there is 'no necessary connection between law and morals' – sometimes also referred to as the 'separability thesis' – has been found puzzling on the basis that Hart 'appears to defend two necessary connections between law and morality, in the connection between rules and justice . . . and in the "minimum content" thesis': see L Green, 'Notes to the Third Edition', in Hart, *The Concept of Law* (n 2) 322, and also Green's 'Introduction' in ibid xxxiii ff. In my view, there is really no reason for puzzlement. First, it seems to me that what Hart means to deny is (as he put it in a later text) 'that there are *any important* necessary connections between law and morality': cf 'Introduction' (n 4) 6, 8–12. The 'connection between rules and justice' that Green mentions seems to be an example of what Hart regards as not particularly 'important'; after all it points to a mere 'germ' of justice: cf *The Concept of Law* (n 2) 206. Furthermore, there are different kinds of 'necessary connections' between law and morality; not all necessary connections are 'necessary' in the same sense. The connection that Hart wished to deny, the one he considered paramount, is the conceptual or definitional connection propounded by natural law theorists such as Gustav Radbruch, who fostered a narrow, morally committed concept of law. Hart's 'minimum content' thesis, on the contrary, points to a different sort of connection between law and morality: an instrumental connection rather than a conceptual one. It points to the minimum *conditions* for the survival of 'our' legal systems, given 'the simple contingent fact that most men most of the time wish to continue in existence', and that human societies are not 'suicide clubs': see *The Concept of Law* (n 2) 191f.

The *multiple contingent connexions* claim draws attention to the several dimensions in which positive legal systems may happen to be related to systems of social and/or critical morality: as to their content, motivation, existence, validity, interpretation, criticism, or instrumentality. Legal systems and systems of morality may also be similarly related to religious outlooks, economic systems, rules of etiquette, and so forth.[52] This suggests that any special, supposedly necessary relationship of conceptual subordination of law to morality (which 'morality', by the way?) will be, so to speak, in the eye of the beholder.

The *conceptual neutrality* claim extols the virtues of a broader, morally neutral concept of law. In contrast with the narrower, morally laden accounts of non-positivist theorists such as Gustav Radbruch (or, in our times, John Finnis and Robert Alexy), a broader, neutral picture is far more serviceable, in Hart's view, for both theoretical and practical purposes.[53]

The *no-commitment* claim, lastly, is the claim that legal theory should keep out of the controversial philosophical issues concerning the ontological status of moral values.[54] This claim plays a key role in shaping Hart's own version of legal positivism *vis-à-vis* both exclusive (or hard) positivism *and* inclusive (or soft) positivism. Soft positivists hold two basic theses. They claim, first, that the validity of legal norms may depend on moral-merit criteria: it is *not* necessarily the case that the identification and content of legal norms does *not* depend on moral arguments. Second, they hold the 'incorporation thesis', as we may call it: the thesis that any legal provision laying down moral-merit criteria of legal validity thereby incorporates into law – that is, into what must count, from the perspective of adjudication, as *pre*-existing law – the moral norms to which that provision refers (together with whatever further norms they may imply). Hard positivists, as is well known, hold just the opposite. They, too, hold two theses. They claim, first, that the validity of legal norms cannot depend on such a test of moral merit: it *is* necessarily the case, they say, that the identification and content of legal norms does *not* depend on moral arguments. Second, whenever a legal system does include a moral-validity provision, such a provision is tantamount to a delegation to judges and other officials of the power to *make* law according to certain moral criteria. Now, it is true that (against Dworkin's reading of his doctrine[55]) Hart portrays himself as a 'soft positivist'.[56] But in fact he endorses only *one* – the first – of the two distinctive claims of soft positivism. As for the second claim, the incorporation thesis, Hart takes a different view; his is ultimately a third ver-

---

[52] *The Concept of Law* (n 2) 185ff, 200ff.
[53] ibid 207ff, 213f.
[54] ibid 250ff, esp at 253f: '[L]egal theory should avoid commitment to controversial philosophical theories of the general status of moral judgments and should leave open . . . the general question of whether they have what Dworkin calls "objective standing"'.
[55] cf R Dworkin, *Law's Empire* (Cambridge, Mass, Harvard University Press, 1986) 31ff, 418f.
[56] In the posthumously published Postscript: cf Hart, *The Concept of Law* (n 2) 250–54.

sion of legal positivism. Roughly, his reasoning runs as follows. First, moral-validity provisions may safely be interpreted as incorporation devices only if the morality they refer to has 'objective standing' (that is, only if it consists of a set of objectively existing moral standards 'out there'). Second, the objective standing of moral norms and values is controversial. Third, soft positivists cannot safely adhere to the incorporation thesis: *qua* legal theorists, they cannot rule out that moral-validity provisions may in fact work as power-conferring rules, that is, as 'directions to courts to *make* law in accordance with morality'.[57] Fourth, and conversely, hard positivists, *qua* legal theorists, must leave open the possibility of moral-validity provisions working as incorporation devices. Fifth, the objective standing of moral values makes no practical difference from the standpoint of judges faced with moral-validity provisions. In any case, their 'duty will be the same: namely, to make the best moral judgment [they] can, on any moral issues [they] may have to decide'.[58]

In summary, Hart's philosophy of legal theory does still represent, here and now, a valuable jurisprudential outlook. Of course, as with any other outlook, it is to be regarded as constantly open to refinement and amendment. Its central ideas, however, seem to outline a useful and reliable model of philosophical inquiry about the law. We may disagree with Hart's theoretical claims, and think that better ones may be set forth and argued for. But this will not necessarily commit us to a repudiation of the Model of Ordinary Analysis. (The Model of Ordinary Analysis, by the way, is strictly a model for *legal theory*. It concerns neither the entire domain of philosophical inquiries about the law – which also includes the development of overarching justificatory theories – nor, evidently, the entire field of legal studies.)

Yet Hart's model has been the target of some radical objections. Let us now briefly consider some of them.

---

[57] ibid 254.

[58] ibid. I have reported Hart's argument on the plain-fact vs soft vs hard positivism issue. This does not mean that I find Hart's argument fully satisfactory. Soft positivism is different from plain-fact positivism (as characterised by Dworkin): while the latter is committed only to formal, procedural ('pedigree') criteria of validity, soft positivism allows for substantive criteria as well. It is also not clear to me that Hart's own version of soft positivism is really different from *hard* positivism. For both views are equally committed to the claim that whenever the law is indeterminate, there is really no law pre-existing the judicial decision, and thus that judges enjoy and exercise discretion (thereby making new law). Now a moral standard included in a constitutional provision (eg 'No cruel punishment allowed') may, like any standard, prove either determinate or indeterminate in the face of any given case at hand. If it proves determinate, its application requires *no moral argument*: judges will simply apply it with its settled and determinate conventional meaning; and if, on the other hand, the standard proves indeterminate, judges must resort to moral argument in order to decide the case: they have to exercise discretion. Since these are Hart's views on indeterminacy and discretion (see, eg, ibid 272ff), his position appears not to be different – save from a notational standpoint – from hard positivism.

IV. IS THE MODEL OF ORDINARY ANALYSIS INADEQUATE FOR DEALING WITH THE CONCEPT OF LAW?

We can think of conceptual analysis as aiming at the explication – that is, the rational reconstruction – of concepts. This is, for example, Eugenio Bulygin's view:

> It is an old analytical tradition to call the process leading from a concept to a better (ie a more exact) one, an *explication* or *rational reconstruction* (Carnap). Different theories of law attempt to formulate a concept of law which is more exact and appropriate according to some theoretical criterion, such as simplicity, fruitfulness, and even presentational elegance.[59]

Joseph Raz objects that such an understanding of conceptual analysis may work for the concepts of the natural sciences, which are descriptive, explanatory concepts, but cannot work for *social* concepts like the concepts of law, legal right, duty, gift, property, marriage, and so forth. For social concepts, Raz claims, are hermeneutic concepts: concepts we use to understand ourselves, other people, and our position in the world. Such concepts are more than mere explanatory tools; they contribute to shaping the very social world that we try to understand, and to which we belong.[60]

Because Bulygin's view of conceptual analysis seems not to be significantly different from Hart's, it may seem that Raz's criticism of Bulygin is equally applicable to Hart's Model of Ordinary Analysis. We must therefore pause to consider whether Hart's model of conceptual analysis is able to cope with social-world-shaping concepts like the concept of law. And the answer is, I think, affirmative. As we saw in section II, Hart has a sophisticated, hermeneutic conception of the 'external' point of view: in order to grasp participants' understanding of their own concepts and institutions, observers must, says Hart, take into account the former's *use* of normative language, putting themselves, as it were, in the user's shoes. Though Hart does not say this explicitly, the distinctions between the observer and the member of a social group, between an 'external' and an 'internal' point of view, point to different roles which may be assumed by the same individual. An 'observer' is not necessarily a *de facto* outsider, akin to a jungle explorer who runs into an unknown tribe; observers may well be actual members of the tribe who temporarily discard their role as insiders and *adopt* an 'external point of view' as a way of getting a

---

[59] E Bulygin, 'Raz y la Teoría del Derecho. Comentarios Sobre "¿Puede Haber una Teoría del Derecho?" de Joseph Raz', in J Raz, R Alexy and E Bulygin, *Una Discusión Sobre la Teoría del Derecho* (Madrid, Marcial Pons, 2007) 107f (my translation).

[60] J Raz, '*Teoría y Conceptos. Réplica a Alexy y Bulygin*', in *Una Discusión Sobre la Teoría del Derecho* (n 57) 119f; see also J Raz, 'Can There Be a Theory of Law?' in his *Between Authority and Interpretation. On the Theory of Law and Practical Reason* (Oxford, Oxford University Press, 2009 [2004]) 17ff.

deeper understanding of their own group's conceptual equipment and institutional setting. Now, Raz claims, as we saw, that legal concepts are social, hermeneutic concepts: concepts that each one of 'us' – who are all participants in some society and some given legal order – uses to understand oneself, other people, and one's position in the world; concepts that are more than mere explanatory tools, for they contribute to shaping the very social world that 'we' seek to understand and to which 'we' belong. But there is nothing about hermeneutic, social concepts, it seems to me (on the basis on my account of the Model of Ordinary Analysis), that makes them unsuitable objects of Hartian philosophical inquiry. On the contrary: the adoption of Hart's hermeneutic external point of view looks like a privileged and reliable way of grasping what such concepts are, developing clarifying accounts thereof, and above all gaining a deeper awareness of their role in shaping the social world. We might even say that only a hermeneutic external perspective is able to lay bare the 'self-complying' capability of 'our' hermeneutic concepts.

V. IS THE MODEL OF ORDINARY ANALYSIS AT ODDS WITH NATURALISM?

One of the most powerful proposals for methodological reform in legal theory advanced in recent years is Brian Leiter's call for a 'naturalized jurisprudence'.[61] Leiter criticises Hart's jurisprudence on three counts. First, Hart's theory is committed to soft positivism; but naturalistic inquiries (such as Segal and Spaeth's 'Attitudinal Model') show hard positivism to be preferable: hard positivism 'captures what law must be if the Attitudinal Model is [as Leiter thinks it is] true and explanatory'.[62] Second, Hart's theory does not adequately account for how ideological attitudes influence judicial decision-making, an aspect which he leaves completely unexplained; Hart focuses instead on the problem of the normativity of law and on judicial 'acceptance' of legal rules.[63]

---

[61] B Leiter, *Naturalizing Jurisprudence. Essays on American Legal Realism and Naturalism in Legal Philosophy* (Oxford, Oxford University Press, 2007).

[62] ibid 189. According to the Attitudinal Model, 'the best explanation for judicial decision-making is to be found in the conjunction of the "facts of the case" and "the ideological attitudes and values of the judges"' (ibid 187). Hard positivism, in turn, argues for 'a notion of the Rule of Recognition whose criteria of legality are exclusively ones of pedigree: a rule (or canon of interpretation) is part of the law by virtue of having a source in legislative enactments, prior court decisions or judicial practice, or constitutional provisions' (ibid 189).

[63] I reconstruct this criticism from the following passage: 'the best causal explanation of decision, the Attitudinal Model, is one that relies centrally on Hermeneutic Concepts: for it is supposed to be the *attitude* of judges towards the *facts* that explains the decision, and "attitudes" are clearly *meaningful* mental states that are assigned a *causal* role in accounting for the outcome (the decision). But a judge's favorable moral attitude towards, e.g., privacy in the home – which might be the attitude explaining some of his votes in search-and-seizure cases – is not the same as the kinds of Hermeneutic Concepts that H.L.A. Hart treats as central to the phenomena of modern legal

Lastly, Hart, committed as he is to conceptual analysis, faces the following dilemma: his theory either amounts to a mere exercise in 'glorified lexicography', in which case it is largely pointless; or it presupposes an unwarrantedly ambitious view of the virtues of conceptual analysis, in which case it necessarily misses its target. Conceptual analysis, Leiter claims, cannot 'illuminate the reality, i.e. the nature of law'; all it can illuminate is 'the nature of our "talk" about law'.[64]

If we take into account our picture – drawn in section II – of Hart's philosophy of legal theory, however, Leiter's objections appear to be unwarranted. To his first objection one may reply that Hart is neither a soft nor a hard positivist. His is, as we saw, a third version of legal positivism; Hart holds that legal theorists, *qua* legal theorists, are to leave open the question of the objective standing of moral values, and that judges, when applying moral-validity ('soft') provisions in cases in which such provisions prove indeterminate, must *in any event* decide by making their best moral judgment on the issue at hand. Indeed, this point suggests that Hart's theory of law may be regarded as being in line with the outcomes of the 'Attitudinal Model' that Leiter endorses. The best moral judgment that judges can make will inevitably reflect their own ideological attitudes and adopted values.[65]

What of Leiter's second objection? A proponent of 'naturalized' jurisprudence takes judicial law-making to be propelled by judges' attitudes. An example would be their 'favorable moral attitude towards . . . privacy in the home'.[66] But what does it mean to have such an attitude? Hart's answer would be, it seems, that it means, roughly, that (some or most) judges *accept*, for moral reasons, the principle of privacy as a paramount normative standard which should both guide social behaviour and provide overwhelming justification for judicial decisions condemnatory of conducts trespassing on privacy. It thus seems, against Leiter's suggestion, that judicial ideologies and moral attitudes can be accounted for in terms of Hart's theory of the internal point of view and rule-acceptance. Hartian 'descriptive sociologists'[67] are accordingly well equipped to account for the very phenomena that the 'Attitudinal Model' purports to emphasise.

Leiter's third objection, in turn, can be met with the reply that Hart appears to be engaged neither in 'glorified' lexicography (whatever that means), for he expressly rejects the view of conceptual analysis as (therapeutic) lexicography; nor in the ambitious enterprise of purporting to discover the 'nature' of law

systems: for example, that official accept some rules from an internal point of view, that is, as imposing obligations on them of compliance': cf ibid 188.

[64] ibid 196.
[65] See also n 58 above, where I claimed the difference between Hart's positivism and hard positivism to be essentially 'notational': a difference in the manner of *presentation* only, and not in substance.
[66] Leiter, *Naturalizing Jurisprudence* (n 59) 188.
[67] See text to n 19 above.

above or *beyond*, as it were, the universe of normative attitudes, words and sentences that make up legal norms and normative language. Remember his no-mystery principle, clarification principle, and conceptual analysis principle, which we encountered in section II. Together, these principles suggest that Hart's model amounts in effect to a third genus of inquiry, namely a combination of linguistic analysis, the hermeneutic standpoint, and descriptive metaphysics. (It is surprising, incidentally, for a proponent of 'naturalized' jurisprudence to assume, as Leiter seemingly does, that beyond that universe of interconnected normative attitudes, actions, words and sentences, there is indeed something that represents the 'nature of law').

VI. THE WISER HEDGEHOG

'The fox knows many things, but the hedgehog knows one big thing': this is the well-known line by Archilochus behind the title of the recent book, *Justice for Hedgehogs*, in which Ronald Dworkin adds yet another link to his criticism of Hartian jurisprudence.[68] Dworkin's interpretivist theory of law is now set forth in the context of (i) a 'one-system', integrated account of the relation between law and morality, which views law as a branch of political morality, and (ii) a unified view of the realm of value, according to which the several values in the various dimensions of human life make up a unitary whole.[69] Let us set aside Dworkin's substantive (and value-laden) proposals, and concentrate instead on his attack on analytic jurisprudence; here are the essentials of his argument.

The 'doctrinal' concept of law – the one at work whenever judges and lawyers ask themselves what the law is, on any given matter, in their jurisdiction – cannot be defined, Dworkin claims, without dealing with the crucial issue of the relation between 'law and morals'. The issue boils down to the following alternative. Is the law made exclusively of 'specific rules enacted in accordance with the community's accepted practices'? Or does it also encompass the implicit 'principles that provide the best moral justification for those enacted rules'?[70] Dworkin follows the latter path. His view is that the doctrinal concept of law is an interpretive concept of political morality. Any 'analysis' of the doctrinal concept of law, accordingly, and whether we like it or not, will

---

[68] R Dworkin, *Justice for Hedgehogs* (Cambridge, Mass, Harvard University Press, 2011) 1.

[69] *Cf*, eg, ibid 5: '[L]aw is a branch of political morality, which is itself a branch of a more general personal morality, which is in turn a branch of a yet more general theory of what it is to live well'; see also ibid 1–19 for a general survey and references to the several parts of Dworkin's 'system', and 400–15 for a summary of his theory of law and morals, meant to 'supplement' the views set forth both in *Law's Empire* (n 53) and in *Justice in Robes* (Cambridge, Mass, Harvard University Press, 2006).

[70] Dworkin, *Justice for Hedgehogs* (n 65) 402.

be an exercise in moral argument, purporting to advance some interpretation of what law is as the only true and correct interpretation, while contesting different interpretations as false and incorrect. There is no way to 'call oneself out' of this game; no viable distinction to be drawn between, on the one hand, avowedly value-laden and interpretive inquiries upon the doctrinal concept of law, and, on the other hand, purported 'descriptive' theories; for it is impossible to deal with the crucial issue of the relations between law and morals without taking sides.[71] Therefore, argues Dworkin, the whole enterprise of 'analytic' jurisprudence – as represented by Hart's work – grounded as it is on the idea that conceptual analysis, by 'making evident the hidden convergent speech practices of ordinary users of the language',[72] will yield value-free clarifications of legal concepts, rests on a mistake. Indeed, Dworkin claims, 'there are no convergent practices to expose', and analytic jurisprudence cannot *but* be a value-laden, interpretive argumentative enterprise, much as it may pretend otherwise.[73]

From the standpoint of Hart's analytic jurisprudence, however, there are several replies that can be made to Dworkin's objections. First, judges' and lawyers' quest for 'the' doctrinal concept of law – 'the' concept that will afford the right answer to the interpretive issue of the relation between their law and some system of morality – is something for descriptive sociologists to record and report. Second, the several competing doctrinal concepts of law that judges and lawyers set forth as outputs of their quest – competing concepts that will reflect different understandings of law, and belong to different conceptual networks – are something for legal theorists to analyse and clarify. (This was exactly what Hart did, for example, when he examined Radbruch's narrow doctrinal concept of law, comparing it with a positivist's broader theoretical concept.[74]) Third, conceptual analysis is not, differently from what Dworkin suggests, an exercise in lexicography; its aim is not to make 'evident the hidden convergent speech practices of ordinary users of the language'; rather – as we have seen – it takes convergent speech practices (as well as the common-sense knowledge to which such practices point) as starting points in its endeavour to further our understanding and to solve persistent puzzles. Fourth, in so doing, analytic legal theory presents itself as an enterprise of thought-clarification that is by design parasitic on on-going attitudes and concepts – which is something very different from engaging in moral, interpretive argument.[75]

---

[71] ibid 404: 'The doctrinal concept of law can only be understood as an interpretive concept . . . So defending an analysis of that concept can only mean defending a controversial theory of political morality'.
[72] ibid.
[73] ibid 403ff.
[74] Hart, *The Concept of Law* (n 2) 207ff.
[75] See also ibid 239–44; Dworkin, *Justice in Robes* (n 66) ch 6.

There is in fact not one, but several hedgehogs around; each one knows, *ex hypothesi*, just one thing – but a big one. If we glance at the world of jurisprudence, we will notice – to stay within the domain of Anglo-American jurisprudence – two competing hedgehogs. One (self-proclaimed) hedgehog is, of course, Ronald Dworkin. The one big thing he claims to know is the unity of value, one aspect of which is the unity of law and morality. The other hedgehog is Hart. The one big thing he knows, however, is not a matter of substantive moral, political, or value theory. It is rather a matter of philosophical methodology. The Model of Ordinary Analysis – with all its several principles, tools, and caveats – is, I suggest, Hart's one big thing. Just how big a thing it is, may be gathered from its capacity to escape from Dworkin's insisting strictures.

VII. CONCLUDING REMARKS

Interpretivism, hermeneutic conceptual analysis, and 'naturalized' jurisprudence are the most powerful post-Hartian views in the philosophy of legal theory. Their objections to the Model of Ordinary Analysis, however – when not misguided or simply beside the point – are modest. Perhaps there is a moral to be drawn from all this: methodologically minded legal theorists would still do better, in the foreseeable future at least, to take Hart's Model seriously, if only in order to make it sharper.

14

Do the 'Persistent Questions' Persist?

Revisiting Chapter I of The Concept of Law

NICOLA LACEY

IT WAS A brilliant idea on the editors' part to put a section on chapter I of *The Concept of Law*[1] at the end of this volume celebrating the fiftieth anniversary of its publication. For on a reappraisal of its beguilingly simple argument, the reader is liable to be struck, forcibly, by the way in which this brief chapter condenses almost every significant idea in the rest of the book. I find myself debating whether this implies that it was written last; or whether, by the time that Hart wrote the final draft of *The Concept of Law*, he had so thoroughly worked through his ideas that he was able to encapsulate them in this elegant, deceptively simple structure – something which gives the book a balance and aesthetic which are surely part of its enduring power.

To anyone educated in a jurisprudential world dominated by Hart's most famous monograph, the task of formulating definitive comments on this chapter is a challenging one. To read it is to read part of my own intellectual history: a text which is so deeply embedded in the way in which I think about law, and which speaks with such eloquent common sense, that it is tricky to find a critical distance. (Though I confess that I wince, anachronistically, at the worldview in which it is natural to speak only of men. I can't honestly imagine that even in 1961, Hart's wife Jenifer would have approved of this had she read the text!).

In what follows, I will raise some questions about the continuing relevance of Hart's three persistent questions; about other questions which might have been on his agenda, or which have found their way onto the jurisprudential agenda in the last half century; and about what light this chapter sheds on the limitations as well as the strengths of Hart's approach.

Like the working notebook which Hart kept during the eight years over which he was working on *The Concept of Law*, this chapter goes straight to the core of the philosophical questions which Hart sees as central to an adequate

[1] HLA Hart, *The Concept of Law*, 3rd edn (Oxford, Oxford University Press, 2012 [1961]).

resolution of the principal issues of jurisprudence. But like much of the rest of the book – and unlike the notebook – it illustrates and moves to a resolution of those questions by setting up earlier mistaken answers and misguided approaches in contrast to which his own approach is delineated. This is a powerful pedagogic and explanatory tool: but I would argue that it sometimes trapped Hart in a framework of limited alternatives. This seems to me particularly true of the first two of the persistent questions: the relationship between law and orders backed by threats, and that between law and morality. The book, like this chapter, sets up a caricature of early positivism, interspersed with the odd hint of legal realism, opposite a caricature of natural law theory, as the Scylla and Charybdis of jurisprudence. This approach lends the impression that Hart's own approach set out in the (symbolically positioned) middle chapters is an inevitable, common-sense conclusion. In particular, the way in which the question about law's relationship with morality is set up strikes me as one of the weakest aspects of the chapter, not least because it fails to advert to an adequate range of possible ways in which legality and morality might be related – an issue canvassed in both Leslie Green's and John Finnis's papers in this volume. Each of the first two persistent questions appears to be driven more by the intended rhetorical structure of the book than by the key insights for which the book remains justly famous. (Indeed Hart himself perhaps hints at this towards the end of the chapter, when he notes somewhat apologetically that his exegesis, which positions positivism before natural law, is determinedly unhistorical.)

I would suggest, then, that the three persistent questions are not all on a level. Indeed in my view the key question for Hart is in fact question number three concerning the relationship between law and rules: What is a rule, and in what sense is law a creature of rules? The aspects of the other two questions in which Hart is really interested (and to which he feels that he has an answer) lay, in his view, in an adequate understanding of law's rule-like quality: in the distinction between rule-based and habitual or forced behaviour; in the varying structure of legal rules; in the distinctive notion of legal obligation; and hence in the different forms of normativity which could characterise rules. But while Hart's theory of law as a system of rules succeeds in resolving many of the deficiencies of both realism and the command theory, and hence in unravelling persistent question number one concerning the relationship between law and orders backed by force, it does far less well on question number two, the relationship between law and morality.

Hart's working notebook (which can now be consulted in the archive at New College, Oxford) shows very clearly that he struggled with this question. The ultimate structure of *The Concept of Law*, with the theory of law as the union of primary and secondary rules with an internal aspect – poised between the Scylla of the Austinian and the Charybdis of the Naturalist caricatures – helped

Hart to avoid quite confronting the puzzle about how his descriptive, social fact theory of law could be reconciled with a fully normative vision of legal obligation or with a conception of legal reasoning as concerned with what *ought* to be decided. In other words, if Hart's argument is that both the existence and the obligatory force of law can be described completely in terms of a set of (admittedly complex) social facts, it appears to espouse a reductionist position at odds with Hart's insistence on the discreteness of law and legal reasoning, or – as Kelsen insisted – to commit the philosophical error of deriving an 'ought' from an 'is'. This is why the critiques which Hart struggled to respond to were those which questioned the pretension to descriptiveness which is so central to the whole conception of *The Concept of Law*. Notable among such critiques were those of John Finnis (particularly the argument mounted in the first chapter of *Natural Law and Natural Rights*,[2] to the effect that Hart's recognition that law is concerned with social stability and peaceful human co-operation implicitly commits him to the view that a core group must have a morally committed internal attitude, and hence to the view that such an attitude counts as the central case of the internal attitude); and – as the Postscript makes painfully apparent – of Ronald Dworkin (in particular the attacks on the descriptive quality of Hart's theory from the publication of *Law's Empire*[3] on).

Would Hart have chosen the same three questions had he been writing *The Concept of Law* today? Clearly not. His approach would have been informed by the significant developments in jurisprudence and indeed in philosophy of the last half century, in particular those bearing on our understanding of law's authority and of law as a system of practical reason.[4] Other contributions to this collection comment in depth on how cutting edge analytical jurisprudence today would have reframed or added to Hart's questions. I would add only that I suspect that had he been writing today, he would have felt less need to demolish the idea that legal theory is a matter of definition. That this task no longer demands the attention of the discerning legal philosopher is of course a token of the very success of this chapter, as of Hart's inaugural lecture,[5] in influencing the way in which jurisprudence is approached.

---

[2] J Finnis, *Natural Law and Natural Rights*, 2nd edn (Oxford, Oxford University Press, 2011); Hart's refusal to give the fully committed internal attitude theoretical priority was, in effect, inconsistent with a notion of law as providing reasons for action whose force is independent of any prediction of the bad consequences of disobedience.

[3] R Dworkin, *Law's Empire* (London, Fontana, 1986). On this aspect of Hart's Postscript, and on his working notebooks, which show him struggling to come to terms with the criticism of a number of other authors as well: see N Lacey, *A Life of H.L.A. Hart: The Nightmare and the Noble Dream* (Oxford, Oxford University Press, 2004) 335–38, 348–53.

[4] See in particular J Raz, *Practical Reason and Norms*, 2nd edn (Oxford, Oxford University Press 1999 [1975]); and *Between Authority and Interpretation: On the Theory of Law and Practical Reason* (Oxford, Oxford University Press, 2009).

[5] HLA Hart, 'Definition and Theory in Jurisprudence' (1954) 70 *Law Quarterly* Review 37; reprinted in Hart's *Essays on Jurisprudence and Philosophy* (Oxford, Clarendon Press, 1983).

But what other questions might Hart have included in this chapter? Here I will mention just two classes of questions to which I have struggled in my own work to find adequate answers in Hartian jurisprudence, and to which answers would have been helpful to me. First, it has always seemed strange to me that while in setting up his puzzle about the nature of law, Hart adverts several times to institutions such as courts and legislatures, none of his questions advert at all to the obvious fact which is reflected in that preliminary discussion, namely the fact that law realises itself in institutional form, and that the nature of that institutional form, and of the social practices by means of which a legal system is operationalised and developed, depends in part on law's articulation with other aspects of social structure, notably the political system.[6] The disembodied or de-institutionalised conception of law which animates *The Concept of Law* differs markedly from the interest in the variety of law's institutional forms disclosed in both Hart's working notebook for *The Concept of Law* and an unpublished paper on discretion circulated to the Harvard Legal Philosophy Discussion Group in 1956 and recently rediscovered by Geoffrey Shaw among the papers of Henry Hart in the Harvard Law School archive, in which the institutional constraints on discretion are implied to be key to explaining its (potential) consistency with the rule of law.[7] Indeed, this de-institutionalised conception of law seems to me to be one of the reasons why Hart's theory struggles to accommodate customary or common law;[8] why his account provides no adequate account of legal systems or even of legal reasoning and adjudication; and why – though it was much to his credit that, unlike most of his theoretical contemporaries, he at least tackled the issue – his treatment of international law is characterised by the missteps analysed by Jeremy Waldron in his contribution to this volume. (As for his treatment of 'primitive' legal systems, the less said the better.[9]) These questions about the institutional, cultural and political conditions of law's power

---

[6] For a further development of this argument, see N Lacey, 'Analytical Jurisprudence versus Descriptive Sociology Revisited' (2006) 84 *Texas Law Review* 945–82, and 'H.L.A. Hart's Rule of Law: The Limits of Philosophy in Historical Perspective' (2007) XXXVI *Quaderni Fiorentini* 1159.

[7] It is an interesting question why Hart's later work was more parsimonious in its analysis of such institutional questions. This issue, inter alia, is discussed in GC Shaw's commentary on Hart's paper, 'H.L.A. Hart's Lost Essay: "Discretion" and the Legal Process School', and in my Introduction, both published alongside Hart's own essay in the *Harvard Law Review* (December 2013). A copy of the original typescript can be found in the papers of Henry Hart, held in the archive at the Special Collections Room, Harvard Law School Library, Box 35, Folder 7. See also N Lacey, 'Institutionalising Responsibility: Implications for Jurisprudence' (2013) 4 *Jurisprudence* 1–19.

[8] On which see AWB Simpson's powerful 'The Common Law and Legal Theory', in Simpson (ed), *Oxford Essays in Jurisprudence. Second Series* (Oxford, Clarendon Press, 1973); see also Simpson's *Reflections on The Concept of Law* (Oxford, Oxford University Press, 2011).

[9] See Lacey, *A Life of H.L.A. Hart* (n 3) 229f; see further, P Fitzpatrick, *The Mythology of Modern Law* (London, Routledge, 1992); B Tamanaha, *A General Jurisprudence of Law and Society* (Oxford, Oxford University Press, 2001).

and authority, like those of the influence of vectors of power on the creation and interpretation of law – questions surely put on the agenda of jurisprudence by the great social theories of Marx, Weber and Durkheim, and ones which claim their place in the jurisprudential canon today in various forms of critical, feminist and sociological legal theory[10] – lurk in the interstices of Hart's argument, but never find their proper place.

Hart's failure to address these questions about the institutional and other conditions of existence of legal authority and of different forms of law is almost certainly related to his concomitant failure to advert to the insights of disciplines complementary to legal philosophy, whose relevance would have been much more apparent to him had he followed his original instinct to place law's institutional form and underpinning at the core of his theory. So, as I argued at some length in Hart's biography and in several subsequent papers,[11] my own view is that *The Concept of Law* is not only a magnificent achievement, but a missed opportunity for a more productive dialogue between the concerns of philosophical jurisprudence and those of disciplines which explicitly concern themselves with the institutional conditions of existence of systems of social norms such as law: of sociological jurisprudence, of anthropology, and of political science, to name merely the most obvious.

I would like to close with an appreciative comment on this chapter. The idea that jurisprudence should be structured around a key set of questions is a fundamentally good one. This may sound obvious. But it is an insight which can be lost in a field crowded with intellectually sophisticated scholarship sometimes distracted from the questions themselves by the temptation to debate the rights and wrongs of other scholars' treatment of those questions (or of other scholars' treatment of other scholars' treatment of those questions, and so on . . .). Herbert Hart would have felt deep satisfaction at the flourishing of analytical jurisprudence which his work engendered; but I suspect that he would have had mixed feelings about the technicality of the field today. Whether or not we think that Hart's persistent questions are the core questions for jurisprudence in the twenty-first century, we should continue to celebrate his vision of jurisprudence, eloquently expressed in and epitomised by chapter I of *The Concept of Law*: elegant and economical in style; accessible to any intelligent reader; and firmly oriented to posing and answering questions about the nature and significance of law.

---

[10] See, eg, R Cotterrell, *Law's Community: Legal Theory in Sociological Perspective* (Oxford, Oxford University Press, 1995); *The Sociology of Law: An Introduction*, 2nd edn (Oxford, Oxford University Press, 1992); C Smart, *Feminism and the Power of Law* (London, Routledge, 1991); N Lacey, *Unspeakable Subjects: Feminist Essays in Legal Theory* (Oxford, Hart Publishing, 1998); W Twining, *General Jurisprudence: Understanding Law from a Global Perspective* (Cambridge, Cambridge University Press, 2009); D Kairys (ed), *The Politics of Law: A Progressive Critique*, 3rd edn (New York, Basic Books, 1998); J Conaghan, *Law and Gender* (Oxford, Clarendon Press, 2013).

[11] See references at nn 6 and 7 above, and 'Philosophy, Political Morality and History: Explaining the Enduring Resonance of the Hart-Fuller Debate' (2008) 83 *New York University Law Review* 1059.

Part III

An Interview with HLA Hart

15
Introductory Note

JUAN RAMÓN DE PÁRAMO

I FIRST MET HLA Hart in Oxford in the summer of 1979. I had recently finished my law degree in Madrid, and in those days Spanish legal philosophy was in a disheartening state. Hart's work was well known – *The Concept of Law* had been excellently translated into Spanish by Genaro Carrió a mere two years after its original publication[1] – but an unappealingly conservative version of natural law theory was still the dominant view. Yet there were some younger scholars, like Alfonso Ruiz Miguel and Liborio Hierro (whose doctoral theses had been on Norberto Bobbio's jurisprudence and on Legal Realism, respectively), who were beginning to broaden the scope of their philosophical interests. Encouraged by the late Gregorio Peces-Barba, I had begun to study Hart's works, and decided to write my doctoral dissertation on the relation between analytic philosophy and general legal theory in Hart's jurisprudence.[2]

During my stay in Oxford I invited Hart to come to Spain, and his first visit would take place the following year. He gave two lectures at the Complutense University of Madrid: 'Between Utility and Rights', which he had recently published;[3] and 'El Nuevo Desafío al Positivismo Jurídico' ('The New Challenge to Legal Positivism'), in which he addressed several of Ronald Dworkin's criticisms of *The Concept of Law*, and which was published in Spanish.[4] In 1987 I invited him again, and it was during that second visit that Hart agreed to this interview, for which he provided written answers. The interview was published, in Spanish translation, in the 1988 volume of *Doxa* – a journal launched in 1984 under Manuel Atienza's direction, and which has played an invaluable role in the renovation of Spanish jurisprudence in the past three decades.

---

[1] HLA Hart, *El Concepto de Derecho*, GR Carrió (trans) (Buenos Aires, Abeledo-Perrot, 1963).
[2] *HLA Hart y la Teoría Analítica del Derecho* (Madrid, Centro de Estudios Constitucionales, 1984).
[3] HLA Hart, 'Between Utility and Rights' (1979) 79 *Columbia Law Review* 828–46.
[4] HLA Hart, 'El Nuevo Desafío al Positivismo Jurídico', L Hierro, F Laporta, and JR de Páramo (trans) (1980) 36 *Sistema* 3–18.

This interview was also published in a German translation (from the Spanish) in *Rechtstheorie* in 1991.[5] Hart's original text, however, remained unpublished – until now.

I have fond memories of HLA Hart, on whose kindness, generosity, and advice I was fortunate to be able to rely. And I shall always remember him strolling down the streets of Ávila while reciting – in Spanish – these verses by San Juan de la Cruz:

> *¡Oh cristalina fuente,*
> *si en esos tus semblantes plateados*
> *formases de repente*
> *los ojos deseados*
> *que tengo en mis entrañas dibujados!*

---

[5] 'Hart's "Concept of Law" nach dreißig Jahren', R Zimmerling (trans) (1991) 22 *Rechtstheorie* 393–414.

16

Answers to Eight Questions
(1988)

HLA HART*

1. *Unlike most philosophers of law, your first professional contact with the law was as a barrister. Was your practice at the Bar during the 1930s important for your later work as a philosopher of law?*

THE SHORT ANSWER to this question is that if I had not practised as a barrister, as I did in London in the years 1932–1940, I would never have become a jurist at all, or written about or taken any interest in jurisprudence or the philosophy of law. But to make this answer intelligible I must say something about my education in the years 1926–1930 as a student at Oxford, and also about my later period as a teacher of philosophy at Oxford between 1946 and 1953.

As a student I studied not law but philosophy, ancient and modern, and ancient history. In my youth it was quite usual in England (though less common now) for those who intended, as I originally did, to follow the profession of law as a barrister to study at university some subject other than law, such as philosophy, history or mathematics or natural science. Indeed many of the most distinguished English judges and lawyers did this and, as a consequence, they, like myself, had no law degree or university education in law. Instead we qualified after leaving university for admission as a practising barrister by a relatively short period of private study sufficient to pass the then not very exacting examination required by the profession. While practising as a barrister, I expected that that would be my lifelong occupation, and I had no thought of becoming an academic. I had however continued since my student days, in my spare time, to take an amateur interest in general philosophy (which had fascinated me as a student) and especially in the main forms of linguistic philosophy which had greatly developed since my student days. By 1940, when I left my practice for war service in the British Intelligence, I had

---

* [Footnotes in square brackets added by the editors of this volume; the remaining footnotes are Hart's own.]

begun to feel that my real interests were not in the law which I practised but in philosophy. This feeling was sharpened by my war time contact with Oxford philosophers, among them Gilbert Ryle and Stuart Hampshire, who were also serving in the British Intelligence.

So it was that when the war ended in 1945 I did not return to my practice as a lawyer but accepted a position at Oxford (where my interest and attainments as a student of philosophy were still remembered) to teach general philosophy. There, as well as lecturing, I took part in regular philosophical discussions with other Oxford philosophers who attended an informal weekly discussion group led by the late Professor JL Austin. Among the many different subjects which we discussed under Austin's stimulating guidance was the general concept of a rule of conduct, which we sought to clarify by considering different systems of rules, legal and non-legal (eg games, social clubs, etc), and by considering the meaning of the different expressions ('following', 'obeying', 'applying') used in conjunction with rules, and by identifying the differences between the various functions of rules such as that of determining the validity of transactions (eg contracts or transfers of property or legislation) contrasted with that of imposing duties or obligations or conferring rights.

In the course of these discussions, and also in the course of arguing with some of my very able Oxford students, I came to see that the methods of analysis and certain distinctions stressed by contemporary English philosophers could profitably be applied to a philosophical study of the law. This was pre-eminently true of their leading idea that the same form of expressions and the same grammatical structures might refer to phenomena between which there were often many irreducible differences and complex relationships. The realisation that this was so served to illumine for me many features of law which had been obscured (or at any rate were not revealed) by traditional English academic jurisprudence taught by lawyers who had little or no contact with philosophy.

In short, the general importance of my eight years of practice as a lawyer for my subsequent work as a legal philosopher was mainly in providing me with a detailed knowledge of some branches of the law as a subject for philosophical reflection to which I could apply some very useful philosophical distinctions and techniques. So my work as a philosopher of law was to some extent the product of a fusion in my mind of various modern philosophical ideas with the knowledge of the law which I had acquired in practice.

2. *During the war not only were you in contact, as you just mentioned, with Ryle and Hampshire, but you were also an active participant in JL Austin's seminar – along with James Urmson, Friedrich Waissman, George Paul, Anthony Woozley, Richard Hare, Peter Strawson, Geoffrey and Mary Warnock, Philippa Foot, and Tony Honoré, among others. This philosophical activity, you say, played a very important role in the development of your own theory of law. Do you think philosophy should be included in legal education?*

Part of my answer to this question is implicit in my answer to Question 1. I certainly think that the study of philosophy is of great importance not only for academic jurists but for those who intend to practise law. The study of philosophy in conjunction with some other subject, and especially in conjunction with the study of law, fosters clarity of thought and expression and develops analytical and critical skills which may be freely transferred to other disciplines. Philosophical study sharpens the powers of argument on any topic. So I would wish to see included in the course of study required for qualification both as a practising lawyer and as a teacher, a short course of modern elementary symbolic logic and a somewhat longer course on the basic issues of moral and political philosophy. For English students, the essentials of this latter study would be the identification of the precise questions about the nature of political authority which Hobbes, Locke, Hume and Rousseau sought to answer, and the evaluation of their different answers.

3. *In 1952 Arthur Goodhart retired from the Chair of Jurisprudence and you were elected as his successor. Yet it was not until 1961, when you were 54 years old, that you completed your major work,* The Concept of Law. *You had published several articles before that, but none seems to have been included in the book. Could you describe its process of gestation?*

The formulation of this question is misleading in suggesting that none of my writings published before *The Concept of Law* were included in that book. It is true that I did not reproduce the actual text of my previous writings, but many of the central theses of my book were expounded in my Holmes Lecture, 'Positivism and the Separation of Law and Morals', given at Harvard in 1957.[1] In that lecture I gave a general critique of imperative theories of law and of the Austinian doctrine of sovereignty. I also argued in that lecture in favour of the conceptual separation of law and morality, and I stressed the 'open-textured' character of many legal rules and the consequent need for the courts to exercise a limited law-creating function or 'discretion'. In my earlier inaugural lecture at Oxford, 'Definition and Theory in Jurisprudence',[2] I advanced two doctrines which were implicit in *The Concept of Law*. These stressed the uselessness of conventional forms of definition in clarifying many concepts and the importance of recognising that there were different forms of rules governing behaviour, between which there were important logical differences.

As to the process of gestation of my work, the main doctrines of *The Concept of Law* were in a sense a by-product of my first lectures as Professor of Jurisprudence at Oxford. At that time (1953) the only original theoretical

---

[1] [HLA Hart, 'Positivism and the Separation of Law and Morals' (1958) 71 *Harvard Law Review* 593–629; reprinted in Hart's *Essays in Jurisprudence and Philosophy* (Oxford, Clarendon Press, 1983) 49–87.]

[2] [HLA Hart, 'Definition and Theory in Jurisprudence' (1953) 70 *Law Quarterly Review* 37–60; reprinted in *Essays in Jurisprudence and Philosophy* (n 1) 21–48.]

work in jurisprudence with which English law students at Oxford were expected to be familiar was Austin's *The Province of Jurisprudence Determined* (1832),[3] though there were a number of secondary general textbooks on jurisprudence which were used to teach students. These usually summarised what were thought to be the main issues of the subject and the main doctrines concerning the nature of law advanced by Plato, Aristotle, Aquinas, and Hobbes. My first lectures at Oxford for law students were actually on Austin, and I found it natural when examining his doctrines to introduce the methods of inquiry and analysis of concepts with which I had become familiar in philosophy and also to relate the subject of law not only to morality but generally to the normative structure of rule-governed behaviour in different fields.

My main criticism of Austin in these early lectures eventually formed the subject of chapter I of *The Concept of Law*, but I soon widened the scope of my lectures to include all the main doctrines of the book. The emergence of *The Concept of Law* from a set of lectures given to students may surprise some readers, but this was very characteristic of the close links between teaching and 'research' and the writing of books, which has always been a prominent (and in my opinion a very valuable) feature of academic work at Oxford.

4. *Would you revise any part of* The Concept of Law?

There are certainly parts of *The Concept of Law* which I recognise need to be corrected and re-written. I am, I regret to say, a somewhat careless writer, and there are a number of instances in my books where I have expressed my views inaccurately, ambiguously or too vaguely. Most of these failures in my exposition concern relatively minor points of detail, but there are some topics of major importance where my exposition is not only confused but incomplete and inconsistent.

The most important of these topics is that of legal obligation. The main source of my error here is the account which I gave in chapter V, section 2 of the general idea of obligation. This account, among other subsidiary errors, wrongly treats obligations of all kinds as arising from social rules which are accepted by the majority of the members of a social group as guides to their conduct and standards of criticism, and are sustained by general demands for conformity and pressure on those who deviate or threaten to deviate. Plainly such an account could at best fit only those obligations which arise, in what I have called a regime of 'primary rules', from *custom-type* rules. But as the rest of my book was concerned to show, in a developed legal system where there are courts and a legislature and constitutional secondary rules of recognition and change, legal obligations frequently also arise under *statute-type* rules enacted

---

[3] [Which Hart had edited: see J Austin, *The Province of Jurisprudence Determined and The Uses of the Study of Jurisprudence*, HLA Hart (ed) (London, Weidenfeld and Nicolson 1954 [1832]).]

by a legislature and applied by courts. Such enacted rules may not be accepted by ordinary members of a society and may not be supported by general social pressure on those who deviate or threaten to deviate. Nonetheless they are recognised by the courts as valid rules of the legal system which courts have to apply to cases coming before them because they satisfy the criteria of validity provided by the secondary rule of recognition which the courts and officials of the system accept. But my account of obligation in *The Concept of Law* fails to give any explanation of how it is that legal obligations arise from such enacted legal rules; moreover, the account I gave even in a regime of primary custom-type rules is defective.

I must therefore give a fresh account of the general idea of obligation and the main features of this account are as follows. Even in the case of a simple regime of custom-type rules, what is necessary to constitute the obligation-imposing rules is not merely that they should in fact be supported by a general demand for conformity and social pressure, but that it should be generally accepted that these are *legitimate* responses to deviations in the sense that they are permitted if not required by the system. Such demands and pressures will not be merely predictable consequences of deviations, but normative consequences, because they are legitimate in this sense. I now think that this idea of a legitimate response to deviation in the form of demands and pressure for conformity is the central component of obligation. This preserves the distinction between a person being merely 'obliged' to act in a certain way because social demand and pressure are the likely consequences of deviation, and 'having an obligation' so to act because such demands and pressure are permitted or required and so legitimate. This idea also reflects the internal point of view of those accepting the rules permitting or requiring such responses.

This revised account of obligation under a simple regime of custom-type rules can be extended to the more complex case of a developed legal system where legal obligations are imposed by statute-type rules enacted by a legislature. Such enacted rules may not be generally accepted by ordinary members of a society, but are recognised as valid rules of the legal system by courts applying the system's secondary rule of recognition which supplies criteria of validity identifying the rules which the courts are to apply to cases coming before them. Such enacted rules imposing obligations need not be and frequently are not supported by general social pressure, but are supported by ancillary rules permitting or requiring officials to respond to deviation with demands and coercive measures to secure conformity. These responses will not be merely predictable consequences of deviation (and indeed may not always be predictable) but will be *legitimate* responses to deviations, since officials are permitted or required to make them. This reflects the internal point of view of officials accepting secondary rules of recognition as identifying the rules which the courts are to apply to cases coming before them.

The best criticisms made of *The Concept of Law* are those which identified the errors in my account of obligation which I have sought to explain here, and I am greatly indebted to the critics[4] who have made them for showing me the error of my ways. But I doubt if the new account presented here will satisfy them. For though it is a new account it is still compatible with the view which I have always held, and which most of my critics reject, that the concept of legal obligation is morally neutral, and that legal and moral obligations are conceptually distinct. In terms of my present account legal obligations exist when demands and social pressure are legitimated by positive legal rules, and moral obligations exist when they are legitimated by moral rules or principles. Though what is legally obligatory may also be and often is morally obligatory, the connections between them when this is so are not necessary or conceptual but contingent. So a man may have a legal obligation to act in a certain way when there is no moral reason for doing so and good moral reasons against doing so.

Most of my critics, I think, would claim that nothing less than the abandonment of my view that the concept of legal obligation is morally neutral will suffice to give an intelligible normative account of obligation, and that it is pointless to insist that a man has a legal obligation to act in a certain way when there are not even prima facie moral reasons why he should so act.

Here, however, I think my critics are mistaken. The point of a theory of legal obligation (and indeed of descriptive jurisprudence in general) is to provide an illuminating form of description of a specific type of social institution which will bring out clearly certain salient features of the institution, which, given the general human condition, are of universal importance. A morally neutral conception of legal obligation serves to mark off the points at which the law itself restricts or permits the restriction of individual freedom. Whether laws are morally good or evil, just or unjust, these are focal points demanding attention as of supreme importance to human beings constituted as they are. So it is not the case, as my critics claim, that a theory of obligation can only make sense if there is some moral ground for the supposed obligation. Of course, those who, like Professor Dworkin, regard jurisprudence or legal theory as a branch of moral theory concerned to state why and under what conditions the enforcement of legal stands is justified, will necessarily reject the morally neutral concept I have sought to elucidate here. But I see no good reason for holding that jurisprudence and legal theory must take this morally justificatory form.

---

[4] These include: Roscoe E Hill, 'Legal Validity and Legal Obligation' (1970) 80 *The Yale Law Journal* 47; Patricia D White, 'HLA Hart on Legal and Moral Obligation' (1974) 73 *Michigan Law Review* 443; and Rodger Beehler, 'The Concept of Law and the Obligation to Obey' (1976) 23 *The American Journal of Jurisprudence* 120.

5. *You retired from the Oxford Chair of Jurisprudence at Oxford in 1968. Your successor, Ronald Dworkin, endorses a very different theory of law to the one you defend in* The Concept of Law. *Was this a welcome theoretical turn? How do you evaluate the latest version of Dworkin's theory as presented in* Law's Empire?[5]

I was delighted when Professor Dworkin was appointed to succeed me as Professor of Jurisprudence at Oxford, though since holders of academic posts at Oxford are not allowed a voice in the selection of their successors I had no share in his actual appointment. Dworkin's great ability, originality, intellectual energy and fertility are manifest in all his published works, which have stimulated many writers on the philosophy of law to examine critically their own theories and the assumptions on which they are based. His main achievement is, I think, to have shown how large parts of the English and American legal systems may be fruitfully treated as if each of these systems were the product of a single coherent and consistent author, concerned to realise in the law a specific political morality which is distinctively liberal, in the sense that it treats all individuals as morally entitled to equal concern and respect, and in it individual basic rights are accorded a priority over collective values.

Where Dworkin and I most differ is that, contrary to my view, Dworkin regards the principles which both approximate most closely to this liberal political morality and also most closely fit the historical positive law of our countries, as themselves *part of the law*, not only when they have been explicitly made into law by a constitution or by legislation or by binding judicial decision, but even when they have not been so made into law, and indeed even when no-one has previously claimed or thought of them as law. In this case, according to Dworkin, these principles are 'implicit' law, but no less binding than explicit law. In his latest work, *Law's Empire*, this implicit law is not merely called, as it was in his earlier work, the 'soundest theory of the law',[6] but law in an 'interpretive' sense,[7] on the footing that the proper (indeed the only) useful way of understanding and interpreting and so of describing the law is to show it in its best moral light. This mix of descriptive elements and evaluation, according to Dworkin, is what interpretation also is in other disciplines, like literature.

This 'interpretive' approach to law seems to me to perpetuate ancient confusions between law and the moral standards that may be used in the criticism of law or as guides to the courts in those 'hard' cases where the explicit law fails to dictate a decision either way, so that there is a gap in the law to be filled by creative judicial decision. Against this confusion, legal philosophers of

---

[5] [Some thoughts – and indeed some sentences – in Hart's reply to this question are resumed in section I of his posthumously published Postscript: *cf The Concept of Law*, 3rd edn (Oxford, Oxford University Press, 2012) 238ff.]

[6] [R Dworkin, *Taking Rights Seriously* (Cambridge, Mass, Harvard University Press, 1977) 66.]

[7] [R Dworkin, *Law's Empire* (Oxford, Hart Publishing, 1986) 87ff.]

the positivist tradition have always protested, on the footing that the status and authority of legal rules as law is normally derived from their source (eg legislative enactment or judicial decision), as to the identity of which there is a general consensus or convention shared by at least the judges of the system. Dworkin does not acknowledge the importance of such judicial consensus, and even welcomes the possibility of a single judge interpreting the law in a creative way without attempting to co-ordinate his interpretation with that of other judges. This indifference to the need for a consensus among judges as to the criterion of valid law and for collective judicial interpretation seems to me one of the major defects of Dworkin's theory; for such consensus is of the utmost importance if incoherence in the decisions of the judiciary as a whole is to be avoided, and if the law is to be a coherent guide to citizens which will enable them to co-ordinate their activities and their behaviour.

Dworkin, in his wide-ranging attack on legal positivism, attributes the importance which the positivist theorist attaches to there being judicial agreement and consensus as to the criteria of valid law to a fallacious theory of meaning or 'semantic' theory. According to Dworkin's version of this theory, there must be agreement as to such criteria, for if there were not, the word 'law' would mean different things to different people, and in using the word they would always be talking past one another, not communicating about the same thing. In those circumstances there could be no intelligible argument or disagreement about what the law of a particular system is or what law in general is. I can only say that such a semantic theory never crossed my mind, and my doctrine of the rule of recognition does not rest on the meaning of the word 'law' or on any theory of meaning. It rests on the consideration about the need for judicial consensus as to the criteria of law, and the requirement that there should be collective interpretations among the judiciary, which I have explained above.

Dworkin rejects all the main doctrines of *The Concept of Law*, but it should be realised that he and I are engaged on different intellectual enterprises and have radically different conceptions of what legal theory or jurisprudence are and what they should do. My aim was to provide a theory of what law is which is both *general* and *descriptive*. It is general in the sense that it is not tied to any particular legal system or legal culture, but seeks to give an explanatory account of law as a complex form of social institution with a normative or rule-governed aspect which, in different cultures and at different times, has taken the same general form and structure in spite of many variations, though many misunderstandings and obscuring myths still calling for clarification and analysis have clustered round it. My account is descriptive in that it is morally neutral and has no justificatory aims; it does not seek to justify or commend on moral grounds the forms and structures which appear in this general account of law, though a clear understanding of these is, I think, an indispensable preliminary to any useful moral criticism of the law. Moreover, unlike Dworkin, whose theory is in essence a theory of adjudication presented as a theory of law, my theory does not seek to say what the law on any point is in any particular system, or to guide judicial decision.

Dworkin seems to see little use for such a general and descriptive jurisprudence. Thus he writes that 'general theories of law, for us, are interpretations of our own judicial practice'[8] and that 'interpretive theories are by their nature addressed to a particular legal culture'.[9] Similarly, he sees no use for a purely descriptive legal theory. His own interpretive form of legal theory combines evaluation and description, and he insists that 'useful theories of law' are 'interpretive',[10] and had earlier written that 'the flat distinction between description and evaluation . . . has enfeebled legal theory'.[11] Surely this depreciatory view of general and descriptive legal theory is excessively narrow, and too exclusively preoccupied with the provision of controversial arguments designed to show how the law of particular communities contributes to the moral justification of their use of collective force. This ignores the need for descriptive analytical and explanatory jurisprudence to answer questions and resolve perplexities and dissipate misunderstandings about the general nature of law to which the existence of developed legal systems have given rise when men have reflected on their knowledge of the law. Such questions are not concerned with the moral justification of the law, but with the structure, constitution and inter-relationship of legal rules and principles and their connection with the use of coercion and with morality. Among such questions are those I attempted, however imperfectly, to answer in my *The Concept of Law*.

6. *You personally met Hans Kelsen, whom you famously debated in 1967. If you were to compare Kelsen and Jeremy Bentham – disregarding the fact that they worked at different times and in different contexts – which of the two ought in your view to be given a more important place in the history of legal philosophy?*

I have little doubt that Bentham was the greatest analytical jurist of the nineteenth century, and Kelsen of the twentieth. But they differ so much in their aims as writers on jurisprudence and in those whom they most wished to influence, in their manner and style of argument, and in their best achievements and worst failings, that they are virtually incommensurable. I do not think, therefore, that an assessment of their comparative merits overall will be meaningful or useful; instead in what follows I shall first attempt to identify some important doctrines that these two great legal theorists had in common;

---

[8] ibid 410.
[9] ibid 102.
[10] ibid.
[11] R Dworkin, *A Matter of Principle* (Oxford, Clarendon Press, 1985) 148.

and then I shall state what in my opinion were the most important lasting contributions to legal theory which these two thinkers made and what were their least successful ventures in this field.

The most obvious common feature of their work is its vast range and scale. Kelsen wrote extensively on the philosophy of law, constitutional law, international law, moral philosophy and political theory. Bentham's range not only includes all these subjects, but extends far wider to embrace detailed studies of such subjects as grammar, linguistics, logic, fallacies, institutions for the relief of poverty, Christianity as the Church of England, birth control and usury, among many other topics.

Secondly, in legal theory both Bentham and Kelsen must be classed as positivists on account of their combination of two important doctrines which they held in common. They both believed in the importance and feasibility of a general descriptive jurisprudence. This, as explained in my answer to Question 4, is concerned not with the law of a particular community or culture, but with the clarification of central features of law as a complex social institution which has taken the same form in different cultures and times and is not concerned with the justification or moral evaluation of the law.

Thirdly, both Bentham and Kelsen held the central positivist doctrine that the existence of law is a matter of social fact and that there are no necessary connections (though many contingent ones) between law and morality. Thus both were opposed to the traditional doctrines of natural law and stressed the need to keep clear the distinction between the law that is and the law that ought to be. Kelsen clung to this view even while holding that law is a social institution with a normative aspect.

The fourth feature common to the work of these two authors is that both, for different reasons, are difficult to read. In Kelsen's case, the reason is that mixed in with the great insights there is much obscurity of expression and some equivocation, so that commentators have differed fundamentally as to the meaning of crucial parts of his doctrines. The difficulty of reading Bentham springs from the fact that despite the bold and illuminating generalisations which he often makes, he had a passion for assembling detail and its arrangement in complex schemes of division and sub-division. He had, it has been said, a lust for classification, and this he applied to subjects such as the variety of human pleasures and pains and the different conditions, social and otherwise, which influence human sensibility to them. His chapter classifying civil and criminal offences and the human interests which they were designed to protect described in minute detail occupies one-third of a book of 300 pages. Bentham himself was aware of the difficulties of reading through this vast classificatory scheme, and spoke of the 'fatigue of wading through' it.[12]

---

[12] [J Bentham, *An Introduction to the Principles of Morals and Legislation*, JH Burns and HLA Hart (ed) (Oxford, Oxford University Press, 1995 [1789]) 5.]

ACHIEVEMENTS

I think Kelsen's greatest achievement as a jurist was to have insisted that all reductive analyses of legal statements (statements of legal rights and duties) must be resisted and the fully normative character of such statements must be maintained. He combined this view of the essentially normative character of legal statements with unwavering acceptance of the view that there is no necessary connection between law and morality. His reconciliation of these two apparently conflicting doctrines involving two different ways in which Kelsen's basic norm may be postulated or accepted contains a great insight, and provides the essentials of an explanation of how it is that the law may be described in terms of rights or duties and validity even by one who does not believe in its morally binding force. This, in my opinion, was a major advance in legal theory, and it has been illuminatingly explained by Raz in terms of a valuable distinction between 'committed' and 'detached' legal statements.[13] The former are normative statements made by one who believes that they have morally binding force; whereas the latter are statements expressing the point of view of one who holds such a belief in their morally binding force, but made by one who does not in fact necessarily share that belief.[14] The latter are characteristic of the normative statements made not by an individual private citizen, but by a legal theorist describing in normative terms the content of the law either of his own present legal system or some past system or some foreign legal system. This explains how it is that normative statements describing the law can consistently be made by a legal theorist even, as Kelsen said, if he is an anarchist. Kelsen somewhat obscures this explanation of the normative language used by the legal theorist in describing the law in normative terms by saying that the theorist presupposes this basic norm 'as a fiction'.

Bentham's greatest achievements as a theorist are, I think, to be found in his many brilliantly original and important contributions to logic and linguistic theory and to the identification of misunderstandings and fallacies which can arise from the very forms of human communication. Chief among these was his elaboration and development, far beyond the works of previous theorists, of what he called the 'Logic of the Will'. This is in effect a logic of imperatives studying the logical relationships of compatibility and incompatibility between commands, prohibitions, permissions to act and permissions to

---

[13] [*cf*, eg, J Raz, *Practical Reason and Norms*, 2nd edn (Oxford, Oxford University Press 1999 [1975]) 170ff; or the essays 'Legal Validity' (1977) and 'The Purity of the Pure Theory' (1981), both reprinted in *The Authority of Law*, 2nd edn (Oxford, Oxford University Press 2009).]

[14] My own view is different: for me committed statements are statements made by one who accepts legal rules as guides of conduct and standards of criticism without necessarily believing that they have moral force; detached statements for me are statements made from the point of view of one who so accepts legal rules as standards by one who does not necessarily himself so accept them.

refrain from acting. Bentham's Logic of the Will commits him to the view that there are no laws which are not either imperative (commands or prohibitions) or permissive. Though I do not share this imperative theory of law, it is clear to me that Bentham's account of it is by far the most profound that has been developed by a philosopher or legal theorist. He was well aware that this imperative character of law is very often not apparent on the face of the law but, as he said, is often 'clouded and concealed from ordinary apprehension'.[15] Very often the law as presented in statutes, codes and treaties is not in imperative language, but appears, as Bentham said, to be 'giving descriptions'.[16] This is true, for example, of legal provisions which define the conditions which constitute a good title to property or determine who has the power to appoint public officials to their offices; but Bentham argues with great ingenuity and plausibility that underlying this surface descriptive appearance of the law there is always a basic imperative structure. To demonstrate this Bentham deploys his doctrine of the individuation of laws, which is among his most original contributions to analytical jurisprudence.[17]

FAILURES

Kelsen's most serious mistakes seem to me to lie in his doctrine that valid laws cannot conflict and all valid laws necessarily form a single system. This was the basis of his so-called 'monistic' theory (which he said was 'inevitable'[18]) according to which international law and all systems of municipal law necessarily form one single system. It is true that in later life (1962) Kelsen came to admit the logical possibility of conflicting valid norms, but he never withdrew or sought to qualify his monistic theory of international law and municipal law.

Kelsen deployed many different arguments in support of his monistic theory, but all of them seem to me to be unsuccessful and indeed to incorporate some major fallacies. His central error was what I shall call his 'content obsession'; this led him to attempt to determine the question whether laws belong to the same or different systems solely by an examination of their content. This error infects his appeal to the fact that international law contains a so-called 'principle of effectiveness'[19] (purporting to legitimate or validate the separate coercive systems of law effective in different territories) to show that on one version of monism municipal laws derive their validity from inter-

---

[15] [J Bentham, *An Introduction to the Principles of Morals and Legislation* (n 12) 305.]
[16] [J Bentham, *Of the Limits of the Penal Branch of Jurisprudence*, P Schofield (ed) (Oxford, Clarendon Press, 2010) 50.]
[17] See also chapter V in my *Essays on Bentham. Jurisprudence and Political Theory* (Oxford, Clarendon Press, 1982).
[18] [H Kelsen, *The Pure Theory of Law*, 2nd edn, M Knight (trans) (Berkeley, University of California Press, 1967 [1960]) 332.]
[19] [ibid 336.]

national law and form one system with it. But the only conclusion to be drawn from these facts is that *for the purposes of international law* and according to international law, municipal laws and international law form a single system, not that they in fact do so. Kelsen's arguments here are no better than the argument that if the Spanish Cortes enacted a law saying that all the laws of Great Britain are valid, it would follow that in fact Spanish Law and English Law were parts of a single system, and not merely that according to Spanish Law and for the purposes of Spanish Law this was so.

It has been said that it takes a man of genius to make a really illuminating mistake, and there certainly is a general lesson of some importance to be learnt from Kelsen's mistake. The lesson is that whether a given law (law B) actually derives its validity from another law (A) purporting to validate the former, and forms part of the same system with it, depends not only on the relationship of validating purport between their content, but on whether or not the courts or law-identifying agencies of the country where law B is recognised as law treat law A as the reason for recognising law B as law.

Bentham's greatest failure, in my opinion, was in his treatment of the concept of individual rights which are not created by positive law. It is true that the doctrine of fundamental natural or human rights as moral limits on the powers of government has, as Bentham argued in his work on *Anarchical Fallacies*,[20] often been expounded in extravagant and confused terms, both in the works of theoretical writers and in various declarations of human rights presented to governments or adopted by them. But Bentham's critique of non-legal rights extends far beyond this. The excesses of the terror in the French revolution seems temporarily to have unbalanced Bentham's normally cool judgment so that he actually recommended that the publication of documents asserting that there are moral or natural rights against governments should be made a criminal offence. Indeed the whole idea that there could be rights which were not creatures of positive law seems to have filled him with a kind of unreasoning fury, possibly because this idea threatened to bring into question utilitarianism as an adequate account of morality.

Sometimes Bentham asserted that a non-legal right was a contradiction in terms, like, as he said, 'a son that never had a father' or 'cold heat',[21] though he offered no proof of the self-contradictory character of non-legal rights. More plausibly, he also objected to the idea of non-legal rights on the grounds that they were indeterminate, that is, that there was no criterion or principle which could determine when such non-legal rights existed.

---

[20] [J Bentham, *Anarchical Fallacies; Being an Examination of the Declaration of Rights Issued During the French Revolution*, in J Bowring (ed), *The Works of Jeremy Bentham*, vol II (Edinburgh, William Tait, 1863).]

[21] [J Bentham, *Supply Without Burden*, in W Stark (ed), *Jeremy Bentham's Economic Writings*, vol 1 (London, Allen & Unwin, 1952 [1793]) 334f.]

This sweeping condemnation of the idea of a right which does not arise from the law is surely excessive and indeed absurd. Even if the appeal to non-legal natural or human rights as elements in political debate or in opposition to the law is dubious, nonetheless non-legal rights are part of ordinary moral assessments which individuals make of each other's conduct. A promise surely creates a moral right for the person to whom the promise is made, and if an owner of property authorises another man to use his property surely that confers upon the latter the right to do so. Such non-legal rights are familiar features of daily life, but Bentham gives no explanation of them as consistent with his general rejection of the idea of a non-legal right.

Much more important than these criticisms is the objection that if the existence of rights separate from the law, according to Bentham, left them without any criterion or identifying mark, why should he have not found in his own utilitarian doctrine (the 'greatest happiness' principle) a sufficient criterion to determine when basic human rights existed? I myself think that there are many objections to such a utilitarian theory, but it is amazing that a thinker of Bentham's stature should have condemned the whole idea of a non-legal right as useless if not nonsensical without carefully considering the possibilities of such a utilitarian theory. It is true that there are scattered hints in Bentham of a theory that statements that men have non-legal natural rights may be viewed as an obscure way of asserting that for reasons of general utility they ought to have certain legal rights. But he deplored such language as dangerously obscure and confused; reasons, even good utilitarian reasons, for wishing that a certain right was established by law are not, itself, a right: 'hunger is not bread'.[22]

I come finally to the question which of these two authors should be treated as more important for study in a department or a faculty of law. Here I would distinguish between law students who have had no previous training in philosophy, particularly moral philosophy, and law students who have had such training. For the former I would prescribe carefully selected parts of Bentham's works, because of the wonderfully high standards of clarity which he maintains even when dealing with abstract issues, and this is, it seems to me, of the greatest value in the education of future philosophers of law. For students who have philosophical training I would prescribe suitable parts of Kelsen's works because of their profundity and power. But works of both authors should be regarded as a matter for critical appraisal on the footing that both of them are fallible as well as writers of genius.

---

[22] [ibid 503.] See also chapter IV in my *Essays on Bentham* (n 16).

7. *During the 1960s, after* The Concept of Law *was published, you occupied yourself mainly with issues in the philosophy of criminal law, the philosophy of punishment, and moral philosophy. The views you defended in* Law, Liberty, and Morality *(1963),* The Morality of the Criminal Law *(1965), and* Punishment and Responsibility *(1968) are close to the tradition of liberal utilitarianism. The climate in Great Britain at the time was one of liberalisation of customs and private morality. Are we nowadays witnessing a conservative reaction in matters of private (and especially sexual) morality?*

I must warn readers of my answer to this question that I have made no systematic or statistical social survey, nor have I had access to any such survey. My answer is therefore based on my own subjective impressions, and on my interpretation of conversations (but only in my own country) with numerous people of different ages, social class, education and occupation. My readers should also know of the possibility that my answer is biased: I have been a lifelong socialist and supporter of the right wing of the British Labour party, and of the partial decriminalisation of homosexual relationships and of abortion which occurred when that party was in power.

It is, I think, clear that since 1979, when the present extreme Conservative government under its rigidly uncompromising leader took power, committed to the restoration of what it calls 'Victorian values' as well as to a 'free market' economic ideology, there has been an increase in the *expression* of opinion hostile to a liberal sexual morality permitting sexual relationships outside marriage, homosexual relations and abortion. But this leaves open the crucial question whether this increased *manifestation* of hostile opinion represents a *reaction*, in the sense of a real increase in the number of those who believe that such practices should not be morally tolerated and, at least in the case of male homosexual relationships and most abortions, should not be legally permitted. An alternative explanation is that there has been no such reaction, but that with a doctrinaire Conservative government, long and firmly in power and determined to propagate 'Victorian values', those who are hostile to a liberal sexual morality, though not increased in numbers, have become bolder and more vociferous, and ready to express their hostility to it in public and to press for measures to prevent its spread.

It may be that, ultimately, this theoretical difference between these two explanations of increased public hostility may cease to be of practical importance, since long sustained criticism of liberal sexual morality and of those who practise it may eventually influence, in a conservative direction, the attitude of many, especially of the young and those who have hitherto had no firm views either way. But the question whether there has been a real reaction, in the sense explained, against liberal sexual morality, and the question whether there has been an increased readiness to express hostility to certain aspects of it, are distinct, and an affirmative answer to the second of these questions does not entail an affirmative answer to the first. I have already given an unqualified affirmative answer to the second question, but I give here only a qualified negative answer to the first.

To explain my answers I will briefly consider separately the bearing of these questions on heterosexual relationships outside marriage, and on homosexual relations. During my eighty years of life, in part owing to the weakened influence of religion among all social classes in my country, extra-marital sexual relationships have not only become increasingly common, but have largely ceased to excite moral criticism or even comment, especially when they have, as often, led to a stable relationship in which the parties set house together. When there are children of such unions, their illegitimacy, in most cases, no longer carries any serious social stigma and there are only vestigial traces of legal disability. In all these respects, the end of my eighty year period presents a very strong contrast with its beginning, and I see no signs of a reaction or reversion to a more restrictive morality for extra-marital sexual relationships.

The prospects for maintaining for homosexual relationships the advances which have been made to a liberal sexual morality cannot be assessed so easily or so confidently. The decriminalisation in 1967 of male homosexual activities, though only partial (extending only to adults, other than members of the armed forces, acting in private), certainly released large numbers from the fear of legal punishment, and encouraged many not only to reveal their sexual orientation, but to campaign against discrimination, eg in employment, and generally to press for equality of treatment and respect with heterosexuals. Homosexuality (of both sexes) has become much more visible throughout British society. Though the cruder forms of abuse and expression of hostility which were quite often heard 25 years ago are no longer common, I think it very probable that this increased visibility and pressure for equality of treatment of practising homosexuals (especially in such matters as admission to the priesthood or facilities for the religious celebration of homosexual unions) has not only excited more open moral condemnation of homosexuals among those already hostile, but has actually led some of those who had not previously thought seriously about homosexuality, or were indifferent to it, to join in such open condemnation.

Two recent developments add to my belief that homosexuals may now face greater intolerance of their way of life. The first is that the present extreme and influential Conservative government has recently initiated legislation, likely to become effective in June this year, forbidding local government authorities (which are responsible for most schools in this country) to 'promote' or support with their funds the promotion of the belief that homosexual relationships (either between men or women) are morally acceptable as alternatives to heterosexual ones. The likely general effect of this legislation may be gauged from the fact that it has already led to proposals for the withdrawal of funds from an educational bookshop which included among its stock of books a very small percentage of homosexual fiction, and has already led to the dismissal (though subsequently cancelled) of a teacher who in answer to a pupil's question stated that he was homosexual.

The second development which may now threaten tolerance is the spread of the AIDS disease. Not all the sources of infection are homosexuals or those infected by them, but homosexuals are likely to be the main focus of fear of infection. This may much intensify pressure for a reversion to a more restrictive sexual morality.

These developments are certainly grounds for thinking that public denunciations of homosexuality will increase; and for thinking, though less confidently, that there will be some real shift in social morality in a restrictive direction. But I am optimistic enough to believe that not all the liberal ground gained hitherto will be lost, and I do not think that in the foreseeable future, the penal legal sanctions which were abolished in 1967 will be reintroduced.

8. *You just mentioned a conservative return to 'Victorian values' promoted by the Conservative party's electoral victory. Do you expect them to win the next election? And apart from these moral issues, have you noticed other changes in British society?*

Most Western European democracies in recent years (with the prominent exceptions of Spain and Greece) have elected Conservative governments, and many of these are committed to more or less drastic modifications of State intervention in their economies and of the scope and scale of redistributive and welfare policies which were aimed at narrowing the gap between rich and poor. Nowhere has this Conservative reaction against previous egalitarian tendencies in government been more severe than in my own country, where an extreme and radical Conservative government avowedly bent on 'destroying socialism' has since 1979 been returned to power in three successive elections. The government under the powerful direction of Mrs Thatcher has recently manifested its hostility to egalitarianism by this year reducing the top rate of income tax from 60% to 40% and thus giving away some two thousand million pounds to the rich at a time when the National Health Service is greatly in need of increasing funds, and cuts have also been made in various forms of State assistance to the poor and unemployed. The ideology underlying these Conservative policies is that great private wealth is not only a necessary but a sufficient condition of ultimate general prosperity and this will in the end 'trickle down' to the poor without State intervention or redistributive taxation. On this footing the best which the ordinary citizen can do to serve his society is to pursue his own interest in a competition for wealth, in which individual enterprise is left as free as possible from State regulation or intervention.

I do not think there can be any single or simple explanation of the widespread rejection of governments pursuing socialist egalitarian policies involving a degree of State intervention in the economy. The countries where this has happened differ too much in their political history in their size and wealth for any such single explanation to be possible. But there are some common features which help to explain this general Conservative reaction: among the most important of these is the sheer difficulty of managing a mixed economy in which capitalist values are tempered by redistributive and welfare policies. The success of such mixed economies calls for much self-discipline and moderation by those who are in employment in pressing for wage increases in societies where there are still very great inequalities of wealth. Such moderation is difficult to maintain over long periods of time, though it is necessary for the maintenance of employment, for profitable industry, for the control of inflation and the viability of State welfare provisions. After a time the failures in these objectives in the form of both unemployment and damaging strikes are remembered, and the earlier successes are forgotten by electors, many of whom then turn to the simplistic Conservative idea that 'market forces' liberated from governmental interference will restore prosperity for all. There are no doubt other factors which increased the difficulties of all governments attempting to run a partly socialised or distributive economy, and the sudden great increase in the last decade in oil prices is no doubt one of such common factors.

In the case of my own country there must be added to these common factors four particular ones which may have parallels in other countries; so I will end by listing them here.

(1) A much publicised division between a moderate centre and right wing, and a militant left wing, have for the last seven years been a persistent feature of the British Labour Party. This has undoubtedly scared many voters who fear that if Labour took power, the Government would be in the hands of wild men bent not only on a vast re-distribution of private wealth, but on a defence policy hostile to the maintenance of British nuclear weapons and to the continuation in Britain of bases for American nuclear forces. There is no doubt that this defence policy, rightly or wrongly, has seemed to many to jeopardise essential British security interests.

(2) In addition to this, division within the Labour Party opposition to the Government has been fragmented by divisions between the Labour Party, on the one hand, and the Alliance parties, and there has been a failure to combine in order to defeat the Conservative government.

(3) A factor of very great importance in England in sustaining the Conservative government's electoral successes has been the Press. The majority of the daily national newspapers, some with huge circulations, is in the hands of capitalist enterprises actively concerned to propagate extreme Conservative views and to belittle or ignore the arguments and criticisms made by the government's opponents.

(4) Through the three Thatcher governments, each secured a vast majority of seats in Parliament at elections, but none ever secured a majority of votes (at the last election it secured 59% of the seats in Parliament, but only 43% of the votes). This is due to the fact that the British electoral system is unique in Europe in having no form of proportional representation or even provision for a second ballot if no party gains an absolute majority of votes. In order to be sure, therefore, of holding power, the government has only to please a minority of voters, and can pursue strongly anti-egalitarian policies and largely ignore the majority, including large numbers of the poor and unemployed who are relatively inarticulate and are unorganised and unable to bring significant pressure on the government.

Index of Names

Alexy, R 260
Almog, J 245
Anscombe, GEM 240
Aquinas, T 182, 197, 201, 229, 238, 282
Archilochus 265
Aristotle 59, 60, 64, 69, 70, 73, 75, 159, 160, 162, 163, 182, 236, 282
Asmis, E 238
Atienza, M 277
Austin, JL 30, 37, 38, 243, 244, 254, 280
Austin, J 6, 7, 9, 15, 16, 21, 22, 42, 43, 45, 46, 47, 52, 57, 58, 59, 61–69, 72–6, 78, 97, 98, 100, 101, 103, 133, 114, 116, 117, 121, 179, 185, 211, 212, 230, 232, 238, 239, 240, 241, 244, 246, 248, 249, 254, 256, 270, 281, 282

Bayles, MD 116
Benn, SI 167
Bentham, J 16, 29, 30, 47, 53, 59, 118, 179, 185, 238, 239, 240, 248, 249, 251, 252, 253, 287–292
Besson, S 211, 221
Bix, B 245
Bjarup, J 238
Blackstone, W 229, 238
Bobbio, N 277
Boyle, J 237
Brink, D 125
Brownlee, K 198
Brownlie, I 217
Buchanan, A 162
Bulygin, E 262

Campbell, T 203
Cane, P 155, 169, 172
Cappelen, H 181
Capps, P 210
Carrió, G 277
Cheng, KY 245
Chiassoni, P 5, 10
Child, R 198
Cicero 201, 238
Cohen, GA 175
Coleman, J 108, 237, 238, 240
Collingwood, RG 227
Conaghan, J 273
Cotterrell, R 86, 273
Coyle, S 237
Cruz, Juan de la 278

Devlin, P 156, 186, 232
Diamond, AS 255
Dicey, AV 194
Duff, A 108
Dumsday, T 245
Dupuy, PM 222
Durkheim, E 273
Dworkin, R 42, 88, 90, 93, 94, 102, 108, 131, 132, 137, 145, 146, 147, 156, 157, 186, 201, 210, 220, 244, 247, 248, 260, 261, 265, 266, 267, 271, 277, 284, 285, 286, 287

Edgeworth, B 86
Eleftheriadis, P 6, 70, 72, 73, 75
Endicott, T 5, 6, 19, 20, 27, 29, 74, 179, 241

Falk, R 210
Finnis, J 6, 18, 35, 74, 85, 86, 108, 157, 158, 163, 167, 189, 190, 199, 220, 231, 232, 235, 236, 238, 241, 260, 270, 271
Fitzpatrick, P 86, 272
Foucault, M 182
Franck, TM 214
Frank, J 239
Foot, P 171, 280
Fuller, LL 8, 35, 39, 87, 90, 91, 93, 94, 149, 238, 239

Gardner, J 8, 86, 87, 92, 93, 116
Gény, F 239
Geuss, R 194
Goldsmith, J 210, 211
Goodhart, AL 240, 281
Gray, JC 239
Green, L 5, 10, 108, 116, 180f, 183ff, 186, 189, 196ff, 199ff, 214, 238, 240, 259, 270
Green, MS 239
Greenberg, M 129, 131, 141, 146, 147, 150
Grotius, H 163

Hacker, PMS 82, 83, 101, 116
Hampshire, S 280
Hare, RM 4, 280
Harris, JW 113
Hart, H 272
Hart, J 15, 269
Hayek, F 90
Henry II 202
Herget, JE 239
Hierro, L 277

Index of Names

Hobbes, T 55, 56, 59, 188, 189, 192, 193, 196, 237, 238, 259, 281, 282
Hoebel, EA 240, 255
Hohfeld, WN 162
Holloway, J 242
Holmes, OW 55, 228, 239
Honoré, T 96, 280
Hooker, R 229
Hume, D 182, 185, 188, 194, 196, 201, 259, 281
Hurley, S 129

Jennings, R 218
Justinian 59, 162, 163

Kant, I 59, 74, 75, 159, 162, 163, 255
Kairys, D 273
Kavka, G 193
Kelsen, H 7, 8, 42, 43, 47, 51, 52, 54, 55, 56, 57, 58, 97, 98, 113, 114, 115, 117, 118, 119, 121, 178, 179, 182, 183, 184, 188, 219, 221, 238, 240, 256, 258, 271, 287–292
Kennedy, D 216
Koh, HH 212
Korsgaard, C 79
Kramer, MH 116, 246
Kripke, S 129, 245

Lacey, N 6, 8, 85, 95, 243, 271, 272, 273
Lamond, G 120, 246
Leiter, B 5, 31, 32, 33, 36, 200, 201, 202, 239, 243, 248, 263, 264, 265
Leslie, SJ 245
Lincoln, A 190
Llewellyn, K 180, 239, 255
Locke, J 59, 159, 163, 182, 201, 256, 281
Lundstedt, V 238
Lyons, D 242

MacCormick, N 101, 111, 116, 171, 188, 203, 240
Magee, B 39
Malinowksi, B 255
Marcus, D 239
Markwick, P 183
Marmor, A 115, 245
Marx, K 195, 273
Mayda, J 239
McRae, DM 210
Mill, JS 162, 163
Moore, GE 37
Moore, M 125
Murphy, L 203
Munzer, S 116

Neale, S 145, 149
Nozick, R 256

O'Neill, O 162, 163
Oberdiek, H 246

Páramo Argüelles, JR de 277
Paul, G 280
Payandeh, M 215, 221
Peces-Barba, G 277
Peters, RS 167
Piddington, R 255
Plato 59, 60, 159, 282
Pope, A 37
Popper, K 202
Posner, E 210, 211
Postema, G 108, 240
Priel, D 245, 246
Putnam, H 245

Radbruch, G 204, 205, 259, 260, 266
Rawls, J 158, 159, 160, 175, 181, 182, 210
Raz, J 35, 92, 101, 102, 108, 111, 112, 115, 121, 137, 142, 167, 181, 183, 221, 243, 244, 245, 248, 262, 263, 271, 289
Rey, G 125
Ristroph, A 212
Rivers, J 210
Rousseau, JJ 59, 281
Ross, A 47, 55, 56, 221
Ruiz Miguel, A 277
Russell, B 39
Ryle, G 280

Sandel, M 159
Scalia, A 147, 149, 150
Schauer, F 5, 243, 245, 246
Schofield, M 61
Searle, JR 242, 243
Sen, A 164
Shapiro, SJ 83, 108, 240, 243, 245
Shaw, GC 272
Sidgwick, H 160, 162
Simmonds, NE 74
Simpson, AWB 58, 86, 272
Smart, C 273
Smith, A 163
Smith, S 24
Soames, S 125, 145, 149, 150
St German, C 229
Stephen, L 194
Stevenson, RL 191
Stavropoulos, N 125, 141, 246
Strauss, L 204
Strawson, PF 82, 83, 251, 252, 256, 280
Sugarman, D 247, 251
Summers RS 37

Tamanaha, B 272
Tasioulas, J 127, 159, 163, 164, 174, 211
Thatcher, M 295, 297

Thompson, EP 195, 196
Tur, RHS 9, 245
Twining, W 239, 273

Urmson, JO 280

Van Doren, J 213
Vico, G 199

Wade, HWR 78
Waissman, F 280
Waldron, J 5, 70, 203, 219, 272
Wallace, S 239
Waluchow, WJ 108
Warnock, GJ 38, 187, 251, 280

Warnock, M 280
Weber, M 250, 273
Whitehead, AN 39
Williams, B 158
Winch, PW 255
Wisdom, J 242
Wittgenstein, L 37, 38, 41, 129, 242, 243
Wolterstorff, N 163
Wood, M 86
Woozley, A 280

Yankah, EN 246
Yowell, P 35

Zagorin, P 238

Index of Subjects

acceptance
of a rule of recognition 65f, 72f, 77, 79, 98f, 101f, 104, 106ff, 110, 112, 114ff, 118, 120, 283
and the existence of a legal system 98, 107f, 121
of legal rules 134, 195, 222, 233, 263f, 282f, 289
of rules of international law 216, 222
of social rules 62ff, 68, 76, 101f, 106, 109, 126f, 232, 264, 282f

adjudication
adjudicative function of the state 20
and the application of legal standards to particular cases 23ff, 77, 90
and the rule of law 90
and correctness 69f, 77
and finality 87f
and ideological attitudes 263
and inclusive legal positivism 260
and judicial discretion 26f, 125, 143, 148f, 261, 272, 281
in constitutional matters 71f
judicial determination of general laws 26ff
particularising functions 24f
rules of adjudication 20, 22, 69f, 77, 79, 81, 85ff, 88f, 100f, 120, 214
as a remedy for the inefficiency of regulation by primary rules 35, 85ff, 88f, 100, 134, 214f
as 'secondary' rules 7, 100f, 120
in international law 214, 216, 219
sanction-free systems of adjudication 244

analogy
and necessary truths 33
and value judgments 34
to central or paradigm cases, method of 5f, 32ff, 236, 242, 253, 258

analysis, conceptual 39, 82, 156f, 162, 245, 248, 251f, 256f, 262, 264ff, 267

anarchism 92, 95, 289

artefactuality of law 31ff, 200ff, 245

Austin, John
'command' (or 'imperative') theory of law 6f, 9, 15f, 22, 42f, 45ff, 52, 57f, 59 61ff, 64ff, 67ff, 72f, 75f, 78, 97f, 100, 116f, 212, 239f, 244, 248
doctrine of sovereignty 57, 61ff, 64ff, 67ff, 72, 78, 97f, 101, 103, 116f, 121, 211, 281

and Hart's rule of recognition 66, 69, 72ff, 76, 78, 97f, 116f
on a 'general habit of obedience' to law 21, 61ff, 64ff, 68, 72, 76, 79, 98, 101, 116, 230

authority
continuity of legislative 61ff, 64f, 101
of law and legal institutions 16, 19ff, 22, 36, 60f, 64f, 66f, 69ff, 74, 78, 101, 117, 181, 195, 197, 271, 272f, 281, 286
practical authority and law-making power 133f

Begriffsjurisprudenz 254

Bentham, Jeremy
achievements and failures 289ff
method of 'paraphrasis' 253
on custom 118
on fictions 253
on legal powers 46f, 53
on the 'proper' use of words 29f

central or paradigm cases, method of 5f, 32ff, 236, 242, 253, 258

coercion 15f, 25, 28, 44, 47ff, 50ff, 70, 100, 141, 184, 193, 229, 231, 236, 239, 247f, 256, 283, 287, 290
and voluntary compliance with law 192f, 195
as a definitional aspect of law 6, 51f, 56ff, 114, 181ff, 229, 239ff, 244ff, 259

'command' (or 'imperative') theory of law 6f, 9, 15f, 22, 42f, 45ff, 52, 57f, 59 61ff, 64ff, 67ff, 72f, 75f, 78, 97f, 100, 116f, 212, 239f, 244, 248

common law
and Hart's theory of law 58, 113, 118, 272

communication, linguistic *see also* **legislation**
linguistic and achievement intentions 145f
linguistic content and legal impact 138, 144ff, 147ff, 150ff

compliance with law
and coercion 192ff, 195f

concepts
and conceptions 159f
conceptual analysis 39, 82, 156f, 162, 245, 248, 251f, 256f, 262, 264ff, 267
conceptual necessity 31, 200f, 241f, 244f

Index of Subjects

constitutional law 6f, 45, 58, 66f, 71ff, 74, 76ff, 83, 117f, 147, 190, 202, 261, 263, 282
  constitutional disagreements 71ff
  continuity with ordinary law 71
  self-referential nature 71, 74
continuity
  of legal systems 72, 77, 98, 107, 114, 190
  of legislative authority 61ff, 64f, 101
conventions
  consensus of conviction vs consensus of convention 157, 232
  conventional morality of a group 132, 186, 231
  conventionalist interpretation of the rule of recognition 108, 286
  social rules and conventional obligations 127ff
correctness
  and adjudication 69f, 77
cricket, rules of 180f, 184, 192
criminal law
  analogy with and orders backed by threats 7, 17, 44ff
  characteristic technique 54
  criminal process 25ff
critical legal theory 273
custom 41, 43, 57f, 84, 96, 98, 103, 118ff, 124, 137f, 177f, 201f, 230, 272, 282f
  in foro and *in pays* 118ff
  in international law 120, 217, 219f

definition
  central or paradigm cases, method of 5f, 32ff, 236, 242, 253, 258
  in jurisprudence 5, 46, 48, 56ff, 204, 227, 236, 242f, 249, 253f, 258, 271, 281
  and the social function(s) of law 57
disagreement 71ff, 142, 160, 286
discretion, judicial 26f, 125, 143, 148f, 261, 272, 281
duty-imposing rules 8, 54, 57, 84, 96, 99, 100, 112, 115
  and power-conferring rules 8, 43, 46, 56f, 96, 100, 112, 115
  as 'primary' rules 35, 66
  as 'secondary' rules 51f

effectiveness of law 21, 105, 107, 112f, 194, 196, 198, 204, 290
  principle of effectiveness in international law 290f
equality 198, 205, 230, 285, 294, 296
  and justice 60, 160ff, 164f, 230,
existence
  of a legal system 6, 9, 16, 22, 71, 77, 87, 107f, 110, 114, 116, 121, 191, 193, 201, 215, 273, 288

  of rules 2, 4, 31, 63f, 87, 99, 104ff, 108, 112ff, 120, 126ff, 131f, 134f, 137, 139, 144, 229f
external point of view 105, 255, 262f
  hermeneutic conception 255, 262f, 265
external aspect of social rules 63, 101
external statements about law 105, 255

feminist legal theory 273
finality
  and adjudication 87f
formalism
  legal 77, 123f, 153, 160
  moral 157, 169f, 172f, 175
Freirechtschule 239
functions
  of the state 20
    adjudicative 20, 281
    executive 6, 20, 24
    legislative 20, 23
    separation of powers 23f, 59f, 73
  particularising functions of legal orders 24f
  social functions of legal rules 7ff, 44, 53f, 85, 280
  and reductionism 7ff, 44ff, 53ff, 57

gaps in the law 69f, 285
generality of law 15ff, 54, 76, 140 *see also* **particularity of law**
  and the rule of law 23, 35f, 90, 93f, 249
  as a necessary feature of law 16, 18, 20, 22, 28f, 34ff, 140
  modes of generality 17ff, 20ff
  moral value 34ff, 76
  use of general terms in legal language 123ff, 140, 142f, 147f, 242, 252

habits
  and social rules 4, 62f, 101, 229f, 234, 270
  John Austin on the 'general habit of obedience' to law 21, 61ff, 64ff, 68, 72, 76, 79, 98, 101, 116, 230
hard cases 285
  and plain cases 124f, 132, 143, 147ff
Hart, HLA
  anti-essentialism 237ff, 241ff, 244ff, 254, 257
  anti-reductionism 4ff, 40f, 42ff, 56, 256, 289
  meta-ethical views 156, 158, 231
  philosophical method 5f, 10, 17, 29ff, 33, 82f, 88, 155f, 200, 204ff, 236, 241ff, 247ff
  The Concept of Law
    intended readership 9, 281f
    'Postscript' (1994) 35, 78, 85, 88, 92, 95, 102, 108, 111, 119, 137, 156f, 185, 209, 231f, 241, 260, 271, 285

ideological attitudes
  and adjudication 263

Index of Subjects   305

inefficiency
  as a 'defect' of regulation by primary rules 35, 85, 89, 100, 214f, 234f
  rules of adjudication as a remedy for 35, 85ff, 88f, 100, 134, 214f
internal aspect of rules 63, 71, 74, 77, 95, 101f, 212, 270
  and critical reflective attitude 63f, 71, 77, 101f
internal point of view 7, 56, 77ff, 102, 105, 107, 109f, 112, 130, 157, 195, 212, 232f, 239, 255, 262, 264, 283, 289
  and the use of normative terminology 63, 102, 109, 255
internal statements of law 105, 126, 255, 289
  and predictions of official action 105
  and the efficacy of the legal system as a whole 105
international law 98, 206, 209ff, 272, 288, 290f
  acceptance of rules of 216, 222
  as a set rather than a system of rules 115, 220f
  as 'primitive' law 209f, 214ff, 217, 222, 272
  custom in 120 217, 219f
  principle of effectiveness 290f
  role of sanctions 209, 211ff, 223
  rule of recognition 209, 219ff
  secondary rules 209, 213ff, 216ff, 219, 221f
  sovereignty as an artefact of 211f

jurisprudence
  branches 249
  educational value 9f, 281, 292
  Hart's 'persistent questions' 3ff, 11, 40, 227ff, 231, 237ff, 247ff, 269ff
  methodology
    central or paradigm cases, method of 5f, 32ff, 236, 242, 253, 258
    definition in jurisprudence 5, 46, 48, 56ff, 204, 227, 236, 242f, 249, 253f, 258, 271, 281
    'genetic-analytic' method 82f, 88f
    jurisprudence and analysis 5, 39, 55f, 82f, 88f, 156, 200, 204, 241ff, 245, 247ff, 251ff, 254ff, 262ff, 265f, 280, 282, 287
    'necessity' in jurisprudence 17, 28ff, 31ff, 34ff, 197, 199ff, 241ff, 244f, 259
  reductionism 4ff, 8f, 39f, 46ff, 256, 271, 289
justice 35, 64, 74, 76, 87, 90f, 141, 144, 155ff, 158ff, 173ff, 196, 230, 234f, 249, 259
  and equality 60, 160ff, 164f, 230,
  and legality 87, 90ff
  and morality 87, 91, 141, 155ff, 158ff, 166f, 173, 175
  and rights 160, 162ff, 165ff, 173ff
  concept and conceptions 159f

  corrective 161, 165f
  distributive 159ff, 163ff, 167
  ideal of a just state 60, 74
  in punishment 26, 166
  in the administration of law 64, 161f

Kelsen, Hans
  achievements and failures 289ff
  doctrine of the basic norm
    and Hart's rule of recognition 97f, 115, 117ff, 121, 219, 221, 289
  'frame-theory' of interpretation 258
  influence on *The Concept of Law* 113f, 117, 121
  on legal norms 7f, 42f, 47, 51f, 54ff, 57f, 182, 258
  on legal validity 113f, 117ff, 178, 188, 290
  on the coerciveness of law 52, 56ff, 182ff, 240
knowledge
  and understanding 1ff, 39, 57, 231, 247, 252, 255f, 262f, 266

language
  and obligation 123ff, 131ff, 141ff, 144ff, 147ff, 150ff
  indeterminacy 76, 125, 131, 135, 139f, 142f, 147ff, 220, 253, 261, 264
    ambiguity 69, 253
    and the indeterminacy of legal obligation 124f, 131ff, 139ff, 142, 147ff, 153
    open texture 253, 281
    vagueness 10, 27, 178, 203, 219, 253
  ordinary language philosophy 10, 17, 29f, 37ff, 204ff, 248, 251ff, 266, 279
  use of general terms in legal language 123ff, 140, 142f, 147ff, 242, 252
law
  and coercion 6, 51f, 56ff, 114, 181ff, 229, 239ff, 244ff, 259
  and content-independent reasons 183
  and individual survival 189ff, 195, 259
  and morality
    demarcation 31ff, 35f, 76, 91f, 172, 177ff, 199ff, 202f, 238, 259ff, 265, 270, 281
    'institutional support' thesis 196ff
    law as a moral idea 73f
    legal enforcement of social morality 156f, 186, 232, 293ff
    moral criteria of legal validity 92ff, 136f, 146f, 153, 206, 260f, 264
    moral need for law 35f, 76, 78, 197, 229, 233ff
    'minimum content' thesis 184ff, 187ff, 190ff, 193ff, 196ff, 199ff, 204ff, 212, 251, 256, 259
    necessary connection(s) 34f, 86f, 89, 91ff, 196ff, 200, 237f, 259f, 284, 288f

law (*cont*):
and morality (*cont*):
presumptive moral bindingness of law 229
artefactuality 31ff , 184, 200ff, 245
as a means 29, 55, 182f, 196ff
as a union of primary and secondary rules 8, 40, 69, 81, 85, 87, 91, 95f, 100, 180, 241, 258, 270
authority of law and legal institutions 16, 19ff, 22, 36, 60f, 64f, 66f, 69ff, 74, 78, 101, 117, 181, 195, 197, 271, 272f, 281, 286
'necessary' features of law 5, 16f, 94, 179ff, 182ff, 191, 202f, 206, 240ff
normative force 16, 63, 105, 112ff, 116, 130f, 172f, 263, 270, 288f
legal impact
of human actions 139, 141, 143, 147
of legislation 138, 144ff, 147ff, 150ff
legal obligation *see* **obligation**
legal officials 7f, 19, 22ff, 27f, 34, 43, 50ff, 53ff, 64f, 68f, 71, 77, 83f, 87, 98f, 105f, 108ff, 113, 115ff, 118ff, 121, 124, 133, 135f, 141f, 195, 230, 255, 260, 264, 283, 290
official side to law 7
importance in jurisprudence 7f, 50ff, 54f, 107ff, 111
who is an official 108, 110ff
legal philosophy *see* **jurisprudence**
legal reasoning 72ff, 78, 271f
and legal validity 72
as practical reasoning 74, 76f
legal rules *see also* **duty-imposing rules, power-conferring rules, primary rules, rule of recognition, rules of adjudication, rules of change, secondary rules, social rules**
acceptance 134, 195, 222, 233, 263f, 282f, 289
social functions 7ff, 44, 53f, 85, 280
and reductionism 7ff, 44ff, 53ff, 57
typological variety 2, 4, 8
vs reducibility to a single type 40ff, 45ff
legal system
as a union of primary and secondary rules 8, 40, 69, 81, 85, 87, 91, 95f, 100, 180, 241, 258, 270
continuity 72, 77, 98, 107, 114, 190
contrasted with a mere 'set' of standards 2, 4, 84, 115ff, 180, 220f, 256
dynamic character 179
existence 6, 9, 16, 22, 77, 107f, 110, 114, 116, 121, 193, 195
and the ideal of the rule of law 23f, 87ff, 90ff, 93f
foundations 66, 73, 78, 97ff, 121, 116, 121

structural features 2, 5f, 7, 10, 40, 61, 82, 98ff, 179f, 210, 250
comprehensive scope 181, 197
independence 2, 19
openness 181
supremacy 2, 19f, 67, 181
unity 77, 107, 114, 116, 121, 220f
legal theory *see* **jurisprudence**
legal validity *see also* **rule of recognition**
and efficacy
of individual rules 52, 113
of the legal system as a whole 105f, 114
and nullity 44f, 47ff, 53
and the normative force of law 105f, 112ff, 115, 135, 289f
and validation by another rule 113, 291
chains of validity 103f, 107, 113, 117f, 121
regress problem 83, 117f
background presuppositions of statements of legal validity 104f
legal positivism as a thesis about 92
moral criteria of legal validity 92ff, 136f, 146f, 153, 206, 260f, 264
persistence across time 18f
qua systemic membership 6, 99, 103, 105f, 112ff, 115, 121, 255, 290f
legality *see* **rule of law**
legislation
as communication 124, 140ff, 144ff, 147ff, 198
legal impact 138, 144ff, 147ff, 150ff
legislative function of the state 20, 23
and the application of legal standards to particular cases 23ff, 77, 90
lex and *ius* 88

methodology of jurisprudence
central or paradigm cases, method of 5f, 32ff, 236, 242, 253, 258
definition in jurisprudence 5, 46, 48, 56ff, 204, 227, 236, 242f, 249, 253f, 258, 271, 281
'genetic-analytic' method 82f, 88f
jurisprudence and analysis 5, 39, 55f, 82f, 88f, 156, 200, 204, 241ff, 245, 247ff, 251ff, 254ff, 262ff, 265f, 280, 282, 287
'necessity' in jurisprudence 17, 28ff, 31ff, 34ff, 197, 199ff, 241ff, 244f, 259
moral obligation *see* **obligation**
morality
and justice 87, 91, 141, 155ff, 158ff, 166f, 173, 175
and law
demarcation 31ff, 35f, 76, 91f, 172, 177ff, 199ff, 202f, 238, 259ff, 265, 270, 281
'institutional support' thesis 196ff
law as a moral idea 73f

'minimum content' thesis 184ff, 187ff, 190ff, 193ff, 196ff, 199f, 204ff, 212, 251, 256, 259
  moral criteria for legal validity 92, 94, 136f, 146f, 153, 206, 260f, 264
  moral need for law 35f, 76, 78, 197, 229, 233ff
  necessary connection(s) 34f, 86f, 89, 91ff, 196ff, 200, 237f, 259f, 284, 288f
  presumptive moral bindingness of law 229
  conventional morality of a group 132, 186, 231
  critical vs positive (social) 75, 127, 156ff, 171, 175, 185, 231f, 260
    legal enforcement of social morality 156f, 186, 232, 293ff
  moral vs other standards of conduct 155, 168ff, 171ff, 185ff

natural law theory 160, 163, 187, 228, 234, 238, 250f, 256f, 259, 270, 277, 288

necessity
  conceptual 31, 197f, 200f, 241f, 244f
  necessary connection(s) between law and morality 34f, 86f, 89, 91ff, 200, 237f, 259f, 284, 288f
  necessary features of law 5, 16f, 94, 179ff, 182ff, 191, 202f, 206, 240ff
  'necessity' in jurisprudence 17, 28ff, 31ff, 34ff, 197, 199ff, 241ff, 244f, 259

normativity of law 16, 18, 63, 112ff, 116, 172f, 263, 270, 288f

nullity
  and legal validity 44f, 47ff, 53
  and power-conferring rules 48f
  and sanctions 46ff, 49f

obligation
  and social pressure 35, 84, 98f, 127, 136, 168, 186, 234, 283
  and social rules 126f, 130f, 173f, 184f, 230ff
  legal obligation
    and language 123ff, 131ff, 141ff, 144ff, 147ff, 150ff
    and moral obligation 3, 116f, 123ff, 130ff, 172, 185f, 178, 185ff, 227ff, 236f, 284
  perfect and imperfect 43
  moral obligation
    and legal obligation 3, 116f, 123ff, 130ff, 172, 185f, 178, 185ff, 227ff, 236f, 284
    perfect and imperfect 162, 173f
  role of actions and practices in bringing about 123ff, 126ff, 131ff, 139ff

ordinary language philosophy 10, 17, 29f, 37ff, 204f, 248, 251ff, 266, 279

open texture 253, 281

particularity of law 16, 19, 22ff, 25ff, 28 *see also* **generality of law**
  and the rule of law 23ff, 25ff, 28, 90
  as a necessary feature of law 16, 25, 28, 35, 77
  importance of particular legal norms 16, 23ff, 26ff, 34ff
  particularising functions of legal orders 24ff

philosophy of law *see* **jurisprudence**

plain cases
  and hard cases 124f, 132, 143, 147ff

point of view
  external 105, 255, 262f
    hermeneutic conception 255, 262f, 265
  internal 7, 56, 77ff, 102, 105, 107, 109f, 112, 130, 157, 195, 212, 232f, 239, 255, 262, 264, 283, 289
  legal 52

positivism, legal 58, 75, 88, 90ff, 93, 204ff, 210f, 221, 234, 237f, 256, 260f, 263f, 266, 270, 277, 286, 288
  and the common law 58
  as a thesis about legal validity 92
  'exclusive' or 'hard' 234, 260f, 263f
  'inclusive' or 'soft' 92f, 234, 260f, 263f
  moral superiority 204ff
  the 'separation' thesis 91ff, 259ff, 288
  the 'sources' thesis 92f, 286, 288

'Postscript' (1994) to *The Concept of Law* 35, 78, 85, 88, 92, 95, 102, 108, 111, 119, 137, 156f, 185, 209, 231f, 241, 260, 271, 285

power-conferring rules 8, 43, 46, 48, 50, 52, 56f, 84, 96, 100f, 112, 114f, 261
  and duty-imposing rules 8, 43, 46, 56f, 96, 100, 112, 115
  and 'secondary' rules 84, 100f, 114
  as 'fragments' of laws 46, 50ff, 53ff

precedent 72, 103f, 117ff, 125, 142ff, 203, 220f
  as custom *in foro* 119

practice theory of rules 102, 126ff, 131ff, 134, 136f

primary rules 35, 40, 51f, 66, 69, 81, 84f, 87, 91, 95f, 98ff, 101f, 106, 115, 120, 180, 190, 199, 214ff, 217, 222, 239, 258, 270, 282f
  and custom-type rules 84, 282f
  defects of regulation by primary rules only 35, 84f, 87f, 98f, 214, 221, 234, 256, 283
  law as a union of primary and secondary rules 8, 40, 69, 81, 85, 87, 91, 95f, 100, 180, 241, 258, 270
  the primary/secondary rules contrast 84, 100f, 114f

punishment 24, 26, 28, 55, 159, 166, 182f, 186, 246, 253, 294
  justice in 26, 166

realism, legal 105f, 113, 230, 238f, 258, 270, 277
  American 228, 238f
  Scandinavian 238
reductionism in jurisprudence 4ff, 8f, 39f, 46ff, 256, 271, 289
  and the social functions of legal rules 7ff, 44, 53f, 85, 280
rights
  and justice 160, 162ff, 165ff, 173ff
  human 174, 210f, 229, 291f
rule of law 25, 27f, 35, 59f, 64, 87, 89ff, 93ff, 147, 187, 206, 243, 249, 272
  and adjudicative finality 87f
  and justice 87, 91
  and legal certainty 35, 87f, 93, 249
  and secondary legal rules 86ff, 89ff
  and separation of powers 23f, 59f, 73
  and the concept of a legal system 87ff, 91ff
  and the generality of law 23, 35f, 90, 93f, 249
  and the particularity of law 23ff, 25ff, 28, 90
  conventionalist interpretation 88, 94
rule of recognition *see also* **legal validity**
  acceptance 65f, 72f, 77, 79, 98f, 101f, 104, 106ff, 110, 112, 114ff, 118, 120, 283
  and the existence of a legal system 98, 107f, 121
  and Hans Kelsen's 'basic norm' 97f, 115, 117ff, 121, 219, 221, 289
  and John Austin's doctrine of sovereignty 66, 69, 72ff, 76, 78, 97f, 116f
  and the efficacy of law 105ff
  and the meaning of 'law' 286
  and the sources of law 6, 102f, 117ff, 203, 263
  and the unity of a legal system 77, 107, 114, 116, 121, 220f
  as a constitutive rule 114f, 120
  as a duty-imposing rule 115f, 120
  as a power-conferring rule 84, 101
  as a second-order rule 20, 22, 65, 81, 85, 98ff, 101f, 106, 114, 282
  conventionalist interpretation 108, 286
  existence as a matter of fact 104f, 118f
    as a social rule 69ff, 101f, 104f, 108ff, 118f, 124, 203
  function(s)
    foundational role 66, 70ff, 73, 76, 78f, 83f, 98, 103ff, 106ff, 111, 116ff, 119ff, 135, 204
    providing criteria for the identification of legal rules 6, 70, 98ff, 102ff, 106f, 112ff, 134ff, 203, 283
  in international law 209, 219ff
  indeterminacy 70f, 76f, 119, 135f
  role of officials 84, 98, 107, 109f, 112, 116f, 120, 283
rule-scepticism 123f, 153, 160, 258

rules *see also* **duty-imposing rules; power-conferring rules; law; legal rules; primary rules; secondary rules; social rules**
  and rule-formulations 143f
  as summary reminders of what should normally be done 131f, 141, 153
  practice theory 102, 126ff, 131ff, 134, 136f
rules of adjudication 20, 22, 69f, 77, 79, 81, 85ff, 88f, 100f, 120, 214
  as a remedy for the inefficiency of regulation by primary rules 85ff, 88f, 100, 134, 214
  as 'secondary' rules 7, 100f, 120
  in international law 214, 216, 219
rules of change 20, 22, 69, 119, 120
  as a remedy for the static character of regulation by primary rules 69, 85, 88f, 100
  as 'secondary' rules 101, 214
  in international law 214, 216, 218f, 222

sanctions *see also* **coercion**
  and evil 47f, 182
  and 'genuine' laws 51ff, 54, 182f
  and nullity 46ff, 49f
  criminal law 7, 26f, 44, 47f, 51ff
  imposition of particular 26f
  in international law 209, 211ff, 223
  sanction-free systems of adjudication 244
secondary rules 22, 40, 51f, 65f, 81, 84ff, 87ff, 95f, 98f, 100ff, 106, 114, 180, 199, 209, 213ff, 216ff, 219, 221f, 239, 241, 258, 270, 282f
  and the rule of law 86ff, 89ff
  in international law 209, 213ff, 216ff, 219, 221f
  law as a union of primary and secondary rules 8, 40, 69, 81, 85, 87, 91, 95f, 100, 180, 241, 258, 270
  the primary/secondary rules contrast 84, 100f, 114
separation of powers 23f, 59f, 73
social functions of legal rules 7ff, 44, 53f, 85, 280
  and reductionism 7ff, 44ff, 53ff, 57
social pressure and obligation 35, 84, 98f, 127, 136, 168, 186, 234, 283
social rules
  acceptance 62ff, 68, 76, 101f, 106, 109, 126f, 232, 264, 282f
  and habits 4, 62f, 101, 229f, 234, 270
  and moral and conventional obligations 126f, 130f, 173f, 184f, 230ff
sociological legal theory 273
sources of law 6, 58, 70, 98, 102f, 106, 117ff, 136f, 203, 219f, 221, 257, 286
  and the rule of recognition 6, 102f, 117ff, 203, 263

sovereignty 59f, 61ff, 64ff, 66ff, 69ff, 73ff, 101, 118f, 209ff, 281
  and international law 209ff
  as an artefact of law 72f, 211f
  John Austin's doctrine of sovereignty 57, 61ff, 64ff, 67ff, 72, 78, 97f, 101, 103, 116f, 121, 211, 281
  legal limits to 66ff
  of Parliament, doctrine of 118f
    as custom *in foro* 119
stasis
  as a 'defect' of regulation by primary rules 69, 84, 100, 234f
  rules of change as a remedy for 69, 85, 88f, 100
state
  adjudicative function 20, 281
  executive function 6, 20, 24
  ideal of a just 60, 74
  legislative function 20, 23
  separation of powers 23f, 59f, 73
statements concerning law
  external statements about law 105, 255
  internal statements of law 105, 126, 255, 289
    and predictions of official action 105
    and the efficacy of the legal system as a whole 105
  committed and detached 289
  use of normative language in describing the law 63, 255, 262, 265, 289

uncertainty *see also* **language**
  as a 'defect' of regulation by primary rules 84, 98f, 234f
  rules of recognition as a remedy for 85, 87ff, 99
understanding
  and knowledge 1ff, 39, 57, 231, 247, 252, 255f, 262f, 266

vagueness 10, 27, 178, 203, 219, 253
virtues
  and law 59ff, 73f

www.ingramcontent.com/pod-product-compliance
Lightning Source LLC
Chambersburg PA
CBHW070749020526
44115CB00032B/1599